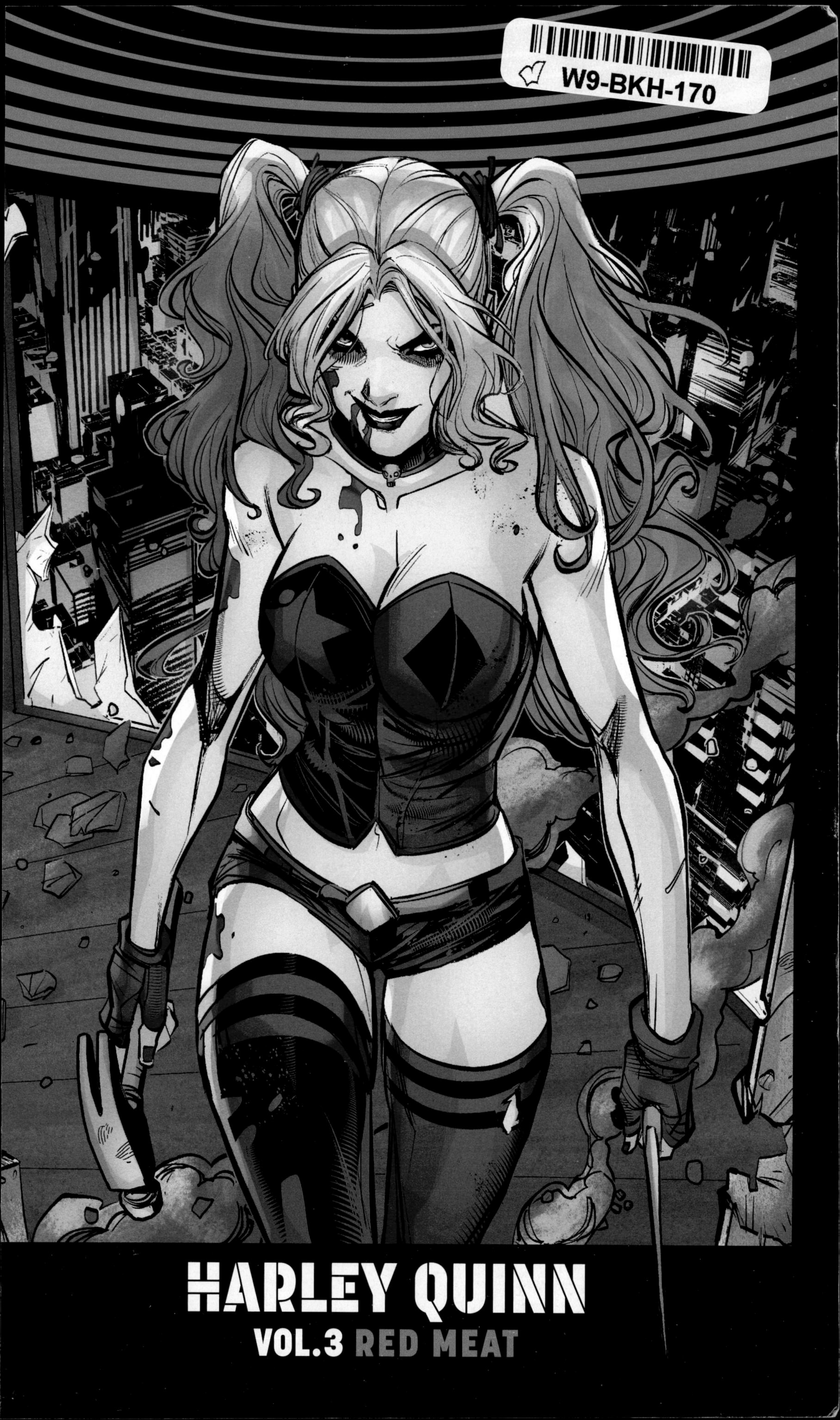

HARLEY QUINN

VOL.3 RED MEAT

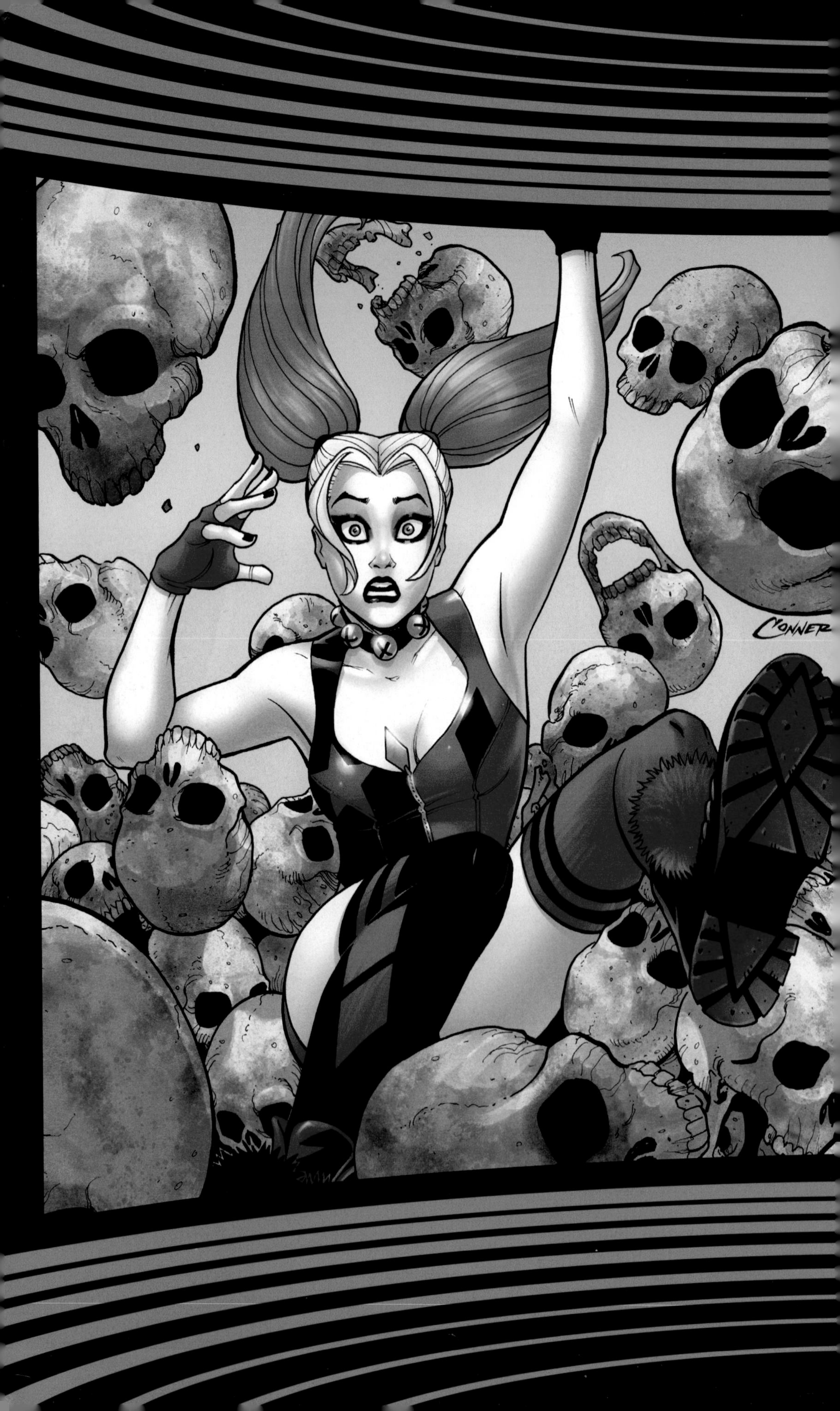
CONNER

HARLEY QUINN
VOL.3 RED MEAT

AMANDA CONNER
JIMMY PALMIOTTI
writers

JOHN TIMMS
JOSEPH MICHAEL LINSNER
KHARI EVANS * MARC DEERING
artists

ALEX SINCLAIR
JEREMIAH SKIPPER
colorists

DAVE SHARPE
letterer

AMANDA CONNER and **ALEX SINCLAIR**
collection cover artists

HARLEY QUINN created by **PAUL DINI** and **BRUCE TIMM**

CHRIS CONROY Editor - Original Series ✳ **DAVE WIELGOSZ** Assistant Editor - Original Series
JEB WOODARD Group Editor - Collected Editions ✳ **ROBIN WILDMAN** Editor - Collected Edition
STEVE COOK Design Director - Books ✳ **MONIQUE GRUSPE** Publication Design

BOB HARRAS Senior VP - Editor-in-Chief, DC Comics

DIANE NELSON President ✳ **DAN DiDIO** Publisher ✳ **JIM LEE** Publisher ✳ **GEOFF JOHNS** President & Chief Creative Officer
AMIT DESAI Executive VP - Business & Marketing Strategy, Direct to Consumer & Global Franchise Management ✳ **SAM ADES** Senior VP - Direct to Consumer
BOBBIE CHASE VP - Talent Development ✳ **MARK CHIARELLO** Senior VP - Art, Design & Collected Editions
JOHN CUNNINGHAM Senior VP - Sales & Trade Marketing ✳ **ANNE DePIES** Senior VP - Business Strategy, Finance & Administration
DON FALLETTI VP - Manufacturing Operations ✳ **LAWRENCE GANEM** VP - Editorial Administration & Talent Relations
ALISON GILL Senior VP - Manufacturing & Operations ✳ **HANK KANALZ** Senior VP - Editorial Strategy & Administration
JAY KOGAN VP - Legal Affairs ✳ **THOMAS LOFTUS** VP - Business Affairs
JACK MAHAN VP - Business Affairs ✳ **NICK J. NAPOLITANO** VP - Manufacturing Administration
EDDIE SCANNELL VP - Consumer Marketing ✳ **COURTNEY SIMMONS** Senior VP - Publicity & Communications
JIM (SKI) SOKOLOWSKI VP - Comic Book Specialty Sales & Trade Marketing ✳ **NANCY SPEARS** VP - Mass, Book, Digital Sales & Trade Marketing

HARLEY QUINN VOL. 3: RED MEAT

Published by DC Comics. Compilation and all new material Copyright © 2017 DC Comics. All Rights Reserved.
Originally published in single magazine form in HARLEY QUINN 14-21. Copyright © 2017 DC Comics.
All Rights Reserved. All characters, their distinctive likenesses and related elements featured in this publication are trademarks of DC Comics.
The stories, characters and incidents featured in this publication are entirely fictional.
DC Comics does not read or accept unsolicited submissions of ideas, stories or artwork.

DC Comics, 2900 West Alameda Ave., Burbank, CA 91505
Printed by LSC Communications, Kendallville, IN, USA. 8/11/17. First Printing.
ISBN: 978-1-4012-7369-9

Library of Congress Cataloging-in-Publication Data is available.

PEFC Certified

Printed on paper from
sustainably managed
forests, controlled
sources

PEFC

PEFC/29-31-337   www.pefc.org

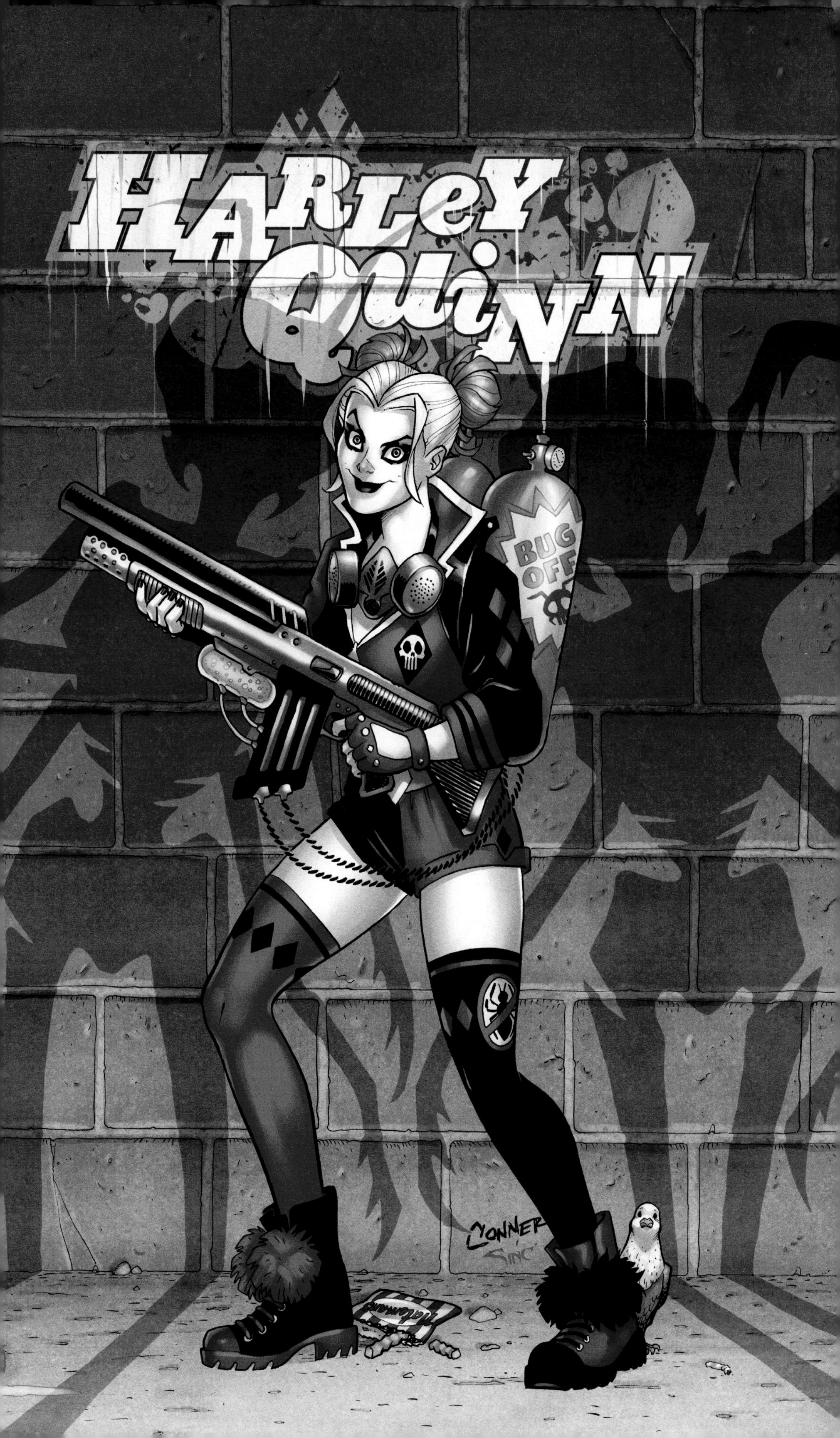

HARLEY QUINN
BUG OFF
CONNER
SINC

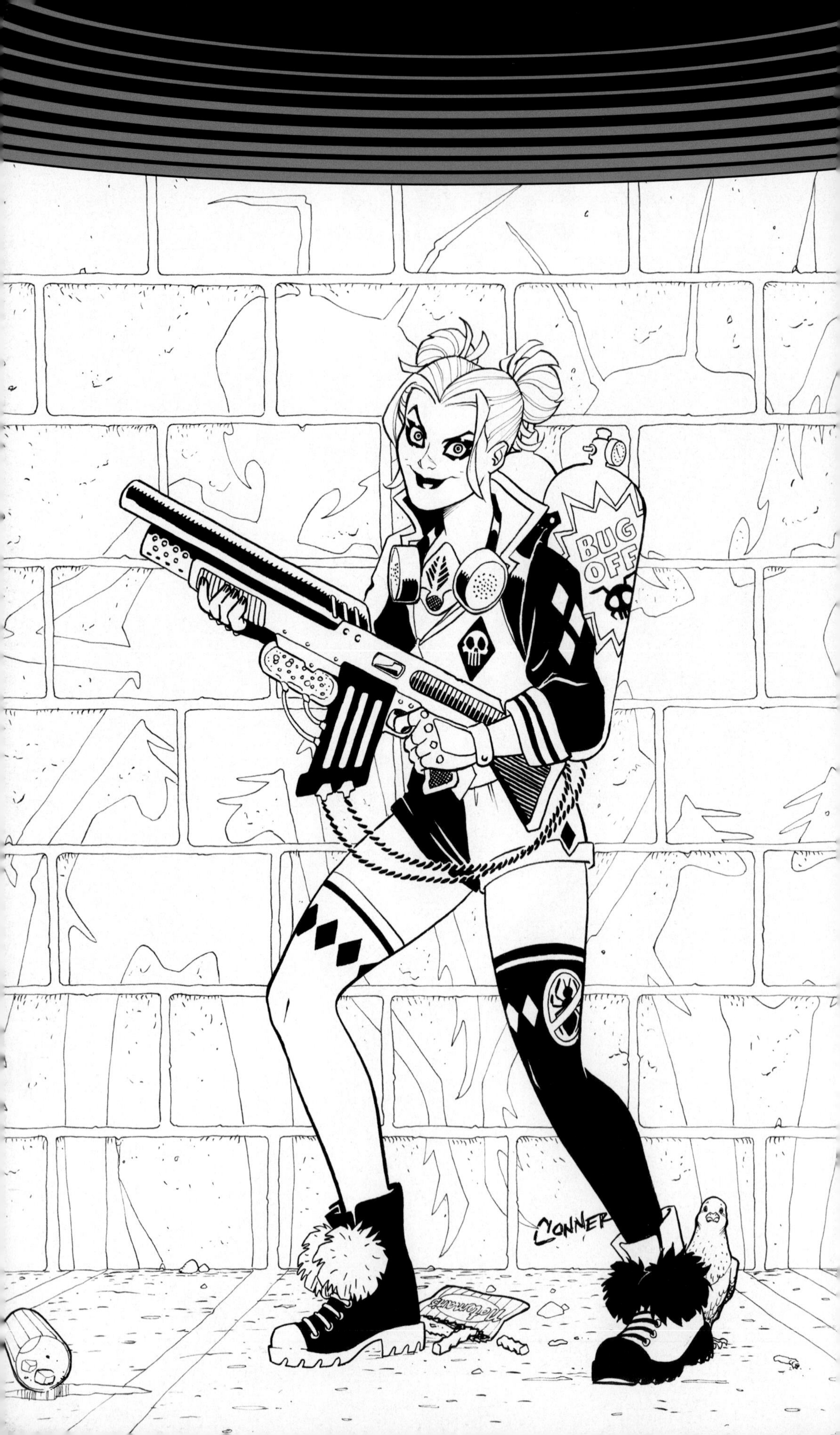
BUG OFF
CONNER

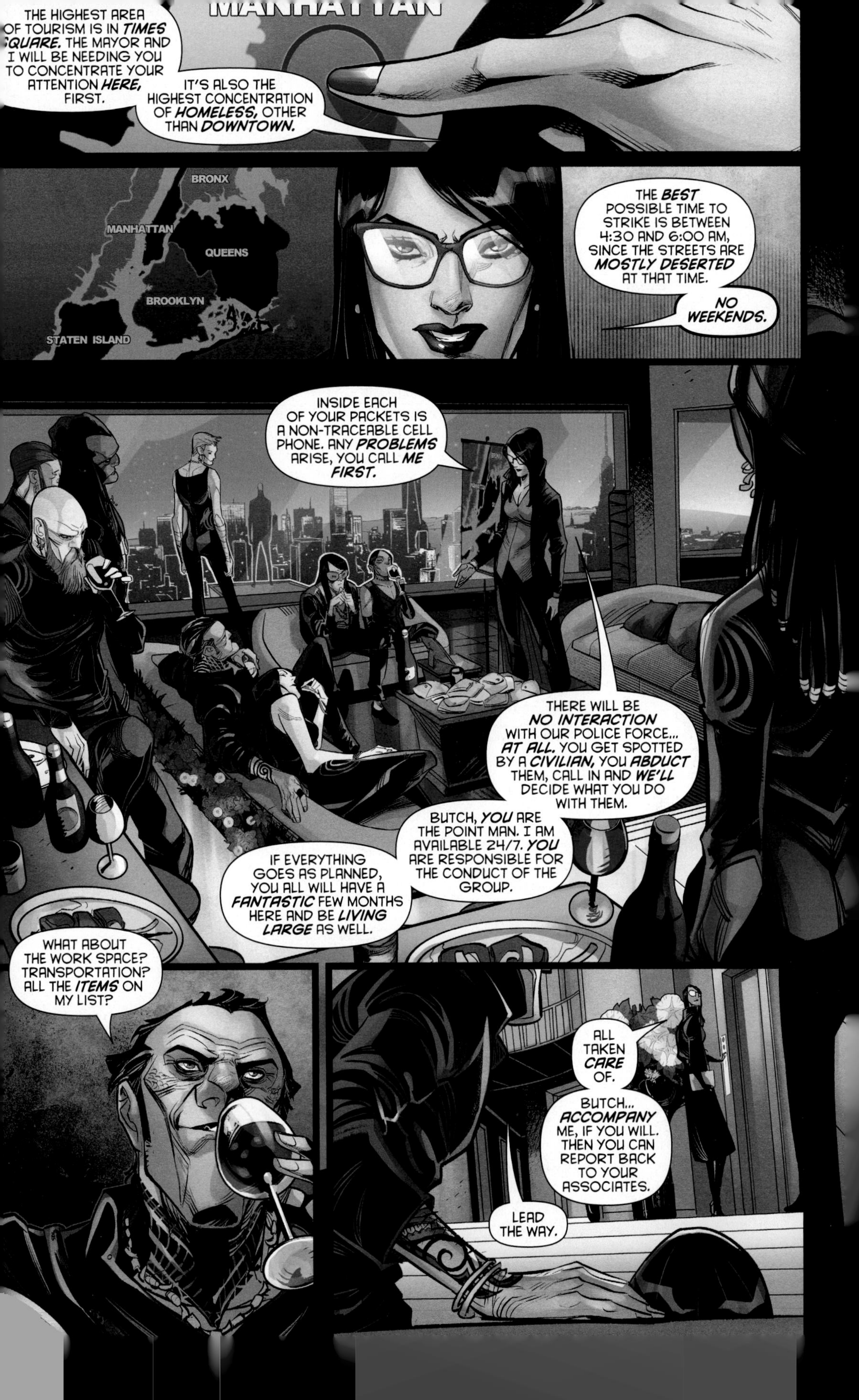

MANHATTAN
THE HIGHEST AREA OF TOURISM IS IN TIMES SQUARE. THE MAYOR AND I WILL BE NEEDING YOU TO CONCENTRATE YOUR ATTENTION HERE, FIRST.
IT'S ALSO THE HIGHEST CONCENTRATION OF HOMELESS, OTHER THAN DOWNTOWN.
BRONX
MANHATTAN
QUEENS
BROOKLYN
STATEN ISLAND
THE BEST POSSIBLE TIME TO STRIKE IS BETWEEN 4:30 AND 6:00 AM, SINCE THE STREETS ARE MOSTLY DESERTED AT THAT TIME.
NO WEEKENDS.
INSIDE EACH OF YOUR PACKETS IS A NON-TRACEABLE CELL PHONE. ANY PROBLEMS ARISE, YOU CALL ME FIRST.
THERE WILL BE NO INTERACTION WITH OUR POLICE FORCE... AT ALL. YOU GET SPOTTED BY A CIVILIAN, YOU ABDUCT THEM, CALL IN AND WE'LL DECIDE WHAT YOU DO WITH THEM.
BUTCH, YOU ARE THE POINT MAN. I AM AVAILABLE 24/7. YOU ARE RESPONSIBLE FOR THE CONDUCT OF THE GROUP.
IF EVERYTHING GOES AS PLANNED, YOU ALL WILL HAVE A FANTASTIC FEW MONTHS HERE AND BE LIVING LARGE AS WELL.
WHAT ABOUT THE WORK SPACE? TRANSPORTATION? ALL THE ITEMS ON MY LIST?
ALL TAKEN CARE OF.
BUTCH... ACCOMPANY ME, IF YOU WILL. THEN YOU CAN REPORT BACK TO YOUR ASSOCIATES.
LEAD THE WAY.

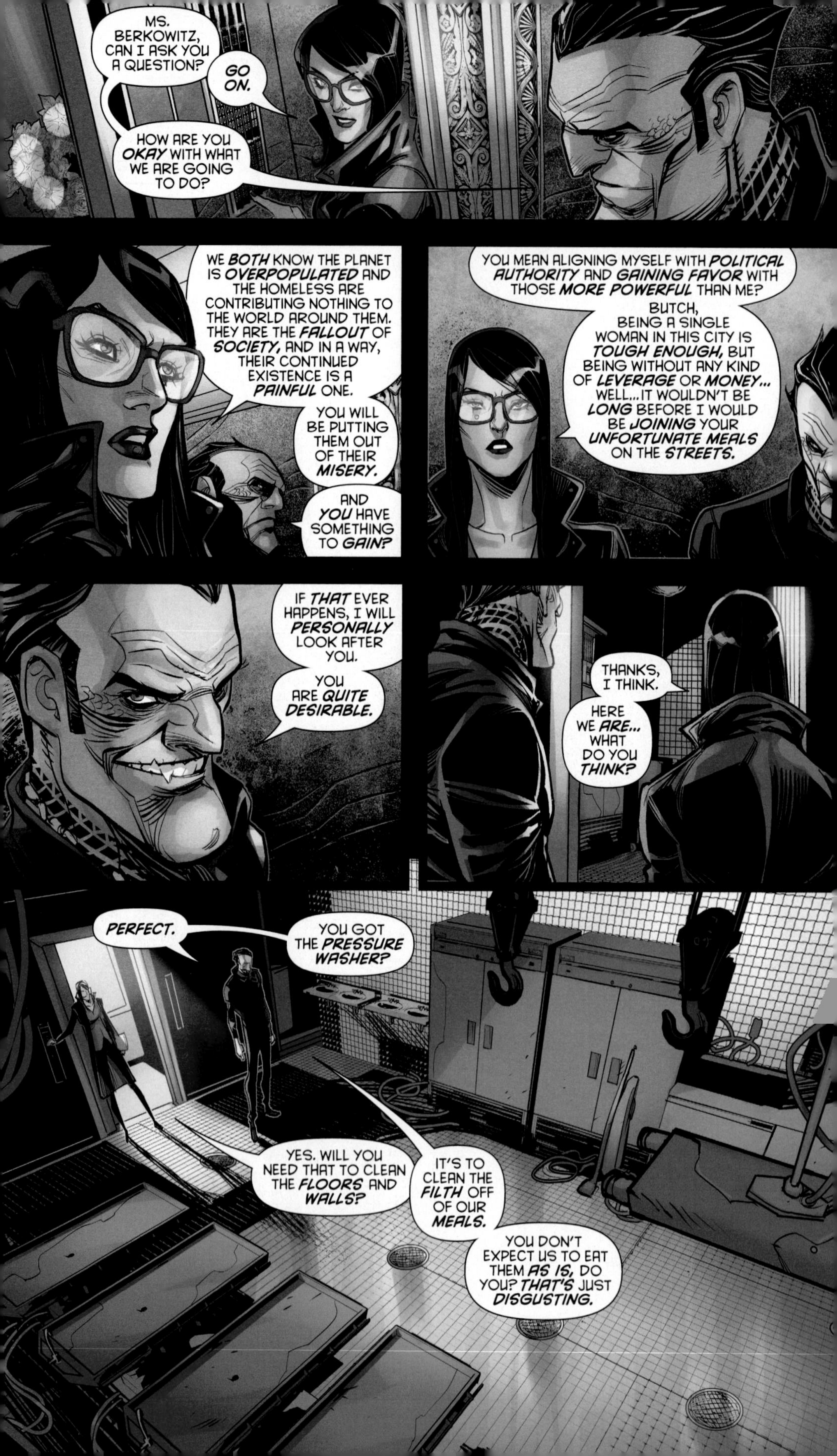

MS. BERKOWITZ, CAN I ASK YOU A QUESTION?
GO ON.
HOW ARE YOU OKAY WITH WHAT WE ARE GOING TO DO?
WE BOTH KNOW THE PLANET IS OVERPOPULATED AND THE HOMELESS ARE CONTRIBUTING NOTHING TO THE WORLD AROUND THEM. THEY ARE THE FALLOUT OF SOCIETY, AND IN A WAY, THEIR CONTINUED EXISTENCE IS A PAINFUL ONE.
YOU WILL BE PUTTING THEM OUT OF THEIR MISERY.
AND YOU HAVE SOMETHING TO GAIN?
YOU MEAN ALIGNING MYSELF WITH POLITICAL AUTHORITY AND GAINING FAVOR WITH THOSE MORE POWERFUL THAN ME?
BUTCH, BEING A SINGLE WOMAN IN THIS CITY IS TOUGH ENOUGH, BUT BEING WITHOUT ANY KIND OF LEVERAGE OR MONEY... WELL...IT WOULDN'T BE LONG BEFORE I WOULD BE JOINING YOUR UNFORTUNATE MEALS ON THE STREETS.
IF THAT EVER HAPPENS, I WILL PERSONALLY LOOK AFTER YOU.
YOU ARE QUITE DESIRABLE.
THANKS, I THINK.
HERE WE ARE... WHAT DO YOU THINK?
PERFECT.
YOU GOT THE PRESSURE WASHER?
YES. WILL YOU NEED THAT TO CLEAN THE FLOORS AND WALLS?
IT'S TO CLEAN THE FILTH OFF OF OUR MEALS.
YOU DON'T EXPECT US TO EAT THEM AS IS, DO YOU? THAT'S JUST DISGUSTING.

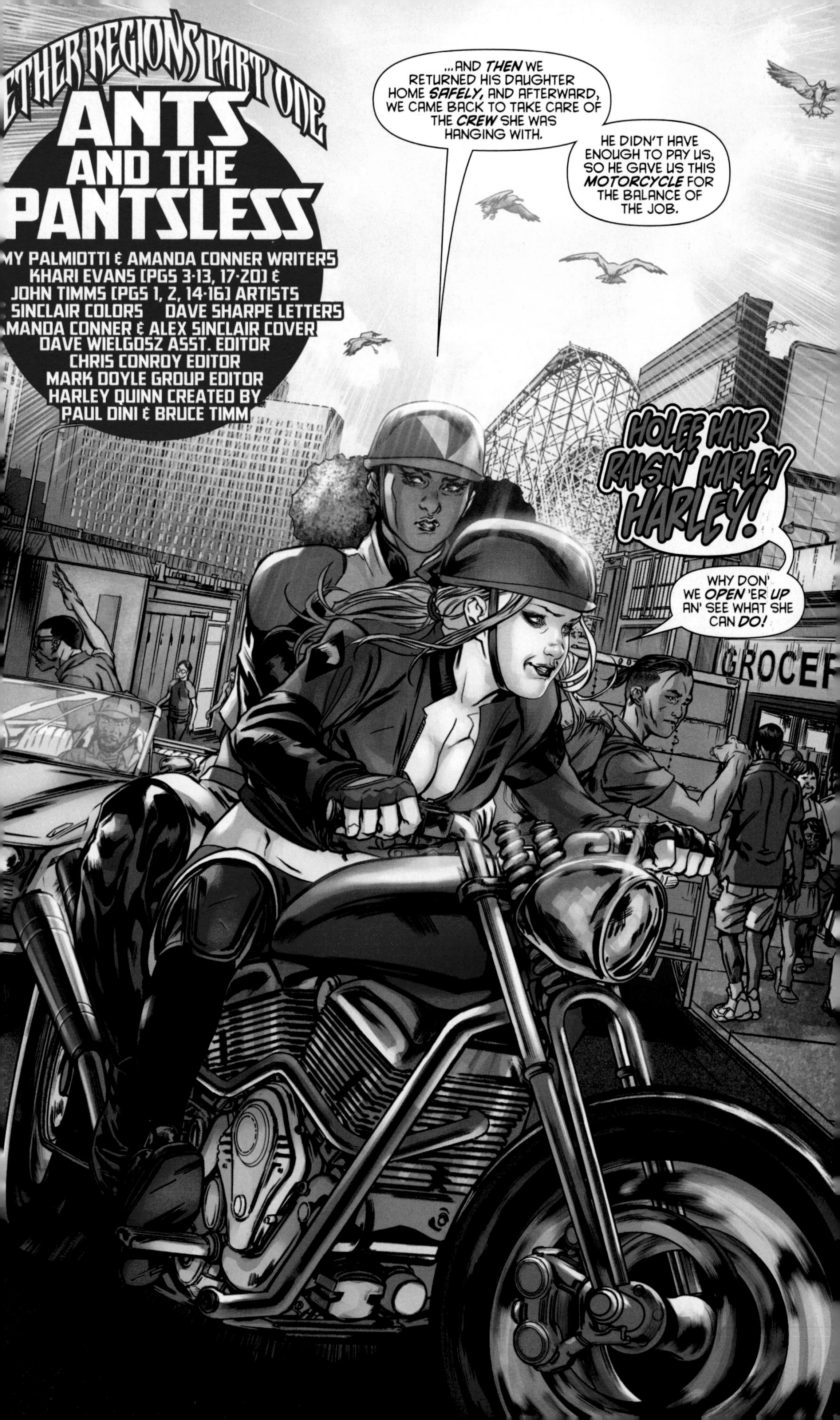

ETHER REGIONS PART ONE
ANTS AND THE PANTSLESS
MY PALMIOTTI & AMANDA CONNER WRITERS
KHARI EVANS [PGS 3-13, 17-20] &
JOHN TIMMS [PGS 1, 2, 14-16] ARTISTS
SINCLAIR COLORS DAVE SHARPE LETTERS
MANDA CONNER & ALEX SINCLAIR COVER
DAVE WIELGOSZ ASST. EDITOR
CHRIS CONROY EDITOR
MARK DOYLE GROUP EDITOR
HARLEY QUINN CREATED BY
PAUL DINI & BRUCE TIMM
...AND THEN WE RETURNED HIS DAUGHTER HOME SAFELY, AND AFTERWARD, WE CAME BACK TO TAKE CARE OF THE CREW SHE WAS HANGING WITH.
HE DIDN'T HAVE ENOUGH TO PAY US, SO HE GAVE US THIS MOTORCYCLE FOR THE BALANCE OF THE JOB.
HOLEE HAIR RAISIN' HARLEY HARLEY!
WHY DON' WE OPEN 'ER UP AN' SEE WHAT SHE CAN DO!
GROCER

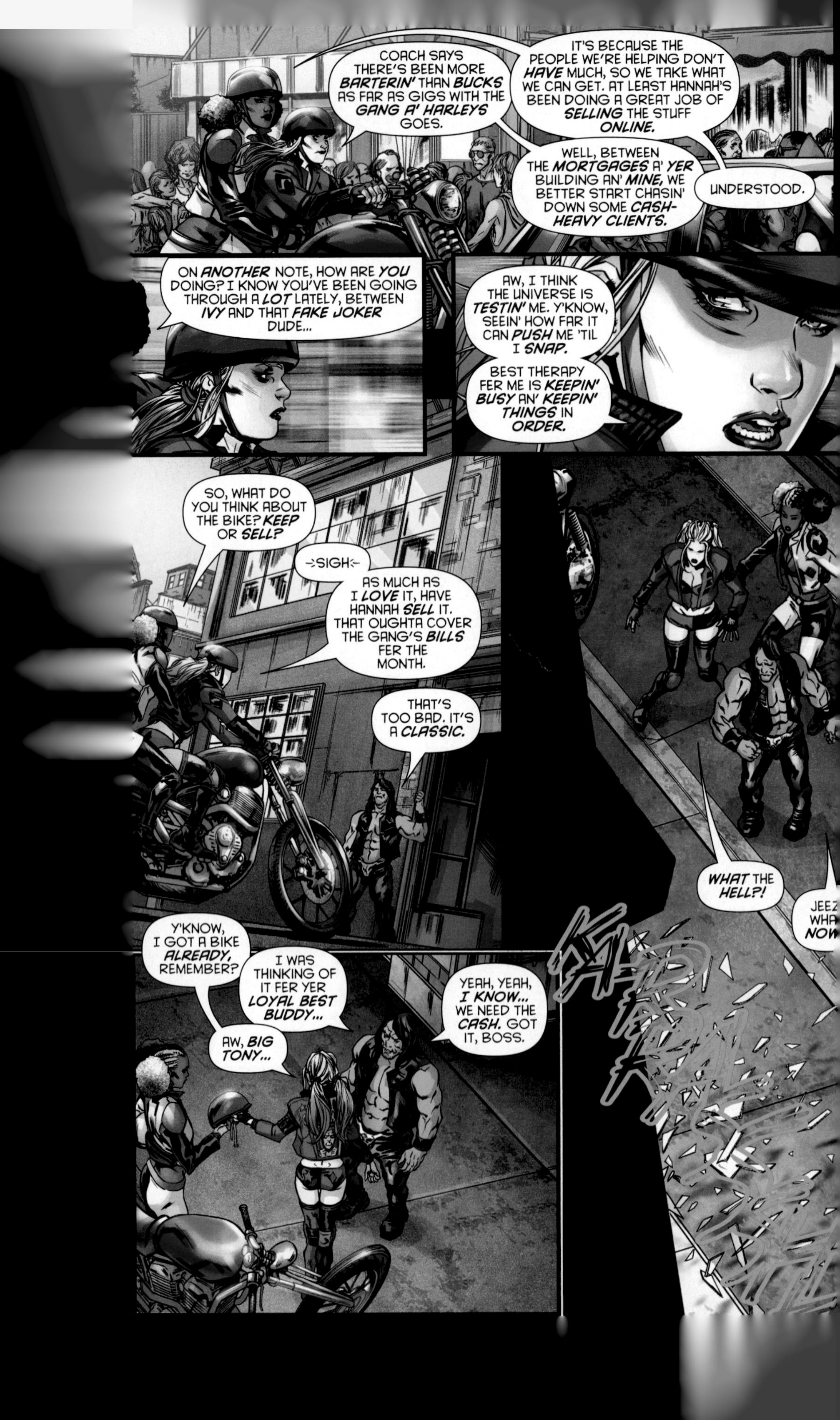

COACH SAYS THERE'S BEEN MORE BARTERIN' THAN BUCKS AS FAR AS GIGS WITH THE GANG A' HARLEYS GOES.
IT'S BECAUSE THE PEOPLE WE'RE HELPING DON'T HAVE MUCH, SO WE TAKE WHAT WE CAN GET. AT LEAST HANNAH'S BEEN DOING A GREAT JOB OF SELLING THE STUFF ONLINE.
WELL, BETWEEN THE MORTGAGES A' YER BUILDING AN' MINE, WE BETTER START CHASIN' DOWN SOME CASH-HEAVY CLIENTS.
UNDERSTOOD.
ON ANOTHER NOTE, HOW ARE YOU DOING? I KNOW YOU'VE BEEN GOING THROUGH A LOT LATELY, BETWEEN IVY AND THAT FAKE JOKER DUDE...
AW, I THINK THE UNIVERSE IS TESTIN' ME. Y'KNOW, SEEIN' HOW FAR IT CAN PUSH ME 'TIL I SNAP.
BEST THERAPY FER ME IS KEEPIN' BUSY AN' KEEPIN' THINGS IN ORDER.
SO, WHAT DO YOU THINK ABOUT THE BIKE? KEEP OR SELL?
-SIGH-
AS MUCH AS I LOVE IT, HAVE HANNAH SELL IT. THAT OUGHTA COVER THE GANG'S BILLS FER THE MONTH.
THAT'S TOO BAD. IT'S A CLASSIC.
Y'KNOW, I GOT A BIKE ALREADY, REMEMBER?
I WAS THINKING OF IT FER YER LOYAL BEST BUDDY...
AW, BIG TONY...
YEAH, YEAH, I KNOW... WE NEED THE CASH. GOT IT, BOSS.
WHAT THE HELL?!

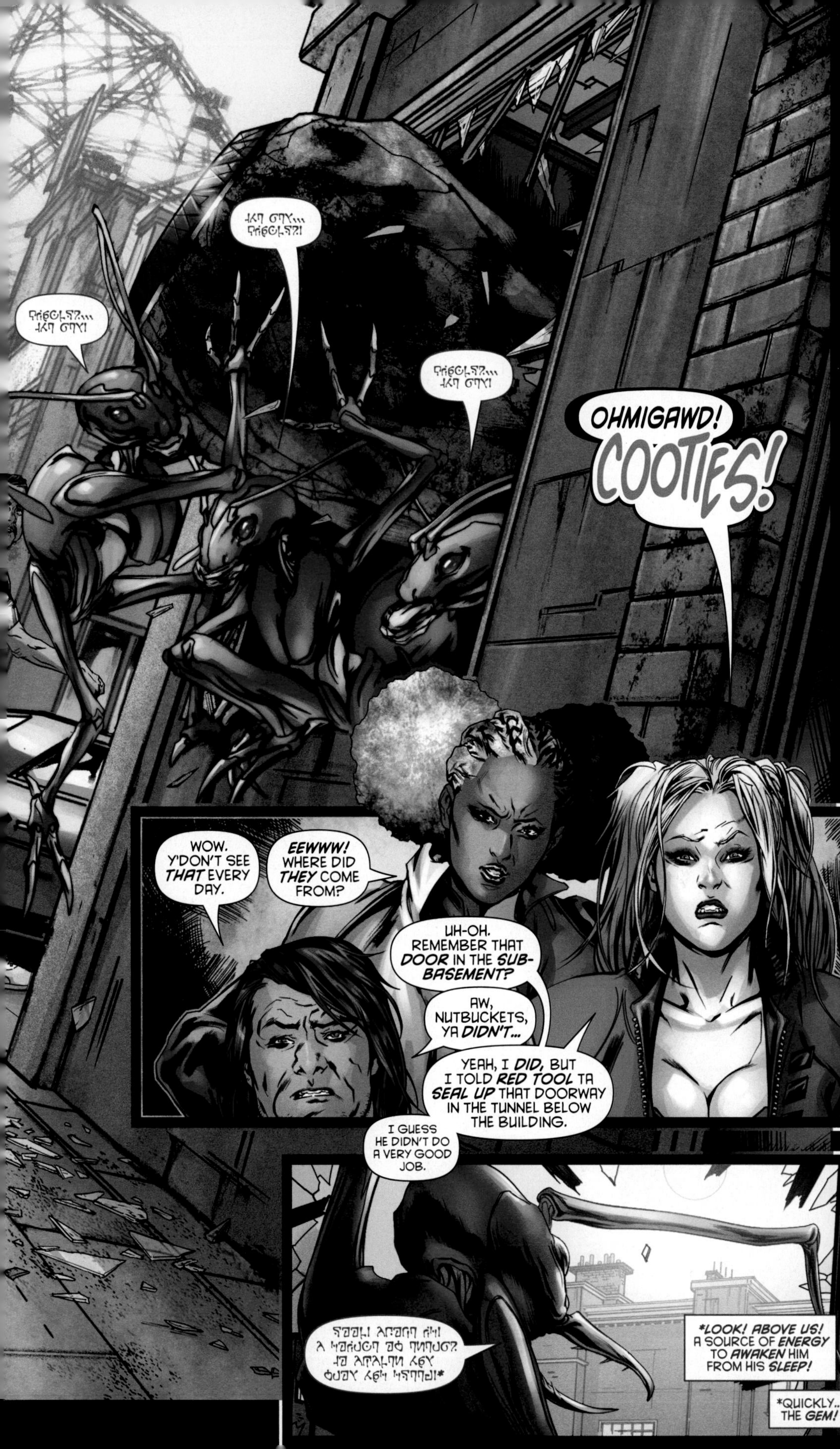
OHMIGAWD! COOTIES!
WOW. Y'DON'T SEE THAT EVERY DAY.
EEWWW! WHERE DID THEY COME FROM?
UH-OH. REMEMBER THAT DOOR IN THE SUB-BASEMENT?
AW, NUTBUCKETS, YA DIDN'T...
YEAH, I DID, BUT I TOLD RED TOOL TA SEAL UP THAT DOORWAY IN THE TUNNEL BELOW THE BUILDING.
I GUESS HE DIDN'T DO A VERY GOOD JOB.
*LOOK! ABOVE US! A SOURCE OF ENERGY TO AWAKEN HIM FROM HIS SLEEP!
*QUICKLY... THE GEM!

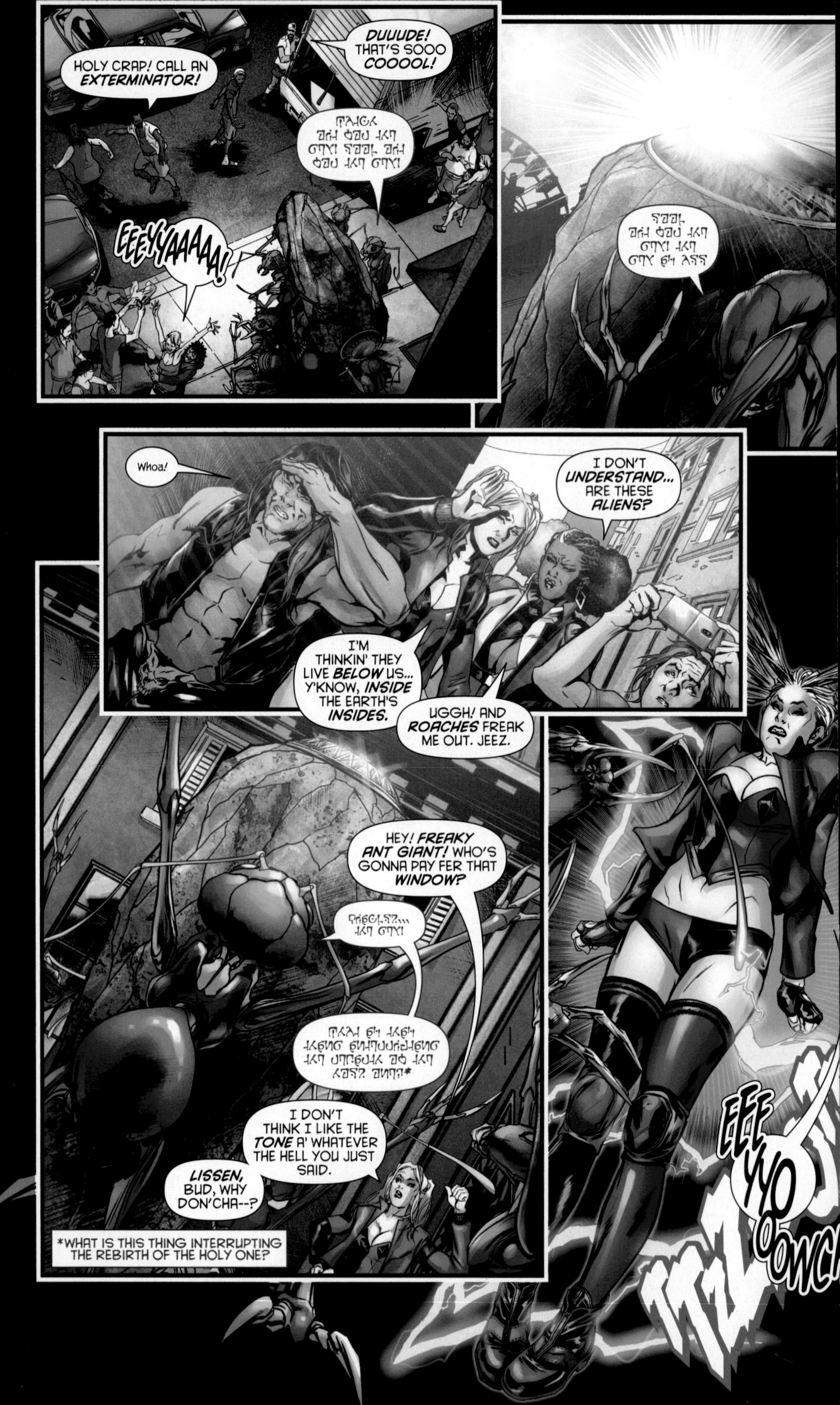

HOLY CRAP! CALL AN EXTERMINATOR!
DUUUDE! THAT'S SOOO COOOOL!
EEEYYAAAAA!
Whoa!
I DON'T UNDERSTAND... ARE THESE ALIENS?
I'M THINKIN' THEY LIVE BELOW US... Y'KNOW, INSIDE THE EARTH'S INSIDES.
UGGH! AND ROACHES FREAK ME OUT. JEEZ.
HEY! FREAKY ANT GIANT! WHO'S GONNA PAY FER THAT WINDOW?
I DON'T THINK I LIKE THE TONE A' WHATEVER THE HELL YOU JUST SAID.
LISSEN, BUD, WHY DON'CHA--?
*WHAT IS THIS THING INTERRUPTING THE REBIRTH OF THE HOLY ONE?
EEEYYOOOWC

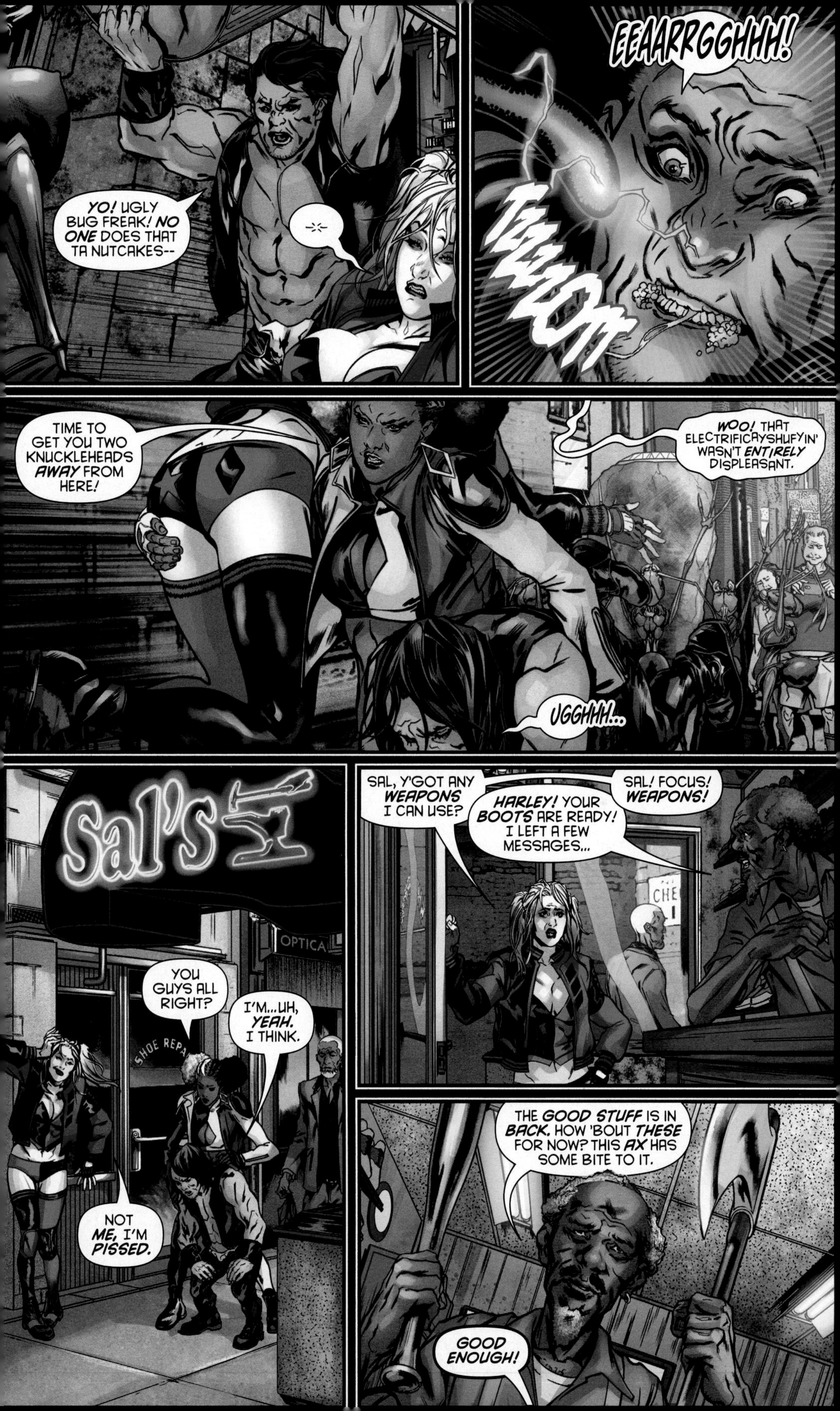

YO! UGLY BUG FREAK! NO ONE DOES THAT TA NUTCAKES--
EEAARRGGHHH!
TZZZOT
TIME TO GET YOU TWO KNUCKLEHEADS AWAY FROM HERE!
WOO! THAT ELECTRIFICAYSHUFYIN' WASN'T ENTIRELY DISPLEASANT.
UGGHHH...
Sal's
OPTICA
SHOE REPA
YOU GUYS ALL RIGHT?
I'M...UH, YEAH. I THINK.
NOT ME, I'M PISSED.
SAL, Y'GOT ANY WEAPONS I CAN USE?
HARLEY! YOUR BOOTS ARE READY! I LEFT A FEW MESSAGES...
SAL! FOCUS! WEAPONS!
THE GOOD STUFF IS IN BACK. HOW 'BOUT THESE FOR NOW? THIS AX HAS SOME BITE TO IT.
GOOD ENOUGH!

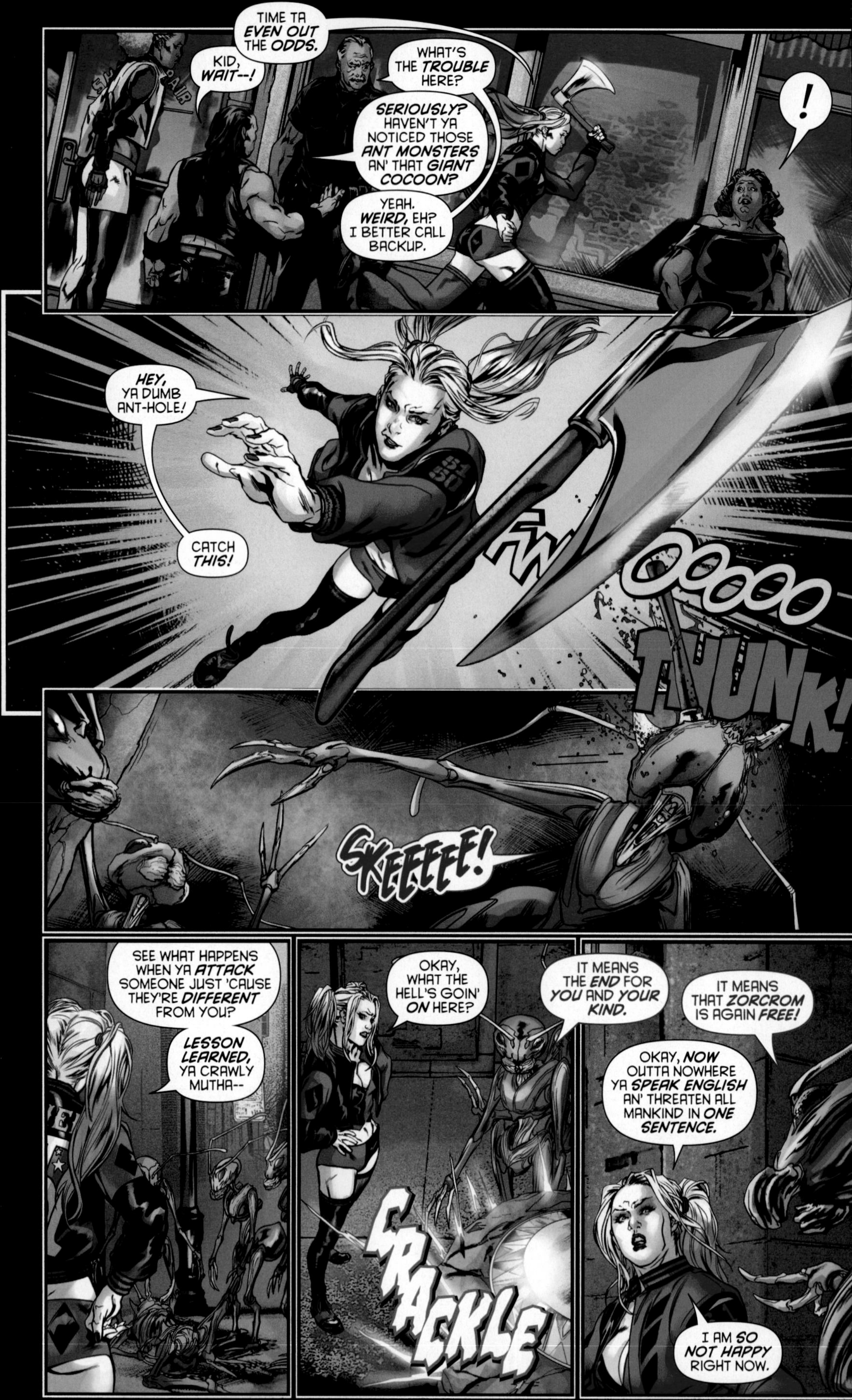
KID, WAIT--!
TIME TA EVEN OUT THE ODDS.
WHAT'S THE TROUBLE HERE?
SERIOUSLY? HAVEN'T YA NOTICED THOSE ANT MONSTERS AN' THAT GIANT COCOON?
YEAH. WEIRD, EH? I BETTER CALL BACKUP.
!
HEY, YA DUMB ANT-HOLE!
CATCH THIS!
FWOOOOOO
THUNK!
SKEEEEE!
SEE WHAT HAPPENS WHEN YA ATTACK SOMEONE JUST 'CAUSE THEY'RE DIFFERENT FROM YOU?
LESSON LEARNED, YA CRAWLY MUTHA--
CRACKLE
OKAY, WHAT THE HELL'S GOIN' ON HERE?
IT MEANS THE END FOR YOU AND YOUR KIND.
IT MEANS THAT ZORCROM IS AGAIN FREE!
OKAY, NOW OUTTA NOWHERE YA SPEAK ENGLISH AN' THREATEN ALL MANKIND IN ONE SENTENCE.
I AM SO NOT HAPPY RIGHT NOW.

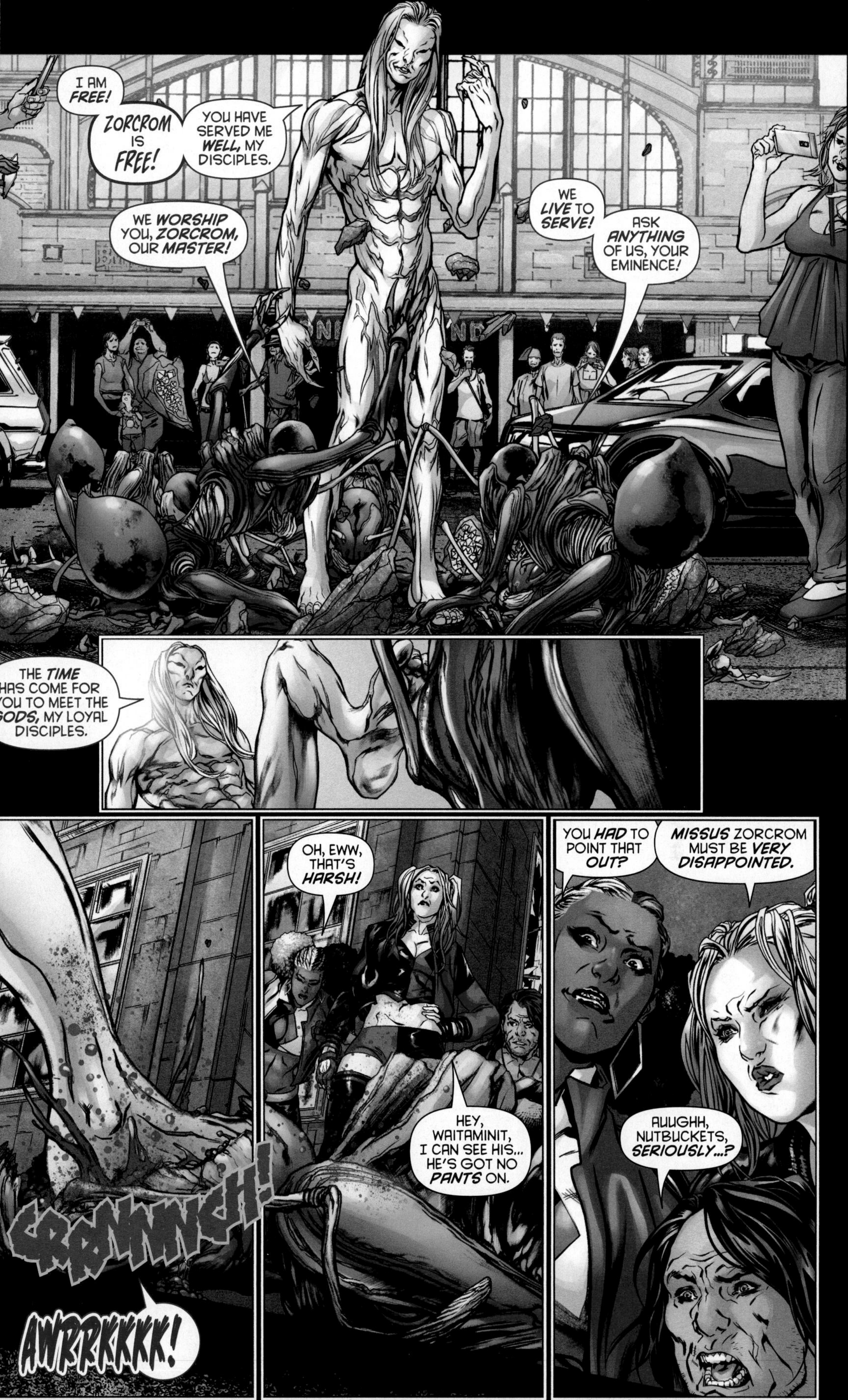

I AM FREE!
ZORCROM IS FREE!
YOU HAVE SERVED ME WELL, MY DISCIPLES.
WE WORSHIP YOU, ZORCROM, OUR MASTER!
WE LIVE TO SERVE!
ASK ANYTHING OF US, YOUR EMINENCE!
THE TIME HAS COME FOR YOU TO MEET THE GODS, MY LOYAL DISCIPLES.
CRONNNCH!
AWRRKKKK!
OH, EWW, THAT'S HARSH!
HEY, WAITAMINIT, I CAN SEE HIS... HE'S GOT NO PANTS ON.
YOU HAD TO POINT THAT OUT?
MISSUS ZORCROM MUST BE VERY DISAPPOINTED.
AUUGHH, NUTBUCKETS, SERIOUSLY...?

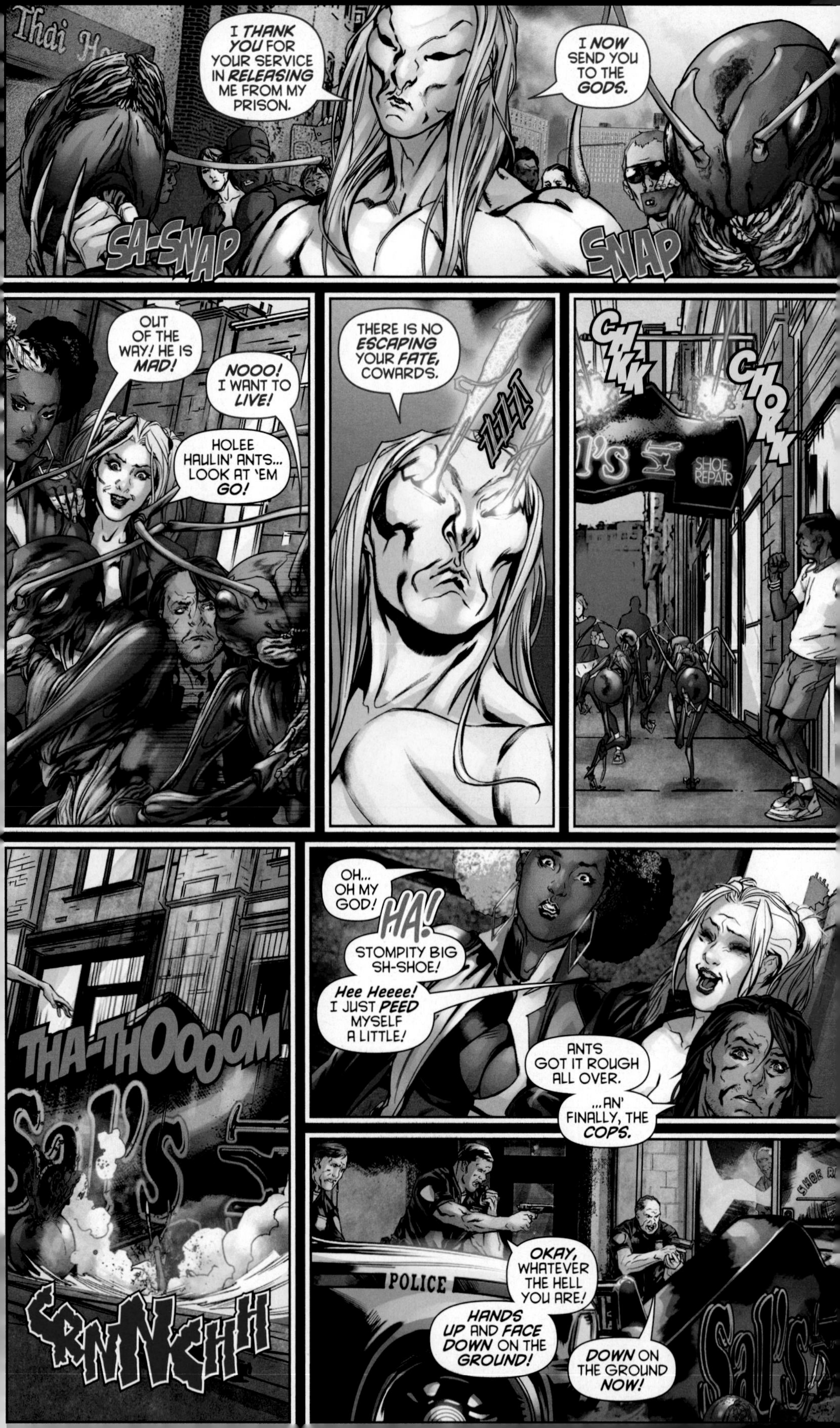
Thai Ho
I THANK YOU FOR YOUR SERVICE IN RELEASING ME FROM MY PRISON.
I NOW SEND YOU TO THE GODS.
SA-SNAP
SNAP
OUT OF THE WAY! HE IS MAD!
NOOO! I WANT TO LIVE!
HOLEE HAULIN' ANTS... LOOK AT 'EM GO!
THERE IS NO ESCAPING YOUR FATE, COWARDS.
CHKK
CHOKK
SHOE REPAIR
THA-THOOOOM
CRNNCHH
OH... OH MY GOD!
HA!
STOMPITY BIG SH-SHOE!
Hee Heeee! I JUST PEED MYSELF A LITTLE!
ANTS GOT IT ROUGH ALL OVER.
...AN' FINALLY, THE COPS.
POLICE
OKAY, WHATEVER THE HELL YOU ARE!
HANDS UP AND FACE DOWN ON THE GROUND!
DOWN ON THE GROUND NOW!

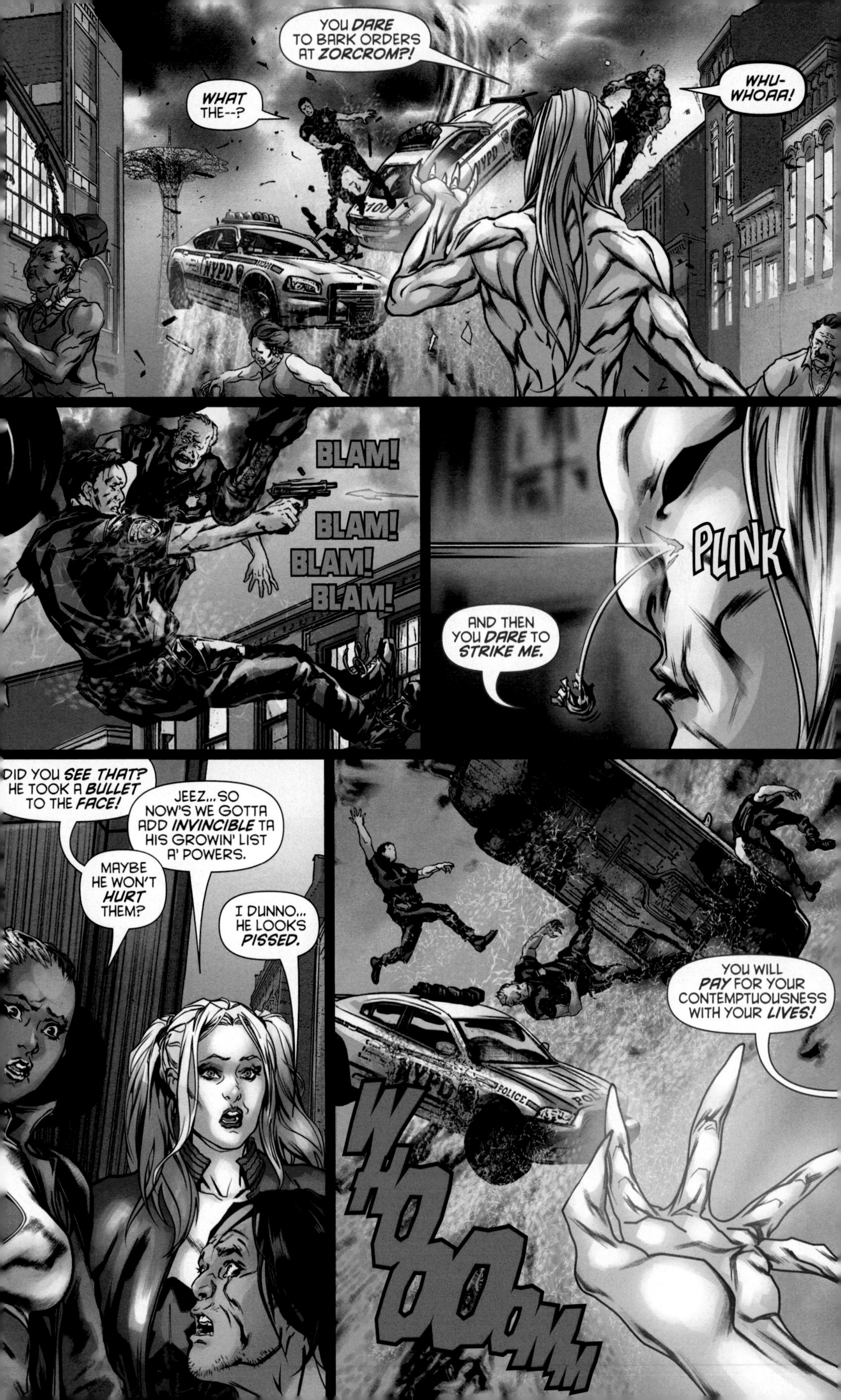

YOU DARE TO BARK ORDERS AT ZORCROM?!
WHAT THE--?
WHU-WHOAA!
BLAM!
BLAM!
BLAM!
BLAM!
PLINK
AND THEN YOU DARE TO STRIKE ME.
DID YOU SEE THAT? HE TOOK A BULLET TO THE FACE!
JEEZ...SO NOW'S WE GOTTA ADD INVINCIBLE TA HIS GROWIN' LIST A' POWERS.
MAYBE HE WON'T HURT THEM?
I DUNNO... HE LOOKS PISSED.
YOU WILL PAY FOR YOUR CONTEMPTUOUSNESS WITH YOUR LIVES!

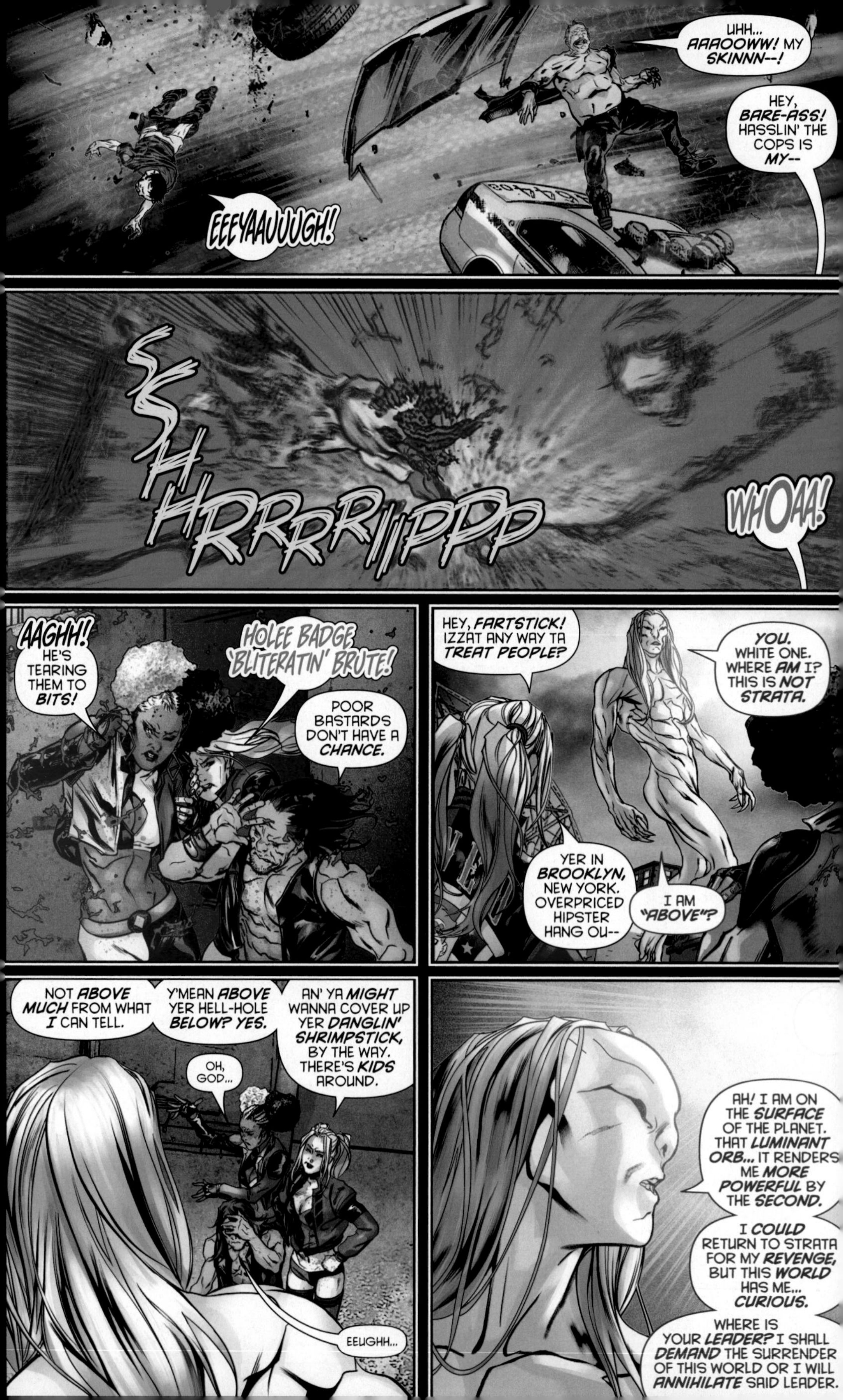
UHH... AAAOOWW! MY SKINNN--!
HEY, BARE-ASS! HASSLIN' THE COPS IS MY--
EEEYAAUUUGH!
SSHHRRRRIIPPPP
WHOAA!
AAGHH! HE'S TEARING THEM TO BITS!
HOLEE BADGE 'BLITERATIN' BRUTE!
POOR BASTARDS DON'T HAVE A CHANCE.
HEY, FARTSTICK! IZZAT ANY WAY TA TREAT PEOPLE?
YOU. WHITE ONE. WHERE AM I? THIS IS NOT STRATA.
YER IN BROOKLYN, NEW YORK. OVERPRICED HIPSTER HANG OU--
I AM "ABOVE"?
NOT ABOVE MUCH FROM WHAT I CAN TELL.
Y'MEAN ABOVE YER HELL-HOLE BELOW? YES.
AN' YA MIGHT WANNA COVER UP YER DANGLIN' SHRIMPSTICK, BY THE WAY. THERE'S KIDS AROUND.
OH, GOD...
EEUGHH...
AH! I AM ON THE SURFACE OF THE PLANET. THAT LUMINANT ORB... IT RENDERS ME MORE POWERFUL BY THE SECOND.
I COULD RETURN TO STRATA FOR MY REVENGE, BUT THIS WORLD HAS ME... CURIOUS.
WHERE IS YOUR LEADER? I SHALL DEMAND THE SURRENDER OF THIS WORLD OR I WILL ANNIHILATE SAID LEADER.

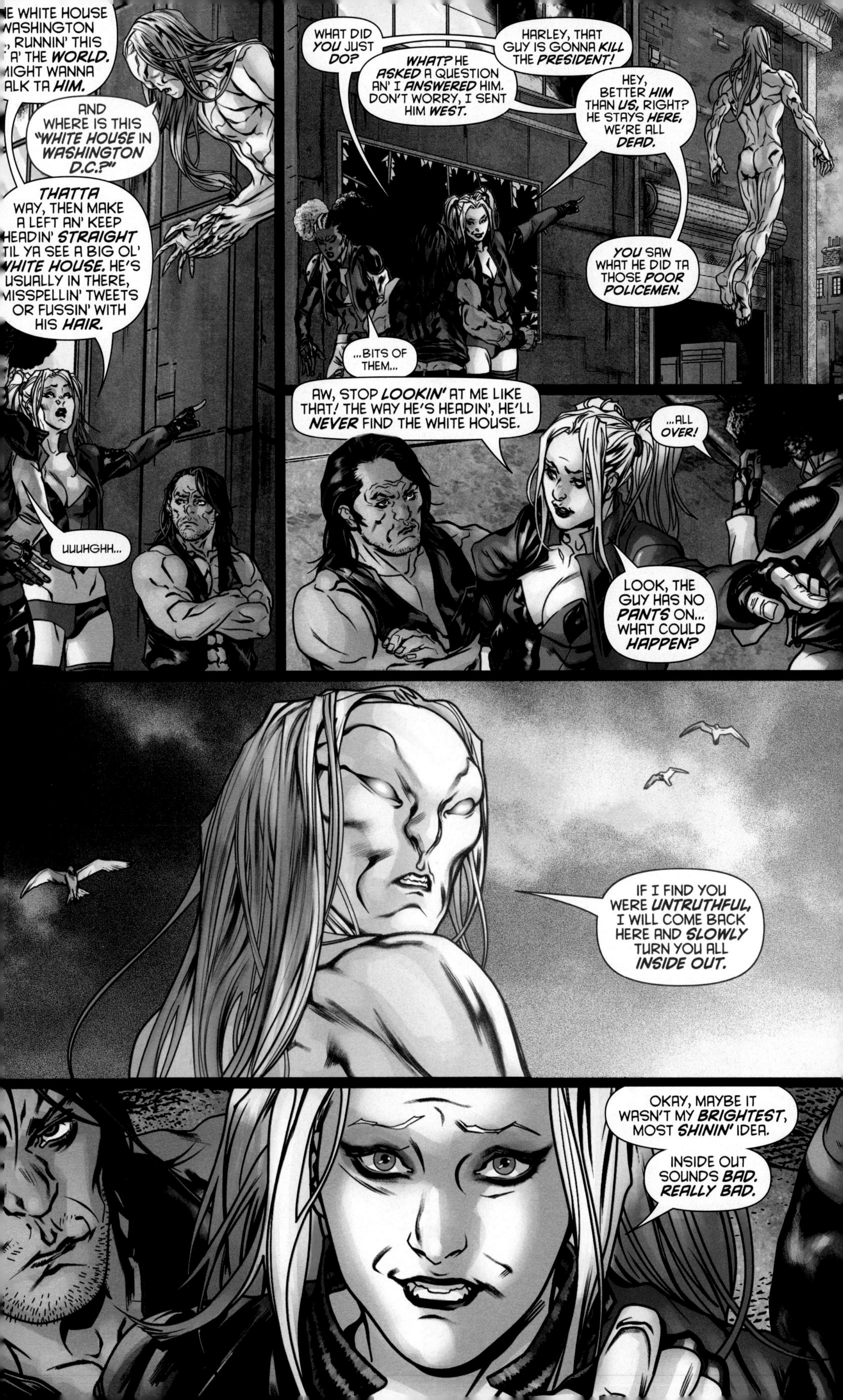

E WHITE HOUSE WASHINGTON , RUNNIN' THIS T A' THE WORLD. MIGHT WANNA ALK TA HIM.
AND WHERE IS THIS "WHITE HOUSE IN WASHINGTON D.C.?"
THATTA WAY, THEN MAKE A LEFT AN' KEEP HEADIN' STRAIGHT TIL YA SEE A BIG OL' WHITE HOUSE. HE'S USUALLY IN THERE, MISSPELLIN' TWEETS OR FUSSIN' WITH HIS HAIR.
UUUHGHH...
WHAT DID YOU JUST DO?
HARLEY, THAT GUY IS GONNA KILL THE PRESIDENT!
WHAT? HE ASKED A QUESTION AN' I ANSWERED HIM. DON'T WORRY, I SENT HIM WEST.
HEY, BETTER HIM THAN US, RIGHT? HE STAYS HERE, WE'RE ALL DEAD.
YOU SAW WHAT HE DID TA THOSE POOR POLICEMEN.
...BITS OF THEM...
AW, STOP LOOKIN' AT ME LIKE THAT! THE WAY HE'S HEADIN', HE'LL NEVER FIND THE WHITE HOUSE.
...ALL OVER!
LOOK, THE GUY HAS NO PANTS ON... WHAT COULD HAPPEN?
IF I FIND YOU WERE UNTRUTHFUL, I WILL COME BACK HERE AND SLOWLY TURN YOU ALL INSIDE OUT.
OKAY, MAYBE IT WASN'T MY BRIGHTEST, MOST SHININ' IDEA.
INSIDE OUT SOUNDS BAD. REALLY BAD.

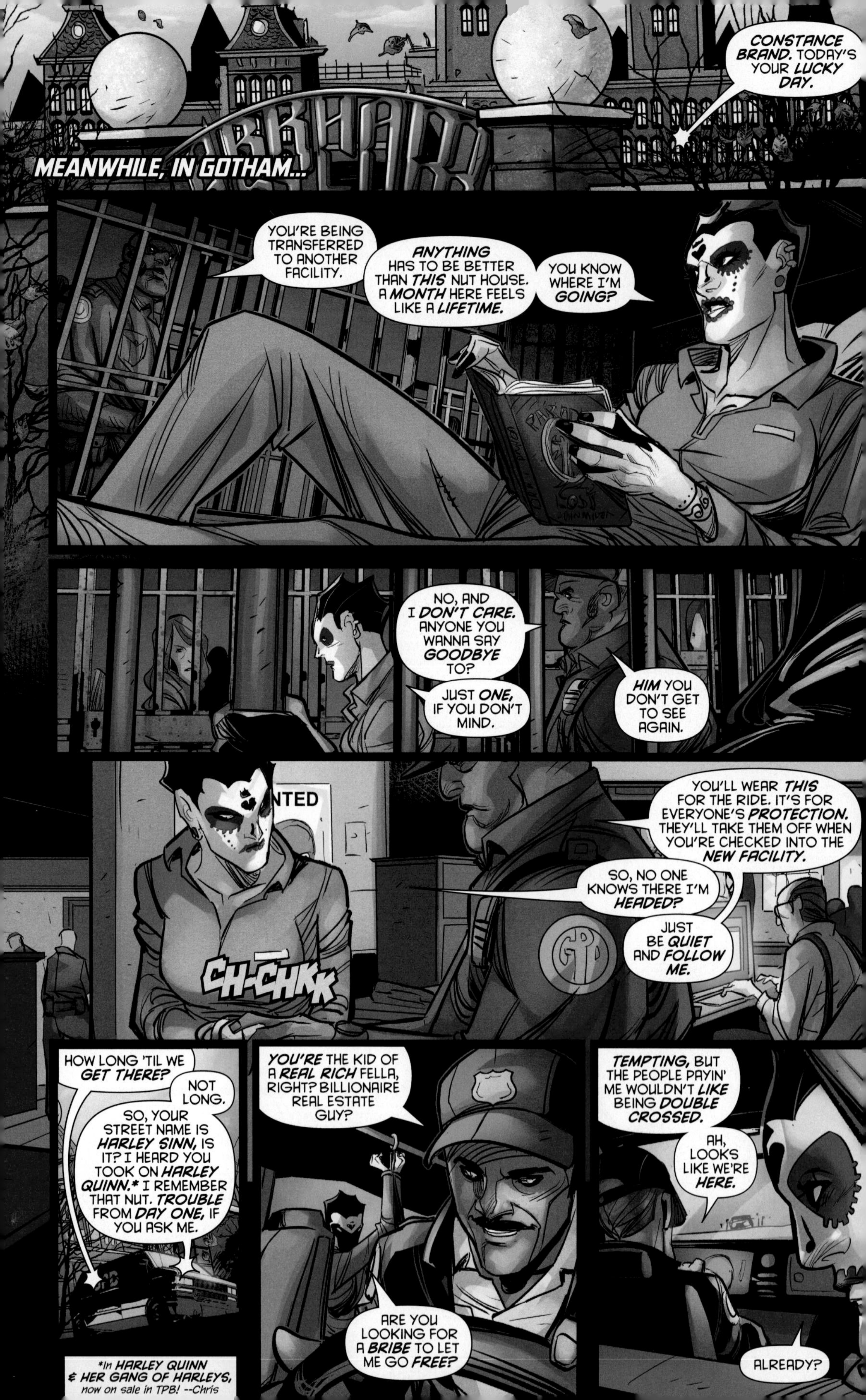
MEANWHILE, IN GOTHAM...
CONSTANCE BRAND. TODAY'S YOUR LUCKY DAY.
YOU'RE BEING TRANSFERRED TO ANOTHER FACILITY.
ANYTHING HAS TO BE BETTER THAN THIS NUT HOUSE. A MONTH HERE FEELS LIKE A LIFETIME.
YOU KNOW WHERE I'M GOING?
NO, AND I DON'T CARE. ANYONE YOU WANNA SAY GOODBYE TO?
JUST ONE, IF YOU DON'T MIND.
HIM YOU DON'T GET TO SEE AGAIN.
YOU'LL WEAR THIS FOR THE RIDE. IT'S FOR EVERYONE'S PROTECTION. THEY'LL TAKE THEM OFF WHEN YOU'RE CHECKED INTO THE NEW FACILITY.
CH-CHKK
SO, NO ONE KNOWS THERE I'M HEADED?
JUST BE QUIET AND FOLLOW ME.
HOW LONG 'TIL WE GET THERE?
NOT LONG.
SO, YOUR STREET NAME IS HARLEY SINN, IS IT? I HEARD YOU TOOK ON HARLEY QUINN.* I REMEMBER THAT NUT. TROUBLE FROM DAY ONE, IF YOU ASK ME.
*In HARLEY QUINN & HER GANG OF HARLEYS, now on sale in TPB! --Chris
YOU'RE THE KID OF A REAL RICH FELLA, RIGHT? BILLIONAIRE REAL ESTATE GUY?
ARE YOU LOOKING FOR A BRIBE TO LET ME GO FREE?
TEMPTING, BUT THE PEOPLE PAYIN' ME WOULDN'T LIKE BEING DOUBLE CROSSED.
AH, LOOKS LIKE WE'RE HERE.
ALREADY?

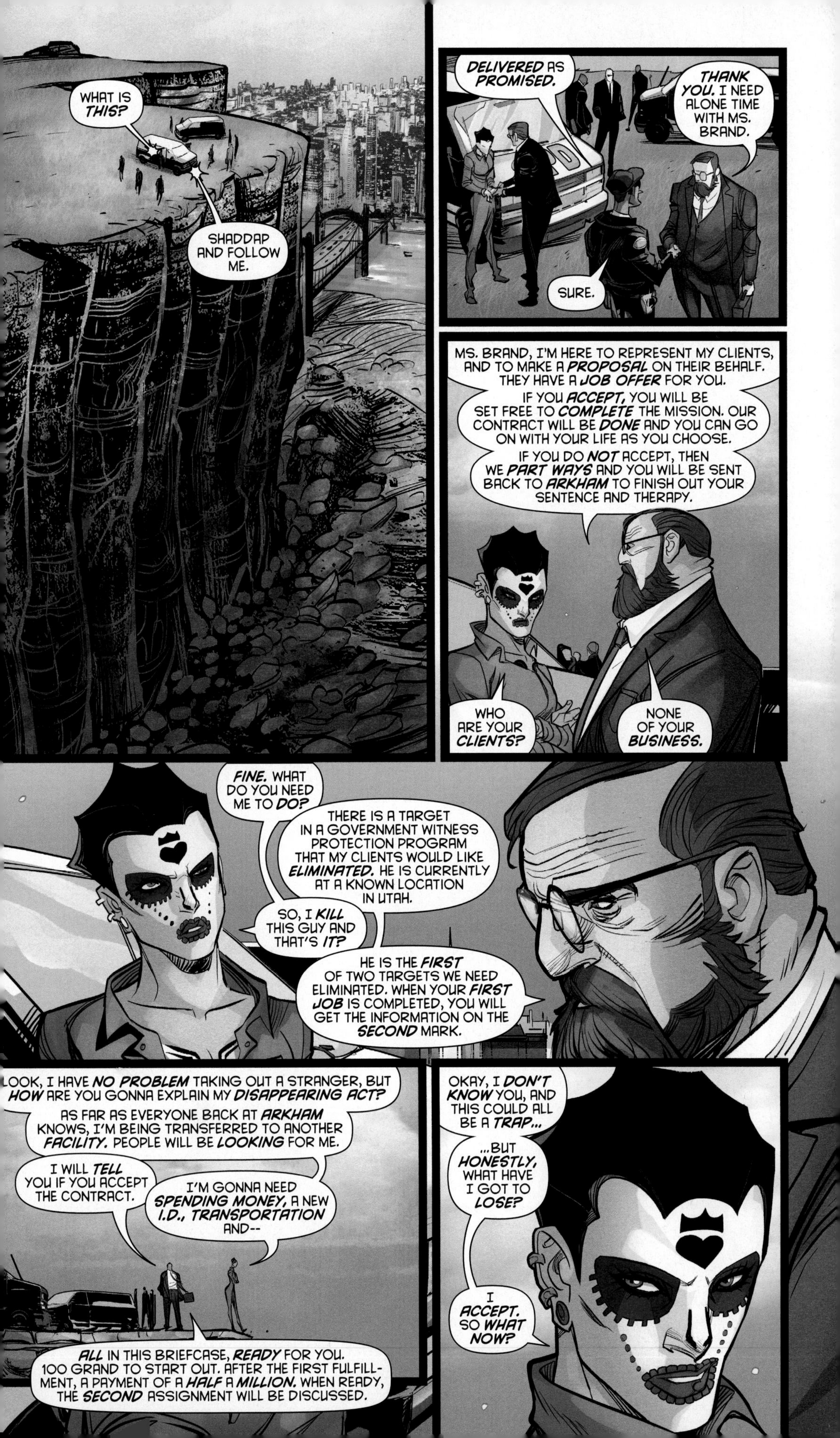
WHAT IS THIS?
SHADDAP AND FOLLOW ME.
DELIVERED AS PROMISED.
THANK YOU. I NEED ALONE TIME WITH MS. BRAND.
SURE.
MS. BRAND, I'M HERE TO REPRESENT MY CLIENTS, AND TO MAKE A PROPOSAL ON THEIR BEHALF. THEY HAVE A JOB OFFER FOR YOU.
IF YOU ACCEPT, YOU WILL BE SET FREE TO COMPLETE THE MISSION. OUR CONTRACT WILL BE DONE AND YOU CAN GO ON WITH YOUR LIFE AS YOU CHOOSE.
IF YOU DO NOT ACCEPT, THEN WE PART WAYS AND YOU WILL BE SENT BACK TO ARKHAM TO FINISH OUT YOUR SENTENCE AND THERAPY.
WHO ARE YOUR CLIENTS?
NONE OF YOUR BUSINESS.
FINE. WHAT DO YOU NEED ME TO DO?
THERE IS A TARGET IN A GOVERNMENT WITNESS PROTECTION PROGRAM THAT MY CLIENTS WOULD LIKE ELIMINATED. HE IS CURRENTLY AT A KNOWN LOCATION IN UTAH.
SO, I KILL THIS GUY AND THAT'S IT?
HE IS THE FIRST OF TWO TARGETS WE NEED ELIMINATED. WHEN YOUR FIRST JOB IS COMPLETED, YOU WILL GET THE INFORMATION ON THE SECOND MARK.
LOOK, I HAVE NO PROBLEM TAKING OUT A STRANGER, BUT HOW ARE YOU GONNA EXPLAIN MY DISAPPEARING ACT?
AS FAR AS EVERYONE BACK AT ARKHAM KNOWS, I'M BEING TRANSFERRED TO ANOTHER FACILITY. PEOPLE WILL BE LOOKING FOR ME.
I WILL TELL YOU IF YOU ACCEPT THE CONTRACT.
I'M GONNA NEED SPENDING MONEY, A NEW I.D., TRANSPORTATION AND--
ALL IN THIS BRIEFCASE, READY FOR YOU. 100 GRAND TO START OUT. AFTER THE FIRST FULFILLMENT, A PAYMENT OF A HALF A MILLION. WHEN READY, THE SECOND ASSIGNMENT WILL BE DISCUSSED.
OKAY, I DON'T KNOW YOU, AND THIS COULD ALL BE A TRAP...
...BUT HONESTLY, WHAT HAVE I GOT TO LOSE?
I ACCEPT. SO WHAT NOW?

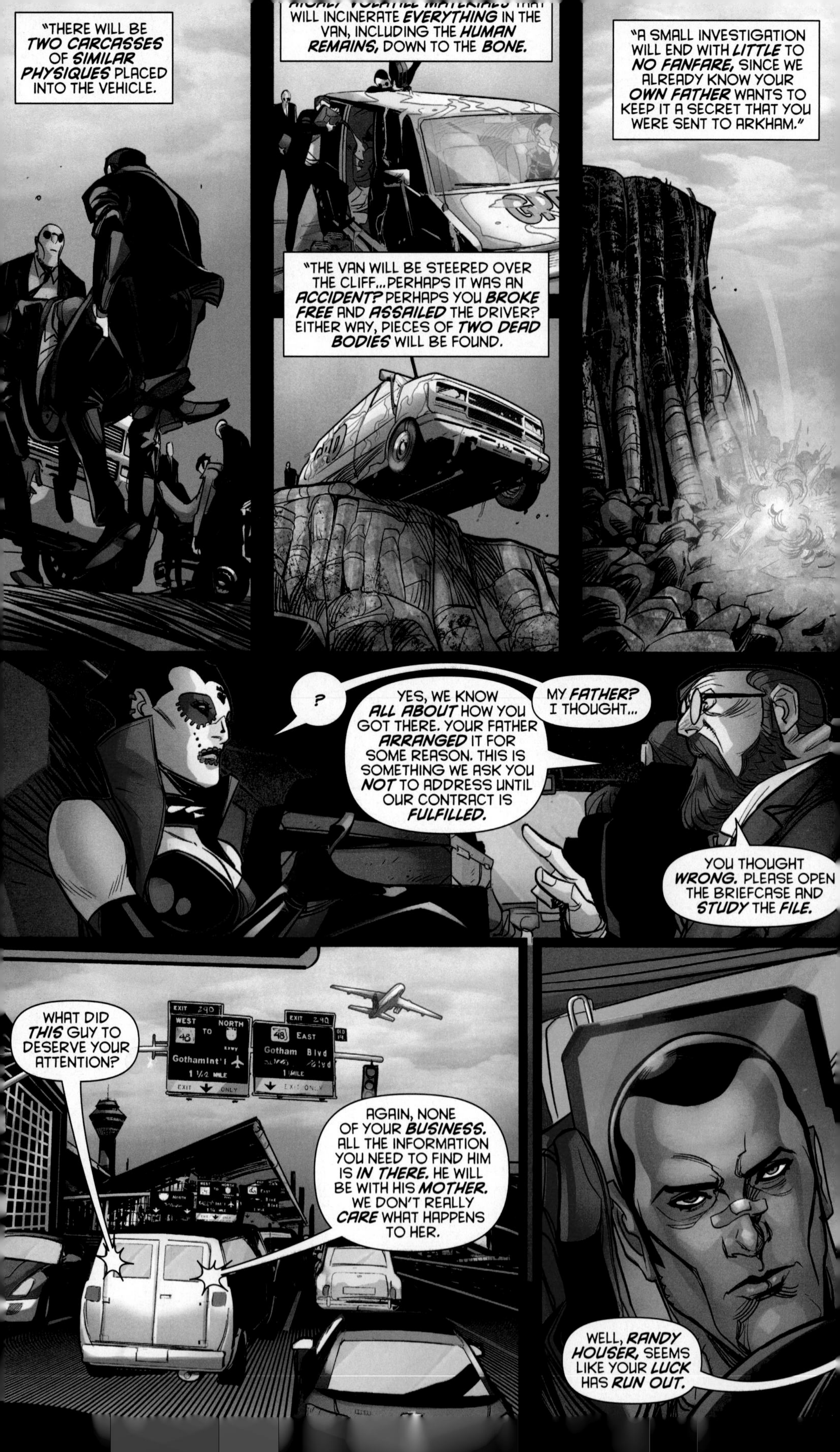

"THERE WILL BE TWO CARCASSES OF SIMILAR PHYSIQUES PLACED INTO THE VEHICLE.
WILL INCINERATE EVERYTHING IN THE VAN, INCLUDING THE HUMAN REMAINS, DOWN TO THE BONE.
"THE VAN WILL BE STEERED OVER THE CLIFF... PERHAPS IT WAS AN ACCIDENT? PERHAPS YOU BROKE FREE AND ASSAILED THE DRIVER? EITHER WAY, PIECES OF TWO DEAD BODIES WILL BE FOUND.
"A SMALL INVESTIGATION WILL END WITH LITTLE TO NO FANFARE, SINCE WE ALREADY KNOW YOUR OWN FATHER WANTS TO KEEP IT A SECRET THAT YOU WERE SENT TO ARKHAM."
?
MY FATHER? I THOUGHT...
YES, WE KNOW ALL ABOUT HOW YOU GOT THERE. YOUR FATHER ARRANGED IT FOR SOME REASON. THIS IS SOMETHING WE ASK YOU NOT TO ADDRESS UNTIL OUR CONTRACT IS FULFILLED.
YOU THOUGHT WRONG. PLEASE OPEN THE BRIEFCASE AND STUDY THE FILE.
EXIT 290
WEST TO NORTH 48
Gotham Int'l 1 1/2 MILE
EXIT ONLY
EXIT 290
48 EAST
Gotham Blvd 1 MILE
EXIT ONLY
WHAT DID THIS GUY TO DESERVE YOUR ATTENTION?
AGAIN, NONE OF YOUR BUSINESS. ALL THE INFORMATION YOU NEED TO FIND HIM IS IN THERE. HE WILL BE WITH HIS MOTHER. WE DON'T REALLY CARE WHAT HAPPENS TO HER.
WELL, RANDY HOUSER, SEEMS LIKE YOUR LUCK HAS RUN OUT.

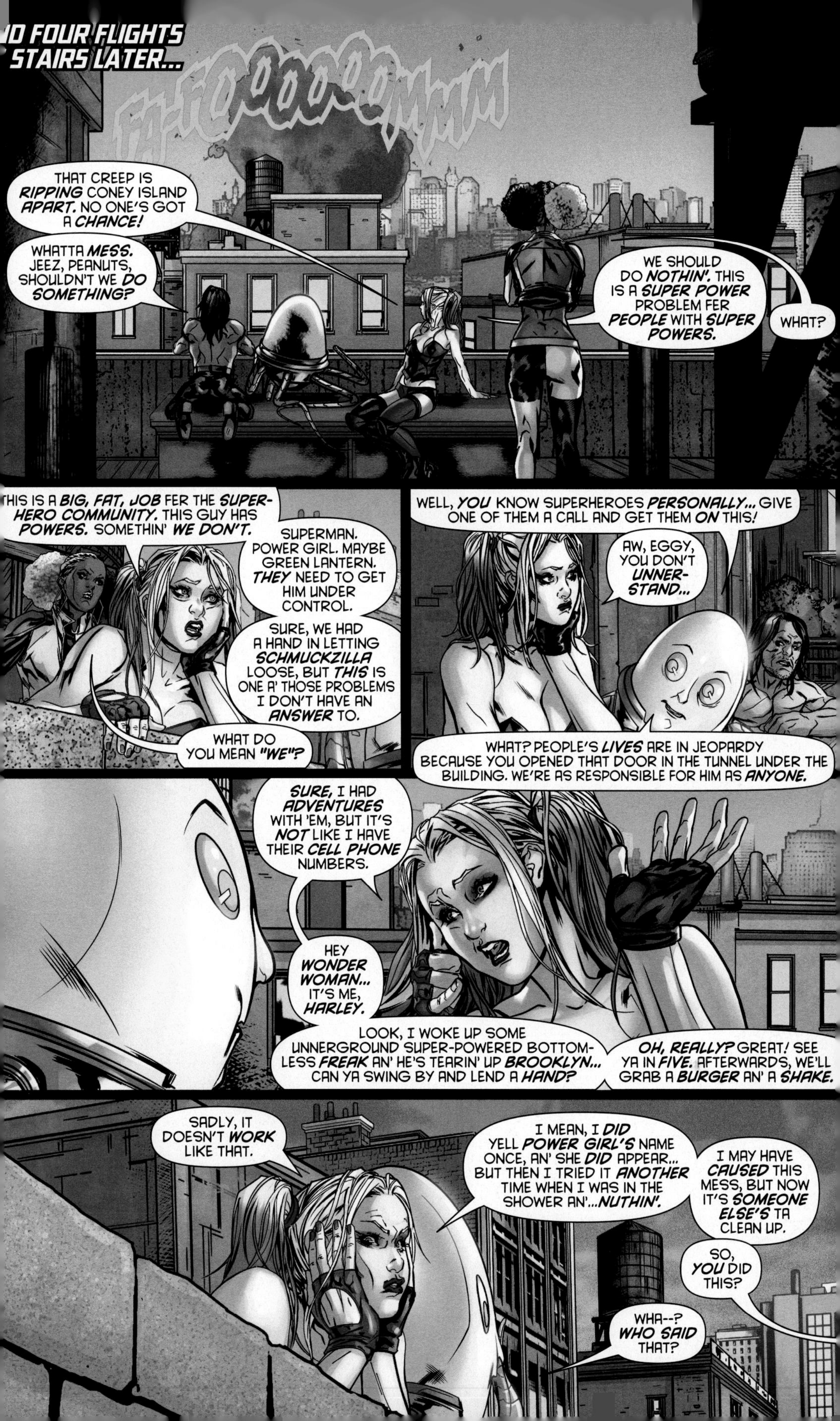

D FOUR FLIGHTS STAIRS LATER...
FA-FOOOOOOOMMM
THAT CREEP IS RIPPING CONEY ISLAND APART. NO ONE'S GOT A CHANCE!
WHATTA MESS. JEEZ, PEANUTS, SHOULDN'T WE DO SOMETHING?
WE SHOULD DO NOTHIN'. THIS IS A SUPER POWER PROBLEM FER PEOPLE WITH SUPER POWERS.
WHAT?
THIS IS A BIG, FAT, JOB FER THE SUPER-HERO COMMUNITY. THIS GUY HAS POWERS. SOMETHIN' WE DON'T.
SUPERMAN. POWER GIRL. MAYBE GREEN LANTERN. THEY NEED TO GET HIM UNDER CONTROL.
SURE, WE HAD A HAND IN LETTING SCHMUCKZILLA LOOSE, BUT THIS IS ONE A' THOSE PROBLEMS I DON'T HAVE AN ANSWER TO.
WHAT DO YOU MEAN "WE"?
WELL, YOU KNOW SUPERHEROES PERSONALLY... GIVE ONE OF THEM A CALL AND GET THEM ON THIS!
AW, EGGY, YOU DON'T UNNER-STAND...
WHAT? PEOPLE'S LIVES ARE IN JEOPARDY BECAUSE YOU OPENED THAT DOOR IN THE TUNNEL UNDER THE BUILDING. WE'RE AS RESPONSIBLE FOR HIM AS ANYONE.
SURE, I HAD ADVENTURES WITH 'EM, BUT IT'S NOT LIKE I HAVE THEIR CELL PHONE NUMBERS.
HEY WONDER WOMAN... IT'S ME, HARLEY.
LOOK, I WOKE UP SOME UNNERGROUND SUPER-POWERED BOTTOM-LESS FREAK AN' HE'S TEARIN' UP BROOKLYN... CAN YA SWING BY AND LEND A HAND?
OH, REALLY? GREAT! SEE YA IN FIVE. AFTERWARDS, WE'LL GRAB A BURGER AN' A SHAKE.
SADLY, IT DOESN'T WORK LIKE THAT.
I MEAN, I DID YELL POWER GIRL'S NAME ONCE, AN' SHE DID APPEAR... BUT THEN I TRIED IT ANOTHER TIME WHEN I WAS IN THE SHOWER AN'...NUTHIN'.
I MAY HAVE CAUSED THIS MESS, BUT NOW IT'S SOMEONE ELSE'S TA CLEAN UP.
SO, YOU DID THIS?
WHA--? WHO SAID THAT?

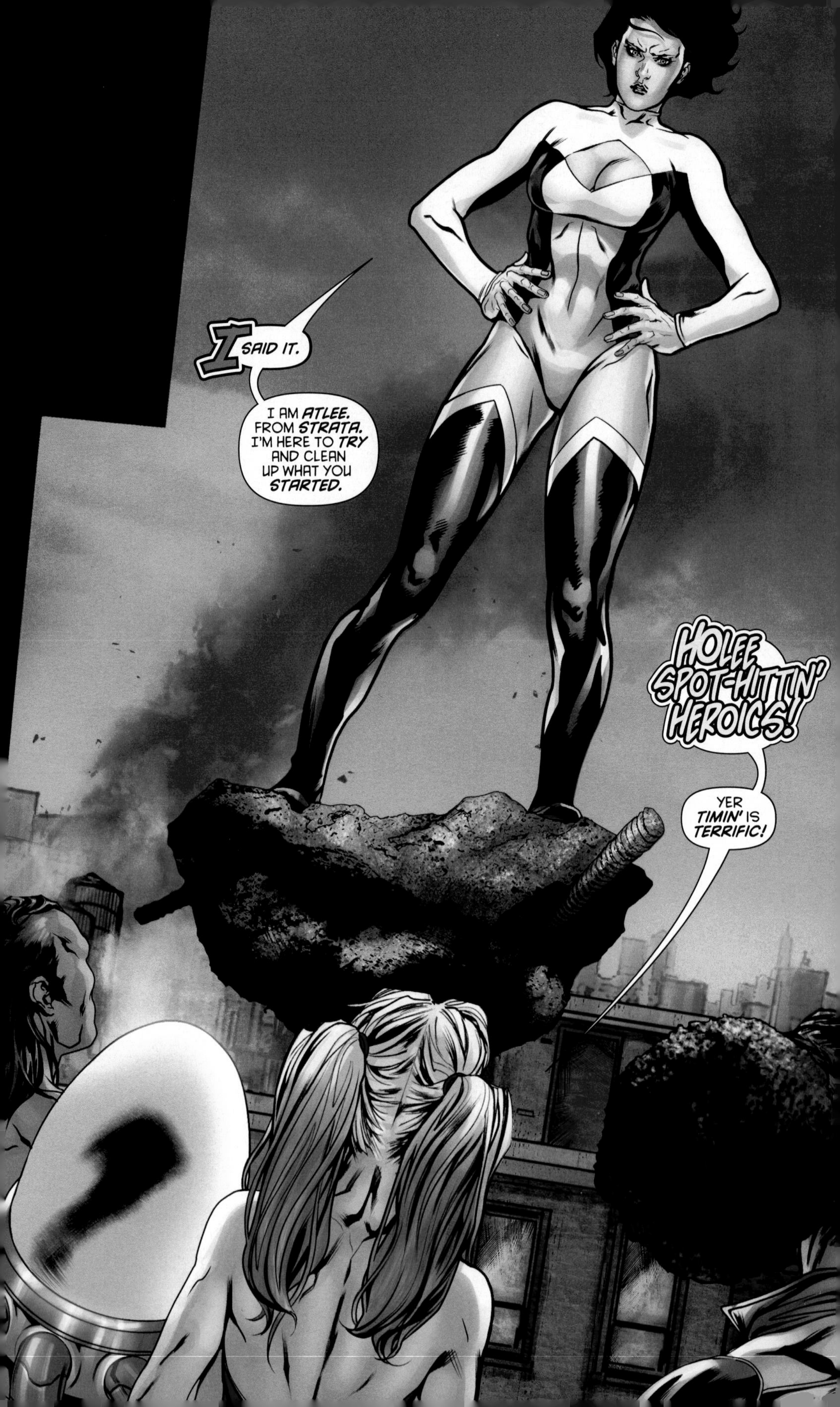

I SAID IT.
I AM ATLEE. FROM STRATA. I'M HERE TO TRY AND CLEAN UP WHAT YOU STARTED.
HOLEE SPOT-HITTIN' HEROICS!
YER TIMIN' IS TERRIFIC!

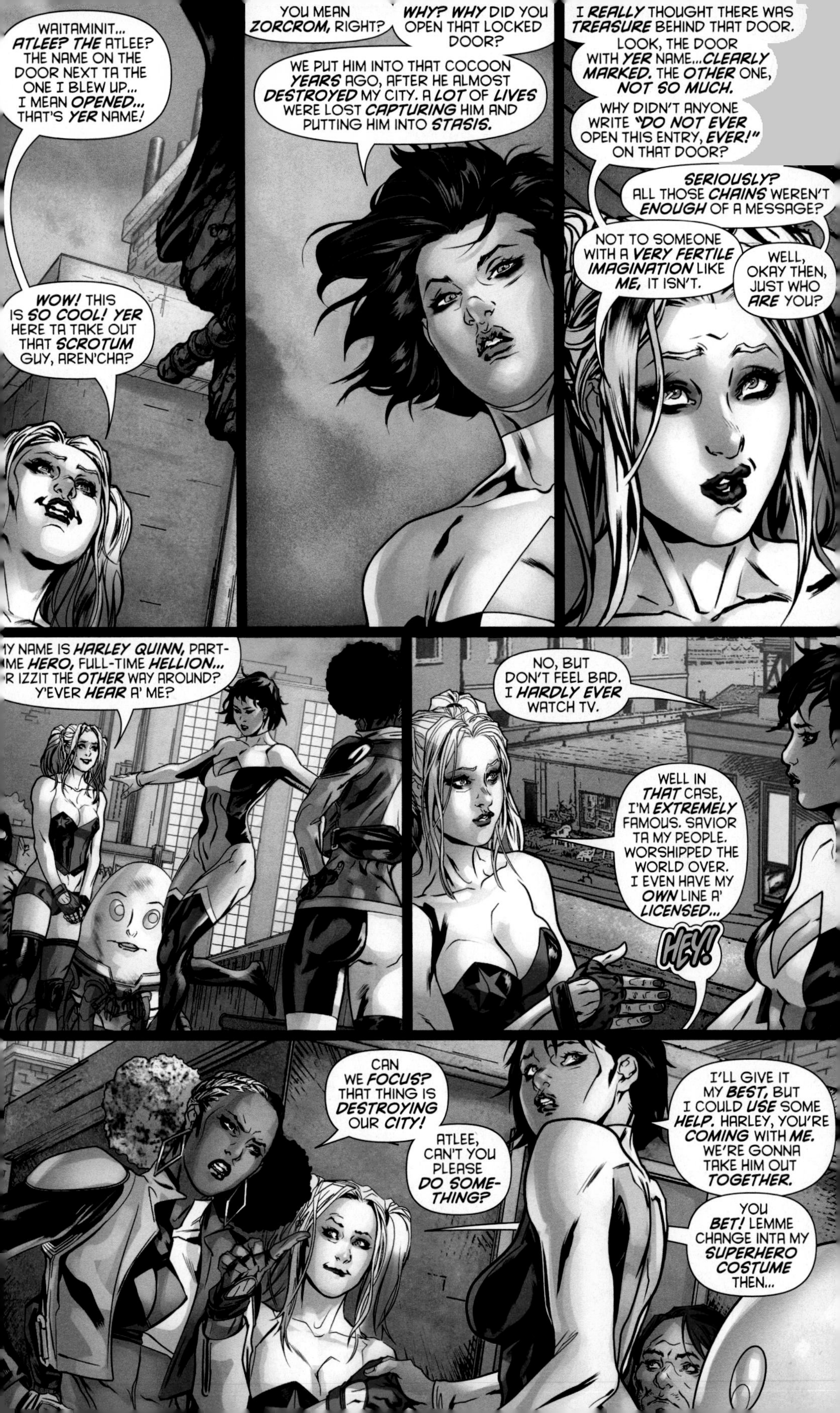
WAITAMINIT... ATLEE? THE ATLEE? THE NAME ON THE DOOR NEXT TA THE ONE I BLEW UP... I MEAN OPENED... THAT'S YER NAME!
WOW! THIS IS SO COOL! YER HERE TA TAKE OUT THAT SCROTUM GUY, AREN'CHA?
YOU MEAN ZORCROM, RIGHT?
WHY? WHY DID YOU OPEN THAT LOCKED DOOR?
WE PUT HIM INTO THAT COCOON YEARS AGO, AFTER HE ALMOST DESTROYED MY CITY. A LOT OF LIVES WERE LOST CAPTURING HIM AND PUTTING HIM INTO STASIS.
I REALLY THOUGHT THERE WAS TREASURE BEHIND THAT DOOR.
LOOK, THE DOOR WITH YER NAME...CLEARLY MARKED. THE OTHER ONE, NOT SO MUCH.
WHY DIDN'T ANYONE WRITE "DO NOT EVER OPEN THIS ENTRY, EVER!" ON THAT DOOR?
SERIOUSLY? ALL THOSE CHAINS WEREN'T ENOUGH OF A MESSAGE?
NOT TO SOMEONE WITH A VERY FERTILE IMAGINATION LIKE ME, IT ISN'T.
WELL, OKAY THEN, JUST WHO ARE YOU?
MY NAME IS HARLEY QUINN, PART-TIME HERO, FULL-TIME HELLION... OR IZZIT THE OTHER WAY AROUND? Y'EVER HEAR A' ME?
NO, BUT DON'T FEEL BAD. I HARDLY EVER WATCH TV.
WELL IN THAT CASE, I'M EXTREMELY FAMOUS. SAVIOR TA MY PEOPLE. WORSHIPPED THE WORLD OVER. I EVEN HAVE MY OWN LINE A' LICENSED...
HEY!
CAN WE FOCUS? THAT THING IS DESTROYING OUR CITY!
ATLEE, CAN'T YOU PLEASE DO SOME-THING?
I'LL GIVE IT MY BEST, BUT I COULD USE SOME HELP. HARLEY, YOU'RE COMING WITH ME. WE'RE GONNA TAKE HIM OUT TOGETHER.
YOU BET! LEMME CHANGE INTA MY SUPERHERO COSTUME THEN...

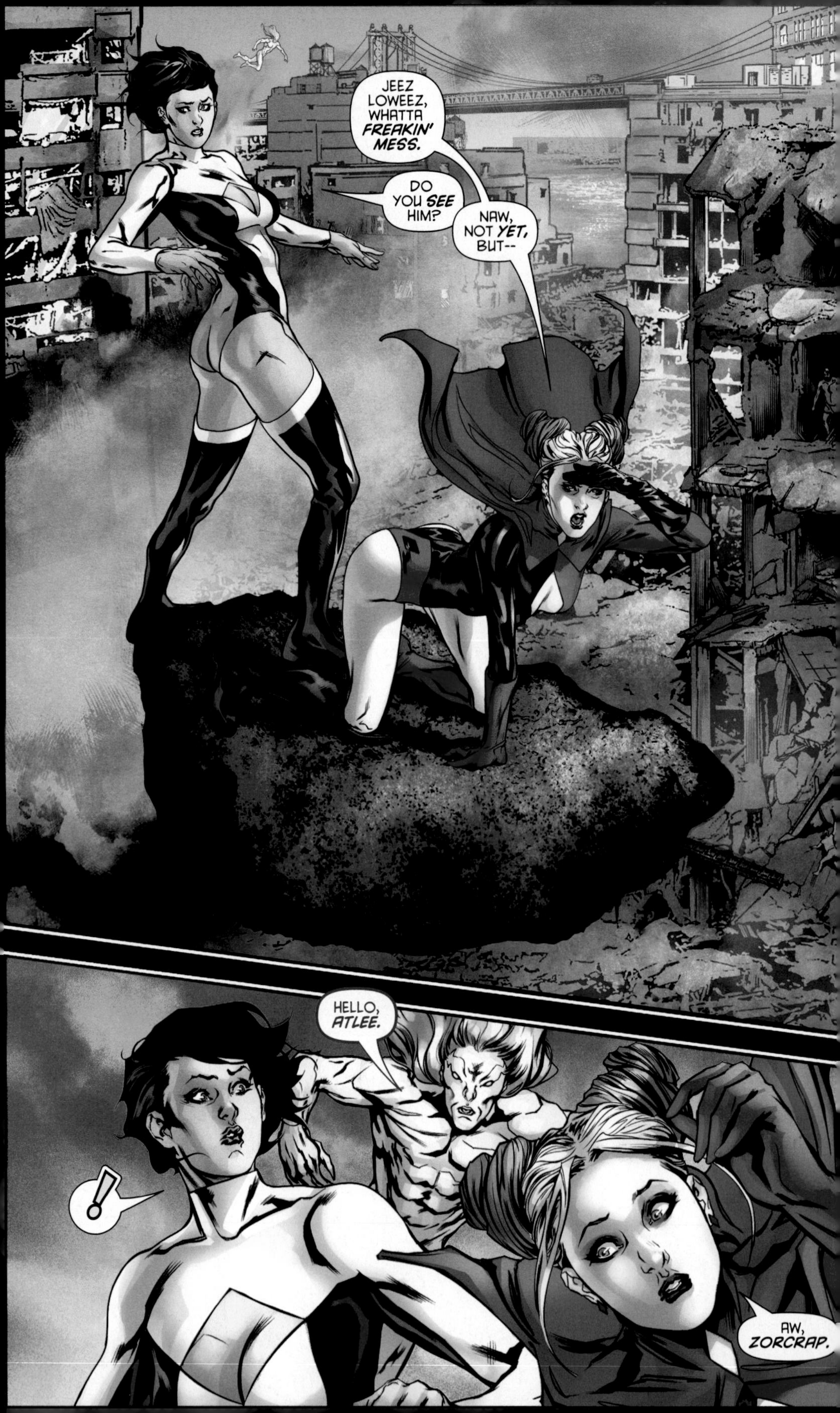
JEEZ LOWEEZ, WHATTA FREAKIN' MESS.
DO YOU SEE HIM?
NAW, NOT YET, BUT--
HELLO, ATLEE.
!
AW, ZORCRAP.

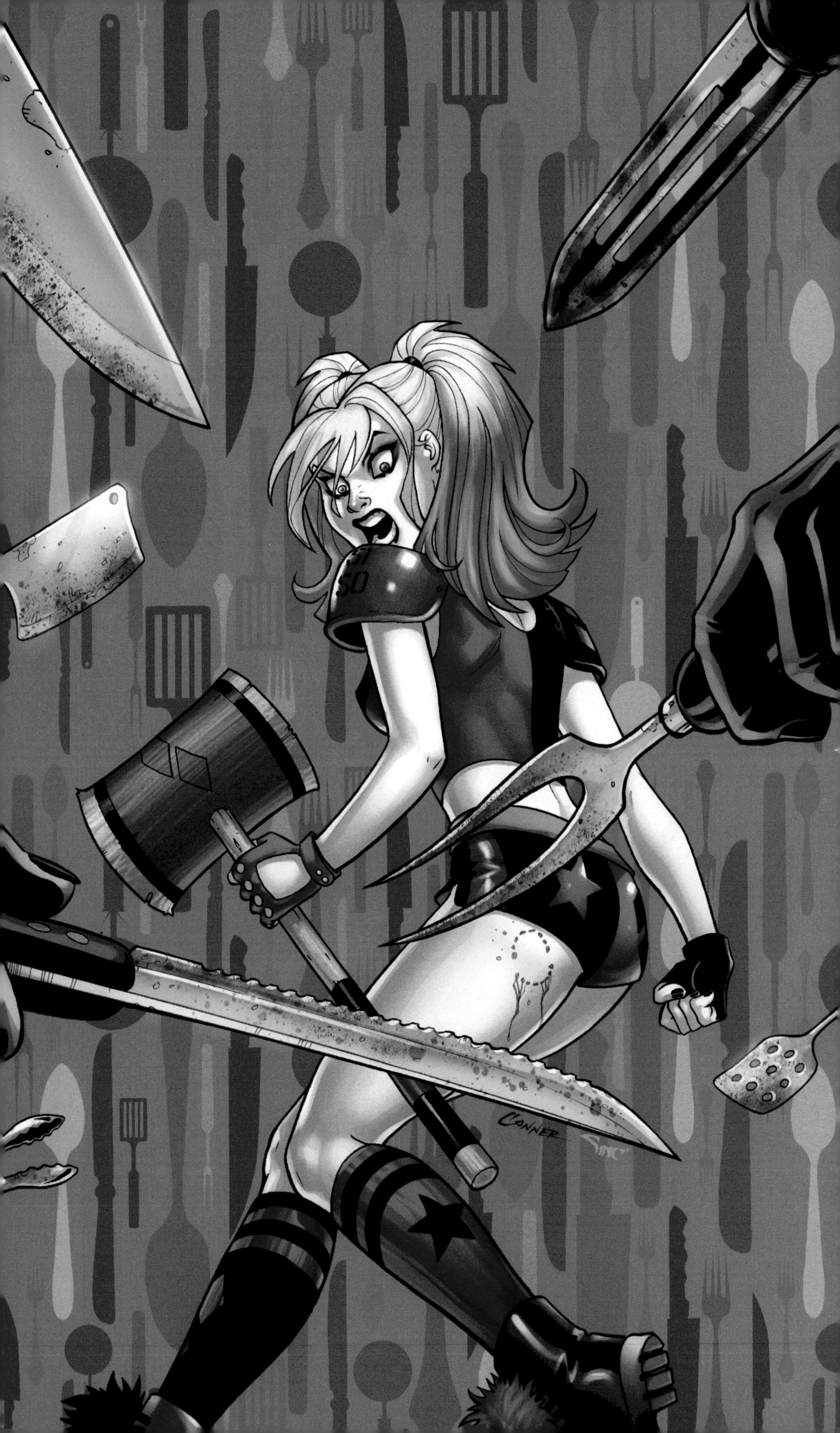
CONNER

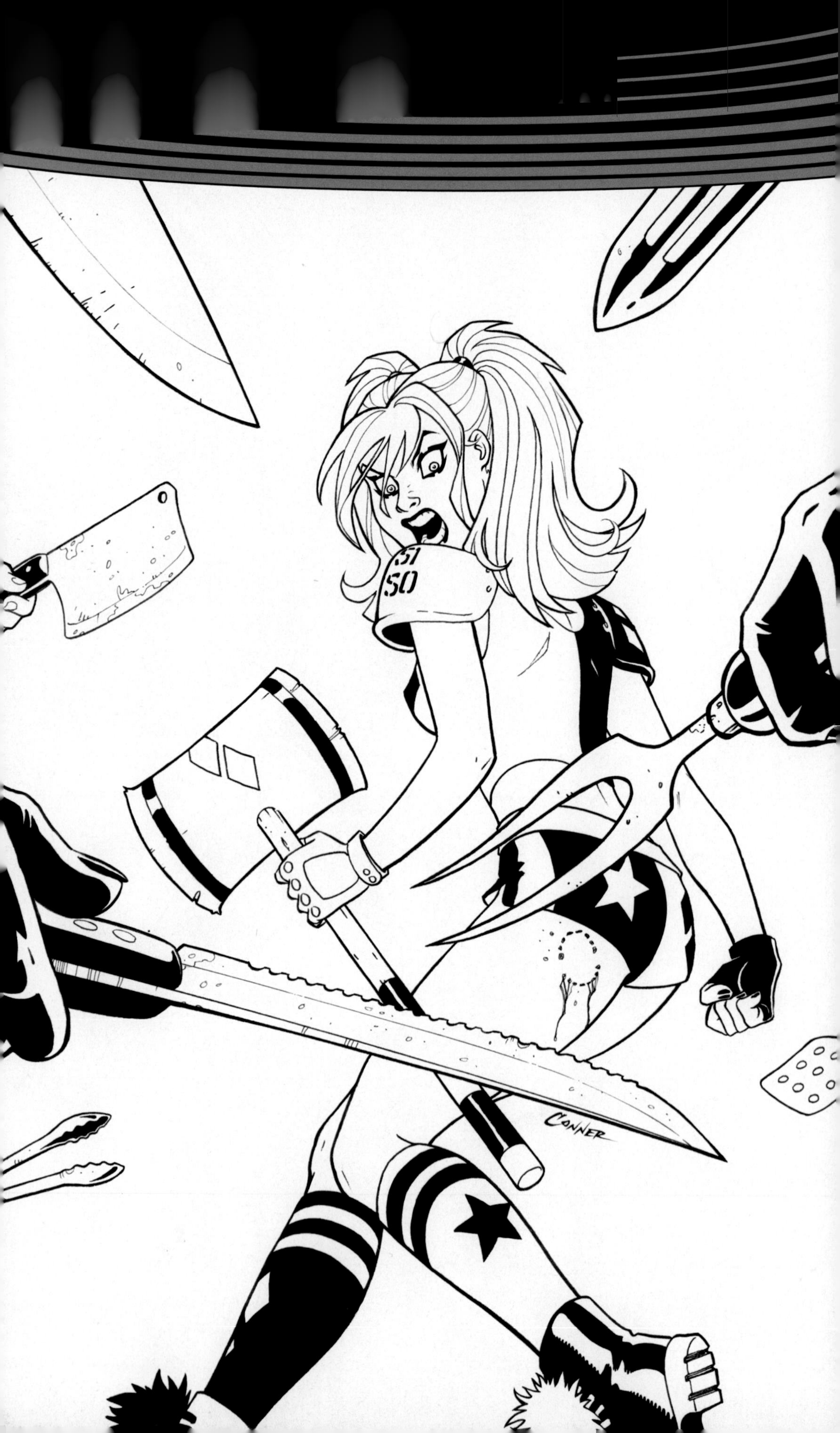
5150
CONNER

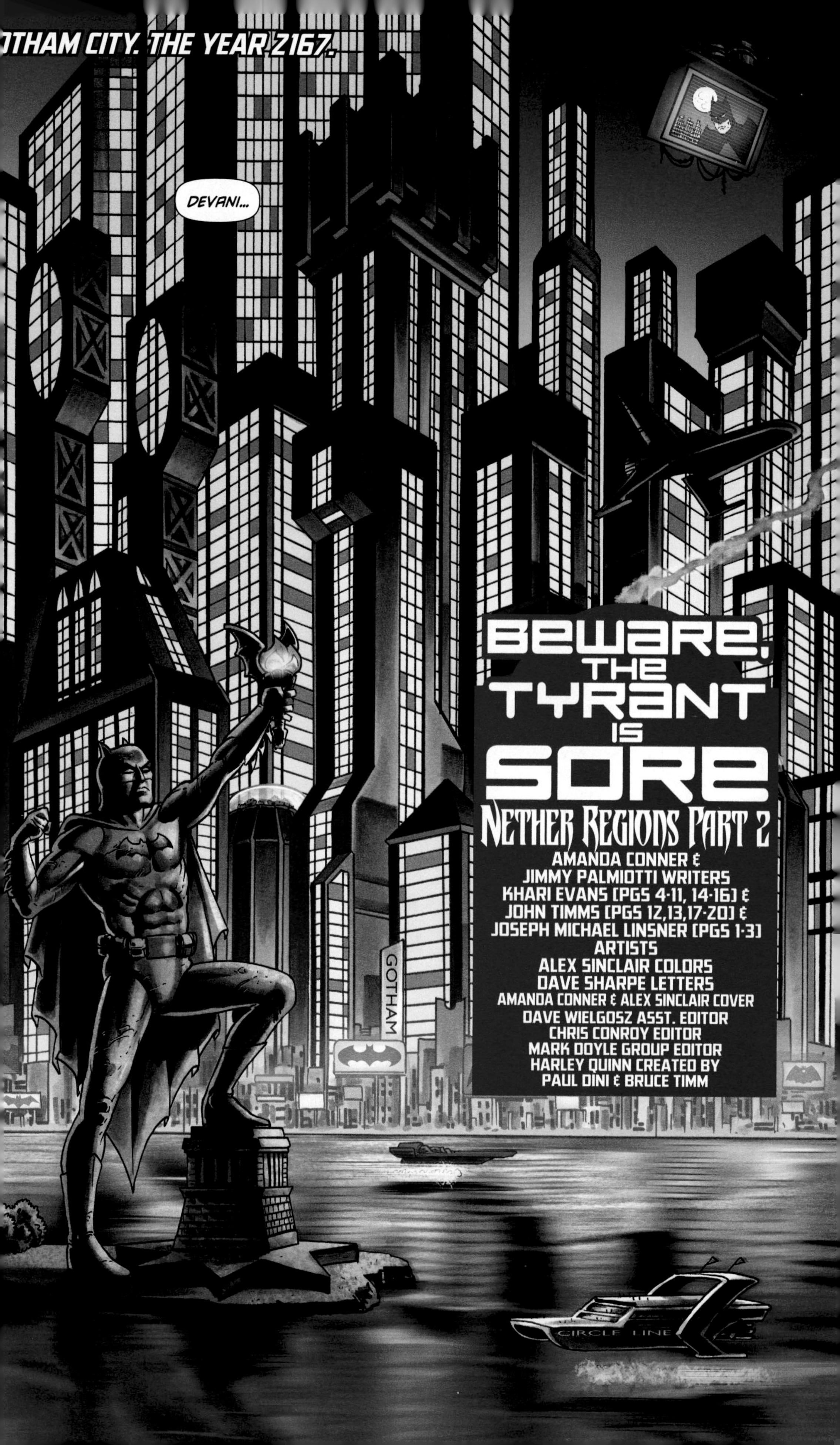

OTHAM CITY. THE YEAR 2167.
DEVANI...
BEWARE, THE TYRANT IS SORE
NETHER REGIONS PART 2
AMANDA CONNER & JIMMY PALMIOTTI WRITERS
KHARI EVANS [PGS 4-11, 14-16] & JOHN TIMMS [PGS 12,13,17-20] & JOSEPH MICHAEL LINSNER [PGS 1-3] ARTISTS
ALEX SINCLAIR COLORS
DAVE SHARPE LETTERS
AMANDA CONNER & ALEX SINCLAIR COVER
DAVE WIELGOSZ ASST. EDITOR
CHRIS CONROY EDITOR
MARK DOYLE GROUP EDITOR
HARLEY QUINN CREATED BY PAUL DINI & BRUCE TIMM
GOTHAM
CIRCLE LINE

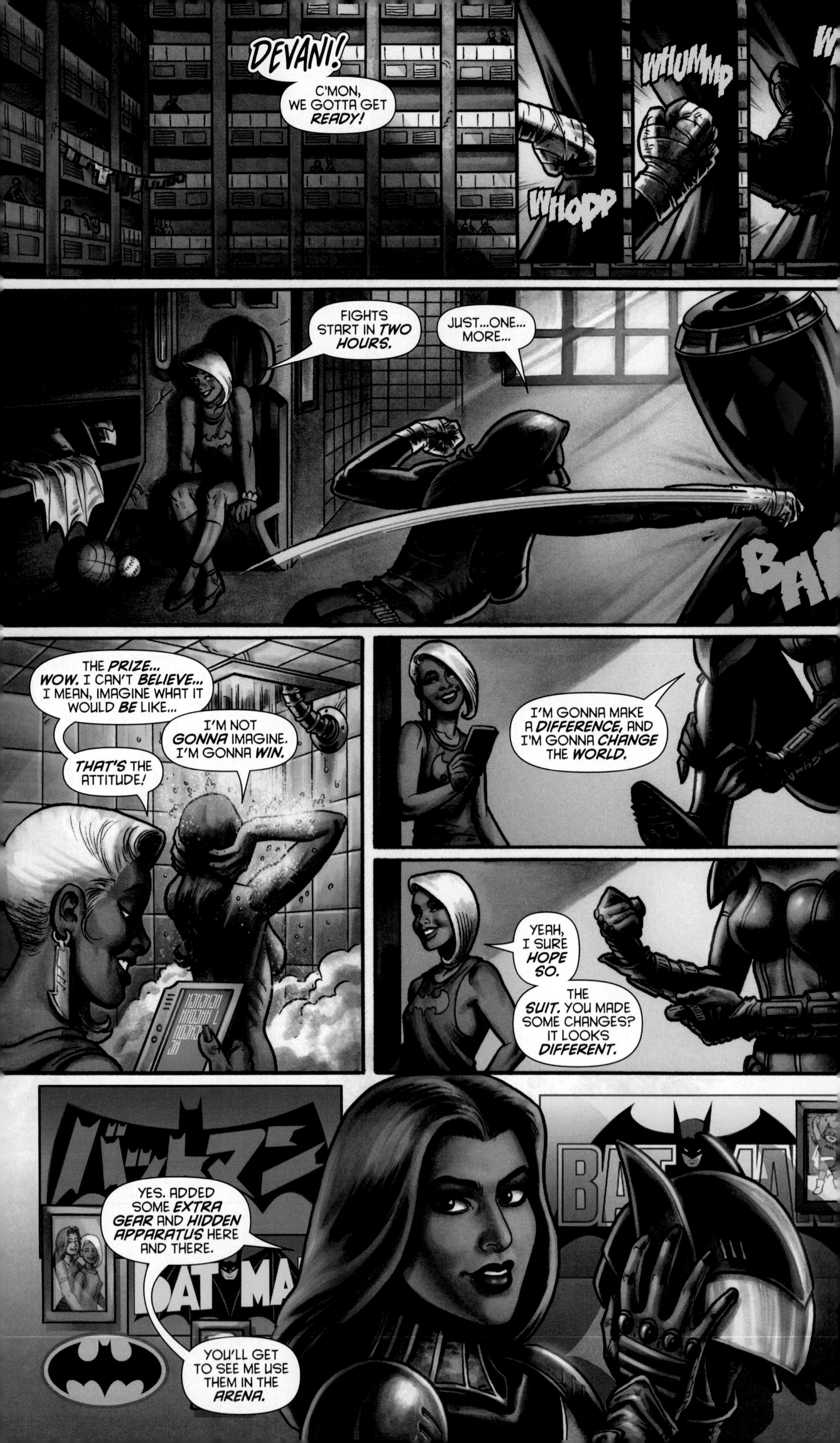
DEVANI!
C'MON, WE GOTTA GET READY!
WHUMMP
WHOPP
FIGHTS START IN TWO HOURS.
JUST...ONE... MORE...
THE PRIZE... WOW. I CAN'T BELIEVE... I MEAN, IMAGINE WHAT IT WOULD BE LIKE...
THAT'S THE ATTITUDE!
I'M NOT GONNA IMAGINE. I'M GONNA WIN.
I'M GONNA MAKE A DIFFERENCE, AND I'M GONNA CHANGE THE WORLD.
YEAH, I SURE HOPE SO.
THE SUIT. YOU MADE SOME CHANGES? IT LOOKS DIFFERENT.
YES. ADDED SOME EXTRA GEAR AND HIDDEN APPARATUS HERE AND THERE.
YOU'LL GET TO SEE ME USE THEM IN THE ARENA.

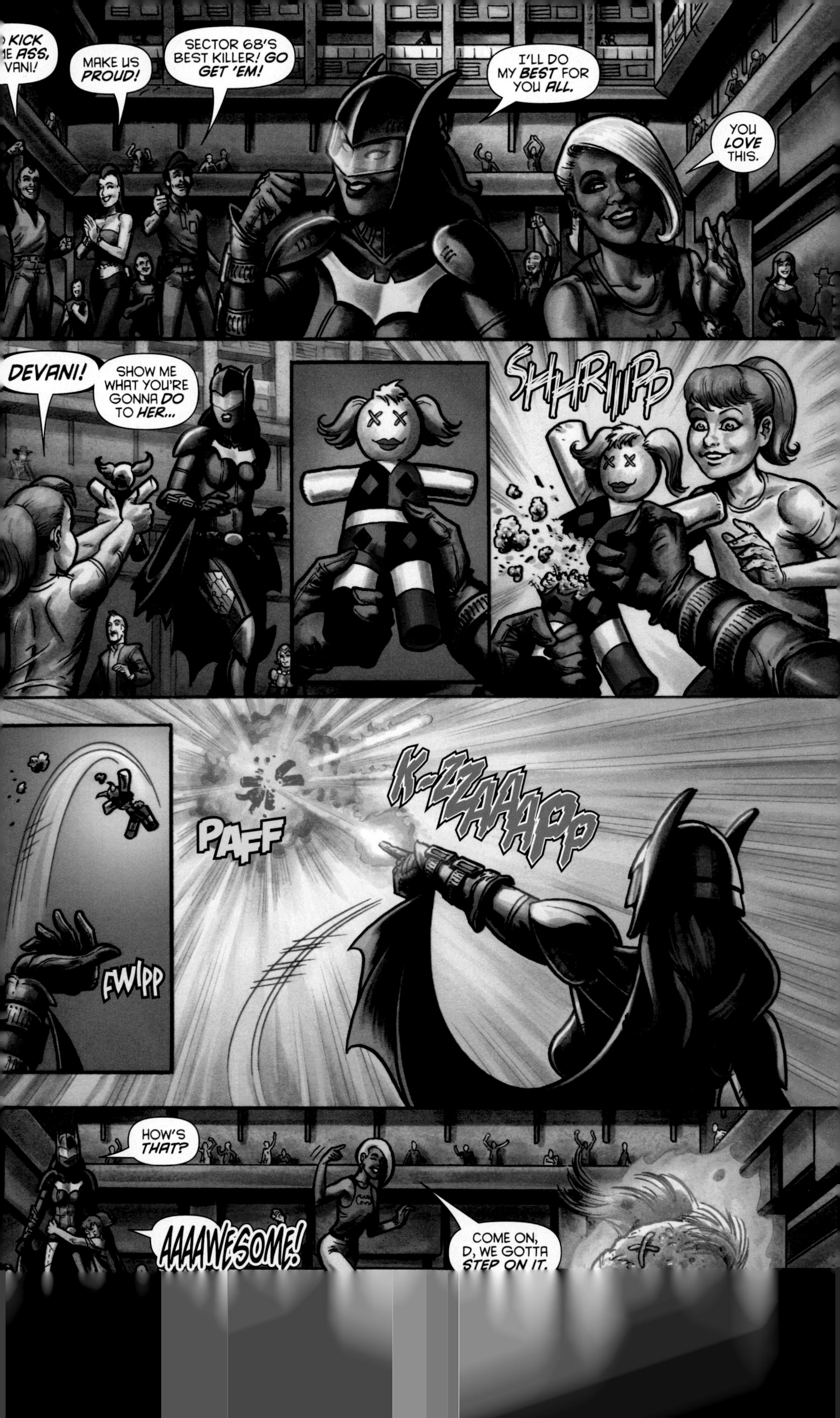

KICK E ASS, VANI!
MAKE US PROUD!
SECTOR 68'S BEST KILLER! GO GET 'EM!
I'LL DO MY BEST FOR YOU ALL.
YOU LOVE THIS.
DEVANI!
SHOW ME WHAT YOU'RE GONNA DO TO HER...
SHHRIIPP
FWIPP
PAFF
K-ZZAAAPP
HOW'S THAT?
AAAAWESOME!
COME ON, D, WE GOTTA STEP ON IT.

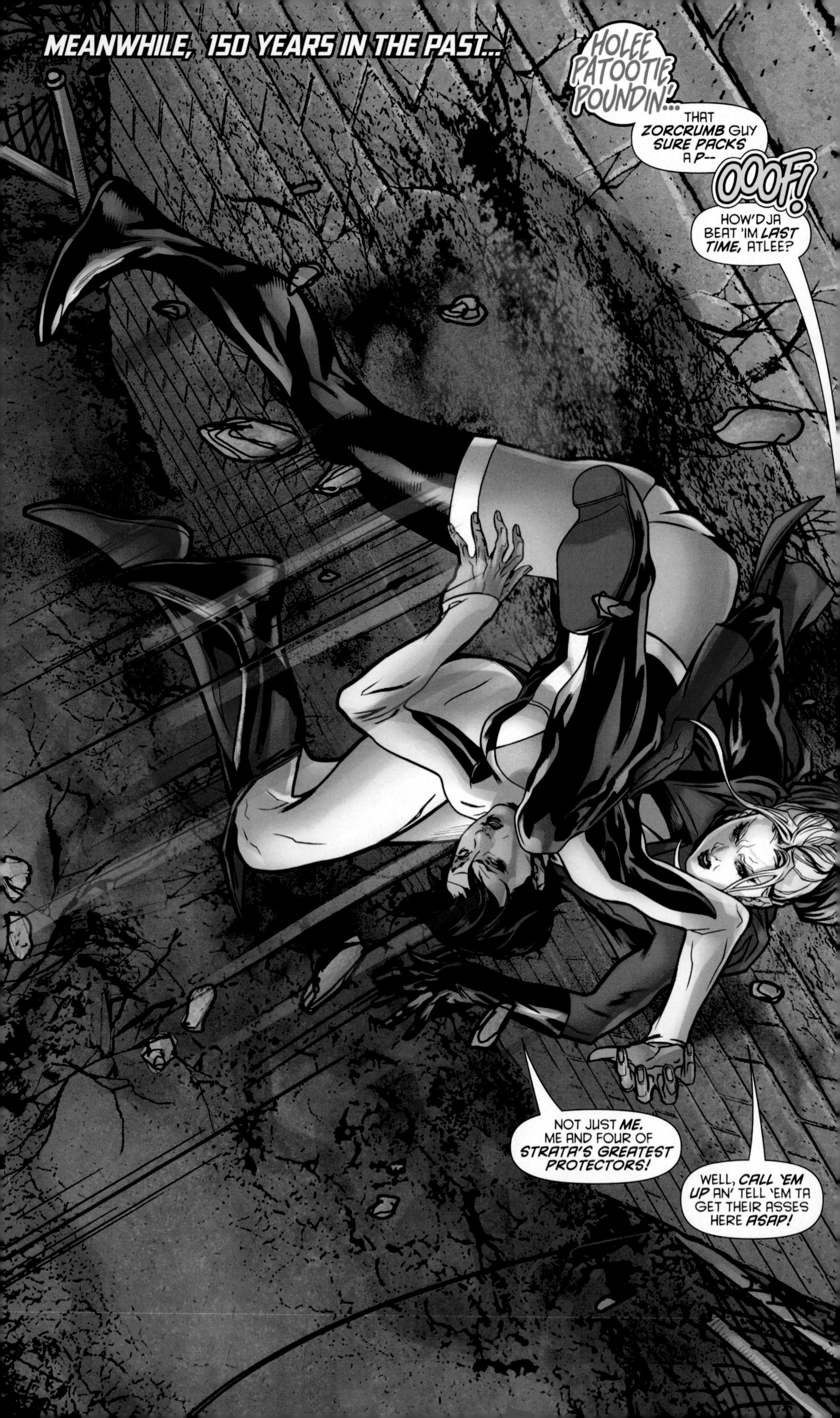
MEANWHILE, 150 YEARS IN THE PAST...
HOLEE PATOOTIE POUNDIN'...
THAT ZORCRUMB GUY SURE PACKS A P--
OOOF!
HOW'DJA BEAT 'IM LAST TIME, ATLEE?
NOT JUST ME. ME AND FOUR OF STRATA'S GREATEST PROTECTORS!
WELL, CALL 'EM UP AN' TELL 'EM TA GET THEIR ASSES HERE ASAP!

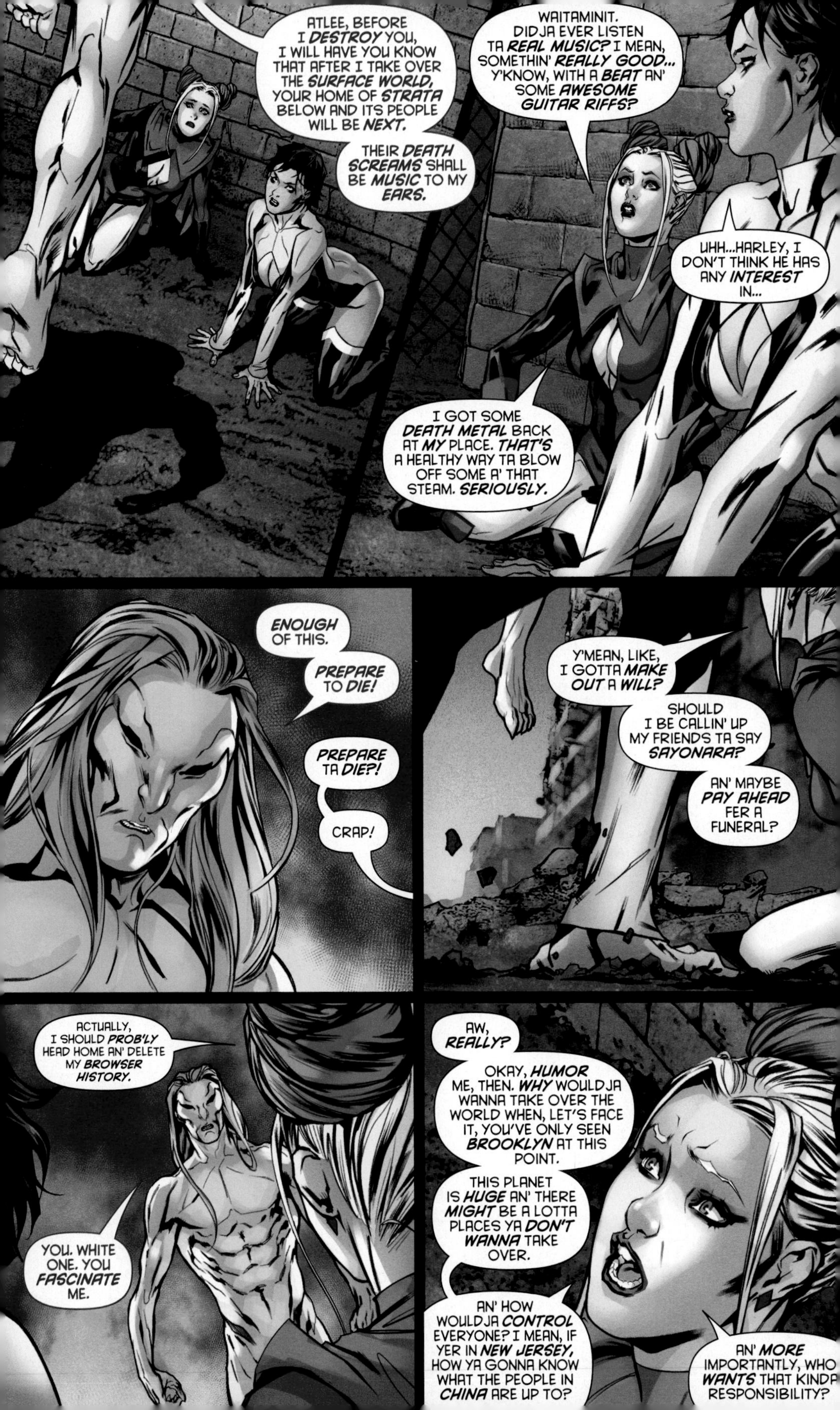
ATLEE, BEFORE I DESTROY YOU, I WILL HAVE YOU KNOW THAT AFTER I TAKE OVER THE SURFACE WORLD, YOUR HOME OF STRATA BELOW AND ITS PEOPLE WILL BE NEXT.
THEIR DEATH SCREAMS SHALL BE MUSIC TO MY EARS.
WAITAMINIT. DIDJA EVER LISTEN TA REAL MUSIC? I MEAN, SOMETHIN' REALLY GOOD... Y'KNOW, WITH A BEAT AN' SOME AWESOME GUITAR RIFFS?
UHH...HARLEY, I DON'T THINK HE HAS ANY INTEREST IN...
I GOT SOME DEATH METAL BACK AT MY PLACE. THAT'S A HEALTHY WAY TA BLOW OFF SOME A' THAT STEAM. SERIOUSLY.
ENOUGH OF THIS.
PREPARE TO DIE!
PREPARE TA DIE?!
CRAP!
Y'MEAN, LIKE, I GOTTA MAKE OUT A WILL?
SHOULD I BE CALLIN' UP MY FRIENDS TA SAY SAYONARA?
AN' MAYBE PAY AHEAD FER A FUNERAL?
ACTUALLY, I SHOULD PROB'LY HEAD HOME AN' DELETE MY BROWSER HISTORY.
YOU. WHITE ONE. YOU FASCINATE ME.
AW, REALLY?
OKAY, HUMOR ME, THEN. WHY WOULDJA WANNA TAKE OVER THE WORLD WHEN, LET'S FACE IT, YOU'VE ONLY SEEN BROOKLYN AT THIS POINT.
THIS PLANET IS HUGE AN' THERE MIGHT BE A LOTTA PLACES YA DON'T WANNA TAKE OVER.
AN' HOW WOULDJA CONTROL EVERYONE? I MEAN, IF YER IN NEW JERSEY, HOW YA GONNA KNOW WHAT THE PEOPLE IN CHINA ARE UP TO?
AN' MORE IMPORTANTLY, WHO WANTS THAT KINDA RESPONSIBILITY?

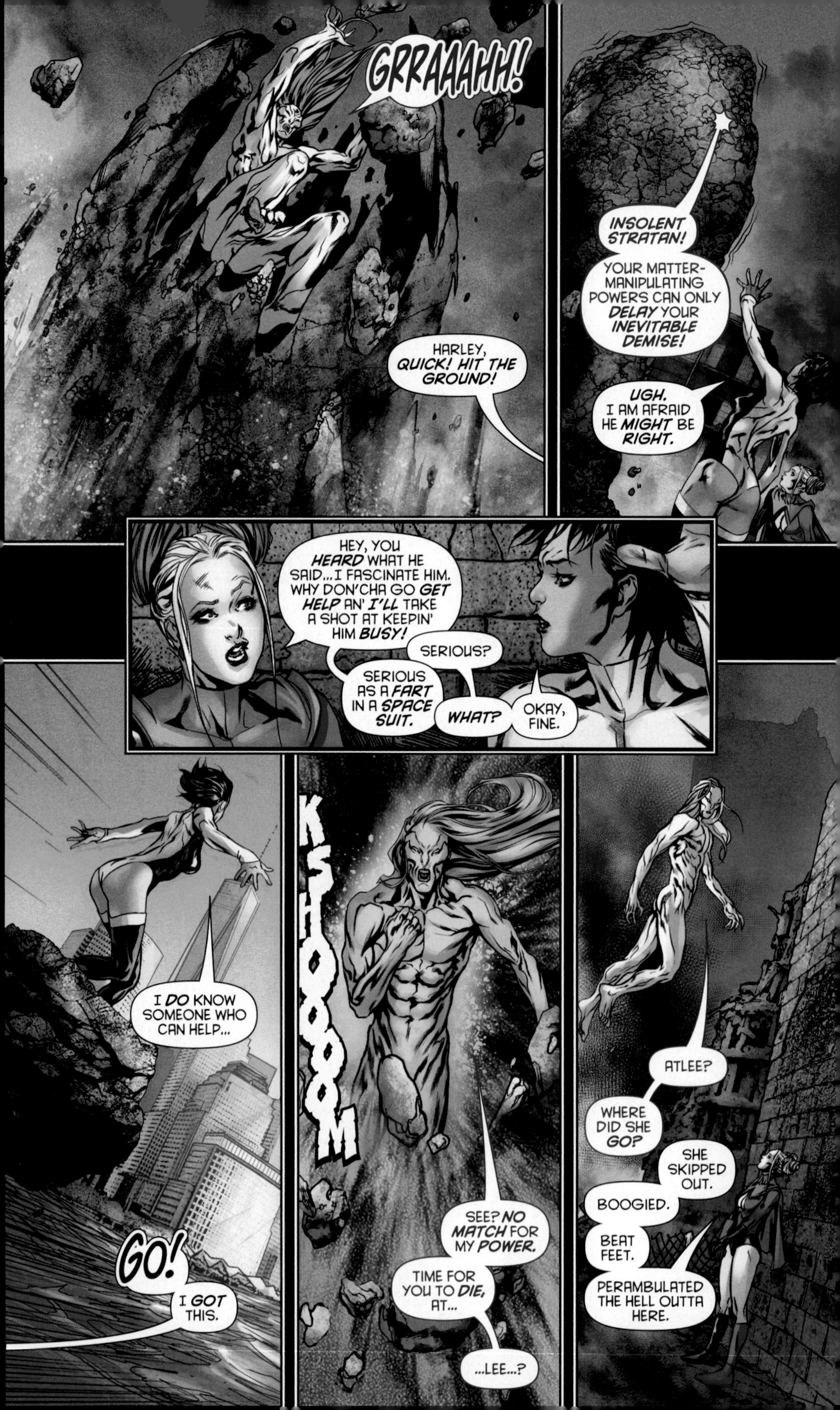

GRRAAAHH!
HARLEY, QUICK! HIT THE GROUND!
INSOLENT STRATAN!
YOUR MATTER-MANIPULATING POWERS CAN ONLY DELAY YOUR INEVITABLE DEMISE!
UGH. I AM AFRAID HE MIGHT BE RIGHT.
HEY, YOU HEARD WHAT HE SAID...I FASCINATE HIM. WHY DON'CHA GO GET HELP AN' I'LL TAKE A SHOT AT KEEPIN' HIM BUSY!
SERIOUS?
SERIOUS AS A FART IN A SPACE SUIT.
WHAT?
OKAY, FINE.
I DO KNOW SOMEONE WHO CAN HELP...
GO!
I GOT THIS.
KSHOOOOOM
SEE? NO MATCH FOR MY POWER.
TIME FOR YOU TO DIE, AT...
...LEE...?
ATLEE?
WHERE DID SHE GO?
SHE SKIPPED OUT.
BOOGIED.
BEAT FEET.
PERAMBULATED THE HELL OUTTA HERE.

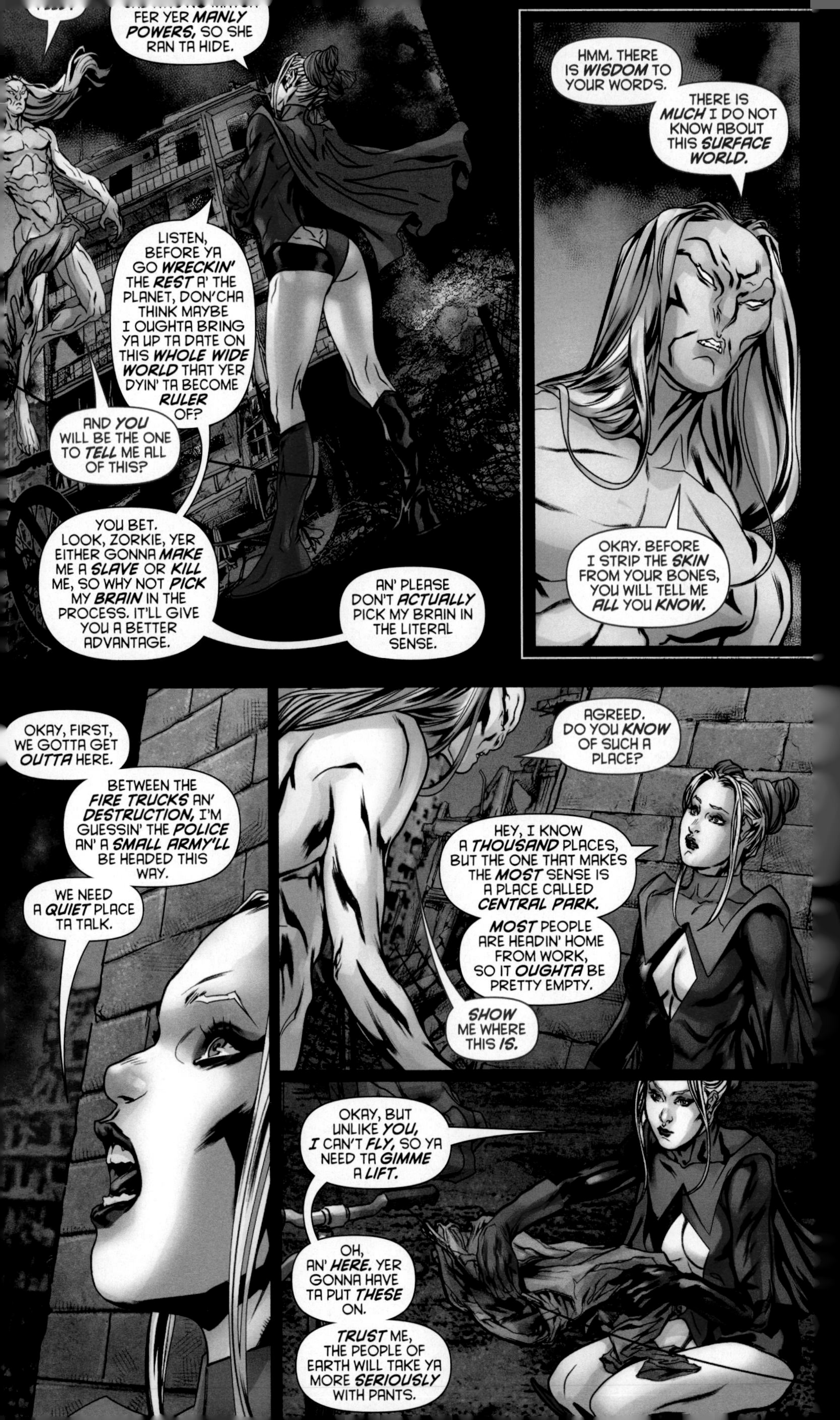
FER YER MANLY POWERS, SO SHE RAN TA HIDE.
LISTEN, BEFORE YA GO WRECKIN' THE REST A' THE PLANET, DON'CHA THINK MAYBE I OUGHTA BRING YA UP TA DATE ON THIS WHOLE WIDE WORLD THAT YER DYIN' TA BECOME RULER OF?
AND YOU WILL BE THE ONE TO TELL ME ALL OF THIS?
YOU BET. LOOK, ZORKIE, YER EITHER GONNA MAKE ME A SLAVE OR KILL ME, SO WHY NOT PICK MY BRAIN IN THE PROCESS. IT'LL GIVE YOU A BETTER ADVANTAGE.
AN' PLEASE DON'T ACTUALLY PICK MY BRAIN IN THE LITERAL SENSE.
HMM. THERE IS WISDOM TO YOUR WORDS.
THERE IS MUCH I DO NOT KNOW ABOUT THIS SURFACE WORLD.
OKAY. BEFORE I STRIP THE SKIN FROM YOUR BONES, YOU WILL TELL ME ALL YOU KNOW.
OKAY, FIRST, WE GOTTA GET OUTTA HERE.
BETWEEN THE FIRE TRUCKS AN' DESTRUCTION, I'M GUESSIN' THE POLICE AN' A SMALL ARMY'LL BE HEADED THIS WAY.
WE NEED A QUIET PLACE TA TALK.
AGREED. DO YOU KNOW OF SUCH A PLACE?
HEY, I KNOW A THOUSAND PLACES, BUT THE ONE THAT MAKES THE MOST SENSE IS A PLACE CALLED CENTRAL PARK.
MOST PEOPLE ARE HEADIN' HOME FROM WORK, SO IT OUGHTA BE PRETTY EMPTY.
SHOW ME WHERE THIS IS.
OKAY, BUT UNLIKE YOU, I CAN'T FLY, SO YA NEED TA GIMME A LIFT.
OH, AN' HERE. YER GONNA HAVE TA PUT THESE ON.
TRUST ME, THE PEOPLE OF EARTH WILL TAKE YA MORE SERIOUSLY WITH PANTS.

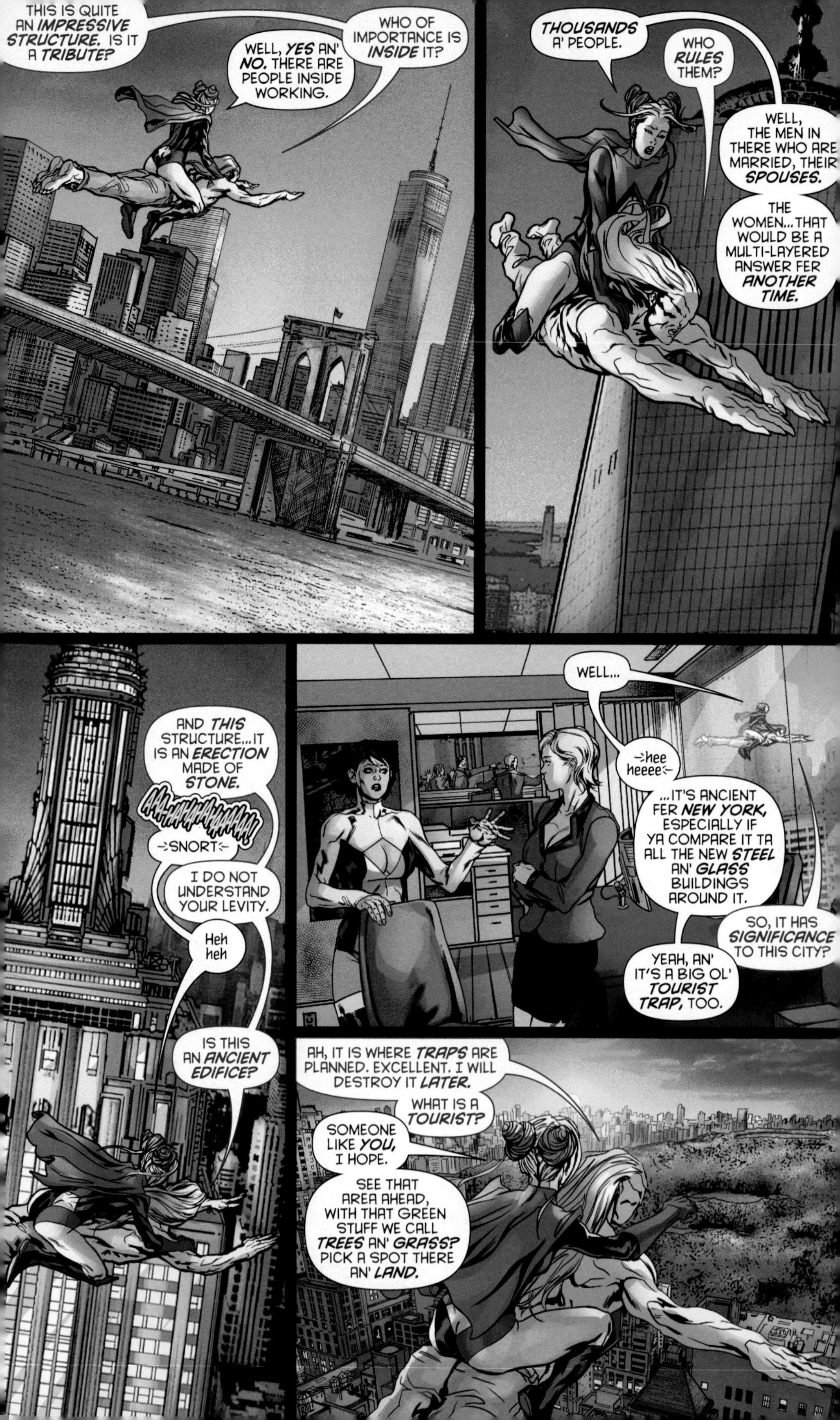
THIS IS QUITE AN IMPRESSIVE STRUCTURE. IS IT A TRIBUTE?
WELL, YES AN' NO. THERE ARE PEOPLE INSIDE WORKING.
WHO OF IMPORTANCE IS INSIDE IT?
THOUSANDS A' PEOPLE.
WHO RULES THEM?
WELL, THE MEN IN THERE WHO ARE MARRIED, THEIR SPOUSES.
THE WOMEN... THAT WOULD BE A MULTI-LAYERED ANSWER FER ANOTHER TIME.
AND THIS STRUCTURE... IT IS AN ERECTION MADE OF STONE.
AAA-HAHAHAHAHAAAAA!
SNORT
I DO NOT UNDERSTAND YOUR LEVITY.
Heh heh
IS THIS AN ANCIENT EDIFICE?
WELL...
hee heeee
...IT'S ANCIENT FER NEW YORK, ESPECIALLY IF YA COMPARE IT TA ALL THE NEW STEEL AN' GLASS BUILDINGS AROUND IT.
SO, IT HAS SIGNIFICANCE TO THIS CITY?
YEAH, AN' IT'S A BIG OL' TOURIST TRAP, TOO.
AH, IT IS WHERE TRAPS ARE PLANNED. EXCELLENT. I WILL DESTROY IT LATER.
WHAT IS A TOURIST?
SOMEONE LIKE YOU, I HOPE.
SEE THAT AREA AHEAD, WITH THAT GREEN STUFF WE CALL TREES AN' GRASS? PICK A SPOT THERE AN' LAND.

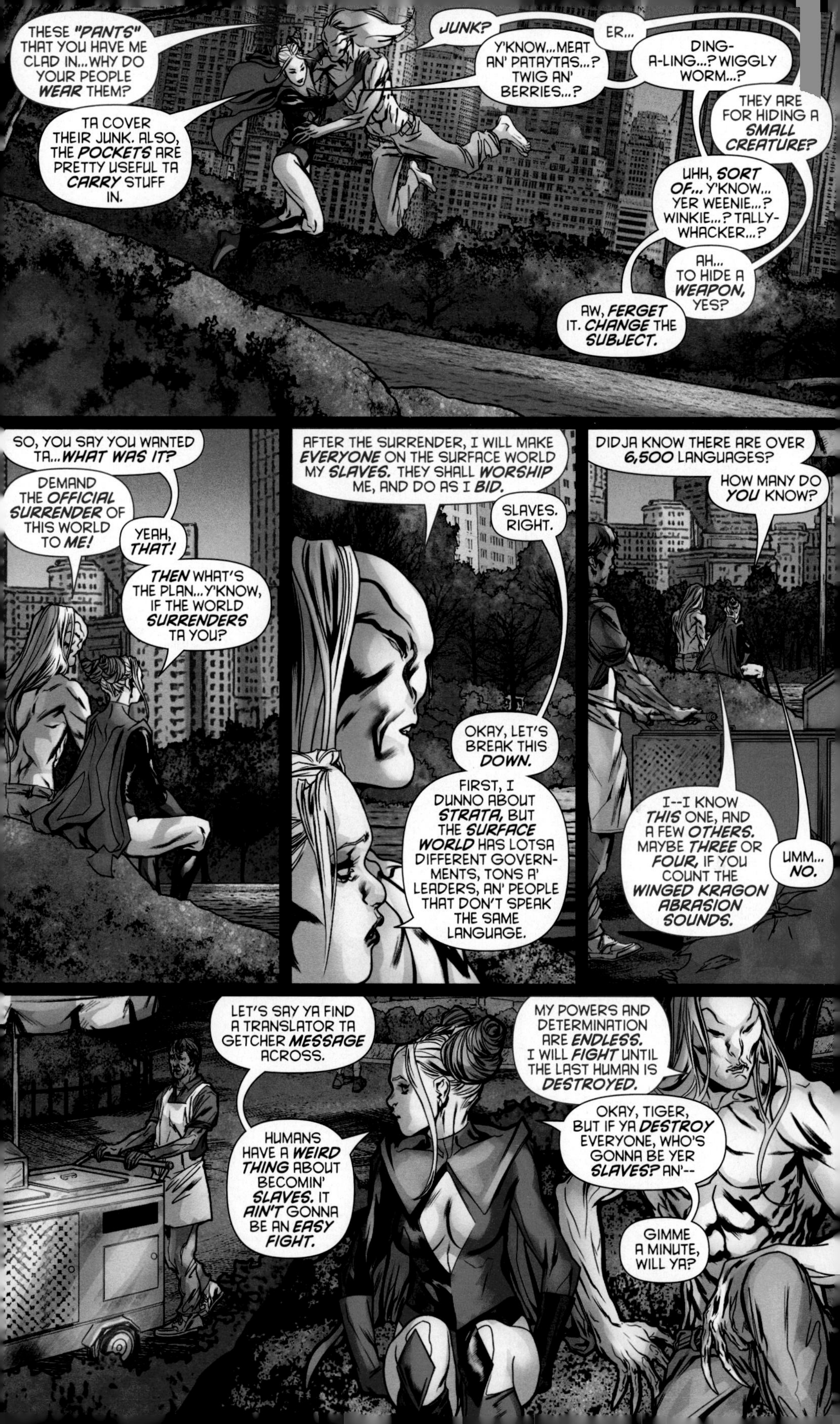
THESE "PANTS" THAT YOU HAVE ME CLAD IN...WHY DO YOUR PEOPLE WEAR THEM?
TA COVER THEIR JUNK. ALSO, THE POCKETS ARE PRETTY USEFUL TA CARRY STUFF IN.
JUNK?
ER...
Y'KNOW...MEAT AN' PATAYTAS...? TWIG AN' BERRIES...?
DING-A-LING...? WIGGLY WORM...?
THEY ARE FOR HIDING A SMALL CREATURE?
UHH, SORT OF... Y'KNOW... YER WEENIE...? WINKIE...? TALLY-WHACKER...?
AH... TO HIDE A WEAPON, YES?
AW, FERGET IT. CHANGE THE SUBJECT.
SO, YOU SAY YOU WANTED TA...WHAT WAS IT?
DEMAND THE OFFICIAL SURRENDER OF THIS WORLD TO ME!
YEAH, THAT!
THEN WHAT'S THE PLAN...Y'KNOW, IF THE WORLD SURRENDERS TA YOU?
AFTER THE SURRENDER, I WILL MAKE EVERYONE ON THE SURFACE WORLD MY SLAVES. THEY SHALL WORSHIP ME, AND DO AS I BID.
SLAVES. RIGHT.
OKAY, LET'S BREAK THIS DOWN.
FIRST, I DUNNO ABOUT STRATA, BUT THE SURFACE WORLD HAS LOTSA DIFFERENT GOVERN-MENTS, TONS A' LEADERS, AN' PEOPLE THAT DON'T SPEAK THE SAME LANGUAGE.
DIDJA KNOW THERE ARE OVER 6,500 LANGUAGES?
HOW MANY DO YOU KNOW?
I--I KNOW THIS ONE, AND A FEW OTHERS. MAYBE THREE OR FOUR, IF YOU COUNT THE WINGED KRAGON ABRASION SOUNDS.
UMM... NO.
LET'S SAY YA FIND A TRANSLATOR TA GETCHER MESSAGE ACROSS.
HUMANS HAVE A WEIRD THING ABOUT BECOMIN' SLAVES. IT AIN'T GONNA BE AN EASY FIGHT.
MY POWERS AND DETERMINATION ARE ENDLESS. I WILL FIGHT UNTIL THE LAST HUMAN IS DESTROYED.
OKAY, TIGER, BUT IF YA DESTROY EVERYONE, WHO'S GONNA BE YER SLAVES? AN'--
GIMME A MINUTE, WILL YA?

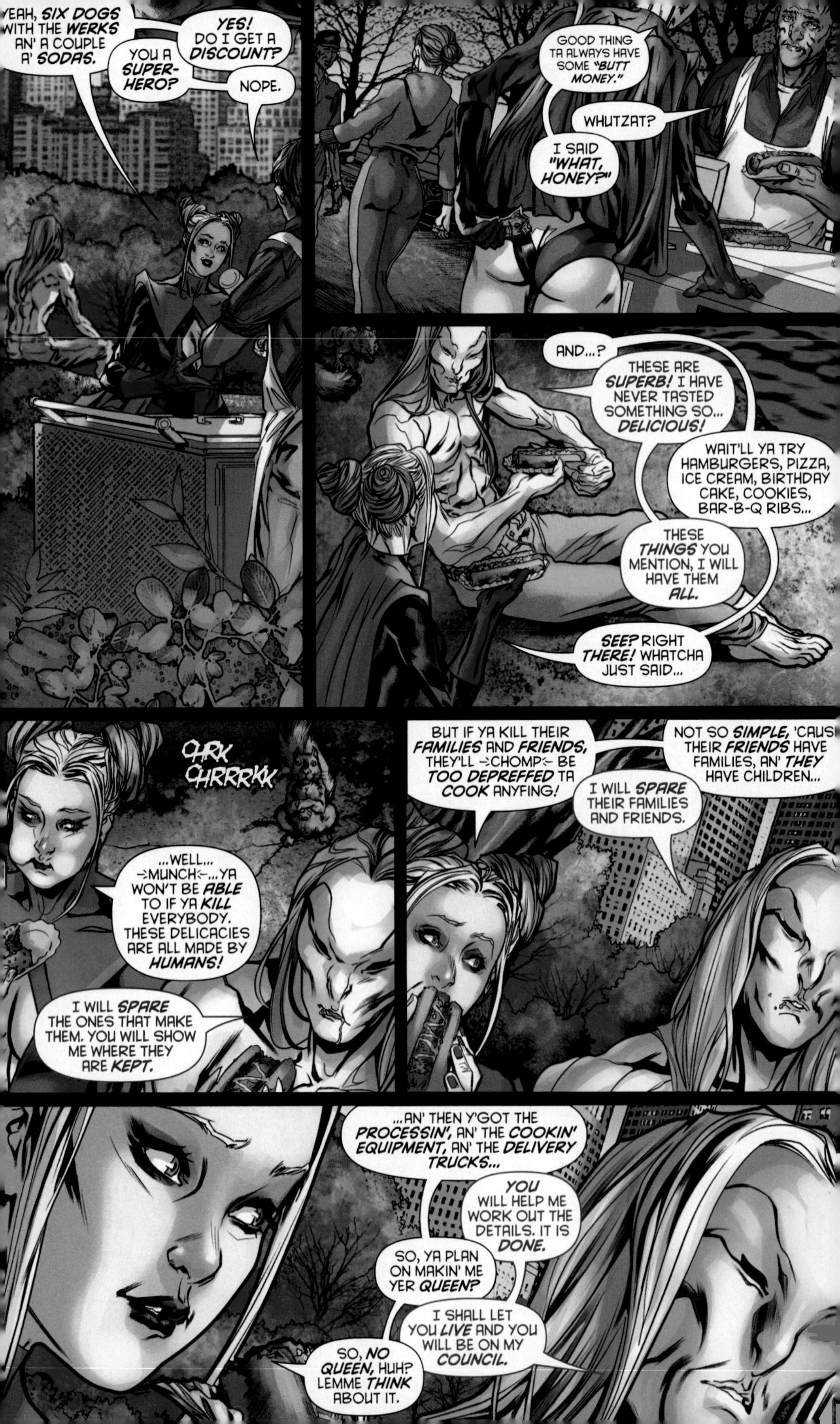
YEAH, SIX DOGS WITH THE WERKS AN' A COUPLE A' SODAS.
YOU A SUPER-HERO?
YES! DO I GET A DISCOUNT?
NOPE.
GOOD THING TA ALWAYS HAVE SOME "BUTT MONEY."
WHUTZAT?
I SAID "WHAT, HONEY?"
AND...?
THESE ARE SUPERB! I HAVE NEVER TASTED SOMETHING SO... DELICIOUS!
WAIT'LL YA TRY HAMBURGERS, PIZZA, ICE CREAM, BIRTHDAY CAKE, COOKIES, BAR-B-Q RIBS...
THESE THINGS YOU MENTION, I WILL HAVE THEM ALL.
SEE? RIGHT THERE! WHATCHA JUST SAID...
CHRK CHRRRKK
...WELL... ⇒MUNCH⇐...YA WON'T BE ABLE TO IF YA KILL EVERYBODY. THESE DELICACIES ARE ALL MADE BY HUMANS!
I WILL SPARE THE ONES THAT MAKE THEM. YOU WILL SHOW ME WHERE THEY ARE KEPT.
BUT IF YA KILL THEIR FAMILIES AND FRIENDS, THEY'LL ⇒CHOMP⇐ BE TOO DEPREFFED TA COOK ANYFING!
I WILL SPARE THEIR FAMILIES AND FRIENDS.
NOT SO SIMPLE, 'CAUS THEIR FRIENDS HAVE FAMILIES, AN' THEY HAVE CHILDREN...
...AN' THEN Y'GOT THE PROCESSIN', AN' THE COOKIN' EQUIPMENT, AN' THE DELIVERY TRUCKS...
YOU WILL HELP ME WORK OUT THE DETAILS. IT IS DONE.
SO, YA PLAN ON MAKIN' ME YER QUEEN?
I SHALL LET YOU LIVE AND YOU WILL BE ON MY COUNCIL.
SO, NO QUEEN, HUH? LEMME THINK ABOUT IT.

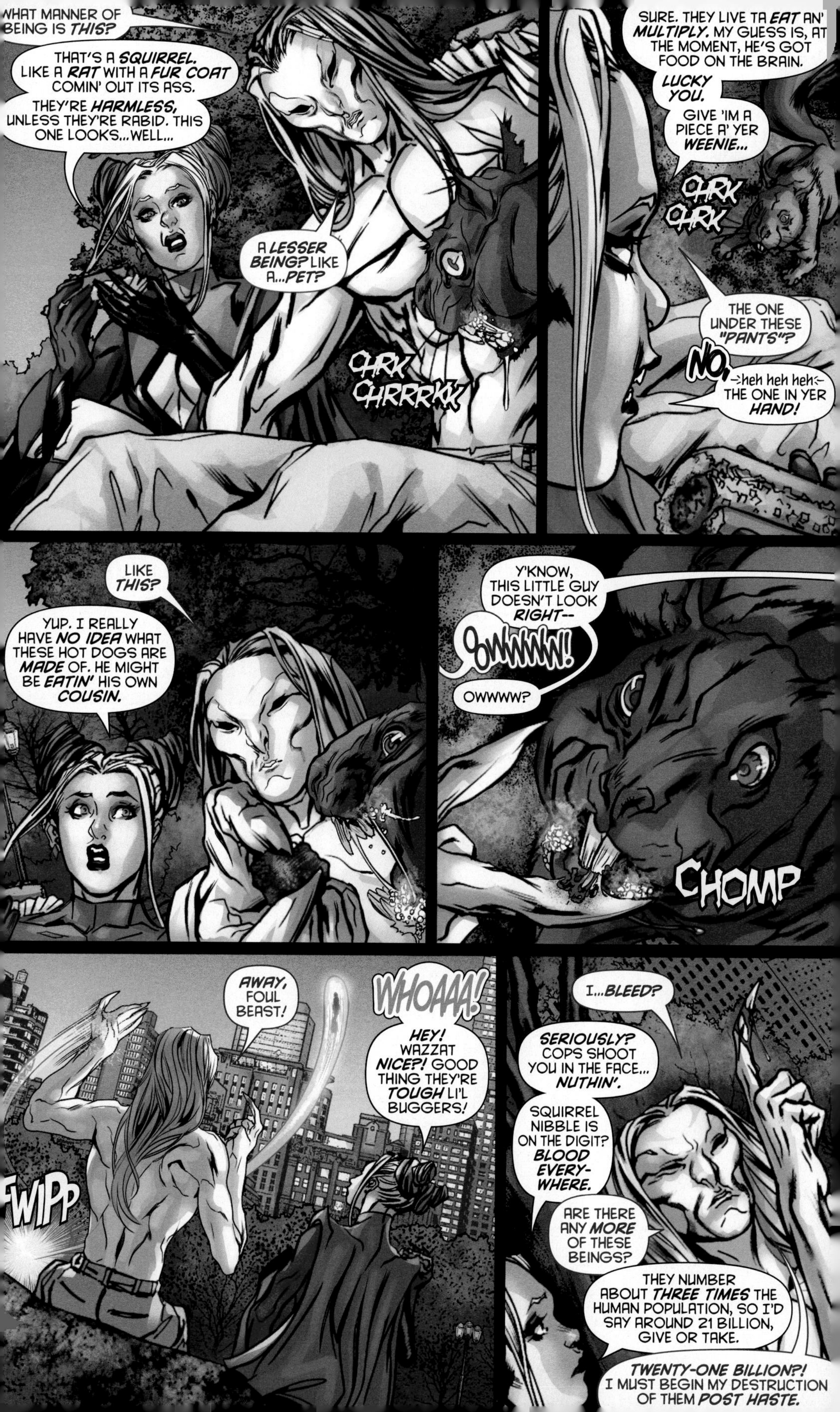
WHAT MANNER OF BEING IS THIS?
THAT'S A SQUIRREL. LIKE A RAT WITH A FUR COAT COMIN' OUT ITS ASS.
THEY'RE HARMLESS, UNLESS THEY'RE RABID. THIS ONE LOOKS...WELL...
A LESSER BEING? LIKE A...PET?
CHRK CHRRRKK
SURE. THEY LIVE TA EAT AN' MULTIPLY. MY GUESS IS, AT THE MOMENT, HE'S GOT FOOD ON THE BRAIN.
LUCKY YOU.
GIVE 'IM A PIECE A' YER WEENIE...
CHRK CHRK
THE ONE UNDER THESE "PANTS"?
NO, -heh heh heh- THE ONE IN YER HAND!
LIKE THIS?
YUP. I REALLY HAVE NO IDEA WHAT THESE HOT DOGS ARE MADE OF. HE MIGHT BE EATIN' HIS OWN COUSIN.
Y'KNOW, THIS LITTLE GUY DOESN'T LOOK RIGHT--
OWWWWW!
OWWWW?
CHOMP
AWAY, FOUL BEAST!
WHOAAA!
HEY! WAZZAT NICE?! GOOD THING THEY'RE TOUGH LI'L BUGGERS!
FWIPP
I...BLEED?
SERIOUSLY? COPS SHOOT YOU IN THE FACE... NUTHIN'.
SQUIRREL NIBBLE IS ON THE DIGIT? BLOOD EVERY-WHERE.
ARE THERE ANY MORE OF THESE BEINGS?
THEY NUMBER ABOUT THREE TIMES THE HUMAN POPULATION, SO I'D SAY AROUND 21 BILLION, GIVE OR TAKE.
TWENTY-ONE BILLION?! I MUST BEGIN MY DESTRUCTION OF THEM POST HASTE.

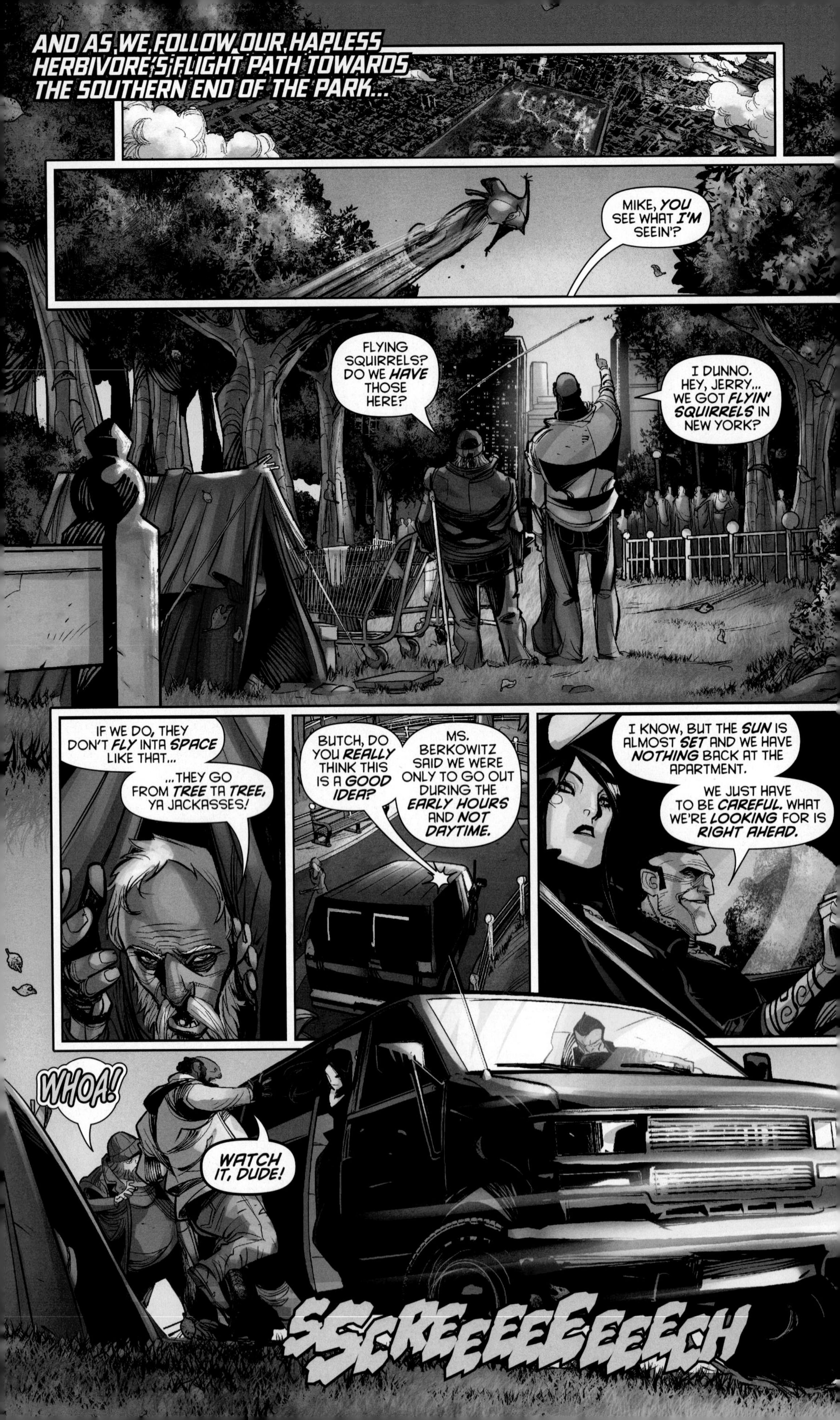

AND AS WE FOLLOW OUR HAPLESS HERBIVORE'S FLIGHT PATH TOWARDS THE SOUTHERN END OF THE PARK...
MIKE, YOU SEE WHAT I'M SEEIN'?
FLYING SQUIRRELS? DO WE HAVE THOSE HERE?
I DUNNO. HEY, JERRY... WE GOT FLYIN' SQUIRRELS IN NEW YORK?
IF WE DO, THEY DON'T FLY INTA SPACE LIKE THAT...
...THEY GO FROM TREE TA TREE, YA JACKASSES!
BUTCH, DO YOU REALLY THINK THIS IS A GOOD IDEA?
MS. BERKOWITZ SAID WE WERE ONLY TO GO OUT DURING THE EARLY HOURS AND NOT DAYTIME.
I KNOW, BUT THE SUN IS ALMOST SET AND WE HAVE NOTHING BACK AT THE APARTMENT.
WE JUST HAVE TO BE CAREFUL. WHAT WE'RE LOOKING FOR IS RIGHT AHEAD.
WHOA!
WATCH IT, DUDE!
SSCREEEEEEEEEECH

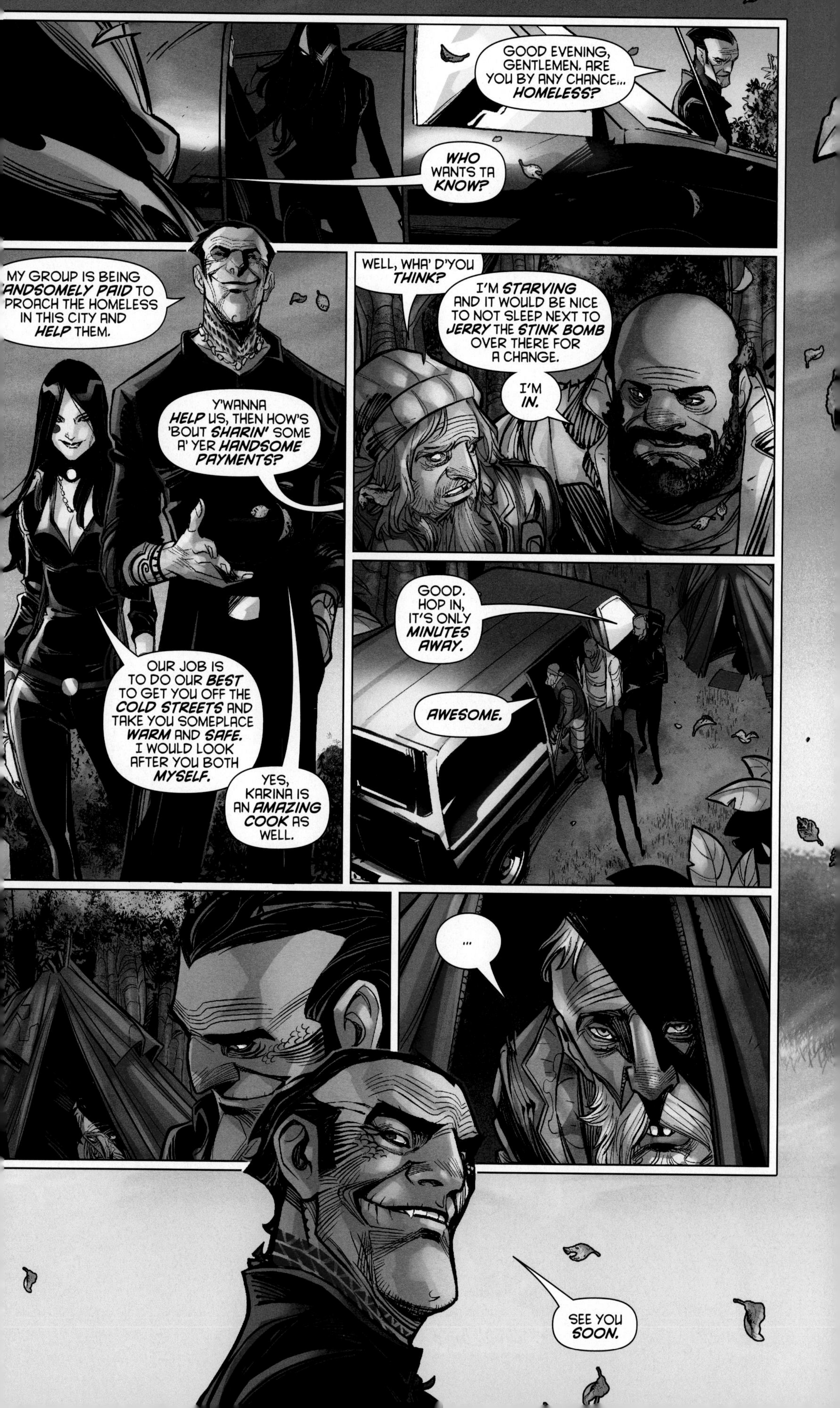
GOOD EVENING, GENTLEMEN. ARE YOU BY ANY CHANCE... HOMELESS?
WHO WANTS TA KNOW?
MY GROUP IS BEING HANDSOMELY PAID TO APPROACH THE HOMELESS IN THIS CITY AND HELP THEM.
Y'WANNA HELP US, THEN HOW'S 'BOUT SHARIN' SOME A' YER HANDSOME PAYMENTS?
OUR JOB IS TO DO OUR BEST TO GET YOU OFF THE COLD STREETS AND TAKE YOU SOMEPLACE WARM AND SAFE. I WOULD LOOK AFTER YOU BOTH MYSELF.
YES, KARINA IS AN AMAZING COOK AS WELL.
WELL, WHA' D'YOU THINK?
I'M STARVING AND IT WOULD BE NICE TO NOT SLEEP NEXT TO JERRY THE STINK BOMB OVER THERE FOR A CHANGE.
I'M IN.
GOOD. HOP IN, IT'S ONLY MINUTES AWAY.
AWESOME.
...
SEE YOU SOON.

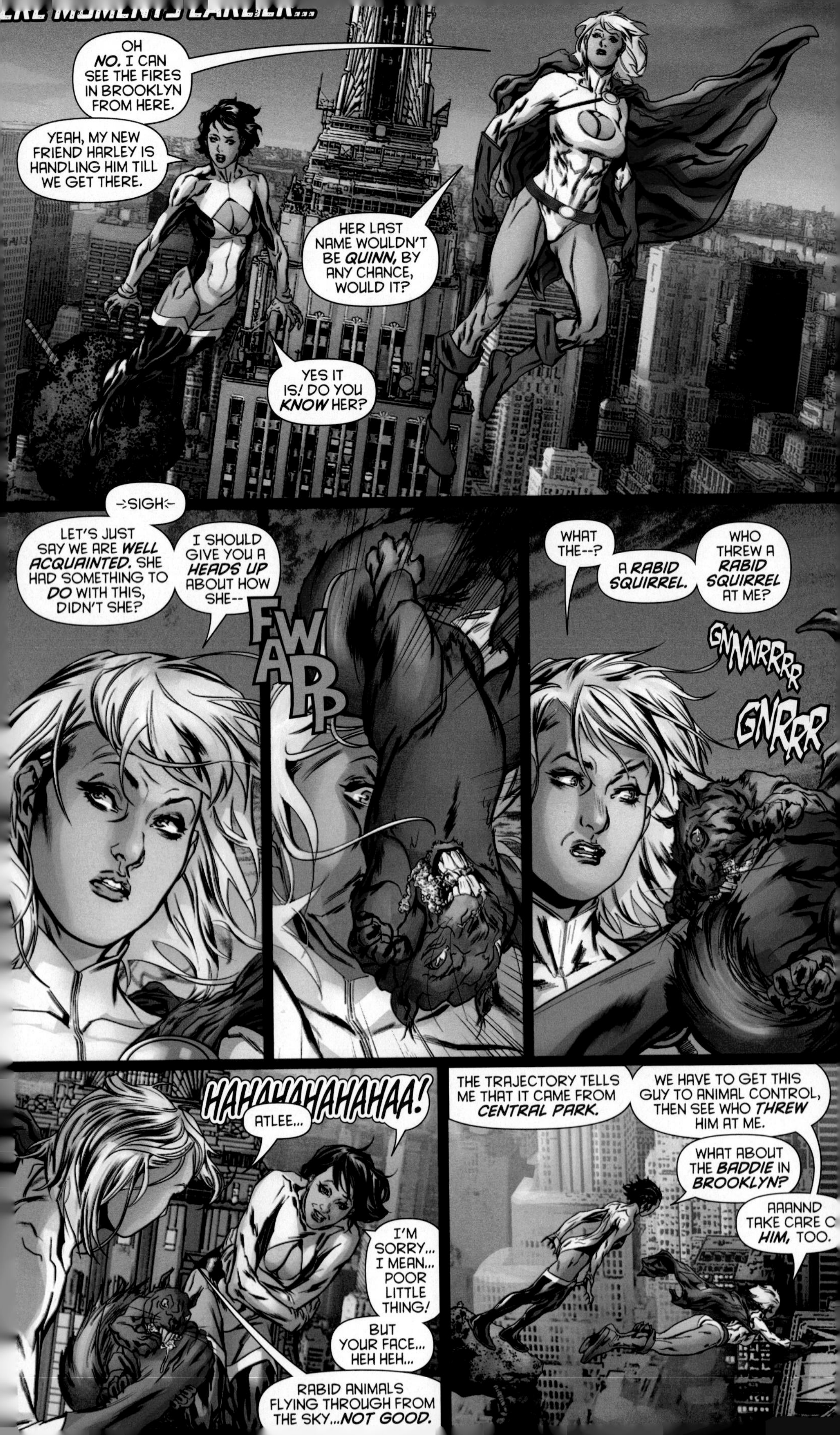
OH NO. I CAN SEE THE FIRES IN BROOKLYN FROM HERE.
YEAH, MY NEW FRIEND HARLEY IS HANDLING HIM TILL WE GET THERE.
HER LAST NAME WOULDN'T BE QUINN, BY ANY CHANCE, WOULD IT?
YES IT IS! DO YOU KNOW HER?
-SIGH-
LET'S JUST SAY WE ARE WELL ACQUAINTED. SHE HAD SOMETHING TO DO WITH THIS, DIDN'T SHE?
I SHOULD GIVE YOU A HEADS UP ABOUT HOW SHE--
FWAPP
WHAT THE--?
A RABID SQUIRREL.
WHO THREW A RABID SQUIRREL AT ME?
GNNNRRRR
GNRRR
HAHAHAHAHAHAA!
ATLEE...
I'M SORRY... I MEAN... POOR LITTLE THING!
BUT YOUR FACE... HEH HEH...
RABID ANIMALS FLYING THROUGH FROM THE SKY...NOT GOOD.
THE TRAJECTORY TELLS ME THAT IT CAME FROM CENTRAL PARK.
WE HAVE TO GET THIS GUY TO ANIMAL CONTROL, THEN SEE WHO THREW HIM AT ME.
WHAT ABOUT THE BADDIE IN BROOKLYN?
AAANND TAKE CARE O HIM, TOO.

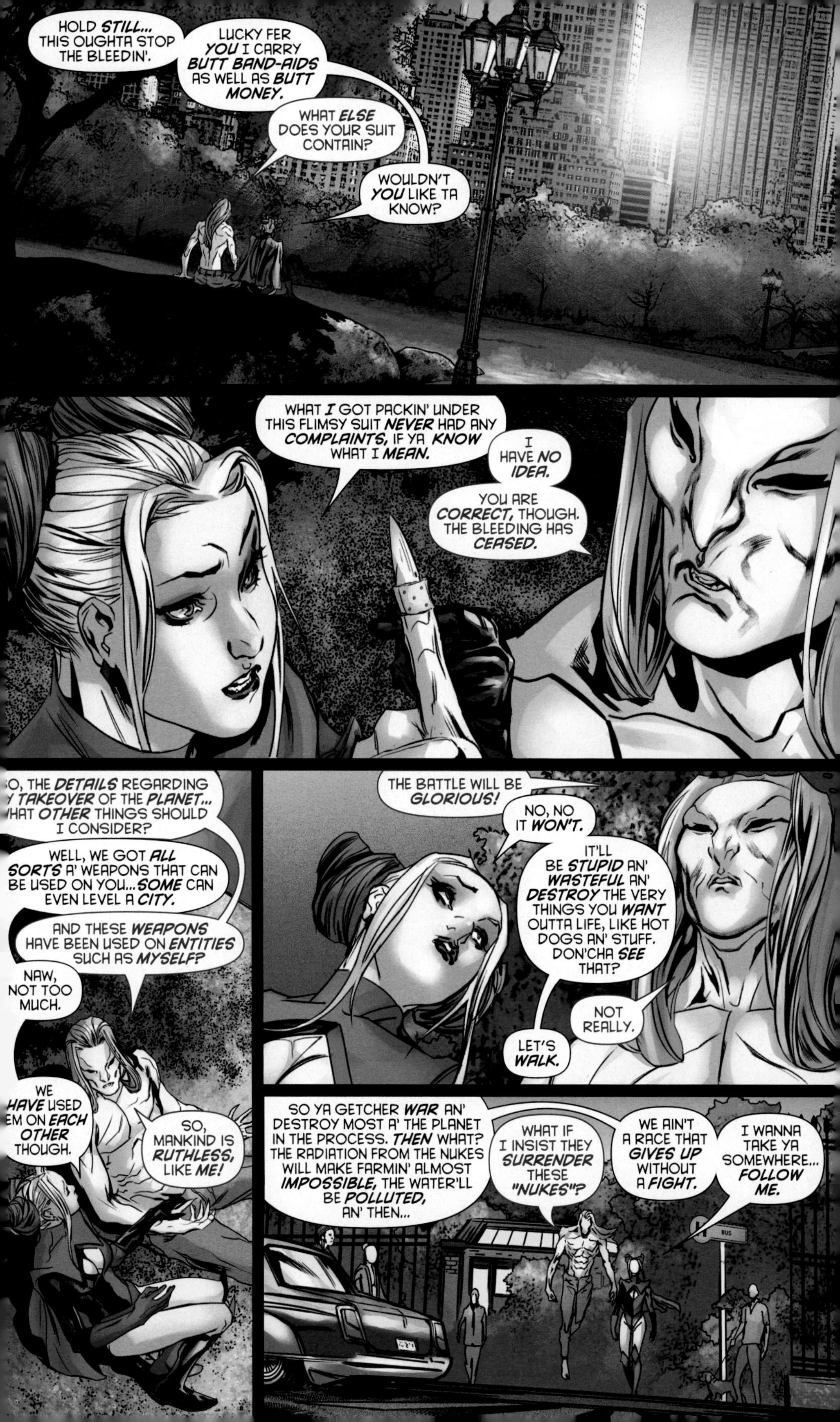

HOLD STILL... THIS OUGHTA STOP THE BLEEDIN'.
LUCKY FER YOU I CARRY BUTT BAND-AIDS AS WELL AS BUTT MONEY.
WHAT ELSE DOES YOUR SUIT CONTAIN?
WOULDN'T YOU LIKE TA KNOW?
WHAT I GOT PACKIN' UNDER THIS FLIMSY SUIT NEVER HAD ANY COMPLAINTS, IF YA KNOW WHAT I MEAN.
I HAVE NO IDEA.
YOU ARE CORRECT, THOUGH. THE BLEEDING HAS CEASED.
O, THE DETAILS REGARDING Y TAKEOVER OF THE PLANET... HAT OTHER THINGS SHOULD I CONSIDER?
WELL, WE GOT ALL SORTS A' WEAPONS THAT CAN BE USED ON YOU...SOME CAN EVEN LEVEL A CITY.
AND THESE WEAPONS HAVE BEEN USED ON ENTITIES SUCH AS MYSELF?
NAW, NOT TOO MUCH.
WE HAVE USED EM ON EACH OTHER THOUGH.
SO, MANKIND IS RUTHLESS, LIKE ME!
THE BATTLE WILL BE GLORIOUS!
NO, NO IT WON'T.
IT'LL BE STUPID AN' WASTEFUL AN' DESTROY THE VERY THINGS YOU WANT OUTTA LIFE, LIKE HOT DOGS AN' STUFF. DON'CHA SEE THAT?
NOT REALLY.
LET'S WALK.
SO YA GETCHER WAR AN' DESTROY MOST A' THE PLANET IN THE PROCESS. THEN WHAT? THE RADIATION FROM THE NUKES WILL MAKE FARMIN' ALMOST IMPOSSIBLE, THE WATER'LL BE POLLUTED, AN' THEN...
WHAT IF I INSIST THEY SURRENDER THESE "NUKES"?
WE AIN'T A RACE THAT GIVES UP WITHOUT A FIGHT.
I WANNA TAKE YA SOMEWHERE... FOLLOW ME.
BUS

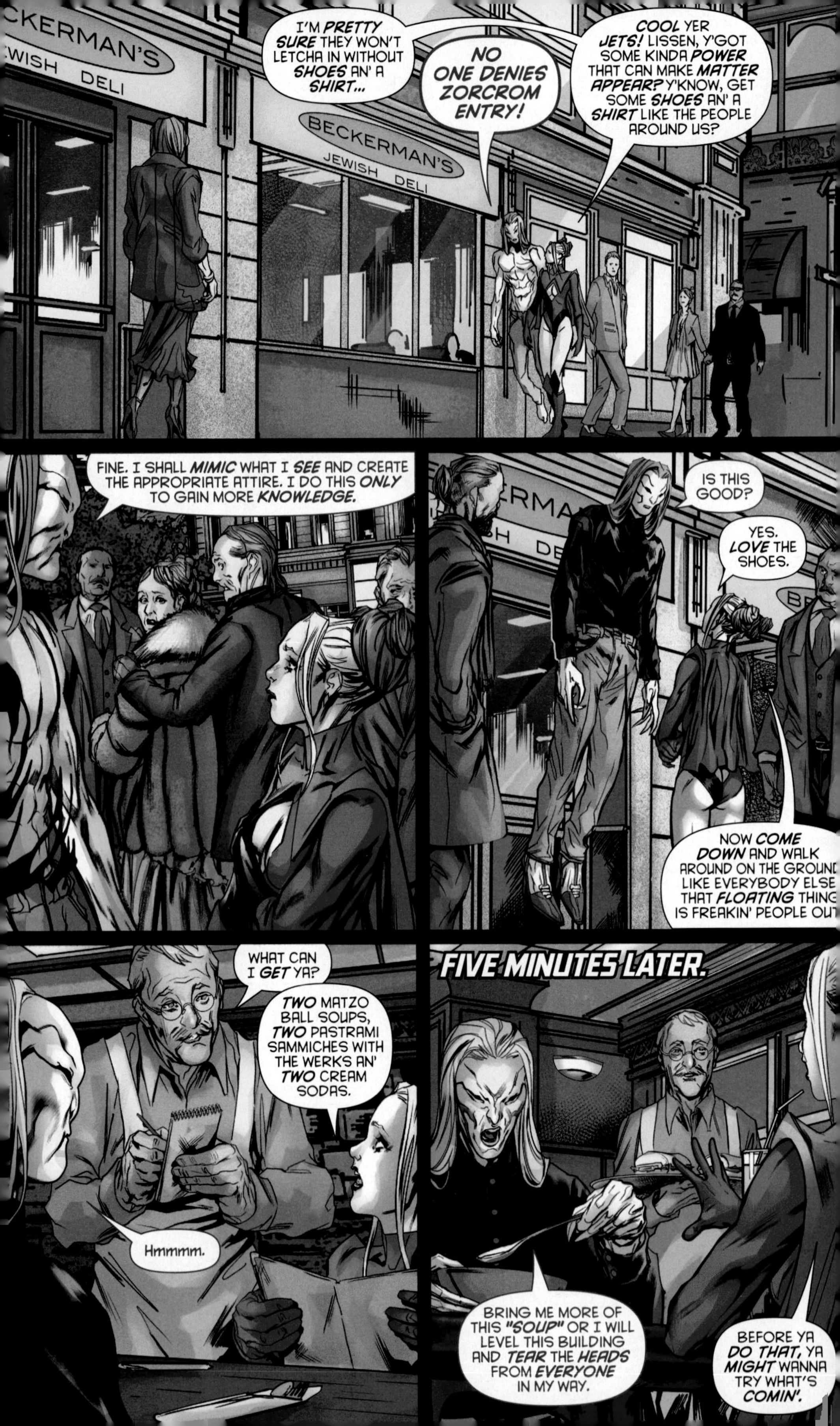
BECKERMAN'S JEWISH DELI
BECKERMAN'S JEWISH DELI
I'M PRETTY SURE THEY WON'T LETCHA IN WITHOUT SHOES AN' A SHIRT...
NO ONE DENIES ZORCROM ENTRY!
COOL YER JETS! LISSEN, Y'GOT SOME KINDA POWER THAT CAN MAKE MATTER APPEAR? Y'KNOW, GET SOME SHOES AN' A SHIRT LIKE THE PEOPLE AROUND US?
FINE. I SHALL MIMIC WHAT I SEE AND CREATE THE APPROPRIATE ATTIRE. I DO THIS ONLY TO GAIN MORE KNOWLEDGE.
IS THIS GOOD?
YES. LOVE THE SHOES.
NOW COME DOWN AND WALK AROUND ON THE GROUND LIKE EVERYBODY ELSE THAT FLOATING THING IS FREAKIN' PEOPLE OUT
WHAT CAN I GET YA?
TWO MATZO BALL SOUPS, TWO PASTRAMI SAMMICHES WITH THE WERKS AN' TWO CREAM SODAS.
Hmmmm.
FIVE MINUTES LATER.
BRING ME MORE OF THIS "SOUP" OR I WILL LEVEL THIS BUILDING AND TEAR THE HEADS FROM EVERYONE IN MY WAY.
BEFORE YA DO THAT, YA MIGHT WANNA TRY WHAT'S COMIN'.

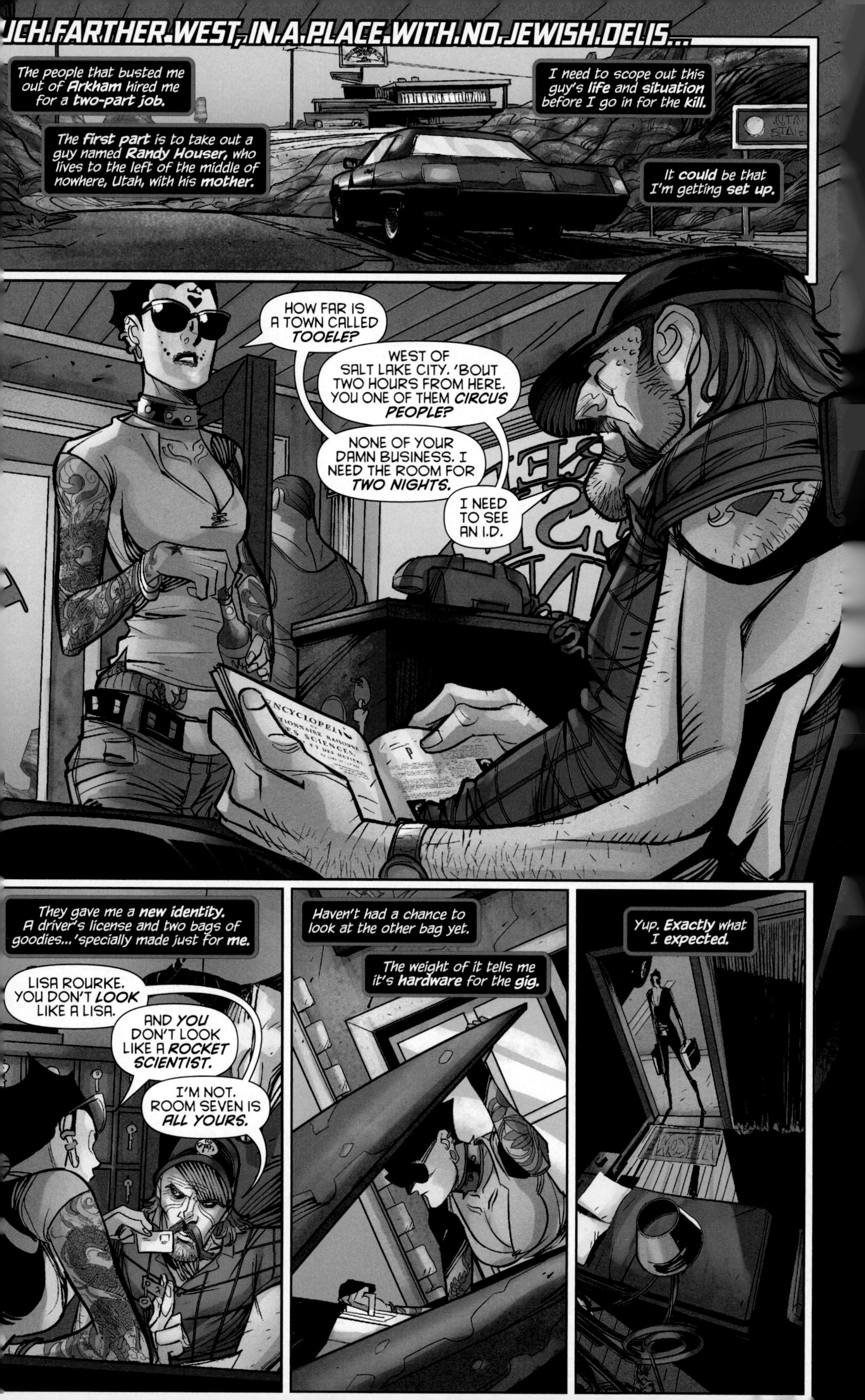

UCH FARTHER WEST, IN A PLACE WITH NO JEWISH DELIS...
The people that busted me out of Arkham hired me for a two-part job.
The first part is to take out a guy named Randy Houser, who lives to the left of the middle of nowhere, Utah, with his mother.
I need to scope out this guy's life and situation before I go in for the kill.
It could be that I'm getting set up.
HOW FAR IS A TOWN CALLED TOOELE?
WEST OF SALT LAKE CITY. 'BOUT TWO HOURS FROM HERE. YOU ONE OF THEM CIRCUS PEOPLE?
NONE OF YOUR DAMN BUSINESS. I NEED THE ROOM FOR TWO NIGHTS.
I NEED TO SEE AN I.D.
They gave me a new identity. A driver's license and two bags of goodies...'specially made just for me.
LISA ROURKE. YOU DON'T LOOK LIKE A LISA.
AND YOU DON'T LOOK LIKE A ROCKET SCIENTIST.
I'M NOT. ROOM SEVEN IS ALL YOURS.
Haven't had a chance to look at the other bag yet.
The weight of it tells me it's hardware for the gig.
Yup. Exactly what I expected.

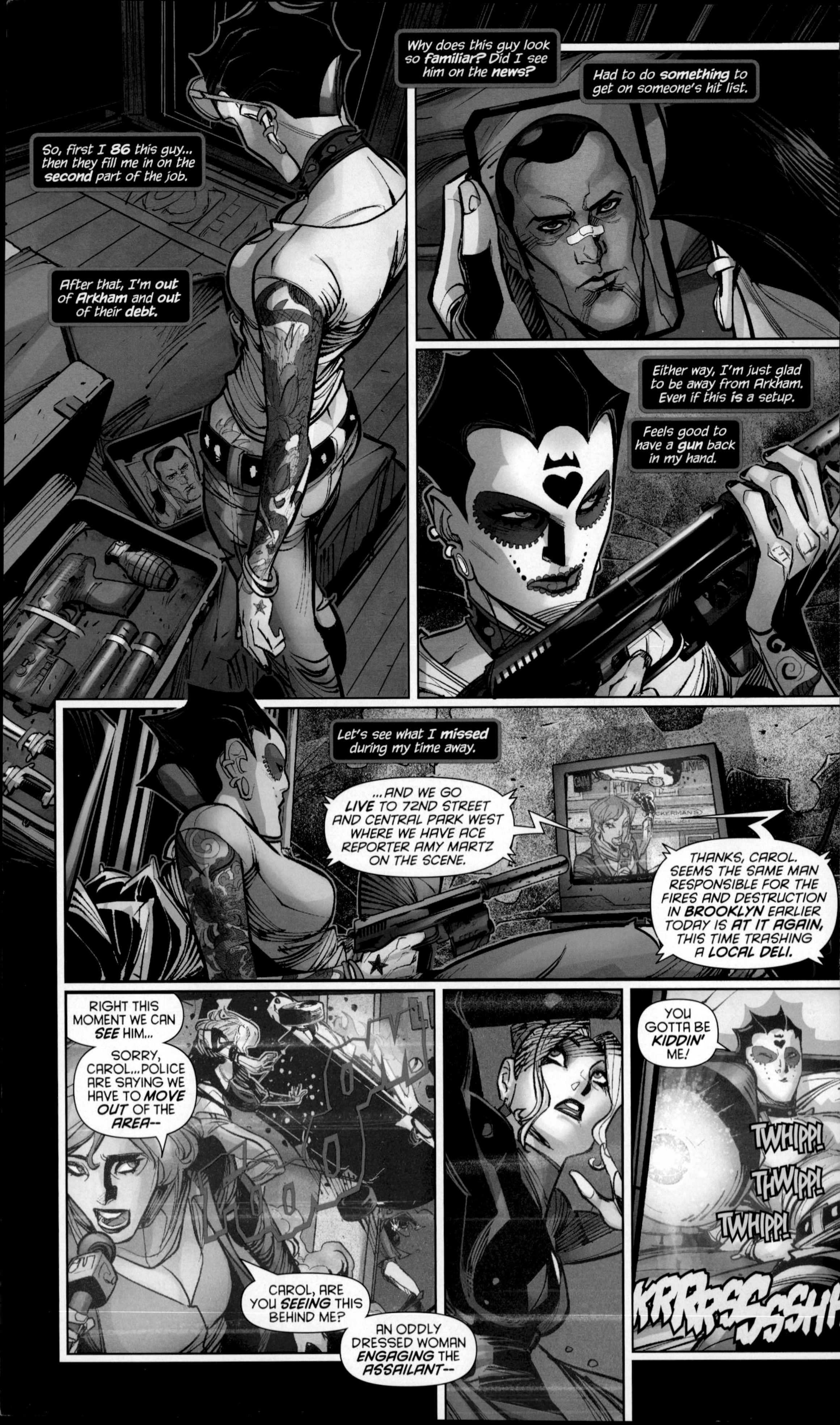
Why does this guy look so familiar? Did I see him on the news?
Had to do something to get on someone's hit list.
So, first I 86 this guy... then they fill me in on the second part of the job.
After that, I'm out of Arkham and out of their debt.
Either way, I'm just glad to be away from Arkham. Even if this is a setup.
Feels good to have a gun back in my hand.
Let's see what I missed during my time away.
...AND WE GO LIVE TO 72ND STREET AND CENTRAL PARK WEST WHERE WE HAVE ACE REPORTER AMY MARTZ ON THE SCENE.
THANKS, CAROL. SEEMS THE SAME MAN RESPONSIBLE FOR THE FIRES AND DESTRUCTION IN BROOKLYN EARLIER TODAY IS AT IT AGAIN, THIS TIME TRASHING A LOCAL DELI.
RIGHT THIS MOMENT WE CAN SEE HIM...
SORRY, CAROL...POLICE ARE SAYING WE HAVE TO MOVE OUT OF THE AREA--
CAROL, ARE YOU SEEING THIS BEHIND ME?
AN ODDLY DRESSED WOMAN ENGAGING THE ASSAILANT--
YOU GOTTA BE KIDDIN' ME!
TWHIPP!
THWIPP!
TWHIPP!
KRRRSSSSHH

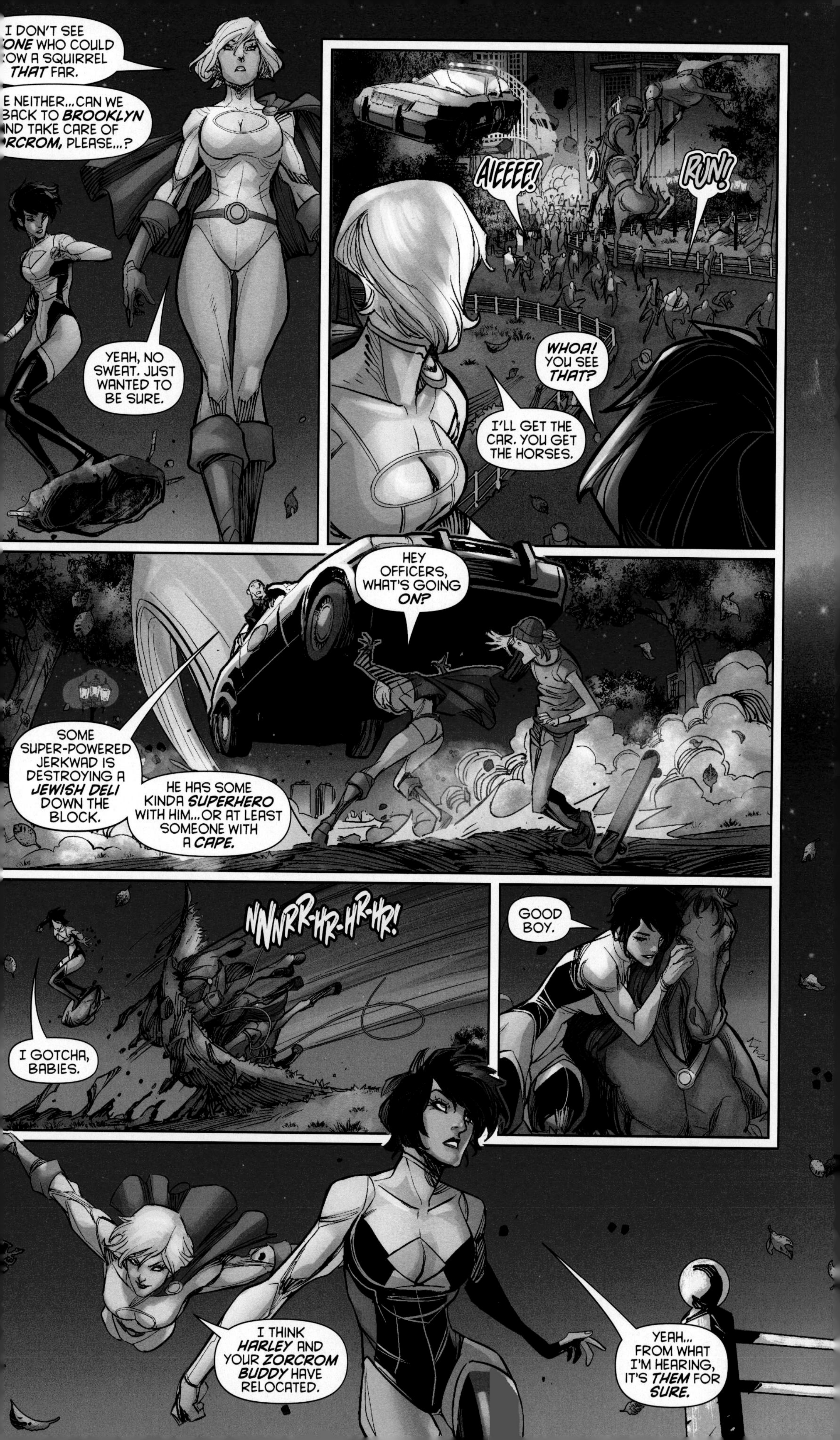
I DON'T SEE ONE WHO COULD ROW A SQUIRREL THAT FAR.
E NEITHER...CAN WE BACK TO BROOKLYN ND TAKE CARE OF RCROM, PLEASE...?
YEAH, NO SWEAT. JUST WANTED TO BE SURE.
AIEEEE!
RUN!
WHOA! YOU SEE THAT?
I'LL GET THE CAR. YOU GET THE HORSES.
HEY OFFICERS, WHAT'S GOING ON?
SOME SUPER-POWERED JERKWAD IS DESTROYING A JEWISH DELI DOWN THE BLOCK.
HE HAS SOME KINDA SUPERHERO WITH HIM...OR AT LEAST SOMEONE WITH A CAPE.
NNNRR-HR-HR-HR!
I GOTCHA, BABIES.
GOOD BOY.
I THINK HARLEY AND YOUR ZORCROM BUDDY HAVE RELOCATED.
YEAH... FROM WHAT I'M HEARING, IT'S THEM FOR SURE.

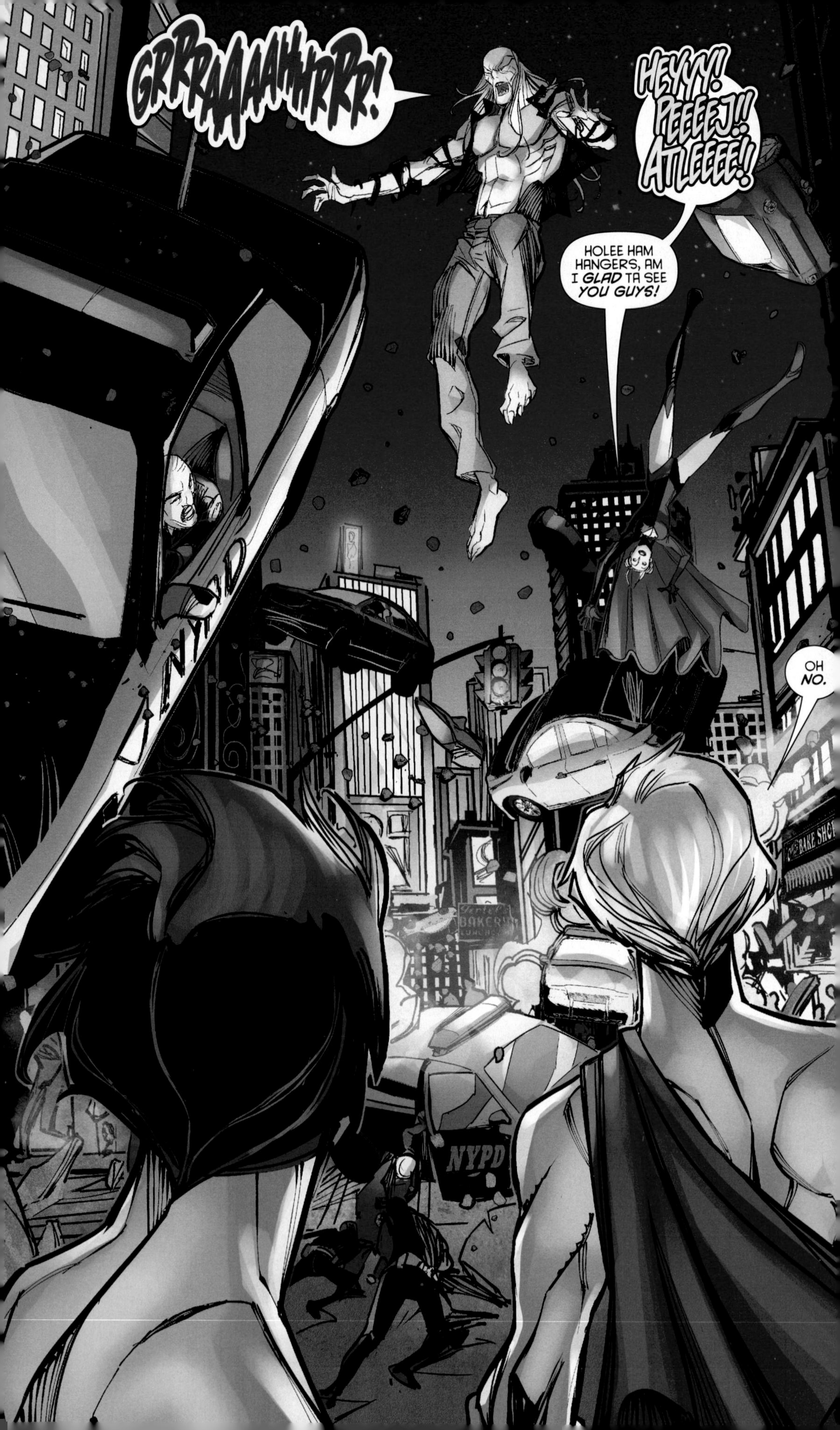
GRRRAAAAHHRRR!
HEYYY! PEEEEJ!! ATLEEEE!!
HOLEE HAM HANGERS, AM I *GLAD* TA SEE *YOU GUYS!*
OH *NO.*
NYPD
NYPD
BAKE SHO

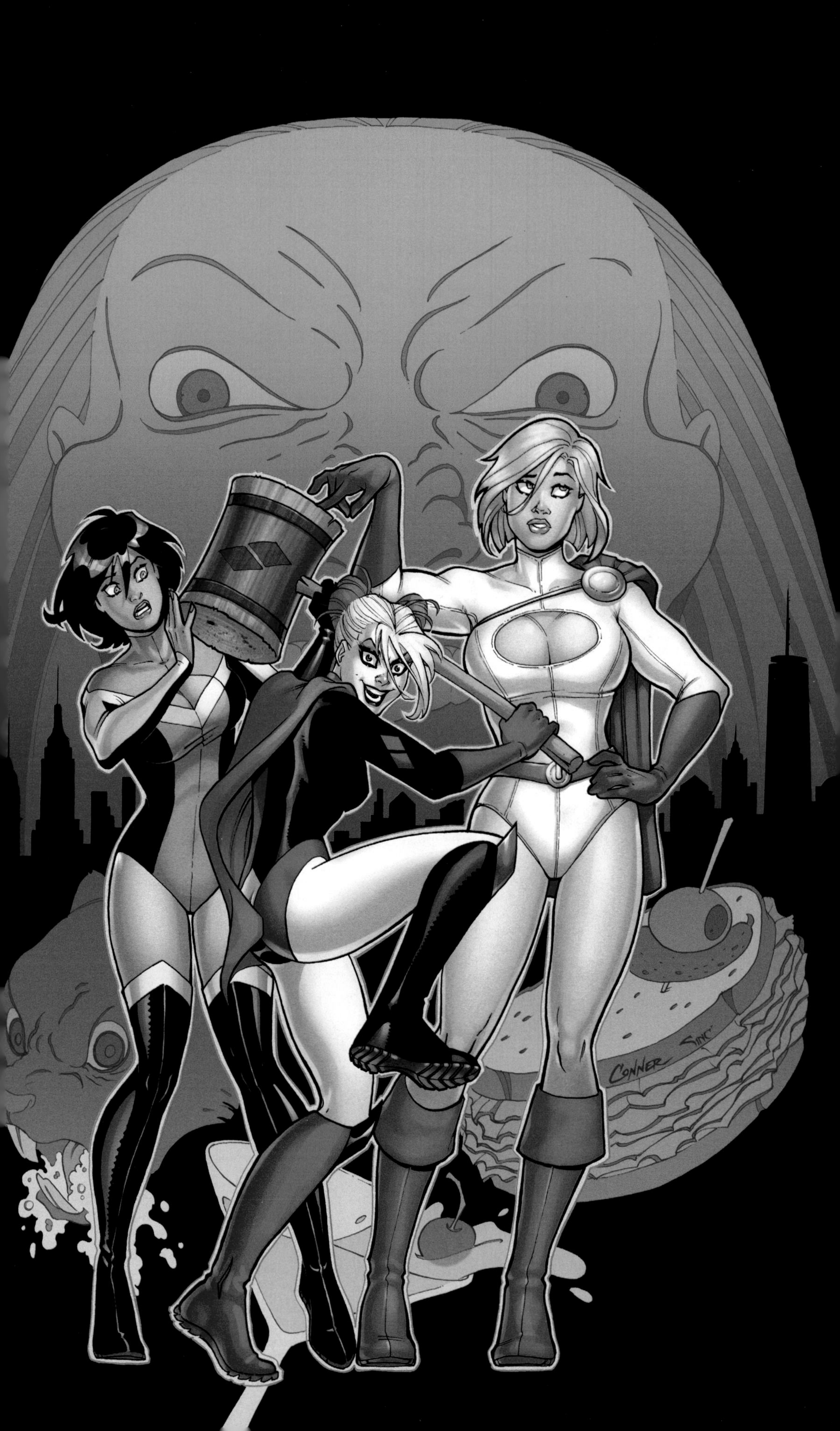
CONNER
SINC

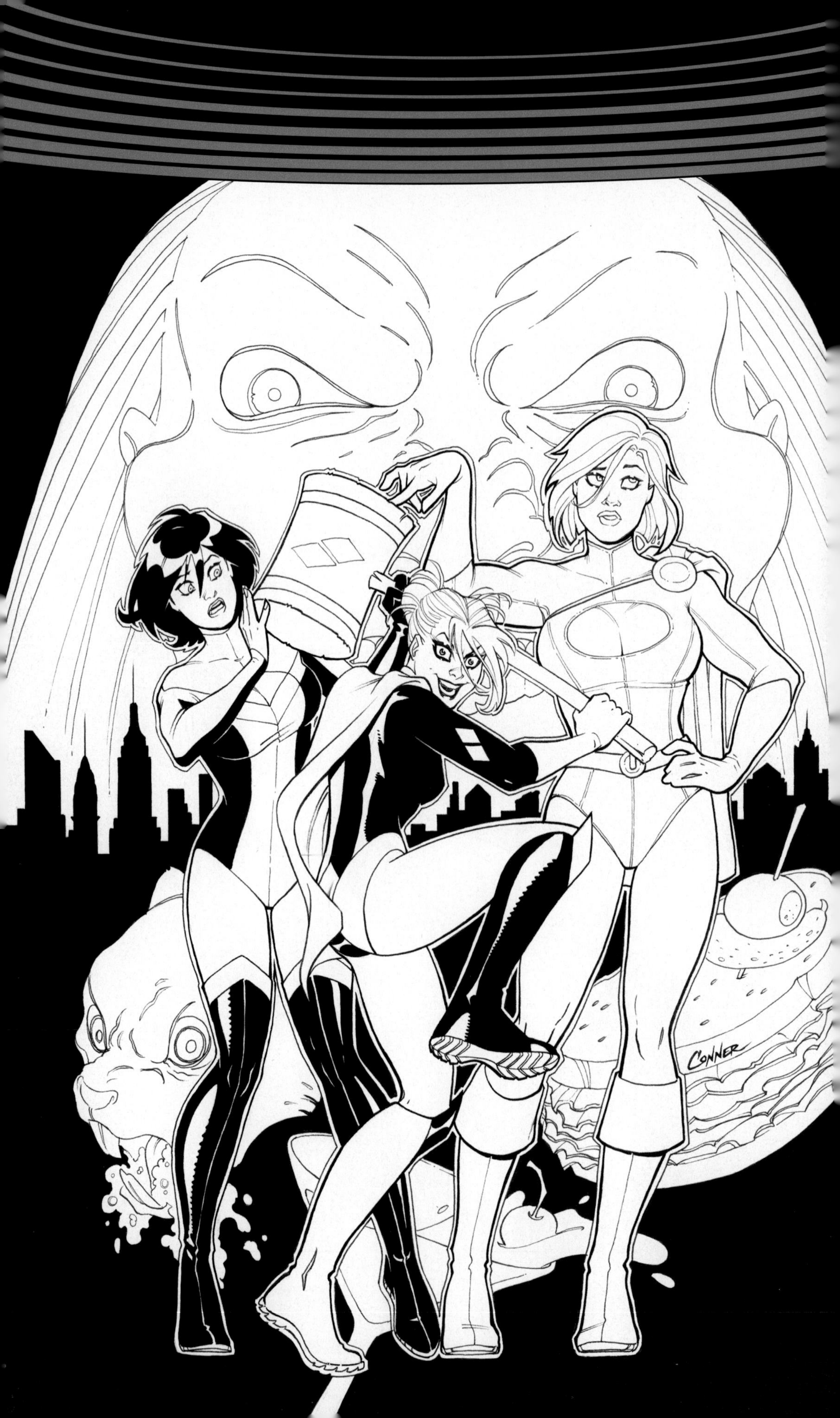
CONNER

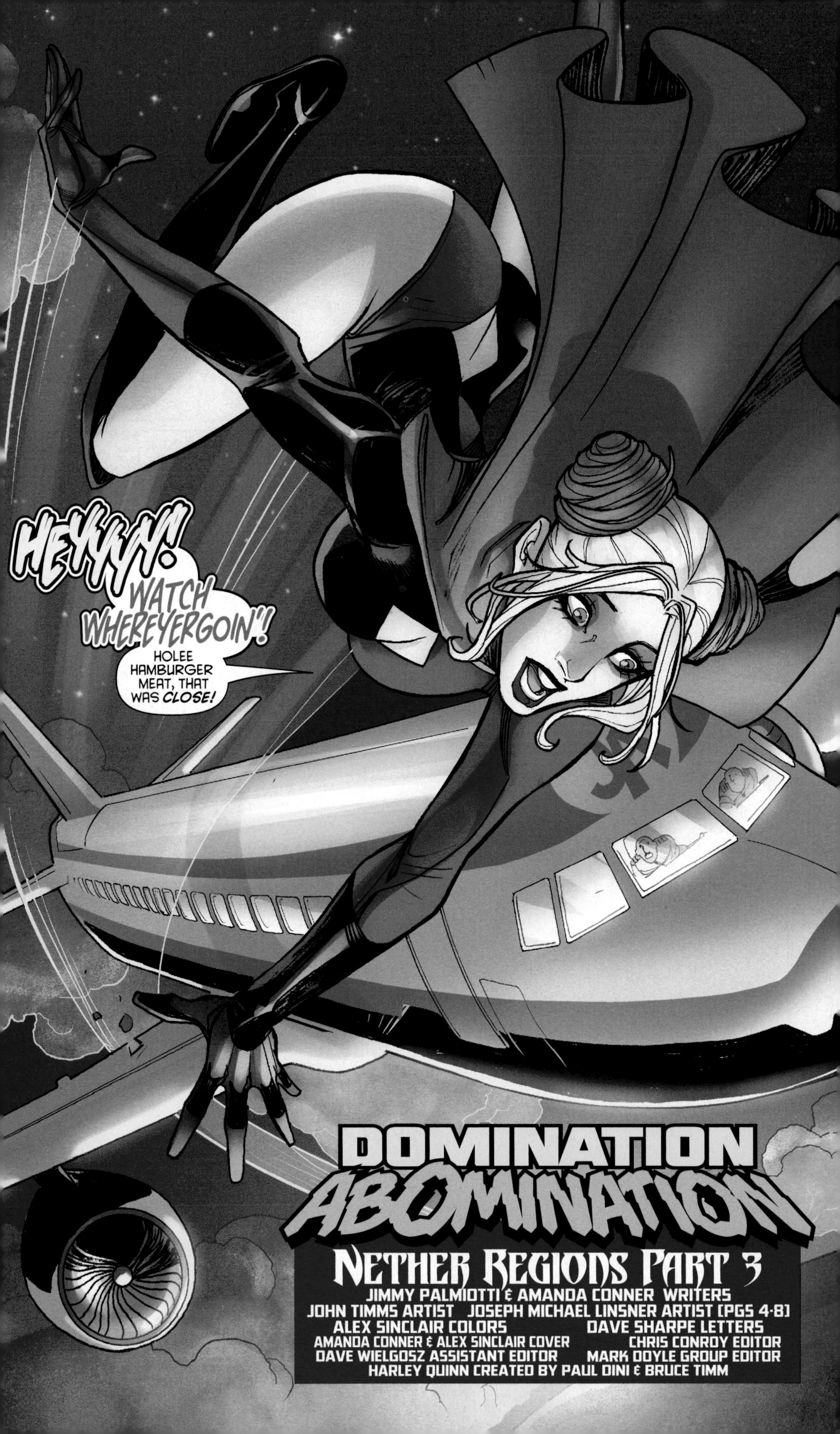

HEYYYY! WATCH WHEREYERGOIN'!
HOLEE HAMBURGER MEAT, THAT WAS CLOSE!
DOMINATION ABOMINATION
NETHER REGIONS PART 3
JIMMY PALMIOTTI & AMANDA CONNER WRITERS
JOHN TIMMS ARTIST JOSEPH MICHAEL LINSNER ARTIST [PGS 4-8]
ALEX SINCLAIR COLORS DAVE SHARPE LETTERS
AMANDA CONNER & ALEX SINCLAIR COVER CHRIS CONROY EDITOR
DAVE WIELGOSZ ASSISTANT EDITOR MARK DOYLE GROUP EDITOR
HARLEY QUINN CREATED BY PAUL DINI & BRUCE TIMM

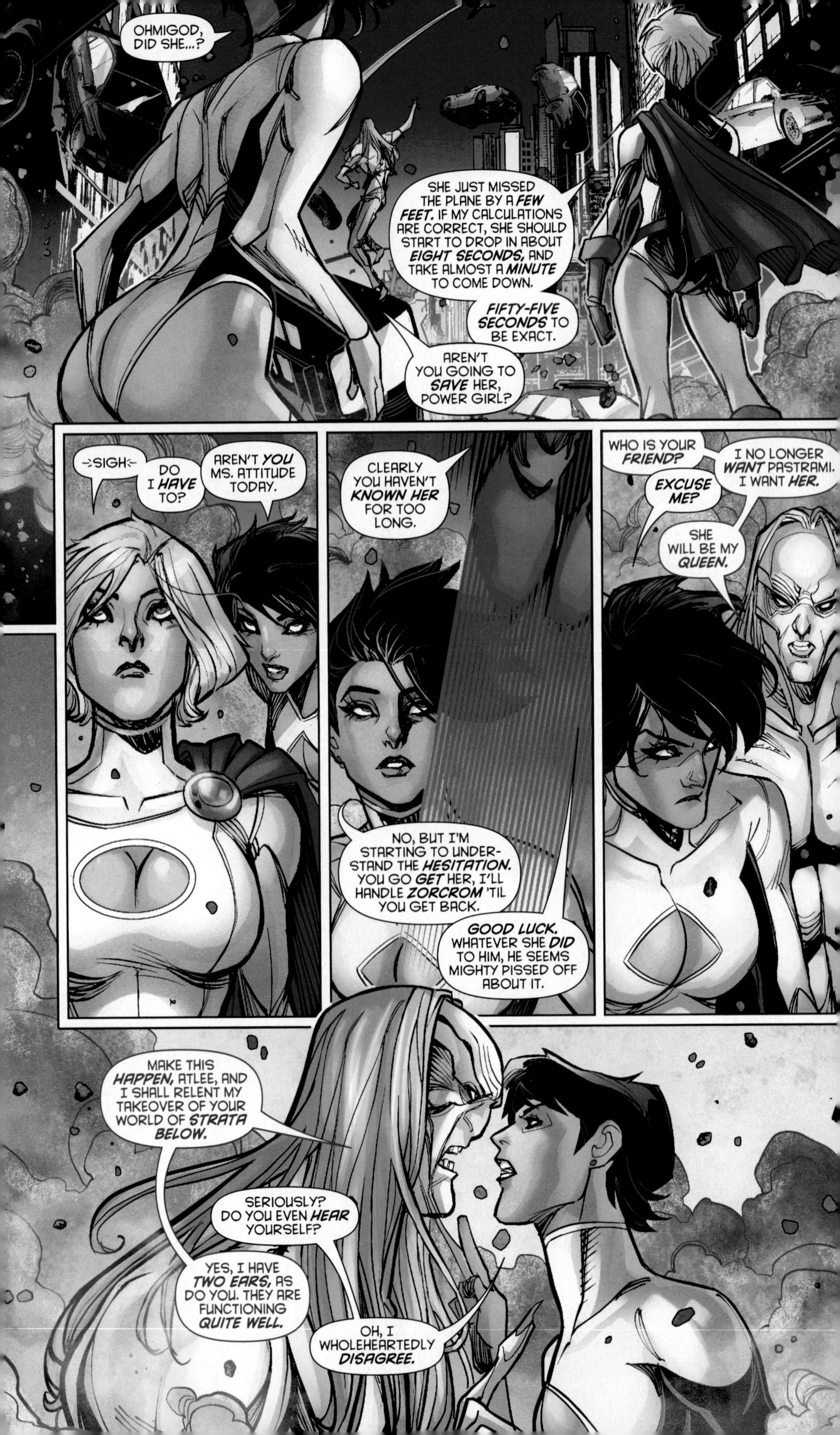

OHMIGOD, DID SHE...?
SHE JUST MISSED THE PLANE BY A FEW FEET. IF MY CALCULATIONS ARE CORRECT, SHE SHOULD START TO DROP IN ABOUT EIGHT SECONDS, AND TAKE ALMOST A MINUTE TO COME DOWN.
FIFTY-FIVE SECONDS TO BE EXACT.
AREN'T YOU GOING TO SAVE HER, POWER GIRL?
-SIGH-
DO I HAVE TO?
AREN'T YOU MS. ATTITUDE TODAY.
CLEARLY YOU HAVEN'T KNOWN HER FOR TOO LONG.
NO, BUT I'M STARTING TO UNDER-STAND THE HESITATION. YOU GO GET HER, I'LL HANDLE ZORCROM 'TIL YOU GET BACK.
GOOD LUCK. WHATEVER SHE DID TO HIM, HE SEEMS MIGHTY PISSED OFF ABOUT IT.
WHO IS YOUR FRIEND?
EXCUSE ME?
I NO LONGER WANT PASTRAMI. I WANT HER.
SHE WILL BE MY QUEEN.
MAKE THIS HAPPEN, ATLEE, AND I SHALL RELENT MY TAKEOVER OF YOUR WORLD OF STRATA BELOW.
SERIOUSLY? DO YOU EVEN HEAR YOURSELF?
YES, I HAVE TWO EARS, AS DO YOU. THEY ARE FUNCTIONING QUITE WELL.
OH, I WHOLEHEARTEDLY DISAGREE.

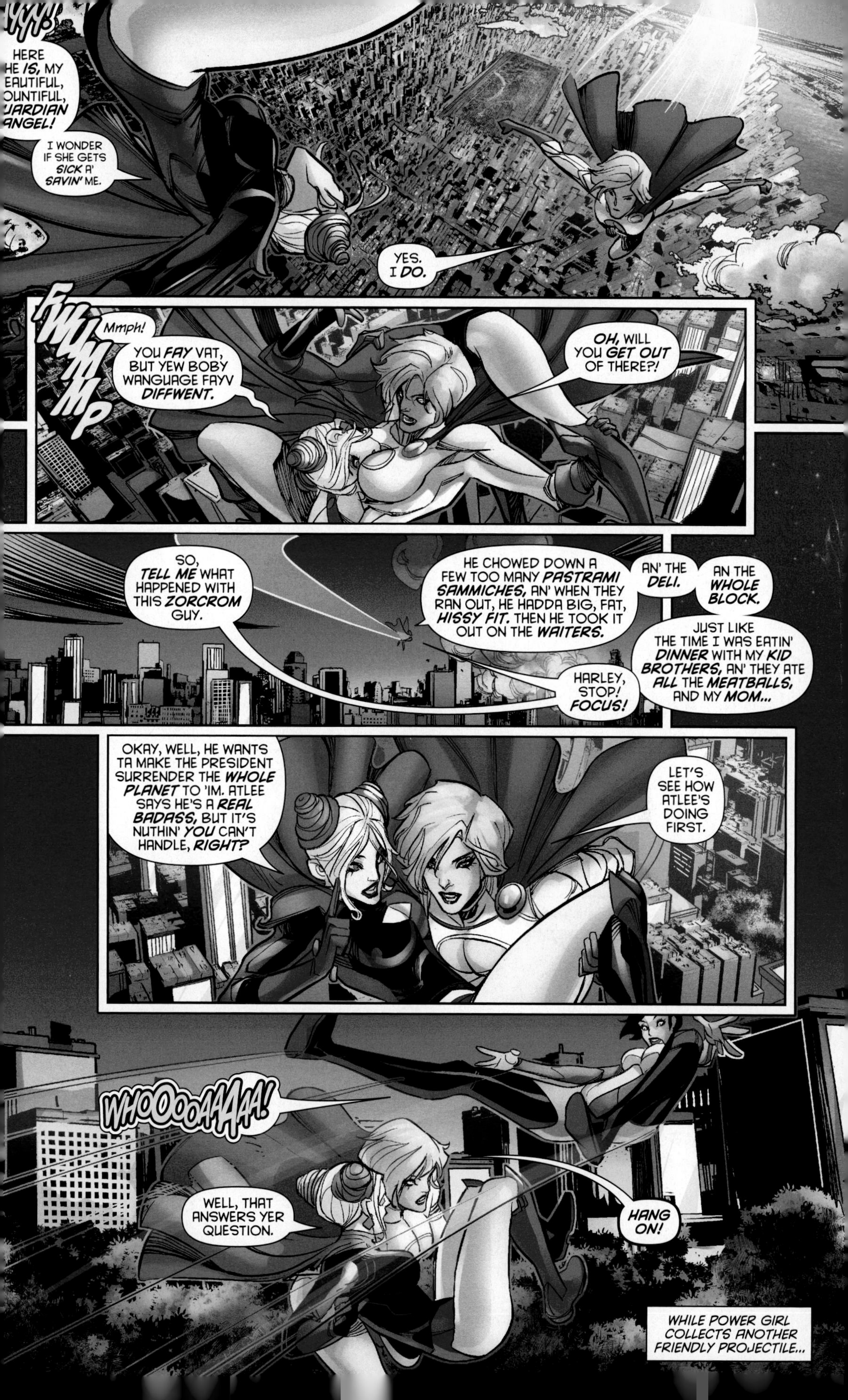
YYY!
HERE HE IS, MY BEAUTIFUL, BOUNTIFUL, GUARDIAN ANGEL!
I WONDER IF SHE GETS SICK A' SAVIN' ME.
YES. I DO.
FWUMMP
Mmph!
YOU FAY VAT, BUT YEW BOBY WANGUAGE FAYV DIFFWENT.
OH, WILL YOU GET OUT OF THERE?!
SO, TELL ME WHAT HAPPENED WITH THIS ZORCROM GUY.
HE CHOWED DOWN A FEW TOO MANY PASTRAMI SAMMICHES, AN' WHEN THEY RAN OUT, HE HADDA BIG, FAT, HISSY FIT. THEN HE TOOK IT OUT ON THE WAITERS.
AN' THE DELI.
AN THE WHOLE BLOCK.
JUST LIKE THE TIME I WAS EATIN' DINNER WITH MY KID BROTHERS, AN' THEY ATE ALL THE MEATBALLS, AND MY MOM...
HARLEY, STOP! FOCUS!
OKAY, WELL, HE WANTS TA MAKE THE PRESIDENT SURRENDER THE WHOLE PLANET TO 'IM. ATLEE SAYS HE'S A REAL BADASS, BUT IT'S NUTHIN' YOU CAN'T HANDLE, RIGHT?
LET'S SEE HOW ATLEE'S DOING FIRST.
WHOOOooAAAAA!
WELL, THAT ANSWERS YER QUESTION.
HANG ON!
WHILE POWER GIRL COLLECTS ANOTHER FRIENDLY PROJECTILE...

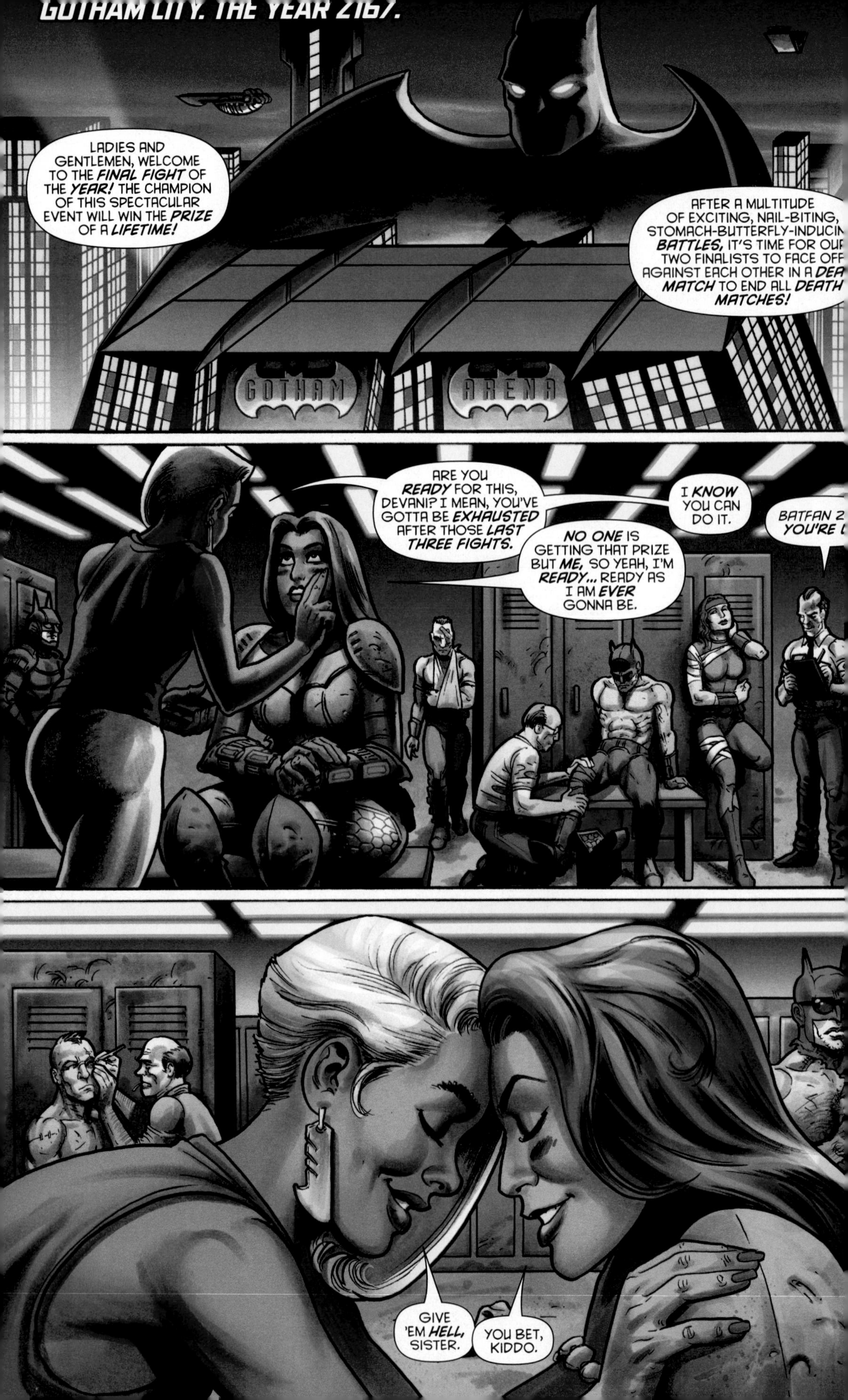
GOTHAM CITY. THE YEAR 2167.
LADIES AND GENTLEMEN, WELCOME TO THE FINAL FIGHT OF THE YEAR! THE CHAMPION OF THIS SPECTACULAR EVENT WILL WIN THE PRIZE OF A LIFETIME!
AFTER A MULTITUDE OF EXCITING, NAIL-BITING, STOMACH-BUTTERFLY-INDUCIN BATTLES, IT'S TIME FOR OUR TWO FINALISTS TO FACE OFF AGAINST EACH OTHER IN A DEA MATCH TO END ALL DEATH MATCHES!
GOTHAM
ARENA
ARE YOU READY FOR THIS, DEVANI? I MEAN, YOU'VE GOTTA BE EXHAUSTED AFTER THOSE LAST THREE FIGHTS.
I KNOW YOU CAN DO IT.
NO ONE IS GETTING THAT PRIZE BUT ME, SO YEAH, I'M READY... READY AS I AM EVER GONNA BE.
BATFAN 2 YOU'RE
GIVE 'EM HELL, SISTER.
YOU BET, KIDDO.

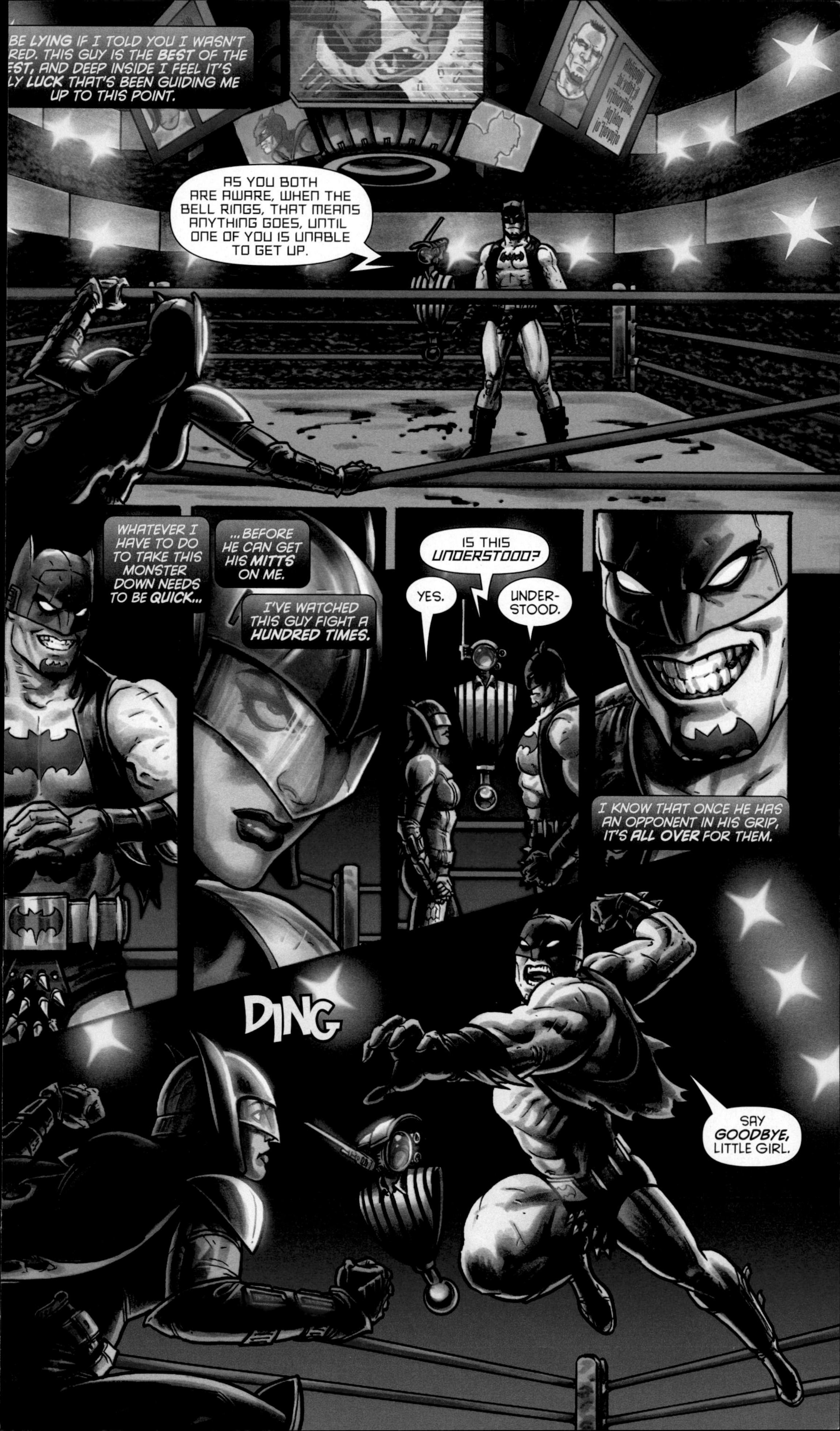
BE LYING IF I TOLD YOU I WASN'T RED. THIS GUY IS THE BEST OF THE EST, AND DEEP INSIDE I FEEL IT'S LY LUCK THAT'S BEEN GUIDING ME UP TO THIS POINT.
AS YOU BOTH ARE AWARE, WHEN THE BELL RINGS, THAT MEANS ANYTHING GOES, UNTIL ONE OF YOU IS UNABLE TO GET UP.
WHATEVER I HAVE TO DO TO TAKE THIS MONSTER DOWN NEEDS TO BE QUICK...
...BEFORE HE CAN GET HIS MITTS ON ME.
I'VE WATCHED THIS GUY FIGHT A HUNDRED TIMES.
IS THIS UNDERSTOOD?
YES.
UNDER-STOOD.
I KNOW THAT ONCE HE HAS AN OPPONENT IN HIS GRIP, IT'S ALL OVER FOR THEM.
DING
SAY GOODBYE, LITTLE GIRL.

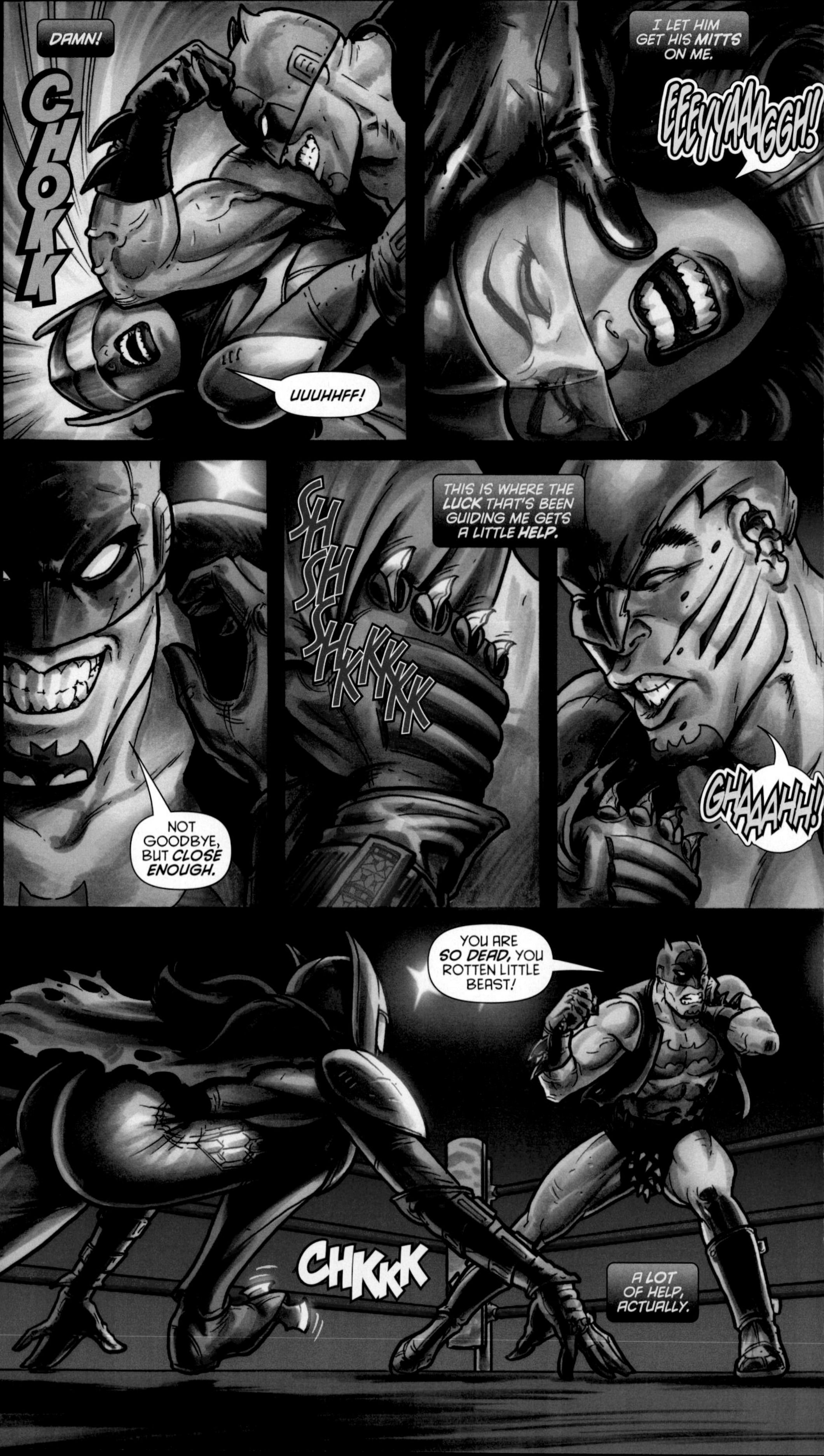
DAMN!
CHOKK
UUUHHFF!
I LET HIM GET HIS MITTS ON ME.
EEEYYAAAGGH!
NOT GOODBYE, BUT CLOSE ENOUGH.
SHSHSHKKKKKK
THIS IS WHERE THE LUCK THAT'S BEEN GUIDING ME GETS A LITTLE HELP.
GHAAAHH!
YOU ARE SO DEAD, YOU ROTTEN LITTLE BEAST!
CHKKK
A LOT OF HELP, ACTUALLY.

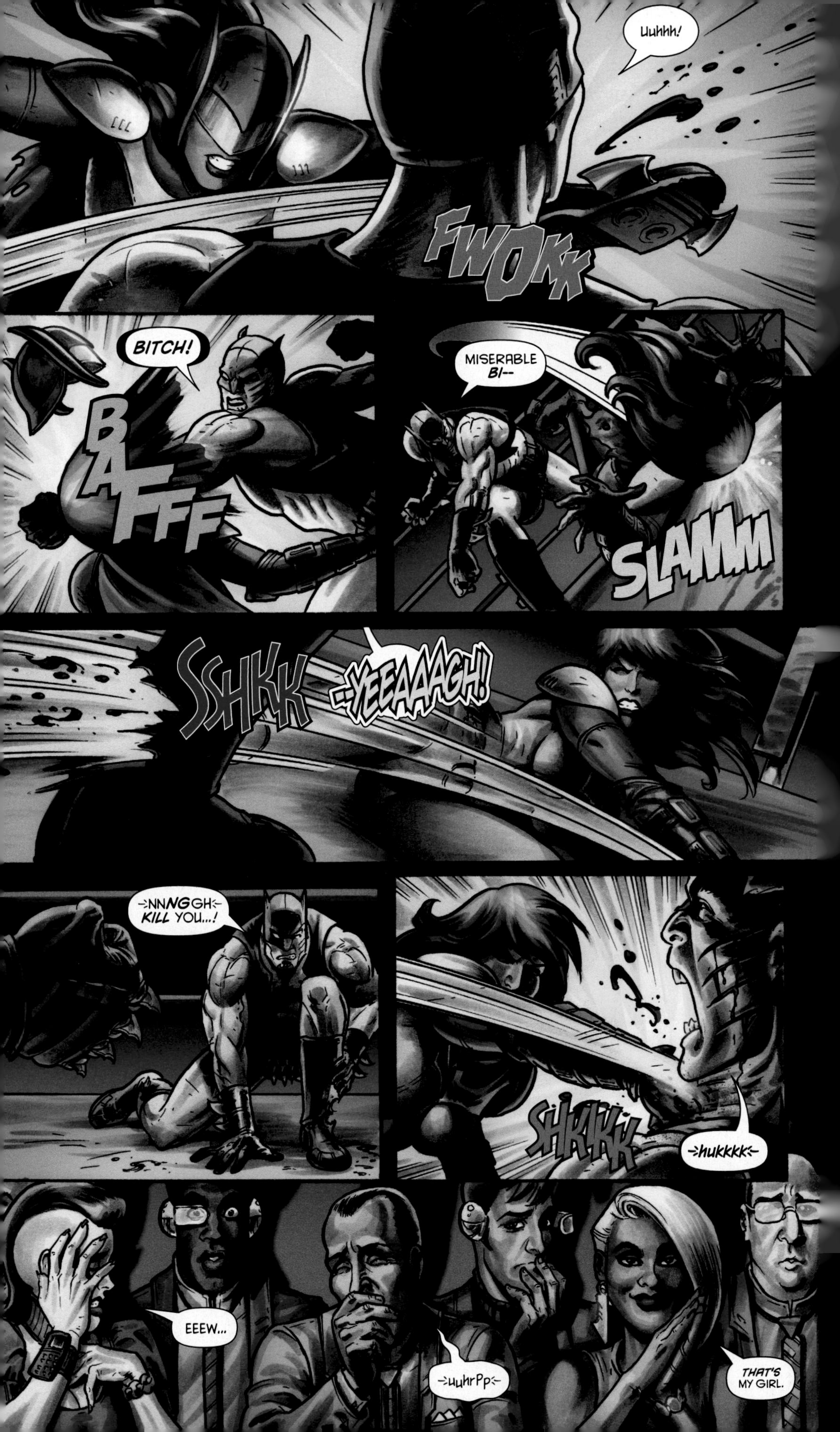
Uuhhh!
FWOKK
BITCH!
BAFFF
MISERABLE BI--
SLAMMM
SSHKK
--YEEAAAGH!
-NNNGGH- KILL YOU...!
SHKKK
-hukkkk-
EEEW...
-uuhrPp-
THAT'S MY GIRL.

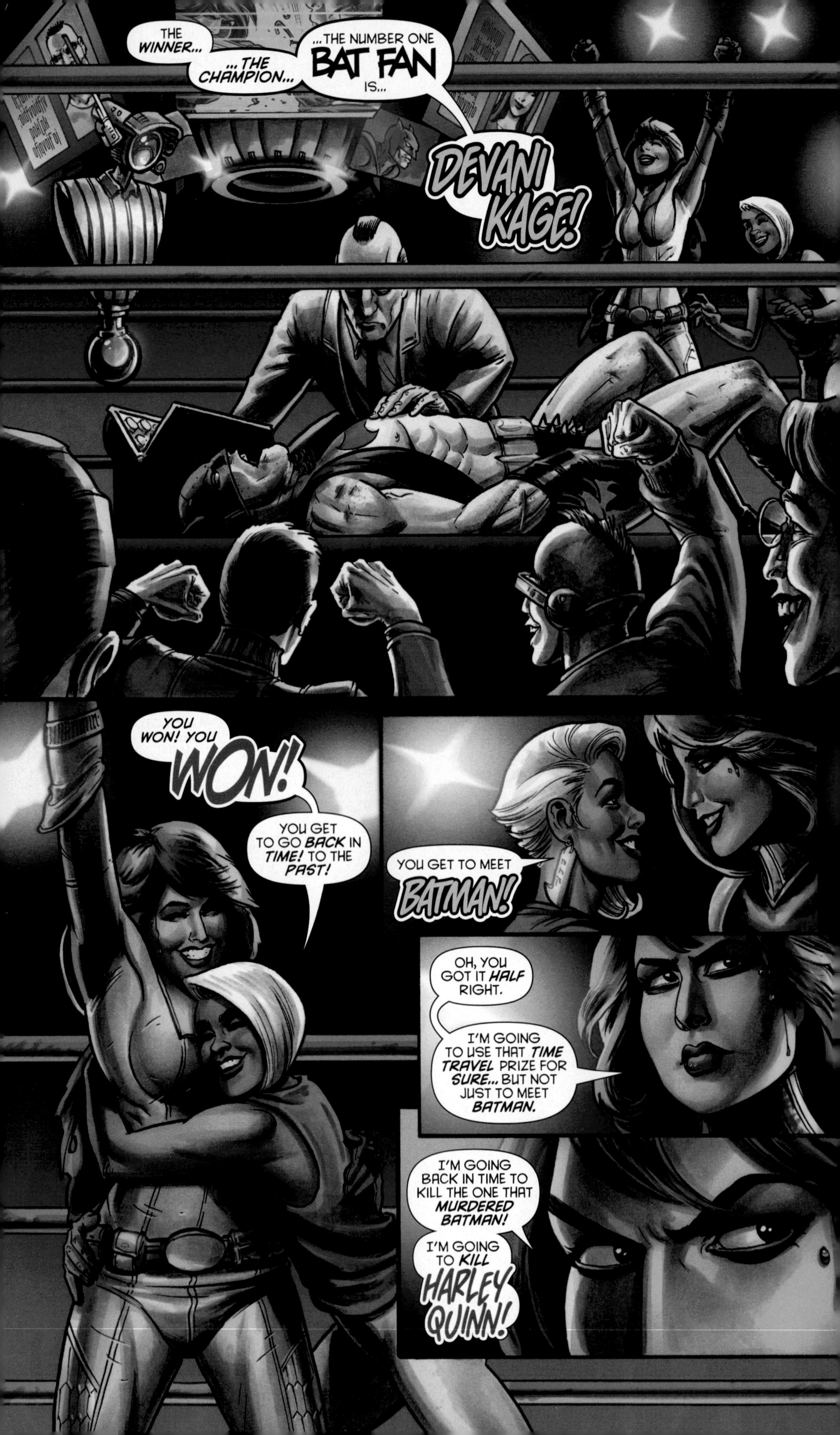
THE WINNER...
...THE CHAMPION...
...THE NUMBER ONE BAT FAN IS...
DEVANI KAGE!
YOU WON! YOU WON!
YOU GET TO GO BACK IN TIME! TO THE PAST!
YOU GET TO MEET BATMAN!
OH, YOU GOT IT HALF RIGHT.
I'M GOING TO USE THAT TIME TRAVEL PRIZE FOR SURE... BUT NOT JUST TO MEET BATMAN.
I'M GOING BACK IN TIME TO KILL THE ONE THAT MURDERED BATMAN!
I'M GOING TO KILL HARLEY QUINN!

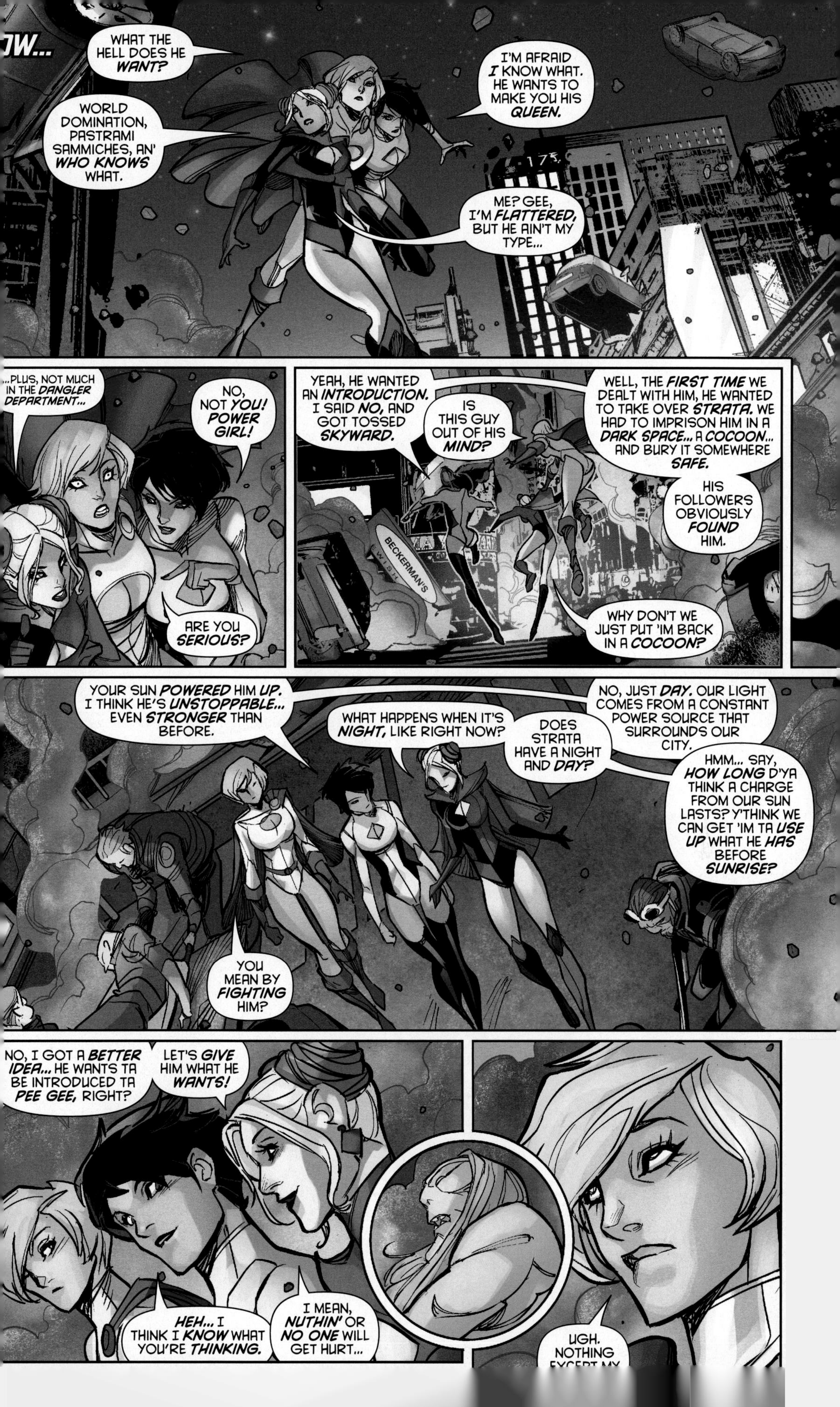
WHAT THE HELL DOES HE *WANT?*
WORLD DOMINATION, PASTRAMI SAMMICHES, AN' *WHO KNOWS* WHAT.
I'M AFRAID *I* KNOW WHAT. HE WANTS TO MAKE YOU HIS *QUEEN.*
ME? GEE, I'M *FLATTERED,* BUT HE AIN'T MY TYPE...
...PLUS, NOT MUCH IN THE *DANGLER DEPARTMENT...*
NO, NOT *YOU! POWER GIRL!*
ARE YOU *SERIOUS?*
YEAH, HE WANTED AN *INTRODUCTION.* I SAID *NO,* AND GOT TOSSED *SKYWARD.*
IS THIS GUY OUT OF HIS *MIND?*
WELL, THE *FIRST TIME* WE DEALT WITH HIM, HE WANTED TO TAKE OVER *STRATA.* WE HAD TO IMPRISON HIM IN A *DARK SPACE...* A *COCOON...* AND BURY IT SOMEWHERE *SAFE.*
HIS FOLLOWERS OBVIOUSLY *FOUND* HIM.
BECKERMAN'S
WHY DON'T WE JUST PUT 'IM BACK IN A *COCOON?*
YOUR SUN *POWERED* HIM *UP.* I THINK HE'S *UNSTOPPABLE...* EVEN *STRONGER* THAN BEFORE.
WHAT HAPPENS WHEN IT'S *NIGHT,* LIKE RIGHT NOW?
DOES STRATA HAVE A NIGHT AND *DAY?*
NO, JUST *DAY.* OUR LIGHT COMES FROM A CONSTANT POWER SOURCE THAT SURROUNDS OUR CITY.
HMM... SAY, *HOW LONG* D'YA THINK A CHARGE FROM OUR SUN LASTS? Y'THINK WE CAN GET 'IM TA *USE UP* WHAT HE *HAS* BEFORE *SUNRISE?*
YOU MEAN BY *FIGHTING* HIM?
NO, I GOT A *BETTER IDEA...* HE WANTS TA BE INTRODUCED TA *PEE GEE,* RIGHT?
LET'S *GIVE* HIM WHAT HE *WANTS!*
HEH... I THINK I *KNOW* WHAT YOU'RE *THINKING.*
I MEAN, *NUTHIN'* OR *NO ONE* WILL GET HURT...
UGH. NOTHING

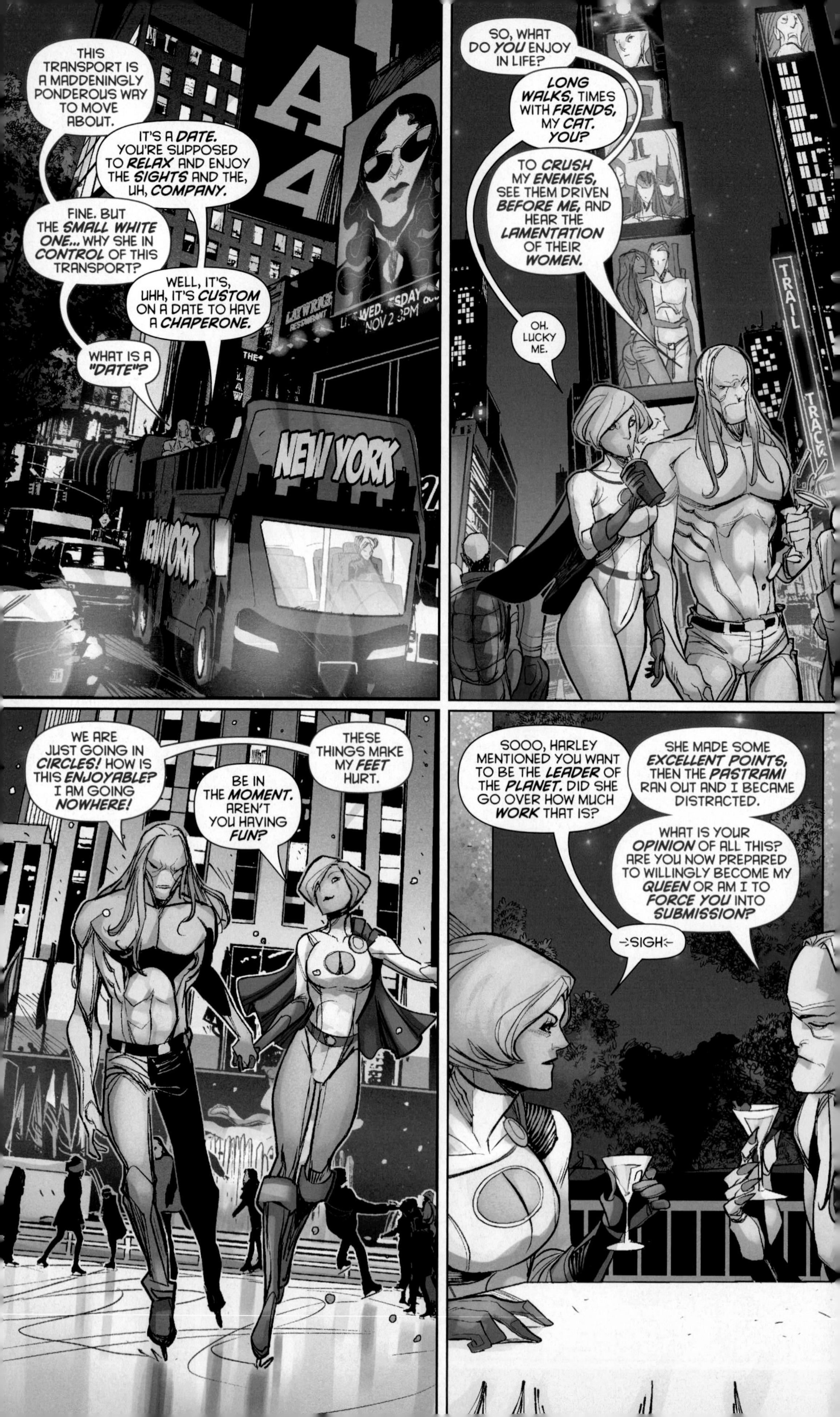
THIS TRANSPORT IS A MADDENINGLY PONDEROUS WAY TO MOVE ABOUT.
IT'S A DATE. YOU'RE SUPPOSED TO RELAX AND ENJOY THE SIGHTS AND THE, UH, COMPANY.
FINE. BUT THE SMALL WHITE ONE... WHY SHE IN CONTROL OF THIS TRANSPORT?
WELL, IT'S, UHH, IT'S CUSTOM ON A DATE TO HAVE A CHAPERONE.
WHAT IS A "DATE"?
NEW YORK
NEW YORK
SO, WHAT DO YOU ENJOY IN LIFE?
LONG WALKS, TIMES WITH FRIENDS, MY CAT. YOU?
TO CRUSH MY ENEMIES, SEE THEM DRIVEN BEFORE ME, AND HEAR THE LAMENTATION OF THEIR WOMEN.
OH. LUCKY ME.
WE ARE JUST GOING IN CIRCLES! HOW IS THIS ENJOYABLE? I AM GOING NOWHERE!
BE IN THE MOMENT. AREN'T YOU HAVING FUN?
THESE THINGS MAKE MY FEET HURT.
SOOO, HARLEY MENTIONED YOU WANT TO BE THE LEADER OF THE PLANET. DID SHE GO OVER HOW MUCH WORK THAT IS?
SHE MADE SOME EXCELLENT POINTS, THEN THE PASTRAMI RAN OUT AND I BECAME DISTRACTED.
WHAT IS YOUR OPINION OF ALL THIS? ARE YOU NOW PREPARED TO WILLINGLY BECOME MY QUEEN OR AM I TO FORCE YOU INTO SUBMISSION?
-SIGH-

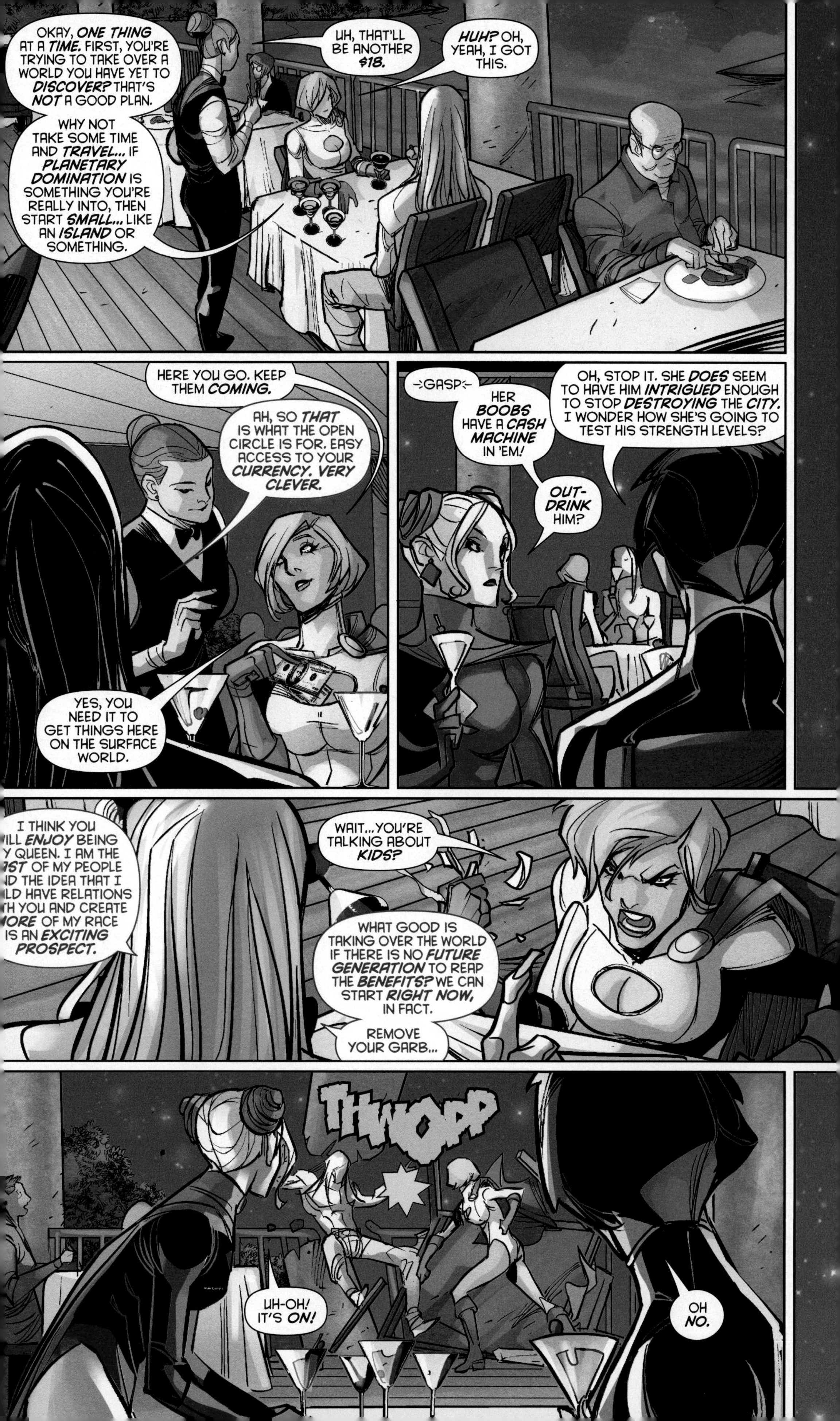
OKAY, ONE THING AT A TIME. FIRST, YOU'RE TRYING TO TAKE OVER A WORLD YOU HAVE YET TO DISCOVER? THAT'S NOT A GOOD PLAN.
WHY NOT TAKE SOME TIME AND TRAVEL... IF PLANETARY DOMINATION IS SOMETHING YOU'RE REALLY INTO, THEN START SMALL... LIKE AN ISLAND OR SOMETHING.
UH, THAT'LL BE ANOTHER $18.
HUH? OH, YEAH, I GOT THIS.
HERE YOU GO. KEEP THEM COMING.
AH, SO THAT IS WHAT THE OPEN CIRCLE IS FOR. EASY ACCESS TO YOUR CURRENCY. VERY CLEVER.
YES, YOU NEED IT TO GET THINGS HERE ON THE SURFACE WORLD.
-GASP-
HER BOOBS HAVE A CASH MACHINE IN 'EM!
OH, STOP IT. SHE DOES SEEM TO HAVE HIM INTRIGUED ENOUGH TO STOP DESTROYING THE CITY. I WONDER HOW SHE'S GOING TO TEST HIS STRENGTH LEVELS?
OUT-DRINK HIM?
I THINK YOU ILL ENJOY BEING Y QUEEN. I AM THE ST OF MY PEOPLE ND THE IDEA THAT I LD HAVE RELATIONS TH YOU AND CREATE ORE OF MY RACE IS AN EXCITING PROSPECT.
WAIT...YOU'RE TALKING ABOUT KIDS?
WHAT GOOD IS TAKING OVER THE WORLD IF THERE IS NO FUTURE GENERATION TO REAP THE BENEFITS? WE CAN START RIGHT NOW, IN FACT.
REMOVE YOUR GARB...
THWOPP
UH-OH! IT'S ON!
OH NO.

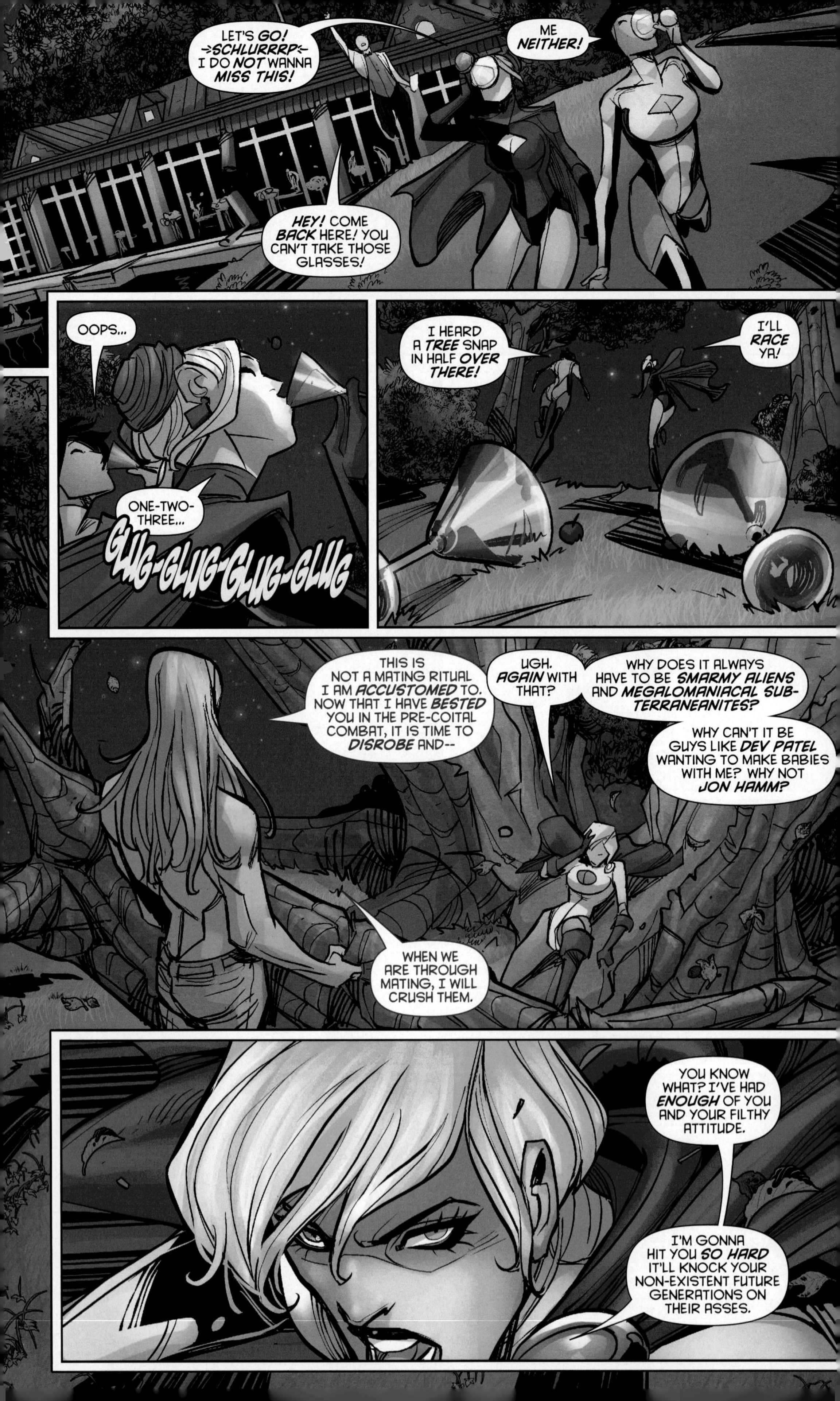
LET'S GO! -SCHLURRRP- I DO NOT WANNA MISS THIS!
ME NEITHER!
HEY! COME BACK HERE! YOU CAN'T TAKE THOSE GLASSES!
OOPS...
ONE-TWO-THREE...
GLUG-GLUG-GLUG-GLUG
I HEARD A TREE SNAP IN HALF OVER THERE!
I'LL RACE YA!
THIS IS NOT A MATING RITUAL I AM ACCUSTOMED TO. NOW THAT I HAVE BESTED YOU IN THE PRE-COITAL COMBAT, IT IS TIME TO DISROBE AND--
UGH. AGAIN WITH THAT?
WHY DOES IT ALWAYS HAVE TO BE SMARMY ALIENS AND MEGALOMANIACAL SUB-TERRANEANITES?
WHY CAN'T IT BE GUYS LIKE DEV PATEL WANTING TO MAKE BABIES WITH ME? WHY NOT JON HAMM?
WHEN WE ARE THROUGH MATING, I WILL CRUSH THEM.
YOU KNOW WHAT? I'VE HAD ENOUGH OF YOU AND YOUR FILTHY ATTITUDE.
I'M GONNA HIT YOU SO HARD IT'LL KNOCK YOUR NON-EXISTENT FUTURE GENERATIONS ON THEIR ASSES.

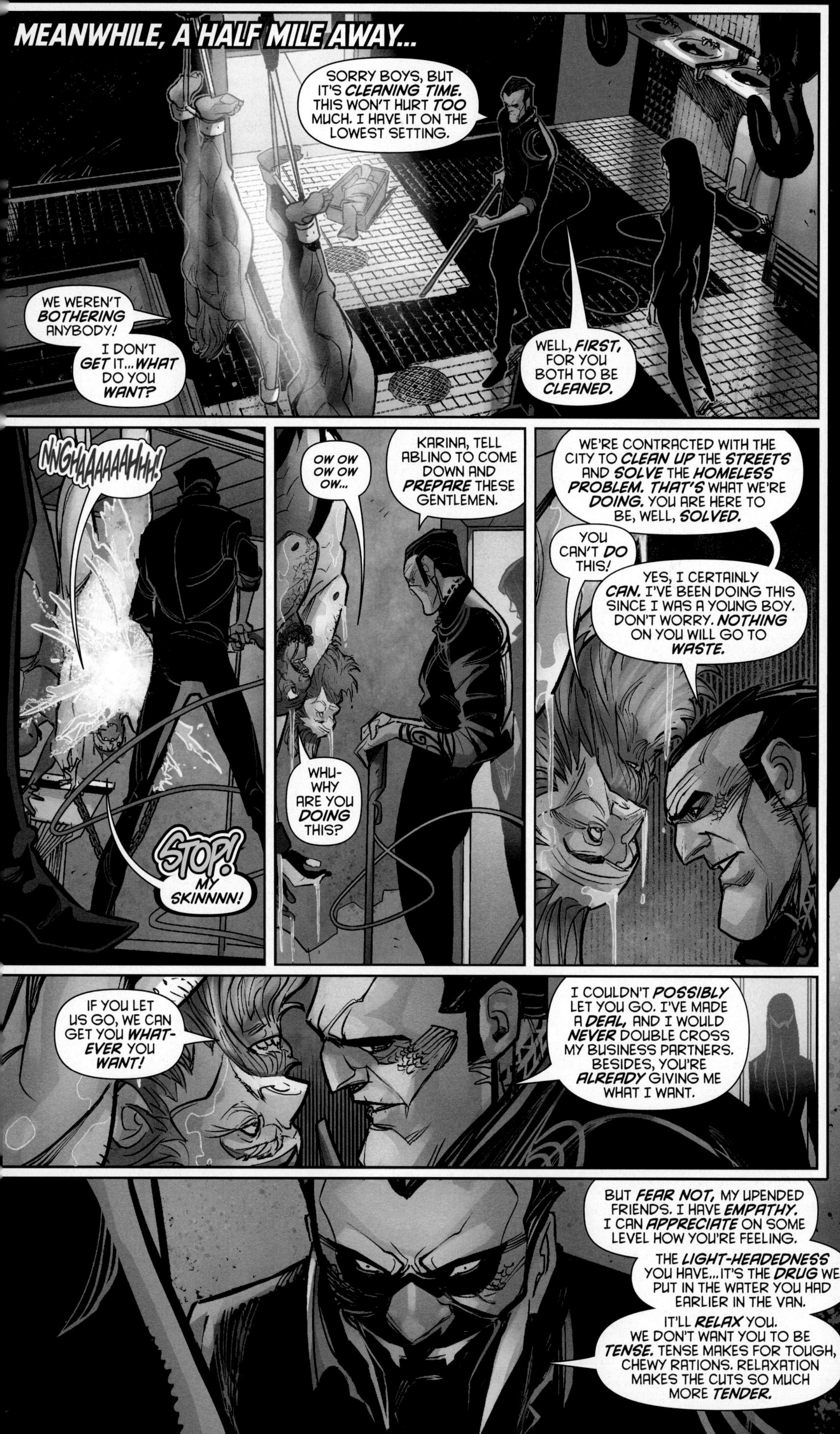

MEANWHILE, A HALF MILE AWAY...
SORRY BOYS, BUT IT'S CLEANING TIME. THIS WON'T HURT TOO MUCH. I HAVE IT ON THE LOWEST SETTING.
WE WEREN'T BOTHERING ANYBODY!
I DON'T GET IT...WHAT DO YOU WANT?
WELL, FIRST, FOR YOU BOTH TO BE CLEANED.
NNGHAAAAAAHHH!
STOP! MY SKINNNN!
OW OW OW OW OW...
KARINA, TELL ABLINO TO COME DOWN AND PREPARE THESE GENTLEMEN.
WHU-WHY ARE YOU DOING THIS?
WE'RE CONTRACTED WITH THE CITY TO CLEAN UP THE STREETS AND SOLVE THE HOMELESS PROBLEM. THAT'S WHAT WE'RE DOING. YOU ARE HERE TO BE, WELL, SOLVED.
YOU CAN'T DO THIS!
YES, I CERTAINLY CAN. I'VE BEEN DOING THIS SINCE I WAS A YOUNG BOY. DON'T WORRY. NOTHING ON YOU WILL GO TO WASTE.
IF YOU LET US GO, WE CAN GET YOU WHAT-EVER YOU WANT!
I COULDN'T POSSIBLY LET YOU GO. I'VE MADE A DEAL, AND I WOULD NEVER DOUBLE CROSS MY BUSINESS PARTNERS. BESIDES, YOU'RE ALREADY GIVING ME WHAT I WANT.
BUT FEAR NOT, MY UPENDED FRIENDS. I HAVE EMPATHY. I CAN APPRECIATE ON SOME LEVEL HOW YOU'RE FEELING.
THE LIGHT-HEADEDNESS YOU HAVE...IT'S THE DRUG WE PUT IN THE WATER YOU HAD EARLIER IN THE VAN.
IT'LL RELAX YOU. WE DON'T WANT YOU TO BE TENSE. TENSE MAKES FOR TOUGH, CHEWY RATIONS. RELAXATION MAKES THE CUTS SO MUCH MORE TENDER.

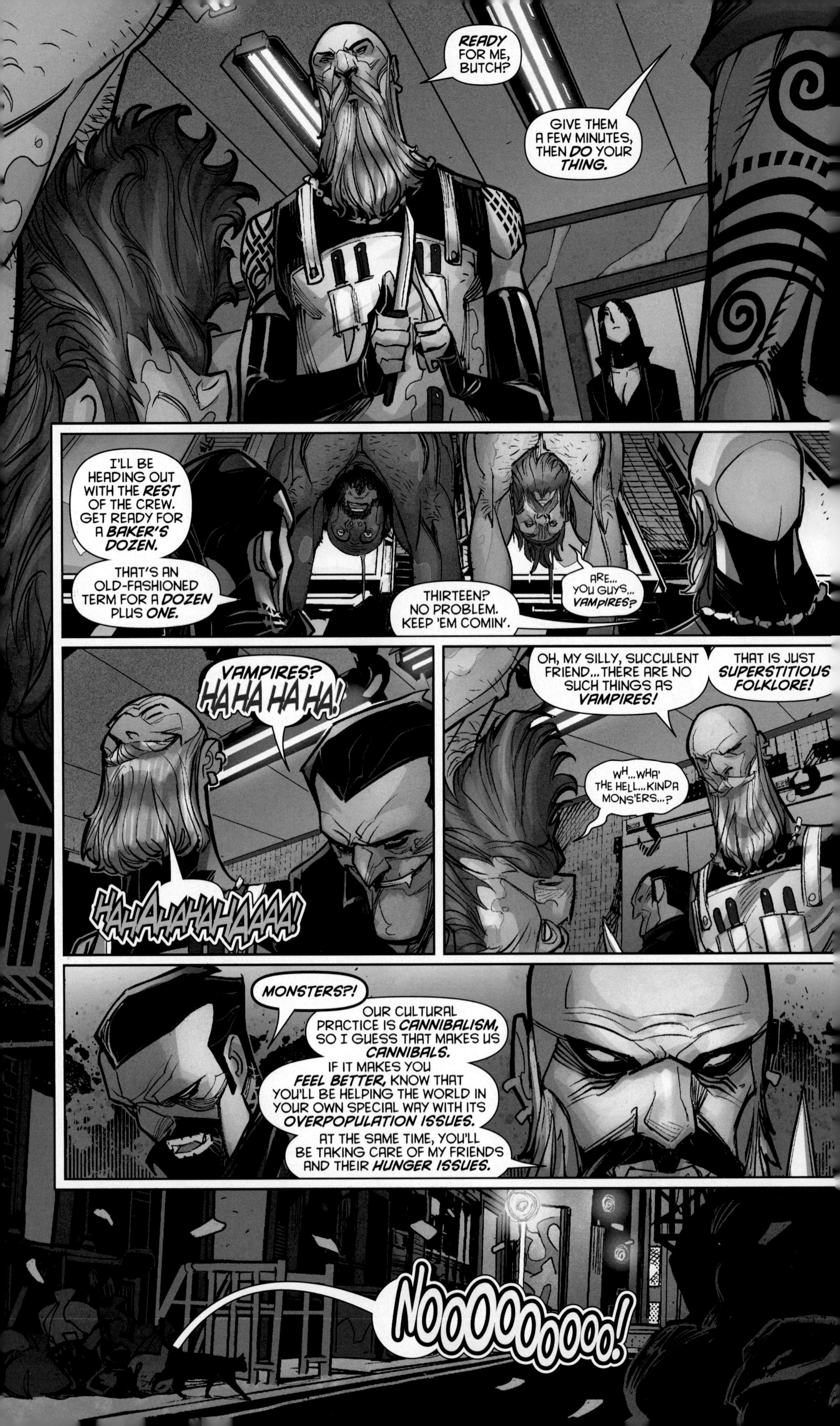

READY FOR ME, BUTCH?
GIVE THEM A FEW MINUTES, THEN DO YOUR THING.
I'LL BE HEADING OUT WITH THE REST OF THE CREW. GET READY FOR A BAKER'S DOZEN.
THAT'S AN OLD-FASHIONED TERM FOR A DOZEN PLUS ONE.
THIRTEEN? NO PROBLEM. KEEP 'EM COMIN'.
ARE... YOU GUYS... VAMPIRES?
VAMPIRES? HAHA HA HA!
HAHAHAHAHÁAAA!
OH, MY SILLY, SUCCULENT FRIEND...THERE ARE NO SUCH THINGS AS VAMPIRES!
THAT IS JUST SUPERSTITIOUS FOLKLORE!
WH...WHA' THE HELL...KINDA MONS'ERS...?
MONSTERS?!
OUR CULTURAL PRACTICE IS CANNIBALISM, SO I GUESS THAT MAKES US CANNIBALS.
IF IT MAKES YOU FEEL BETTER, KNOW THAT YOU'LL BE HELPING THE WORLD IN YOUR OWN SPECIAL WAY WITH ITS OVERPOPULATION ISSUES.
AT THE SAME TIME, YOU'LL BE TAKING CARE OF MY FRIENDS AND THEIR HUNGER ISSUES.
NOOOOOOOOOO!

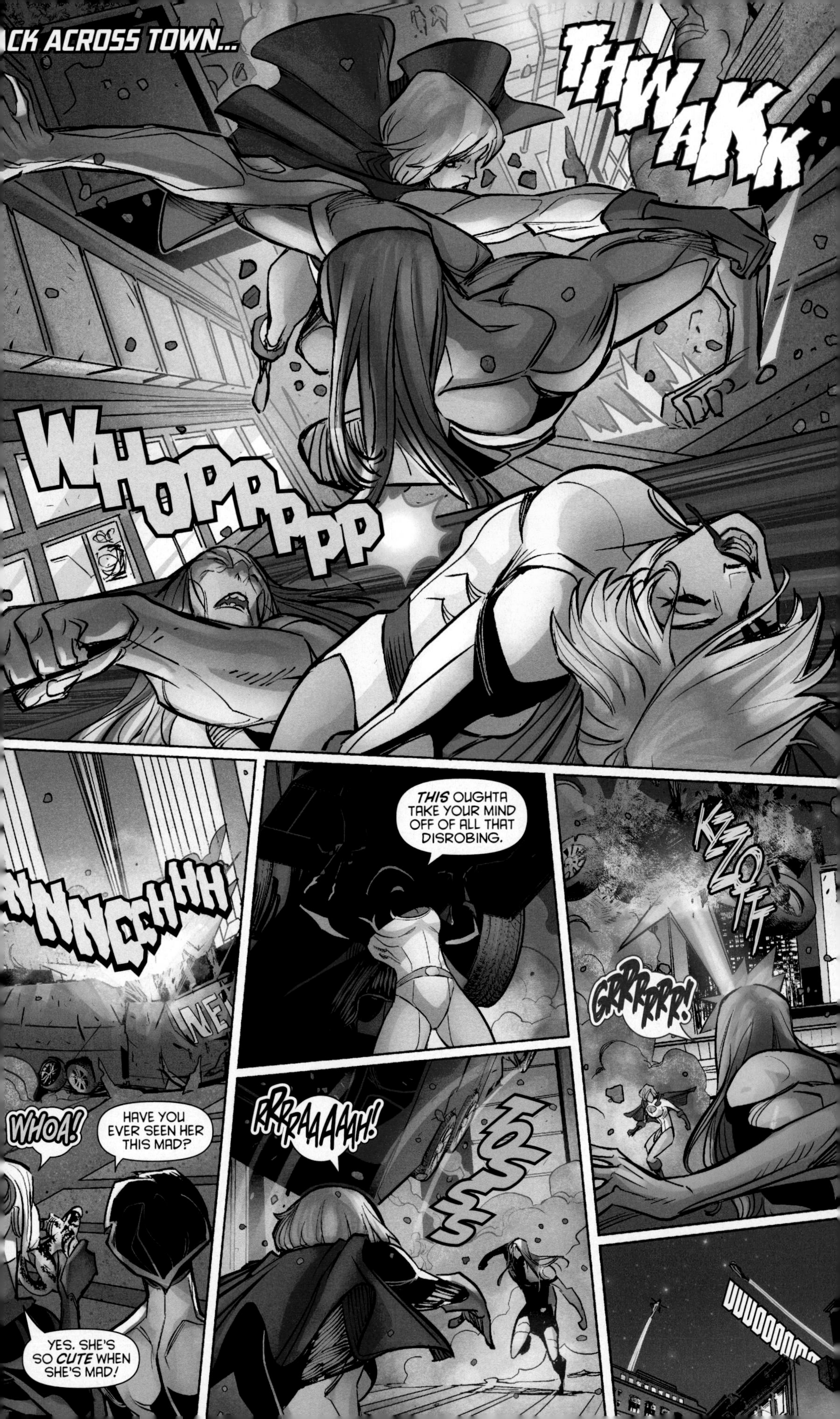
...CK ACROSS TOWN...
THWAKK
WHOPRRPPP
NNNNGCHHH
THIS OUGHTA TAKE YOUR MIND OFF OF ALL THAT DISROBING.
KRZOTT
GRRRRRP!
WHOA!
HAVE YOU EVER SEEN HER THIS MAD?
RRRRAAAAAH!
TOSSS
YES. SHE'S SO CUTE WHEN SHE'S MAD!
VVVOOOOOO

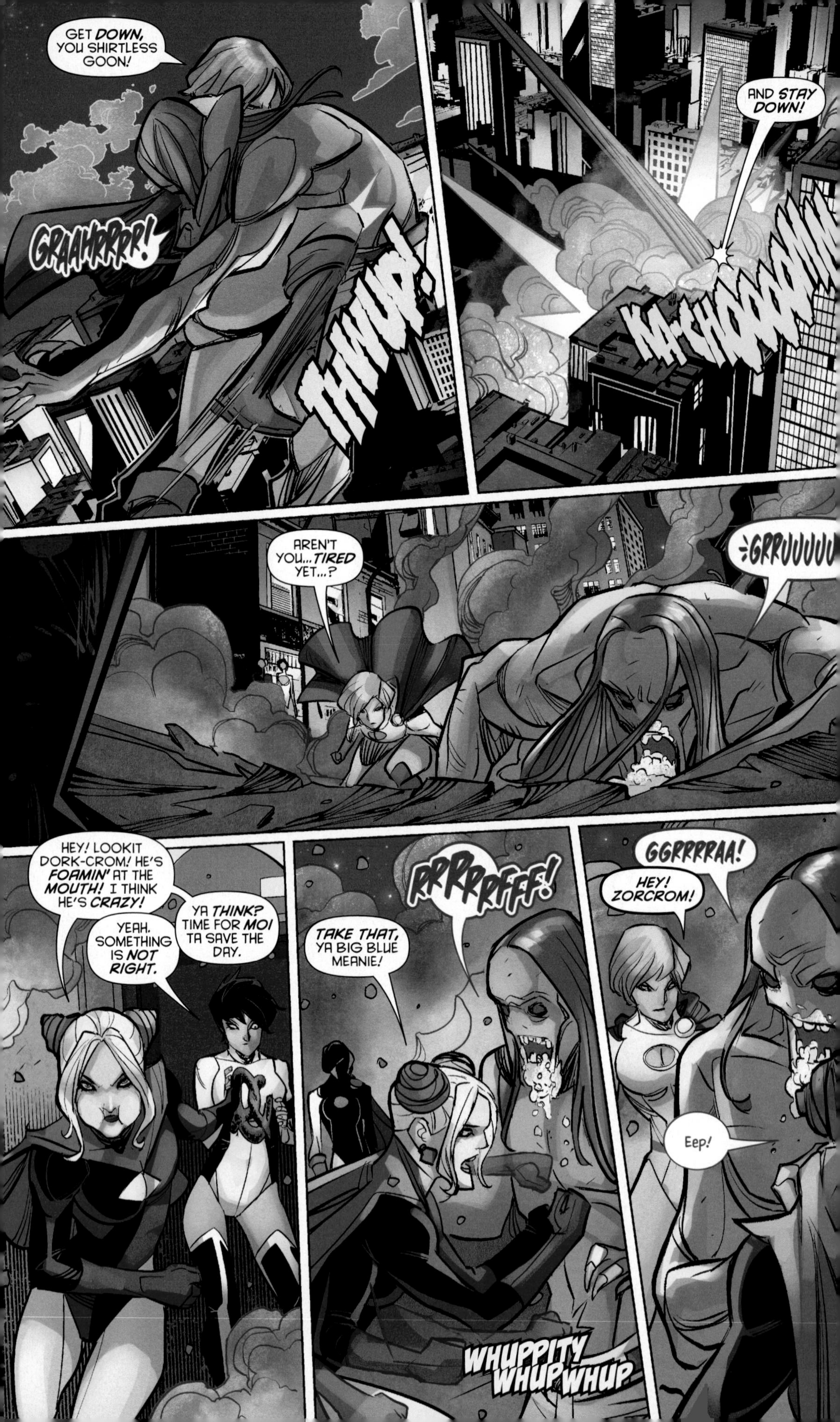
GET DOWN, YOU SHIRTLESS GOON!
GRAAHRRRR!
THWUD!
AND STAY DOWN!
KA-CHOOOM
AREN'T YOU...TIRED YET...?
GRRUUUUU
HEY! LOOKIT DORK-CROM! HE'S FOAMIN' AT THE MOUTH! I THINK HE'S CRAZY!
YEAH. SOMETHING IS NOT RIGHT.
YA THINK? TIME FOR MOI TA SAVE THE DAY.
RRRRRFFF!
TAKE THAT, YA BIG BLUE MEANIE!
GGRRRRAA!
HEY! ZORCROM!
Eep!
WHUPPITY WHUP WHUP

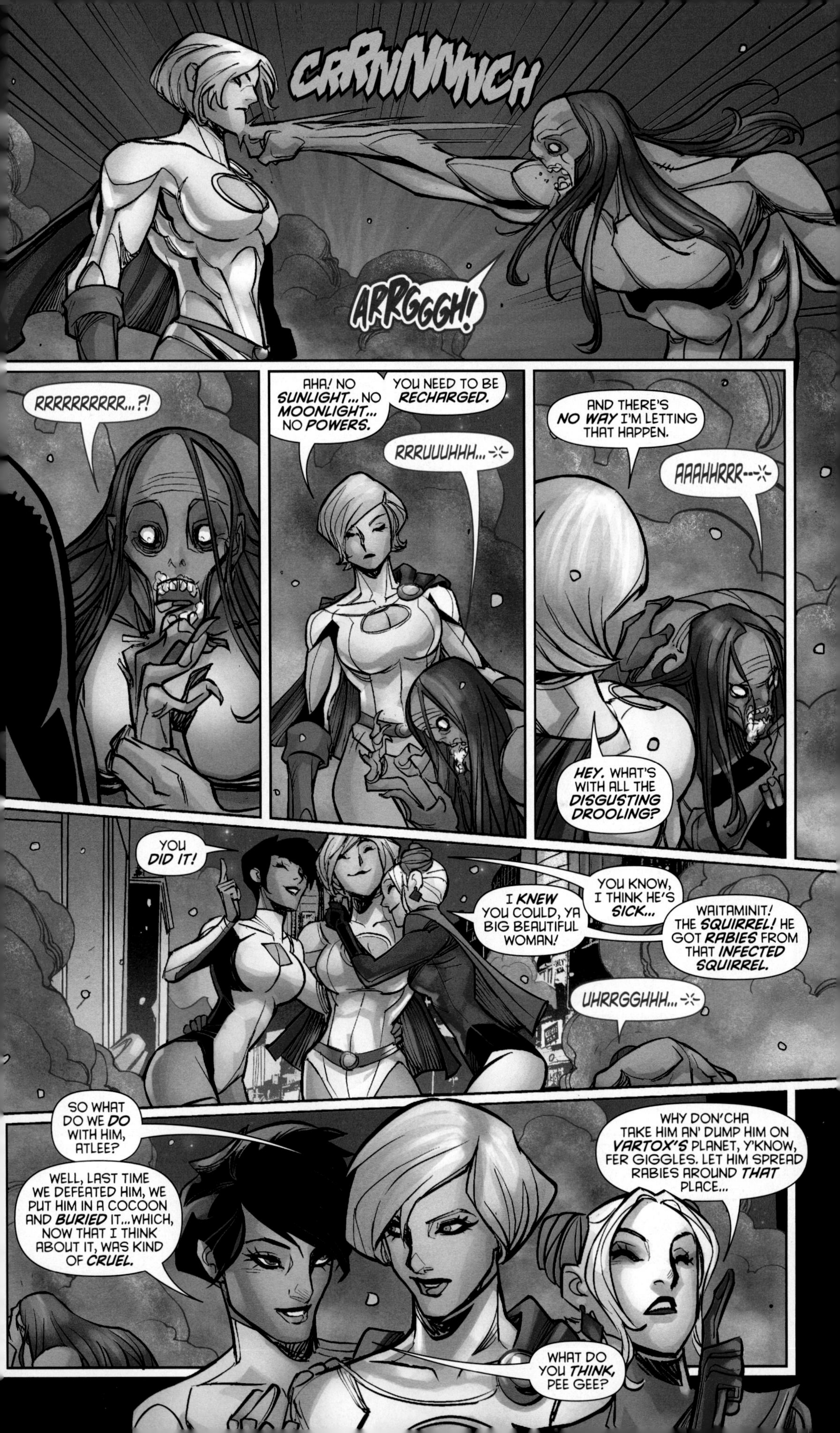

CRRNNNNCH
ARRGGGH!
RRRRRRRRRR...?!
AHA! NO SUNLIGHT... NO MOONLIGHT... NO POWERS.
YOU NEED TO BE RECHARGED.
RRRUUUHHH...
AND THERE'S NO WAY I'M LETTING THAT HAPPEN.
AAAHHRRR--
HEY. WHAT'S WITH ALL THE DISGUSTING DROOLING?
YOU DID IT!
I KNEW YOU COULD, YA BIG BEAUTIFUL WOMAN!
YOU KNOW, I THINK HE'S SICK...
WAITAMINIT! THE SQUIRREL! HE GOT RABIES FROM THAT INFECTED SQUIRREL.
UHRRGGHHH...
SO WHAT DO WE DO WITH HIM, ATLEE?
WELL, LAST TIME WE DEFEATED HIM, WE PUT HIM IN A COCOON AND BURIED IT...WHICH, NOW THAT I THINK ABOUT IT, WAS KIND OF CRUEL.
WHY DON'CHA TAKE HIM AN' DUMP HIM ON VARTOX'S PLANET, Y'KNOW, FER GIGGLES. LET HIM SPREAD RABIES AROUND THAT PLACE...
WHAT DO YOU THINK, PEE GEE?

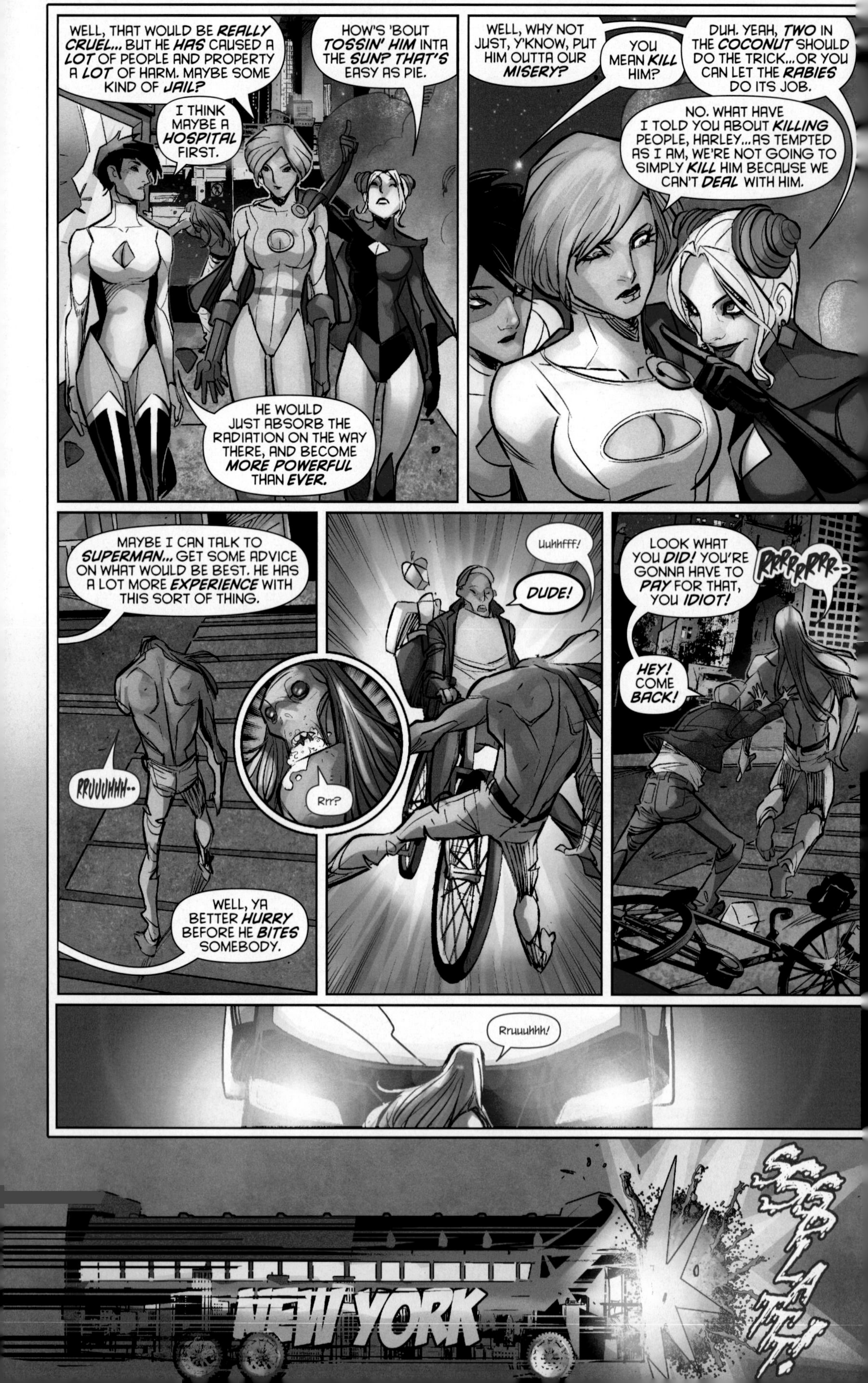

WELL, THAT WOULD BE REALLY CRUEL... BUT HE HAS CAUSED A LOT OF PEOPLE AND PROPERTY A LOT OF HARM. MAYBE SOME KIND OF JAIL?
I THINK MAYBE A HOSPITAL FIRST.
HOW'S 'BOUT TOSSIN' HIM INTA THE SUN? THAT'S EASY AS PIE.
HE WOULD JUST ABSORB THE RADIATION ON THE WAY THERE, AND BECOME MORE POWERFUL THAN EVER.
WELL, WHY NOT JUST, Y'KNOW, PUT HIM OUTTA OUR MISERY?
YOU MEAN KILL HIM?
DUH. YEAH, TWO IN THE COCONUT SHOULD DO THE TRICK...OR YOU CAN LET THE RABIES DO ITS JOB.
NO. WHAT HAVE I TOLD YOU ABOUT KILLING PEOPLE, HARLEY...AS TEMPTED AS I AM, WE'RE NOT GOING TO SIMPLY KILL HIM BECAUSE WE CAN'T DEAL WITH HIM.
MAYBE I CAN TALK TO SUPERMAN... GET SOME ADVICE ON WHAT WOULD BE BEST. HE HAS A LOT MORE EXPERIENCE WITH THIS SORT OF THING.
RRUUUHHH--
Rrr?
WELL, YA BETTER HURRY BEFORE HE BITES SOMEBODY.
Uuhhfff!
DUDE!
LOOK WHAT YOU DID! YOU'RE GONNA HAVE TO PAY FOR THAT, YOU IDIOT!
RRRRRRRR--
HEY! COME BACK!
Rruuuhhh!
NEW YORK
SPLAT!

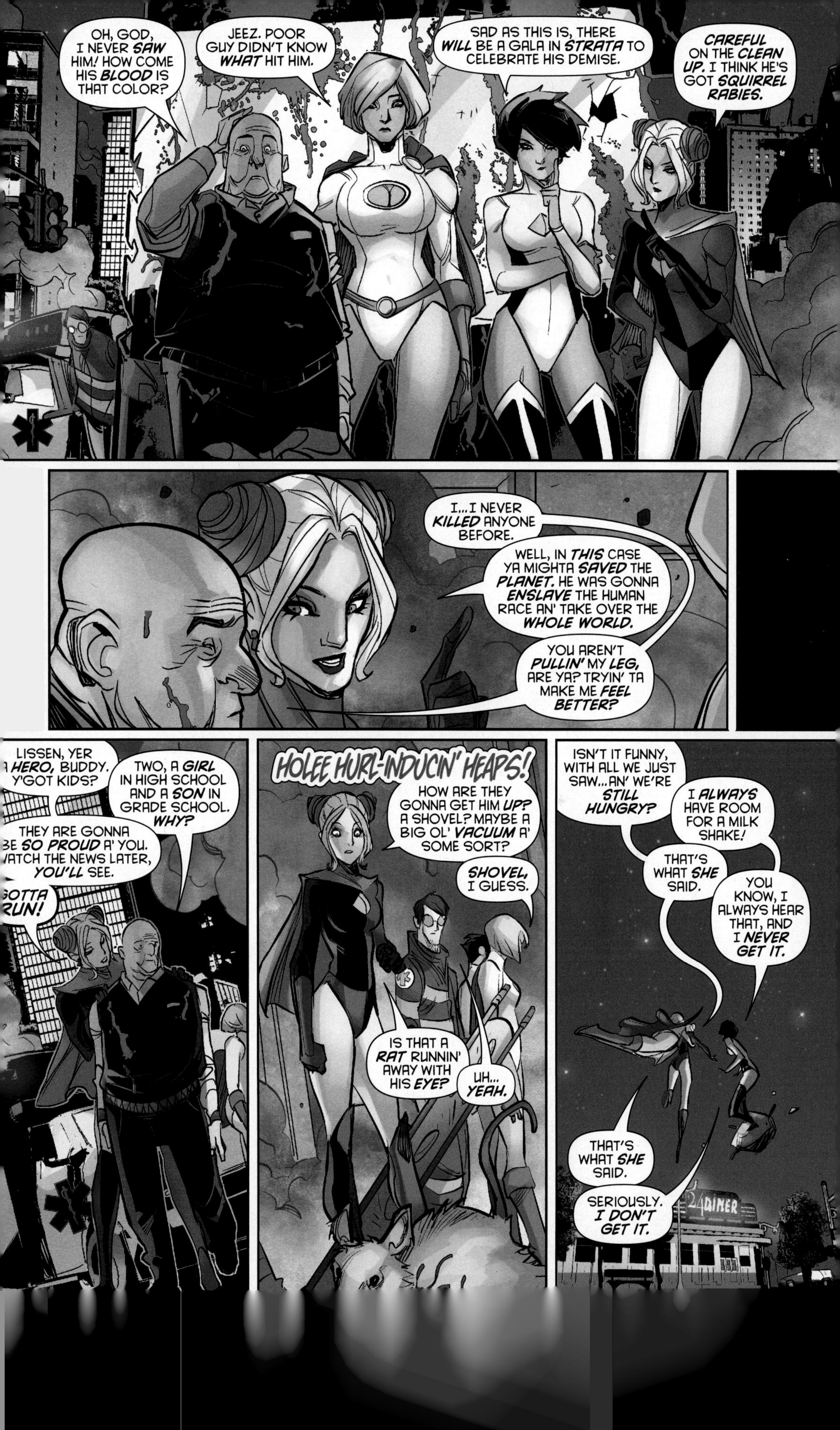

OH, GOD, I NEVER SAW HIM! HOW COME HIS BLOOD IS THAT COLOR?
JEEZ. POOR GUY DIDN'T KNOW WHAT HIT HIM.
SAD AS THIS IS, THERE WILL BE A GALA IN STRATA TO CELEBRATE HIS DEMISE.
CAREFUL ON THE CLEAN UP. I THINK HE'S GOT SQUIRREL RABIES.
I...I NEVER KILLED ANYONE BEFORE.
WELL, IN THIS CASE YA MIGHTA SAVED THE PLANET. HE WAS GONNA ENSLAVE THE HUMAN RACE AN' TAKE OVER THE WHOLE WORLD.
YOU AREN'T PULLIN' MY LEG, ARE YA? TRYIN' TA MAKE ME FEEL BETTER?
LISSEN, YER A HERO, BUDDY. Y'GOT KIDS?
TWO, A GIRL IN HIGH SCHOOL AND A SON IN GRADE SCHOOL. WHY?
THEY ARE GONNA BE SO PROUD A' YOU. WATCH THE NEWS LATER, YOU'LL SEE.
GOTTA RUN!
HOLEE HURL-INDUCIN' HEAPS!
HOW ARE THEY GONNA GET HIM UP? A SHOVEL? MAYBE A BIG OL' VACUUM A' SOME SORT?
SHOVEL, I GUESS.
IS THAT A RAT RUNNIN' AWAY WITH HIS EYE?
UH... YEAH.
ISN'T IT FUNNY, WITH ALL WE JUST SAW...AN' WE'RE STILL HUNGRY?
I ALWAYS HAVE ROOM FOR A MILK SHAKE!
THAT'S WHAT SHE SAID.
YOU KNOW, I ALWAYS HEAR THAT, AND I NEVER GET IT.
THAT'S WHAT SHE SAID.
SERIOUSLY. I DON'T GET IT.
24 DINER

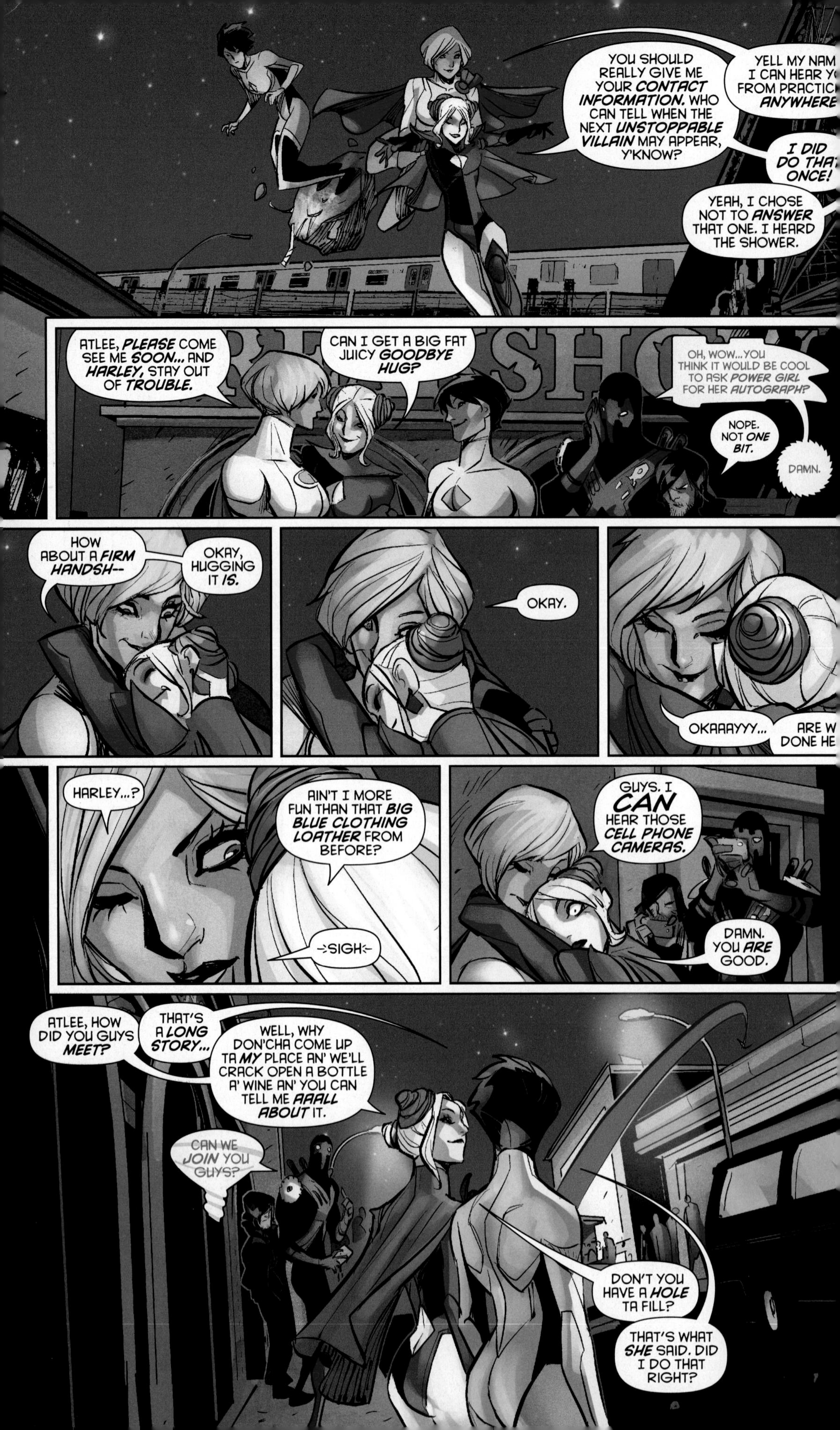

YOU SHOULD REALLY GIVE ME YOUR CONTACT INFORMATION. WHO CAN TELL WHEN THE NEXT UNSTOPPABLE VILLAIN MAY APPEAR, Y'KNOW?
YELL MY NAM
I CAN HEAR Y
FROM PRACTIC
ANYWHERE
I DID DO THA
ONCE!
YEAH, I CHOSE NOT TO ANSWER THAT ONE. I HEARD THE SHOWER.
ATLEE, PLEASE COME SEE ME SOON... AND HARLEY, STAY OUT OF TROUBLE.
CAN I GET A BIG FAT JUICY GOODBYE HUG?
OH, WOW...YOU THINK IT WOULD BE COOL TO ASK POWER GIRL FOR HER AUTOGRAPH?
NOPE. NOT ONE BIT.
DAMN.
HOW ABOUT A FIRM HANDSH--
OKAY, HUGGING IT IS.
OKAY.
OKAAAYYY...
ARE W
DONE HE
HARLEY...?
AIN'T I MORE FUN THAN THAT BIG BLUE CLOTHING LOATHER FROM BEFORE?
->SIGH<-
GUYS. I CAN HEAR THOSE CELL PHONE CAMERAS.
DAMN. YOU ARE GOOD.
ATLEE, HOW DID YOU GUYS MEET?
THAT'S A LONG STORY...
WELL, WHY DON'CHA COME UP TA MY PLACE AN' WE'LL CRACK OPEN A BOTTLE A' WINE AN' YOU CAN TELL ME AAALL ABOUT IT.
CAN WE JOIN YOU GUYS?
DON'T YOU HAVE A HOLE TA FILL?
THAT'S WHAT SHE SAID. DID I DO THAT RIGHT?

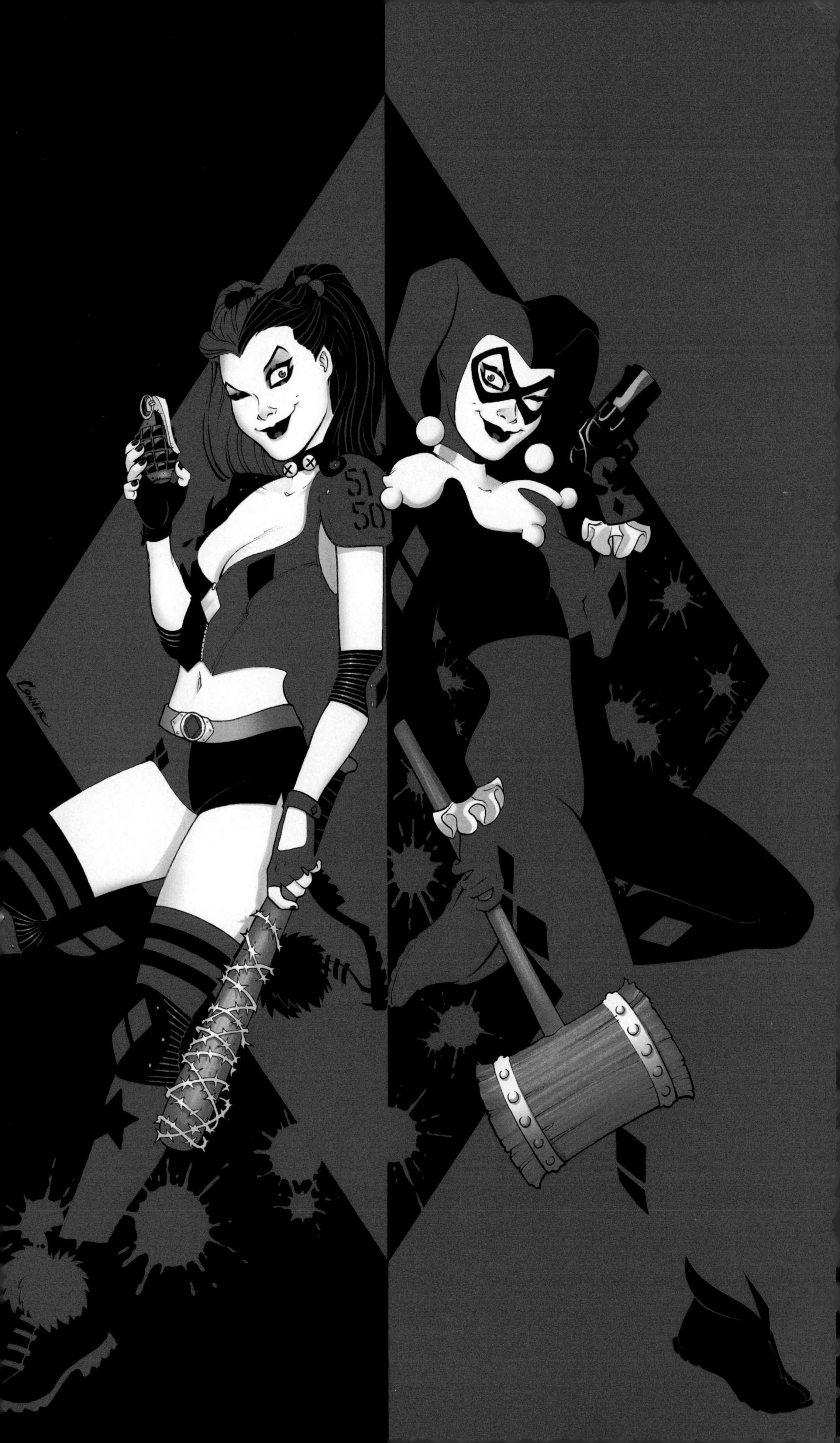
51
50
CONNER

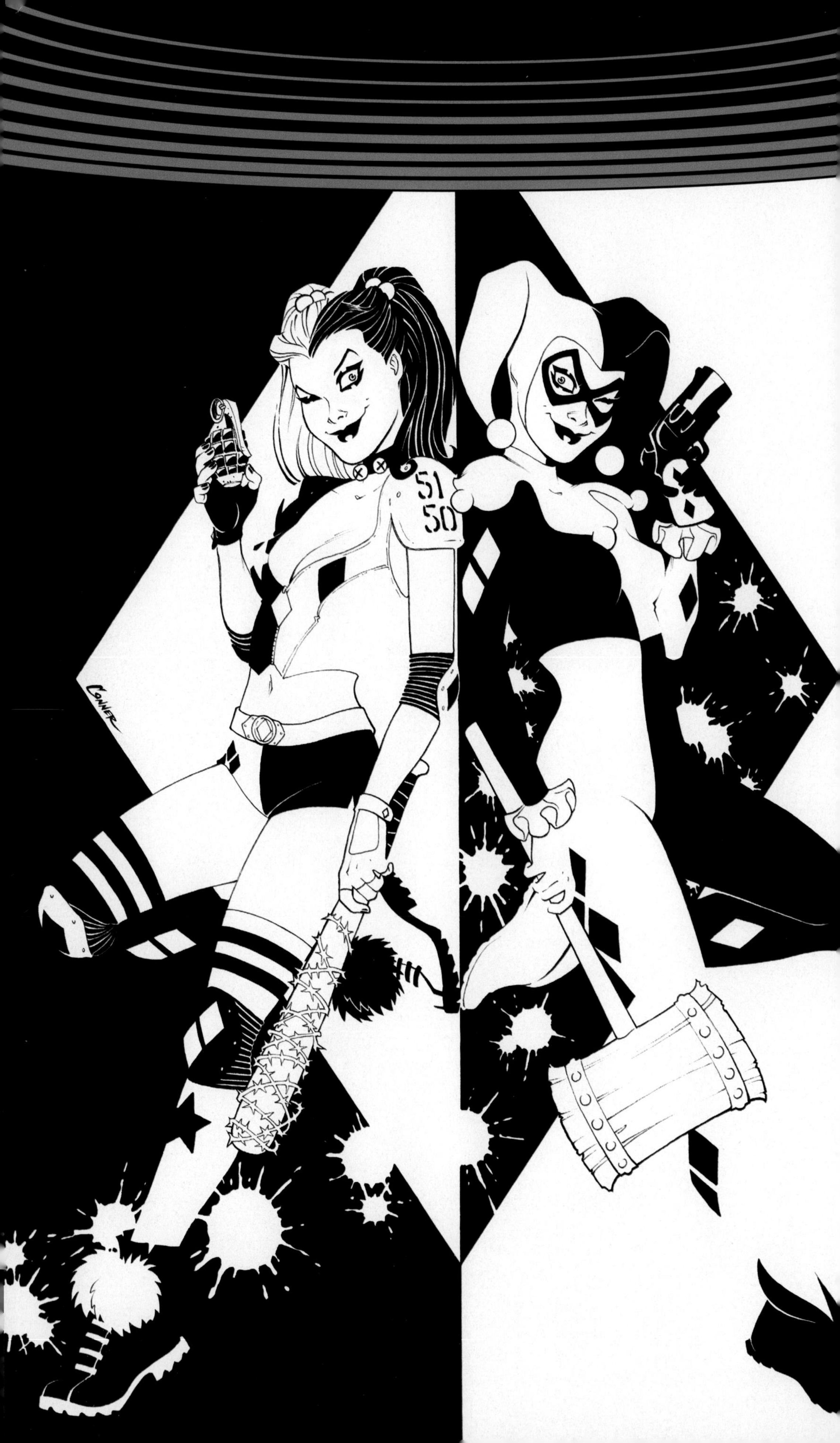
CONNER
51
50

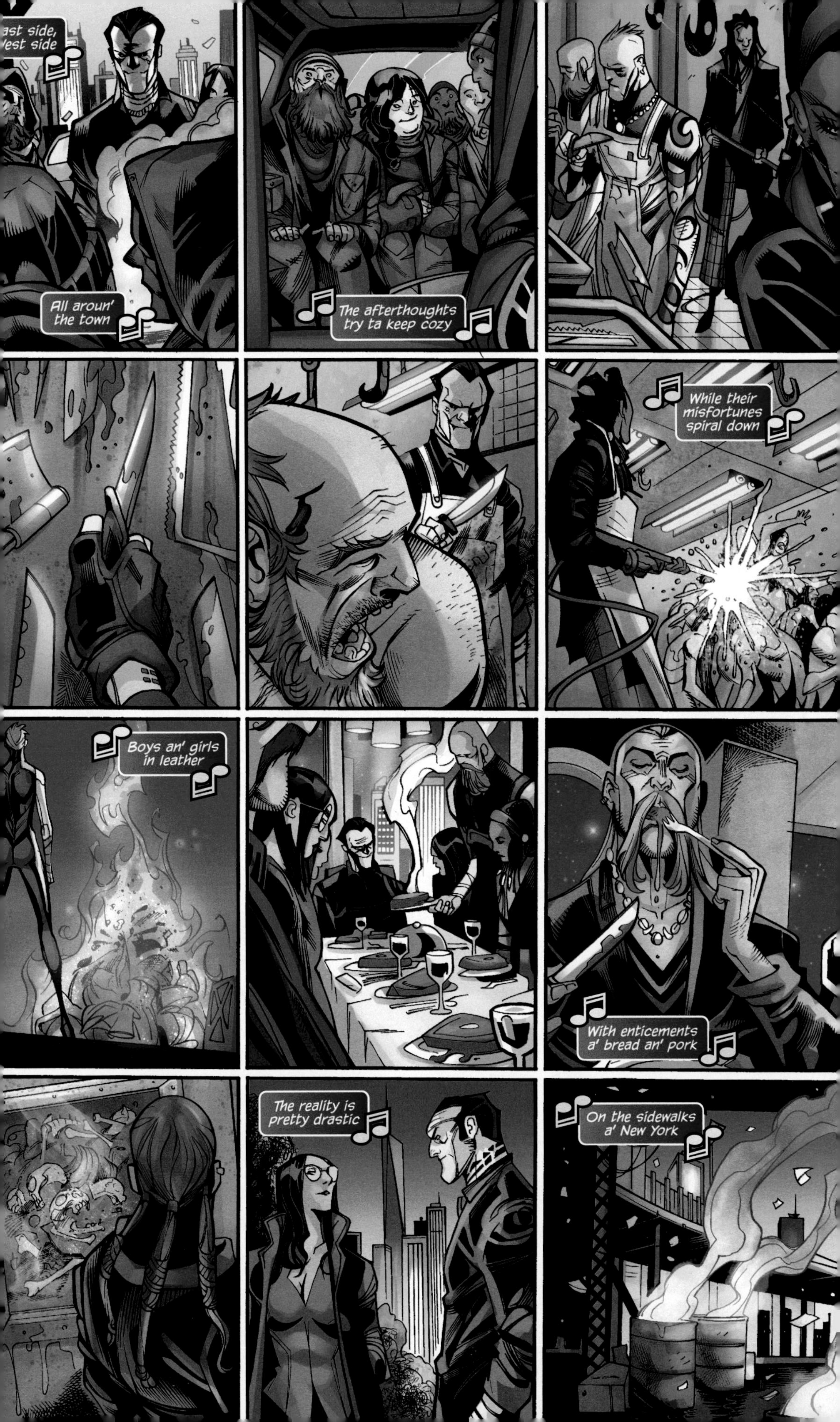
ast side,
Vest side
All aroun' the town
The afterthoughts try ta keep cozy
While their misfortunes spiral down
Boys an' girls in leather
With enticements a' bread an' pork
The reality is pretty drastic
On the sidewalks a' New York

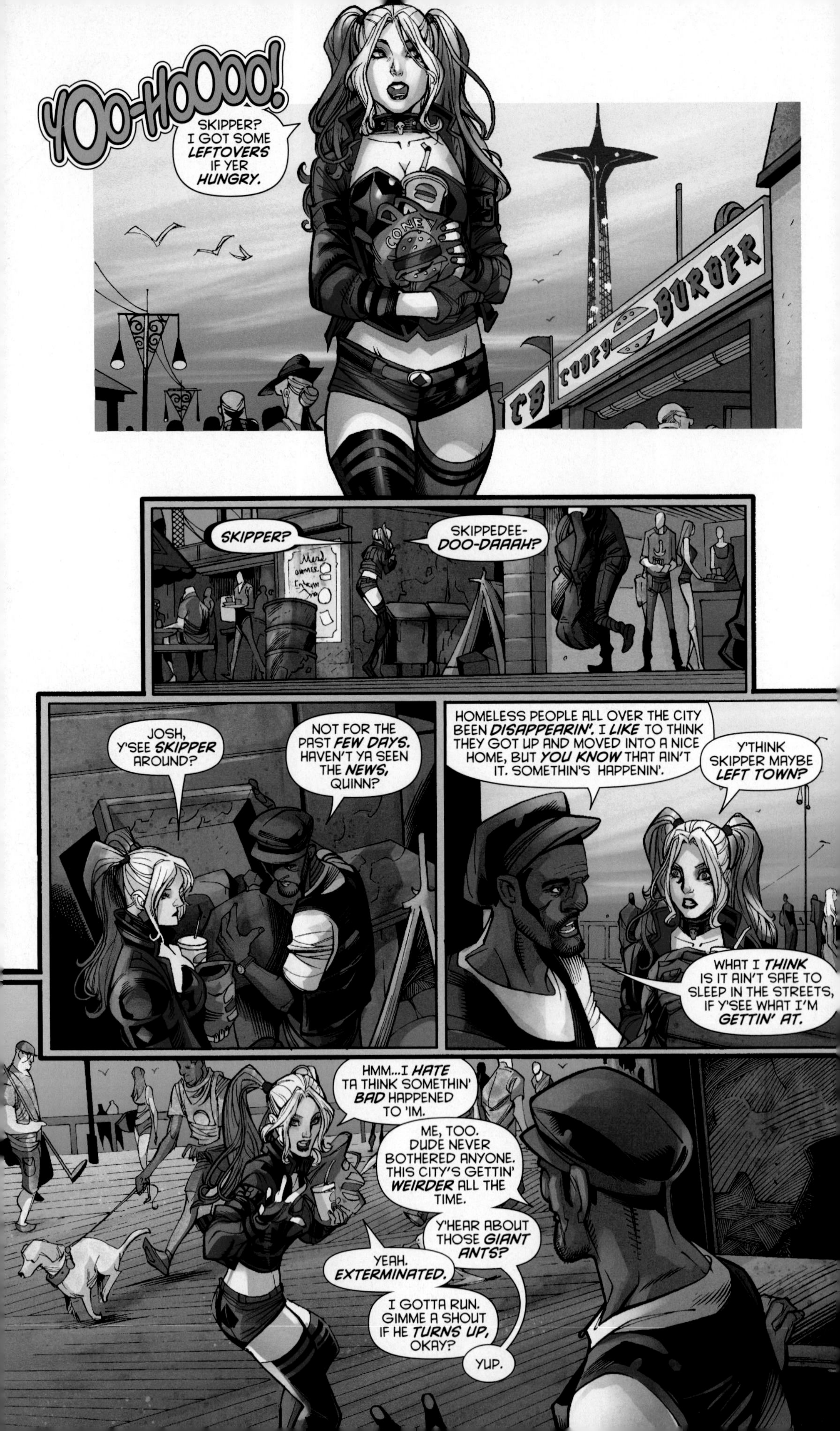
YOO-HOOOO!
SKIPPER? I GOT SOME LEFTOVERS IF YER HUNGRY.
CONEY
CB
CONEY BURGER
SKIPPER?
SKIPPEDEE-DOO-DAAAH?
JOSH, Y'SEE SKIPPER AROUND?
NOT FOR THE PAST FEW DAYS. HAVEN'T YA SEEN THE NEWS, QUINN?
HOMELESS PEOPLE ALL OVER THE CITY BEEN DISAPPEARIN'. I LIKE TO THINK THEY GOT UP AND MOVED INTO A NICE HOME, BUT YOU KNOW THAT AIN'T IT. SOMETHIN'S HAPPENIN'.
Y'THINK SKIPPER MAYBE LEFT TOWN?
WHAT I THINK IS IT AIN'T SAFE TO SLEEP IN THE STREETS, IF Y'SEE WHAT I'M GETTIN' AT.
HMM...I HATE TA THINK SOMETHIN' BAD HAPPENED TO 'IM.
ME, TOO. DUDE NEVER BOTHERED ANYONE. THIS CITY'S GETTIN' WEIRDER ALL THE TIME.
Y'HEAR ABOUT THOSE GIANT ANTS?
YEAH. EXTERMINATED.
I GOTTA RUN. GIMME A SHOUT IF HE TURNS UP, OKAY?
YUP.

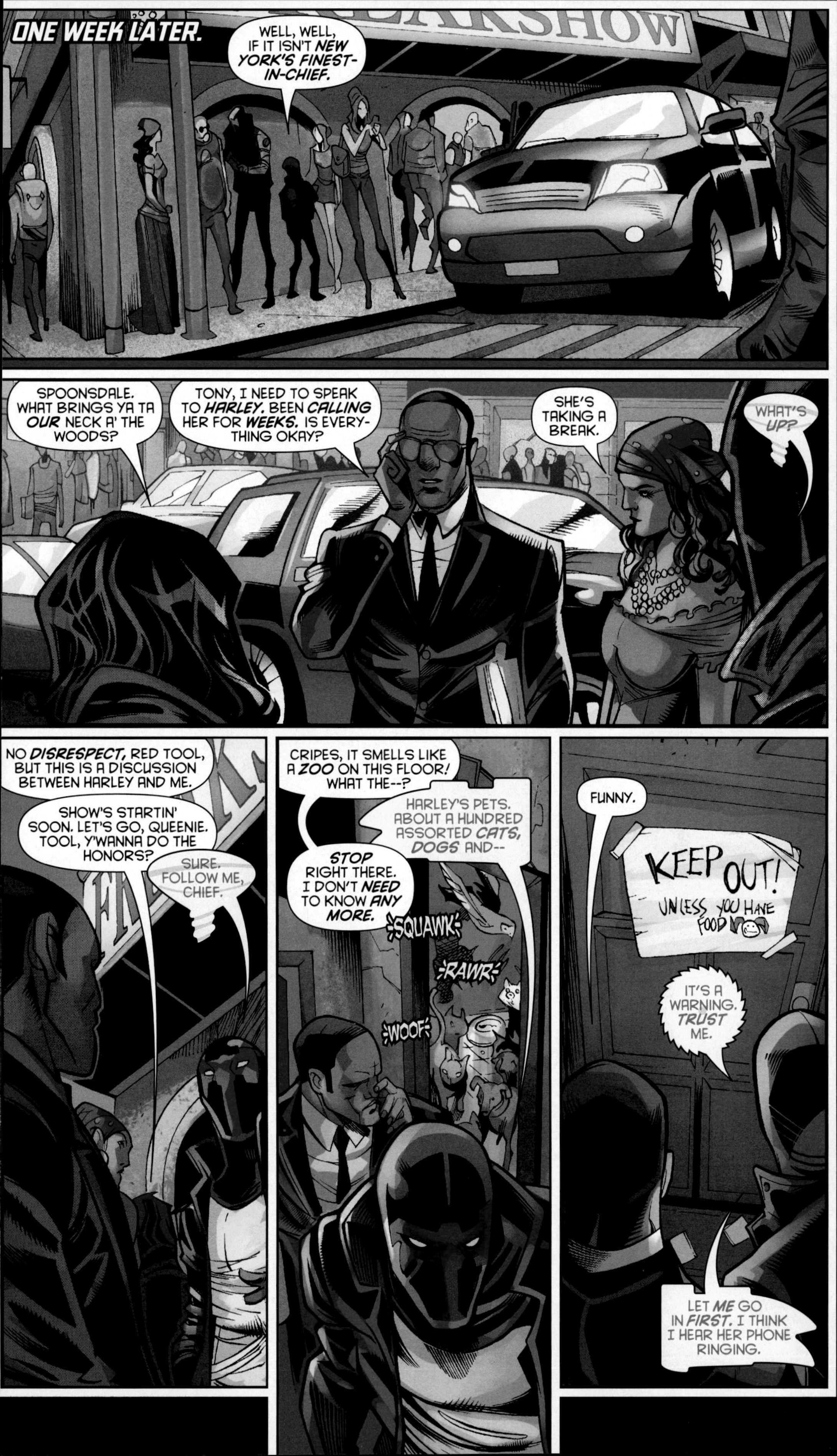
ONE WEEK LATER.
WELL, WELL, IF IT ISN'T NEW YORK'S FINEST-IN-CHIEF.
SPOONSDALE. WHAT BRINGS YA TA OUR NECK A' THE WOODS?
TONY, I NEED TO SPEAK TO HARLEY. BEEN CALLING HER FOR WEEKS. IS EVERY-THING OKAY?
SHE'S TAKING A BREAK.
WHAT'S UP?
NO DISRESPECT, RED TOOL, BUT THIS IS A DISCUSSION BETWEEN HARLEY AND ME.
SHOW'S STARTIN' SOON. LET'S GO, QUEENIE. TOOL, Y'WANNA DO THE HONORS?
SURE. FOLLOW ME, CHIEF.
CRIPES, IT SMELLS LIKE A ZOO ON THIS FLOOR! WHAT THE--?
HARLEY'S PETS. ABOUT A HUNDRED ASSORTED CATS, DOGS AND--
STOP RIGHT THERE. I DON'T NEED TO KNOW ANY MORE.
SQUAWK
RAWR
WOOF
FUNNY.
KEEP OUT!
UNLESS YOU HAVE FOOD
IT'S A WARNING. TRUST ME.
LET ME GO IN FIRST. I THINK I HEAR HER PHONE RINGING.

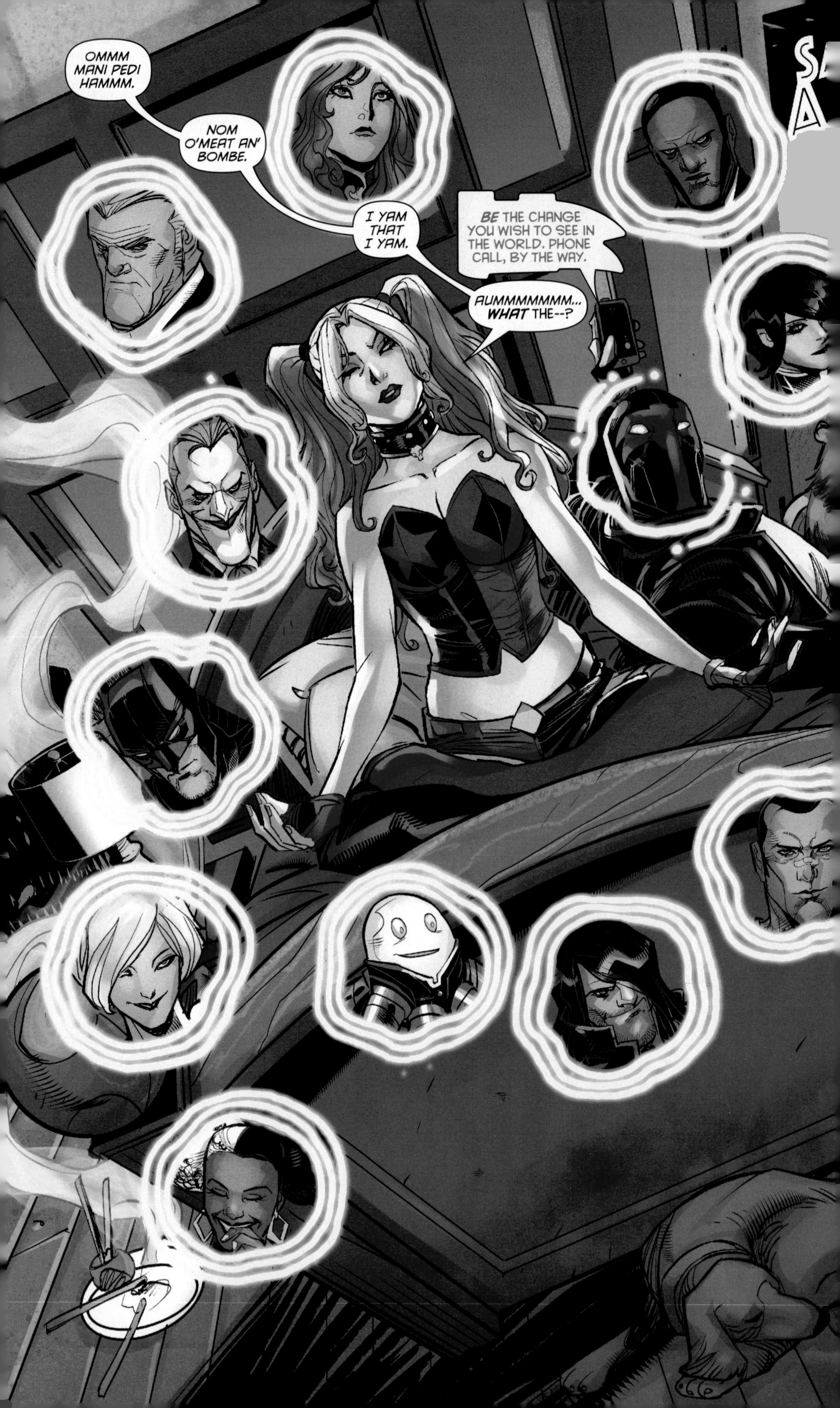
OMMM MANI PEDI HAMMM.
NOM O'MEAT AN' BOMBE.
I YAM THAT I YAM.
BE THE CHANGE YOU WISH TO SEE IN THE WORLD. PHONE CALL, BY THE WAY.
AUMMMMMMM... WHAT THE--?

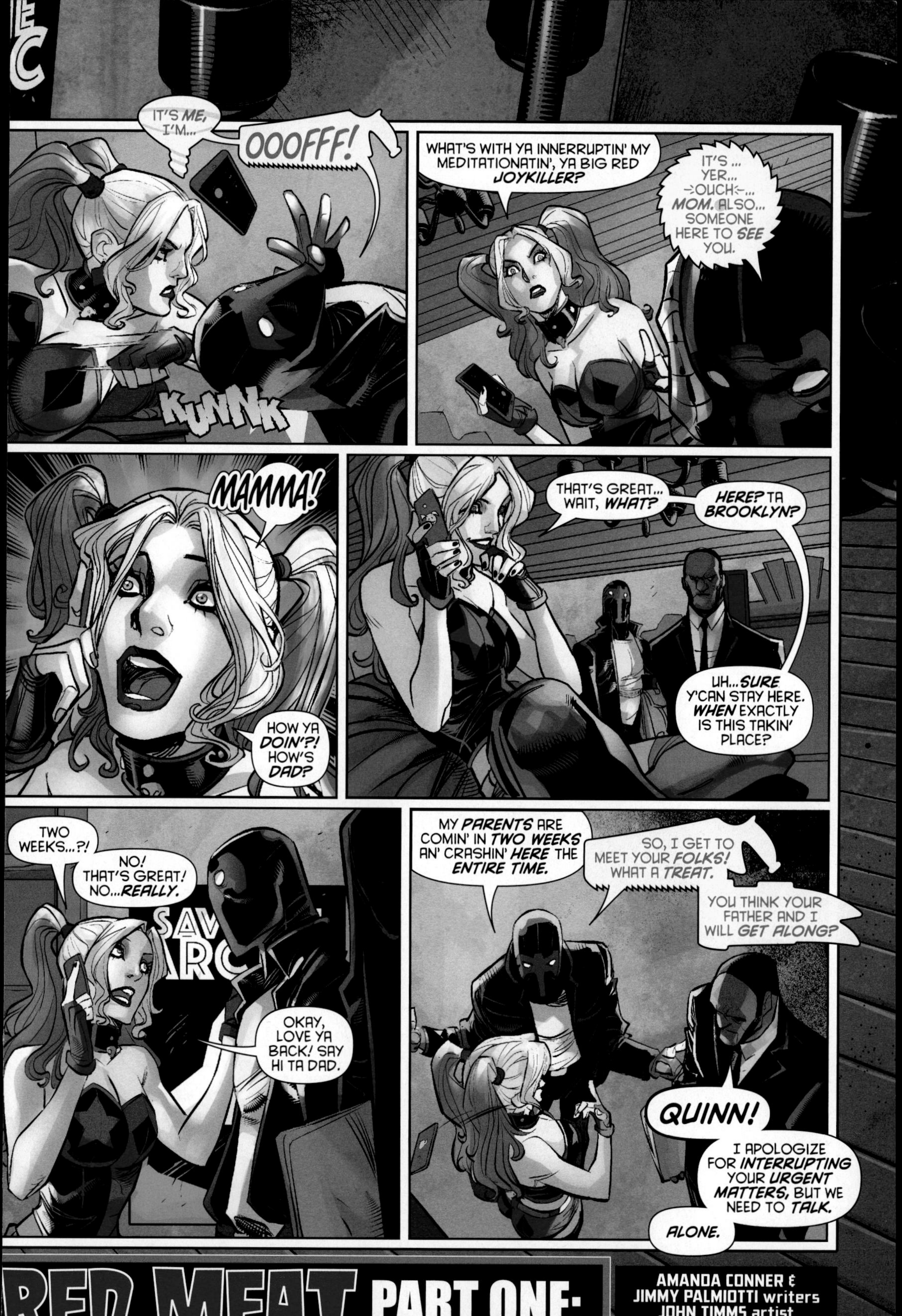
IT'S ME, I'M...
OOOFFF!
KUNNK
WHAT'S WITH YA INNERRUPTIN' MY MEDITATIONATIN', YA BIG RED JOYKILLER?
IT'S ... YER... -OUCH-... MOM. ALSO... SOMEONE HERE TO SEE YOU.
MAMMA!
HOW YA DOIN'?! HOW'S DAD?
THAT'S GREAT... WAIT, WHAT?
HERE? TA BROOKLYN?
UH...SURE Y'CAN STAY HERE. WHEN EXACTLY IS THIS TAKIN' PLACE?
TWO WEEKS...?!
NO! THAT'S GREAT! NO...REALLY.
OKAY, LOVE YA BACK! SAY HI TA DAD.
MY PARENTS ARE COMIN' IN TWO WEEKS AN' CRASHIN' HERE THE ENTIRE TIME.
SO, I GET TO MEET YOUR FOLKS! WHAT A TREAT.
YOU THINK YOUR FATHER AND I WILL GET ALONG?
QUINN!
I APOLOGIZE FOR INTERRUPTING YOUR URGENT MATTERS, BUT WE NEED TO TALK.
ALONE.

RED MEAT PART ONE: MANTRA MIX-UP

AMANDA CONNER & JIMMY PALMIOTTI writers
JOHN TIMMS artist
MARC DEERING inks Pgs 1-3, 7, 8
ALEX SINCLAIR colors
DAVE SHARPE letters
AMANDA CONNER & ALEX SINCLAIR cover artists
DAVE WIELGOSZ asst. editor
CHRIS CONROY editor
MARK DOYLE group editor
HARLEY QUINN created by PAUL DINI & BRUCE TIMM

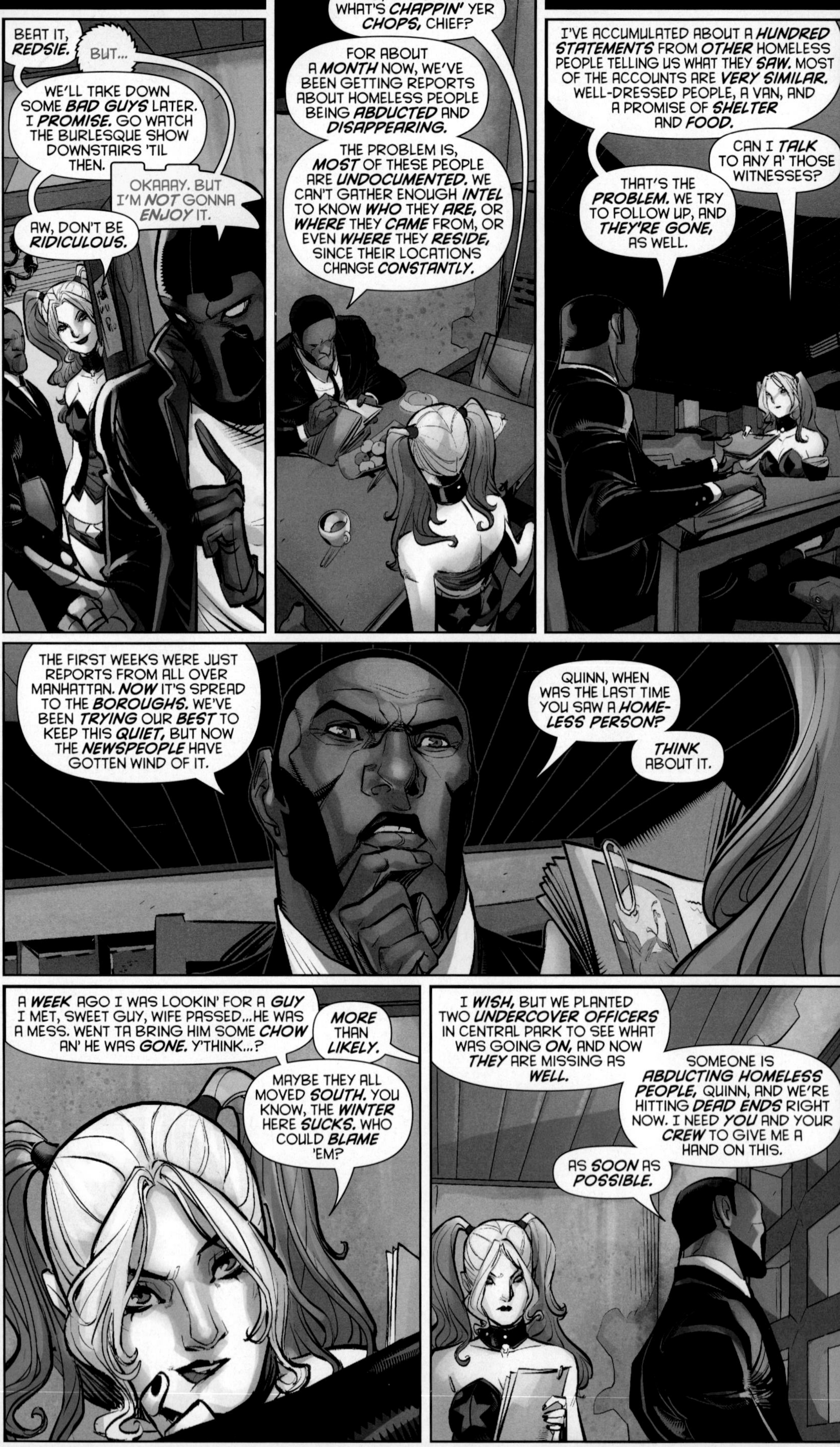
BEAT IT, REDSIE.
BUT...
WE'LL TAKE DOWN SOME BAD GUYS LATER. I PROMISE. GO WATCH THE BURLESQUE SHOW DOWNSTAIRS 'TIL THEN.
OKAAAY. BUT I'M NOT GONNA ENJOY IT.
AW, DON'T BE RIDICULOUS.
SO, SPOONSIE... WHAT'S CHAPPIN' YER CHOPS, CHIEF?
FOR ABOUT A MONTH NOW, WE'VE BEEN GETTING REPORTS ABOUT HOMELESS PEOPLE BEING ABDUCTED AND DISAPPEARING.
THE PROBLEM IS, MOST OF THESE PEOPLE ARE UNDOCUMENTED. WE CAN'T GATHER ENOUGH INTEL TO KNOW WHO THEY ARE, OR WHERE THEY CAME FROM, OR EVEN WHERE THEY RESIDE, SINCE THEIR LOCATIONS CHANGE CONSTANTLY.
I'VE ACCUMULATED ABOUT A HUNDRED STATEMENTS FROM OTHER HOMELESS PEOPLE TELLING US WHAT THEY SAW. MOST OF THE ACCOUNTS ARE VERY SIMILAR. WELL-DRESSED PEOPLE, A VAN, AND A PROMISE OF SHELTER AND FOOD.
CAN I TALK TO ANY A' THOSE WITNESSES?
THAT'S THE PROBLEM. WE TRY TO FOLLOW UP, AND THEY'RE GONE, AS WELL.
THE FIRST WEEKS WERE JUST REPORTS FROM ALL OVER MANHATTAN. NOW IT'S SPREAD TO THE BOROUGHS. WE'VE BEEN TRYING OUR BEST TO KEEP THIS QUIET, BUT NOW THE NEWSPEOPLE HAVE GOTTEN WIND OF IT.
QUINN, WHEN WAS THE LAST TIME YOU SAW A HOME-LESS PERSON?
THINK ABOUT IT.
A WEEK AGO I WAS LOOKIN' FOR A GUY I MET, SWEET GUY, WIFE PASSED...HE WAS A MESS. WENT TA BRING HIM SOME CHOW AN' HE WAS GONE. Y'THINK...?
MORE THAN LIKELY.
MAYBE THEY ALL MOVED SOUTH. YOU KNOW, THE WINTER HERE SUCKS. WHO COULD BLAME 'EM?
I WISH, BUT WE PLANTED TWO UNDERCOVER OFFICERS IN CENTRAL PARK TO SEE WHAT WAS GOING ON, AND NOW THEY ARE MISSING AS WELL.
SOMEONE IS ABDUCTING HOMELESS PEOPLE, QUINN, AND WE'RE HITTING DEAD ENDS RIGHT NOW. I NEED YOU AND YOUR CREW TO GIVE ME A HAND ON THIS.
AS SOON AS POSSIBLE.

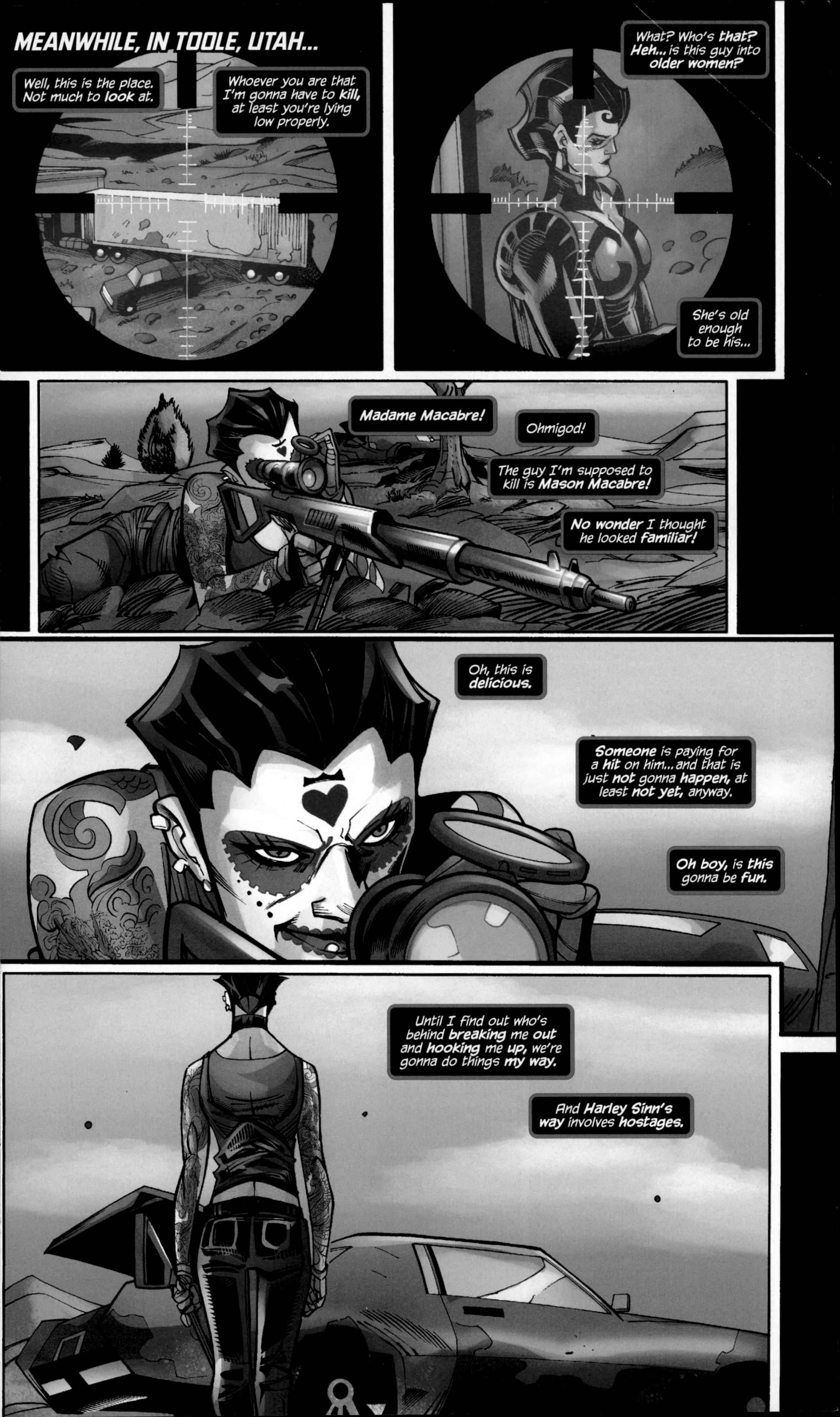
MEANWHILE, IN TOOLE, UTAH...
Well, this is the place. Not much to look at.
Whoever you are that I'm gonna have to kill, at least you're lying low properly.
What? Who's that? Heh... is this guy into older women?
She's old enough to be his...
Madame Macabre!
Ohmigod!
The guy I'm supposed to kill is Mason Macabre!
No wonder I thought he looked familiar!
Oh, this is delicious.
Someone is paying for a hit on him... and that is just not gonna happen, at least not yet, anyway.
Oh boy, is this gonna be fun.
Until I find out who's behind breaking me out and hooking me up, we're gonna do things my way.
And Harley Sinn's way involves hostages.

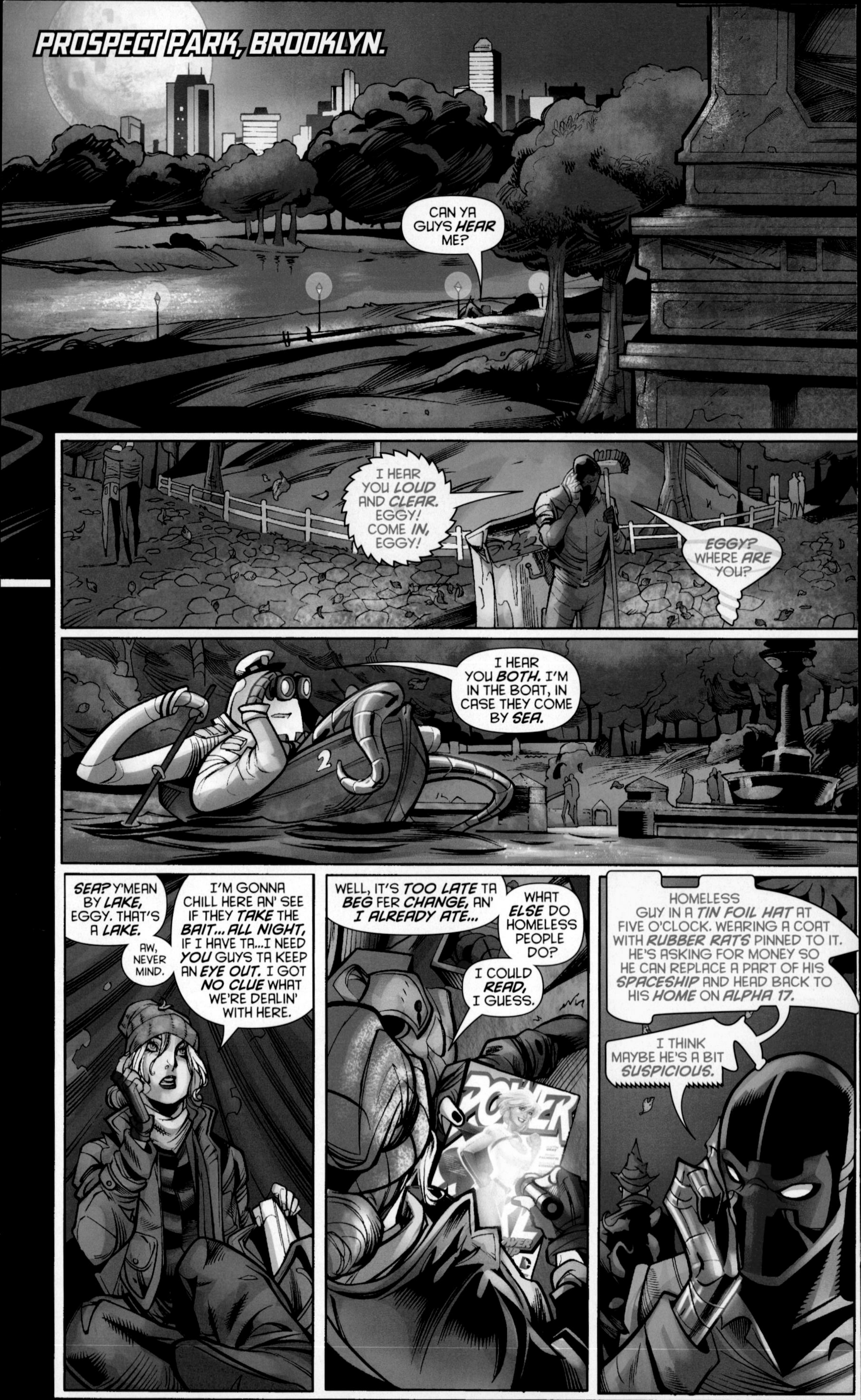

PROSPECT PARK, BROOKLYN.
CAN YA GUYS HEAR ME?
I HEAR YOU LOUD AND CLEAR. EGGY! COME IN, EGGY!
EGGY? WHERE ARE YOU?
I HEAR YOU BOTH. I'M IN THE BOAT, IN CASE THEY COME BY SEA.
SEA? Y'MEAN BY LAKE, EGGY. THAT'S A LAKE.
AW, NEVER MIND.
I'M GONNA CHILL HERE AN' SEE IF THEY TAKE THE BAIT... ALL NIGHT, IF I HAVE TA...I NEED YOU GUYS TA KEEP AN EYE OUT. I GOT NO CLUE WHAT WE'RE DEALIN' WITH HERE.
WELL, IT'S TOO LATE TA BEG FER CHANGE, AN' I ALREADY ATE...
WHAT ELSE DO HOMELESS PEOPLE DO?
I COULD READ, I GUESS.
HOMELESS GUY IN A TIN FOIL HAT AT FIVE O'CLOCK. WEARING A COAT WITH RUBBER RATS PINNED TO IT. HE'S ASKING FOR MONEY SO HE CAN REPLACE A PART OF HIS SPACESHIP AND HEAD BACK TO HIS HOME ON ALPHA 17.
I THINK MAYBE HE'S A BIT SUSPICIOUS.

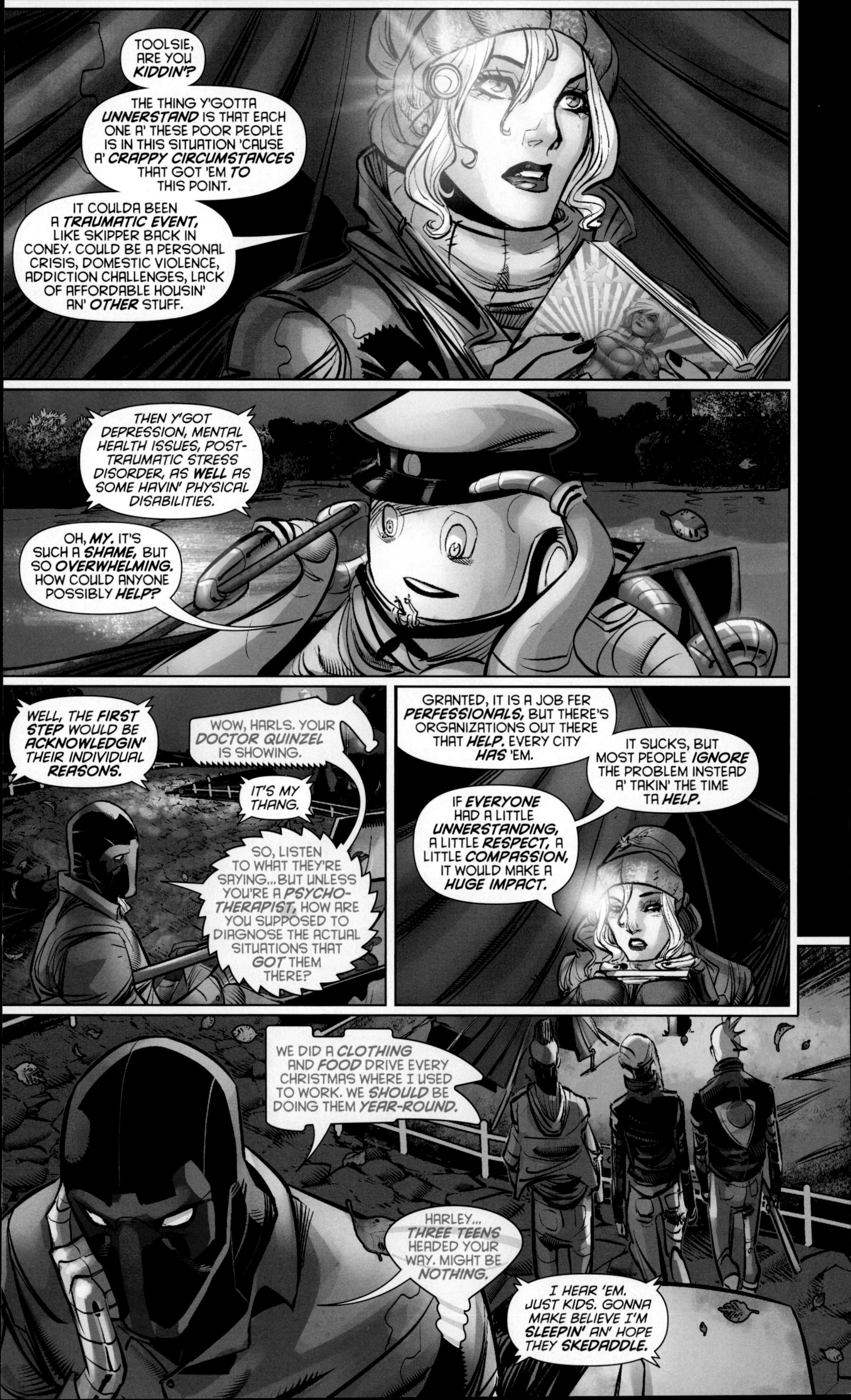
TOOLSIE, ARE YOU KIDDIN'?
THE THING Y'GOTTA UNNERSTAND IS THAT EACH ONE A' THESE POOR PEOPLE IS IN THIS SITUATION 'CAUSE A' CRAPPY CIRCUMSTANCES THAT GOT 'EM TO THIS POINT.
IT COULDA BEEN A TRAUMATIC EVENT, LIKE SKIPPER BACK IN CONEY. COULD BE A PERSONAL CRISIS, DOMESTIC VIOLENCE, ADDICTION CHALLENGES, LACK OF AFFORDABLE HOUSIN' AN' OTHER STUFF.
THEN Y'GOT DEPRESSION, MENTAL HEALTH ISSUES, POST-TRAUMATIC STRESS DISORDER, AS WELL AS SOME HAVIN' PHYSICAL DISABILITIES.
OH, MY. IT'S SUCH A SHAME, BUT SO OVERWHELMING. HOW COULD ANYONE POSSIBLY HELP?
WELL, THE FIRST STEP WOULD BE ACKNOWLEDGIN' THEIR INDIVIDUAL REASONS.
WOW, HARLS. YOUR DOCTOR QUINZEL IS SHOWING.
IT'S MY THANG.
SO, LISTEN TO WHAT THEY'RE SAYING...BUT UNLESS YOU'RE A PSYCHO-THERAPIST, HOW ARE YOU SUPPOSED TO DIAGNOSE THE ACTUAL SITUATIONS THAT GOT THEM THERE?
GRANTED, IT IS A JOB FER PERFESSIONALS, BUT THERE'S ORGANIZATIONS OUT THERE THAT HELP. EVERY CITY HAS 'EM.
IT SUCKS, BUT MOST PEOPLE IGNORE THE PROBLEM INSTEAD A' TAKIN' THE TIME TA HELP.
IF EVERYONE HAD A LITTLE UNNERSTANDING, A LITTLE RESPECT, A LITTLE COMPASSION, IT WOULD MAKE A HUGE IMPACT.
WE DID A CLOTHING AND FOOD DRIVE EVERY CHRISTMAS WHERE I USED TO WORK. WE SHOULD BE DOING THEM YEAR-ROUND.
HARLEY... THREE TEENS HEADED YOUR WAY. MIGHT BE NOTHING.
I HEAR 'EM. JUST KIDS. GONNA MAKE BELIEVE I'M SLEEPIN' AN' HOPE THEY SKEDADDLE.

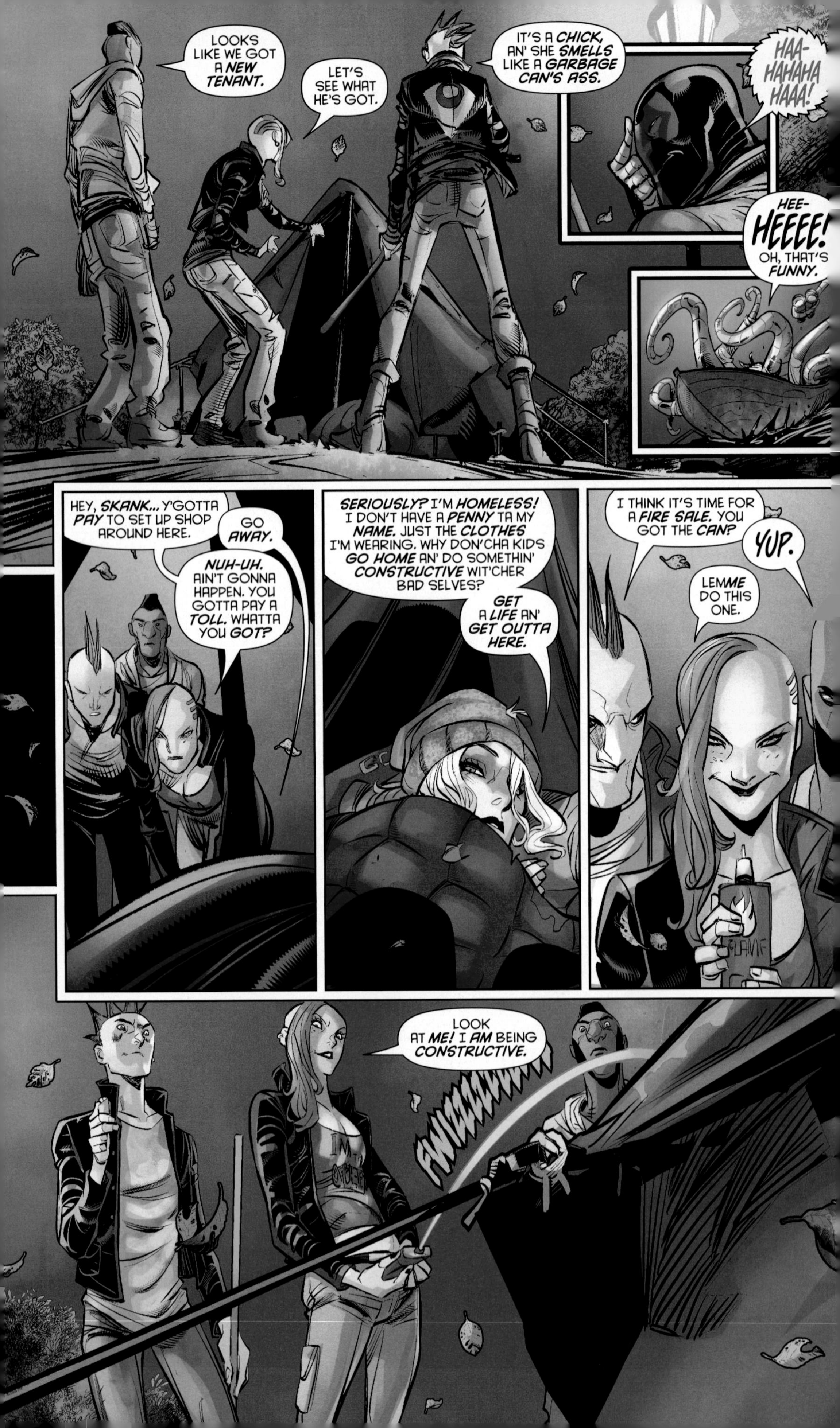

LOOKS LIKE WE GOT A NEW TENANT.
LET'S SEE WHAT HE'S GOT.
IT'S A CHICK, AN' SHE SMELLS LIKE A GARBAGE CAN'S ASS.
HAA-HAHAHA HAAA!
HEE-HEEEE! OH, THAT'S FUNNY.
HEY, SKANK... Y'GOTTA PAY TO SET UP SHOP AROUND HERE.
GO AWAY.
NUH-UH. AIN'T GONNA HAPPEN. YOU GOTTA PAY A TOLL. WHATTA YOU GOT?
SERIOUSLY? I'M HOMELESS! I DON'T HAVE A PENNY TA MY NAME. JUST THE CLOTHES I'M WEARING. WHY DON'CHA KIDS GO HOME AN' DO SOMETHIN' CONSTRUCTIVE WIT'CHER BAD SELVES?
GET A LIFE AN' GET OUTTA HERE.
I THINK IT'S TIME FOR A FIRE SALE. YOU GOT THE CAN?
YUP.
LEMME DO THIS ONE.
LOOK AT ME! I AM BEING CONSTRUCTIVE.

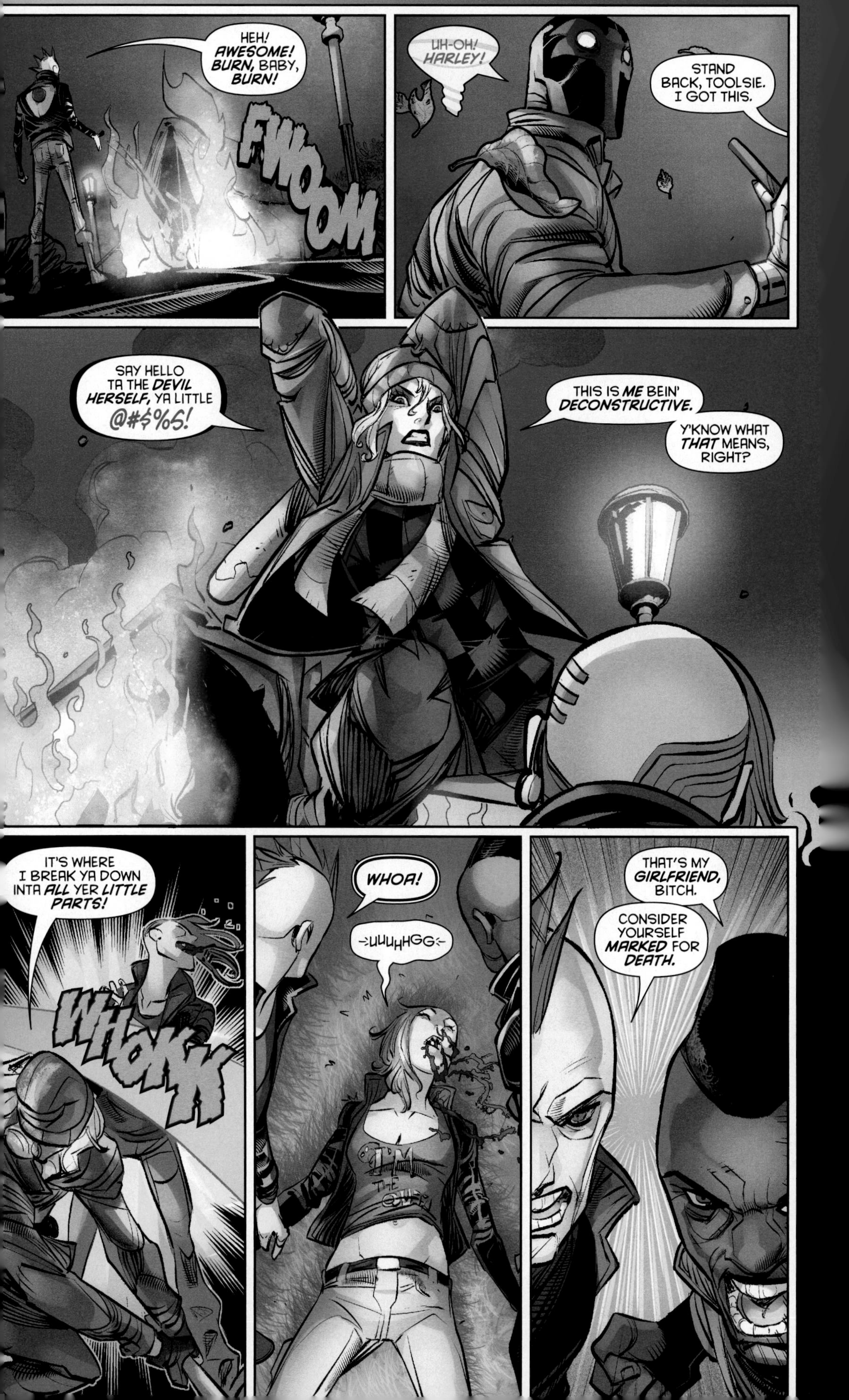
HEH! AWESOME! BURN, BABY, BURN!
FWOOM
UH-OH! HARLEY!
STAND BACK, TOOLSIE. I GOT THIS.
SAY HELLO TA THE DEVIL HERSELF, YA LITTLE @#$%$!
THIS IS ME BEIN' DECONSTRUCTIVE.
Y'KNOW WHAT THAT MEANS, RIGHT?
IT'S WHERE I BREAK YA DOWN INTA ALL YER LITTLE PARTS!
WHOKK
WHOA!
UUUHHGG
THAT'S MY GIRLFRIEND, BITCH.
CONSIDER YOURSELF MARKED FOR DEATH.

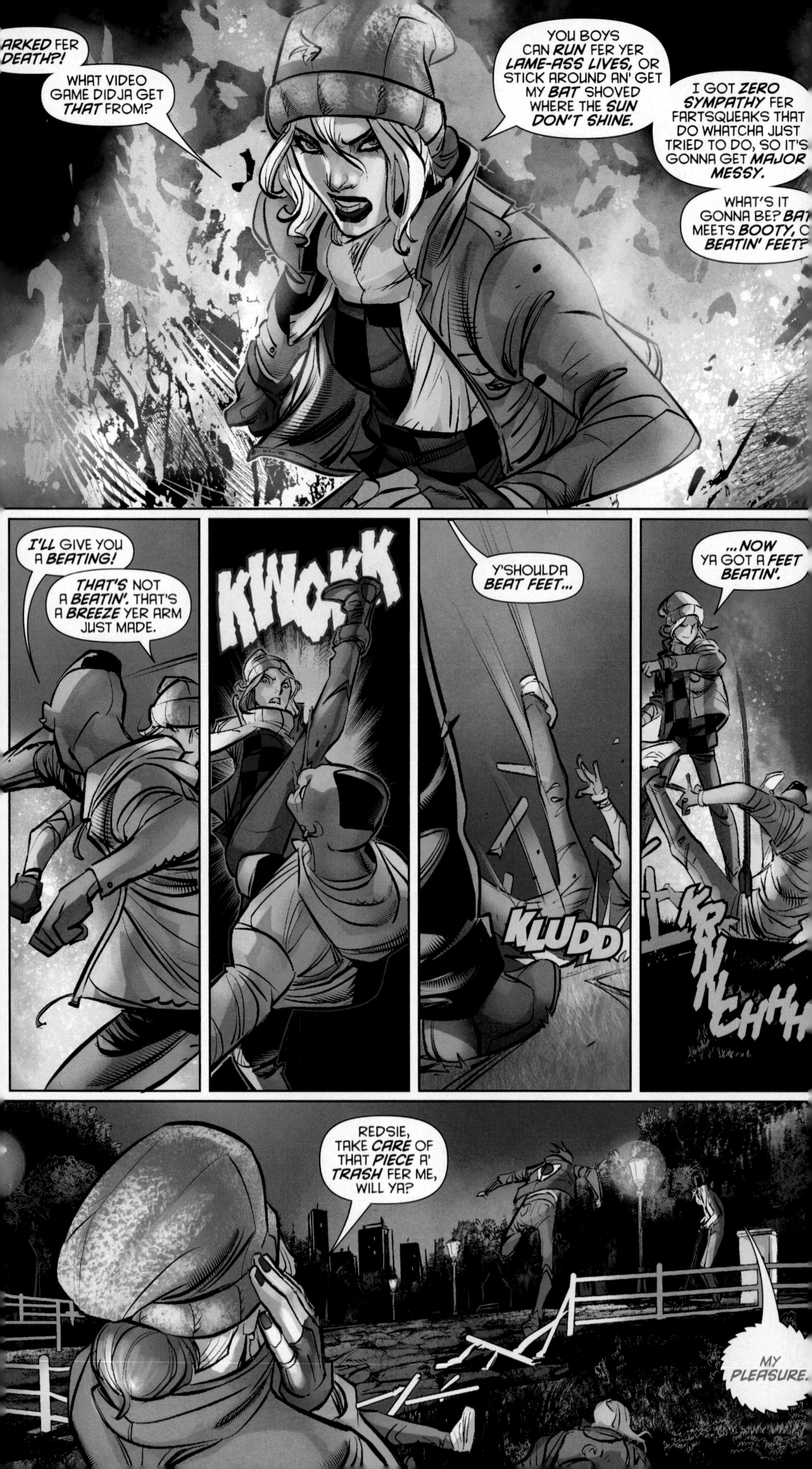
ARKED FER DEATH?!
WHAT VIDEO GAME DIDJA GET THAT FROM?
YOU BOYS CAN RUN FER YER LAME-ASS LIVES, OR STICK AROUND AN' GET MY BAT SHOVED WHERE THE SUN DON'T SHINE.
I GOT ZERO SYMPATHY FER FARTSQUEAKS THAT DO WHATCHA JUST TRIED TO DO, SO IT'S GONNA GET MAJOR MESSY.
WHAT'S IT GONNA BE? BAT MEETS BOOTY, OR BEATIN' FEET?
I'LL GIVE YOU A BEATING!
THAT'S NOT A BEATIN'. THAT'S A BREEZE YER ARM JUST MADE.
KWOKK
Y'SHOULDA BEAT FEET...
KLUDD
...NOW YA GOT A FEET BEATIN'.
KRNCHHH
REDSIE, TAKE CARE OF THAT PIECE A' TRASH FER ME, WILL YA?
MY PLEASURE.

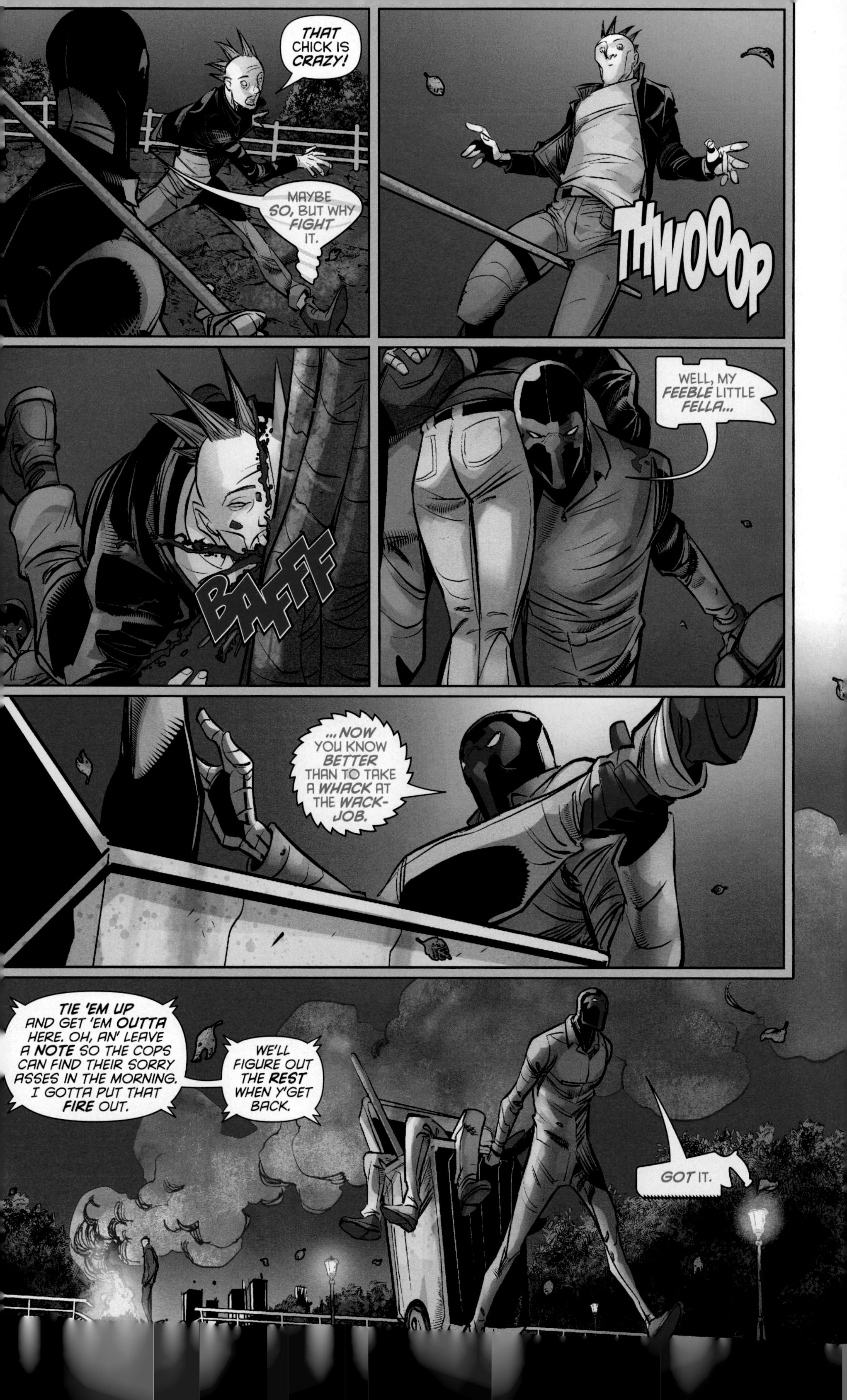
THAT CHICK IS CRAZY!
MAYBE SO, BUT WHY FIGHT IT.
THWOOOP
BAFFF
WELL, MY FEEBLE LITTLE FELLA...
...NOW YOU KNOW BETTER THAN TO TAKE A WHACK AT THE WACK-JOB.
TIE 'EM UP AND GET 'EM OUTTA HERE. OH, AN' LEAVE A NOTE SO THE COPS CAN FIND THEIR SORRY ASSES IN THE MORNING. I GOTTA PUT THAT FIRE OUT.
WE'LL FIGURE OUT THE REST WHEN Y'GET BACK.
GOT IT.

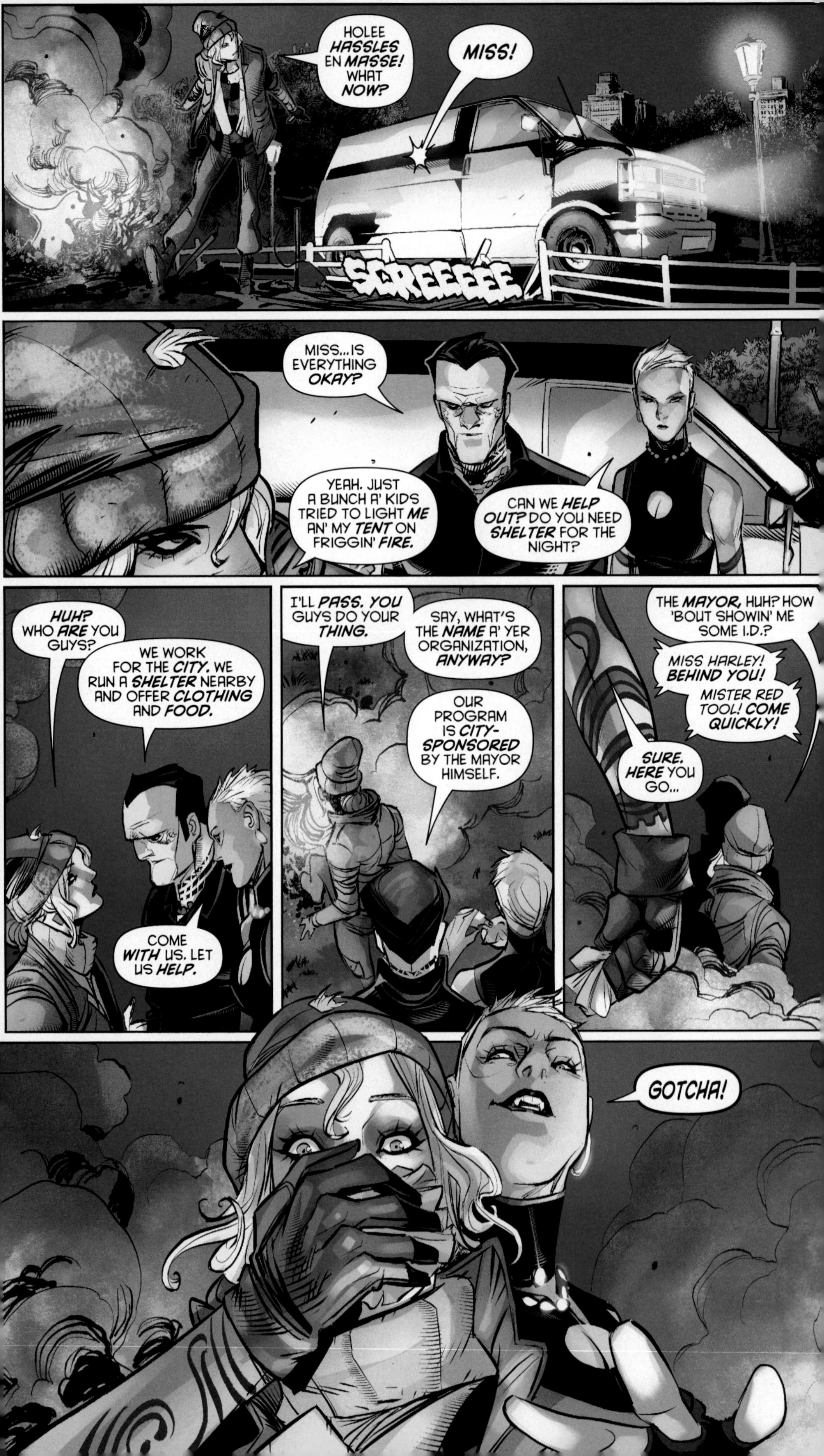
HOLEE HASSLES EN MASSE! WHAT NOW?
MISS!
SCREEEEEE
MISS...IS EVERYTHING OKAY?
YEAH. JUST A BUNCH A' KIDS TRIED TO LIGHT ME AN' MY TENT ON FRIGGIN' FIRE.
CAN WE HELP OUT? DO YOU NEED SHELTER FOR THE NIGHT?
HUH? WHO ARE YOU GUYS?
WE WORK FOR THE CITY. WE RUN A SHELTER NEARBY AND OFFER CLOTHING AND FOOD.
COME WITH US. LET US HELP.
I'LL PASS. YOU GUYS DO YOUR THING.
SAY, WHAT'S THE NAME A' YER ORGANIZATION, ANYWAY?
OUR PROGRAM IS CITY-SPONSORED BY THE MAYOR HIMSELF.
THE MAYOR, HUH? HOW 'BOUT SHOWIN' ME SOME I.D.?
MISS HARLEY! BEHIND YOU!
MISTER RED TOOL! COME QUICKLY!
SURE. HERE YOU GO...
GOTCHA!

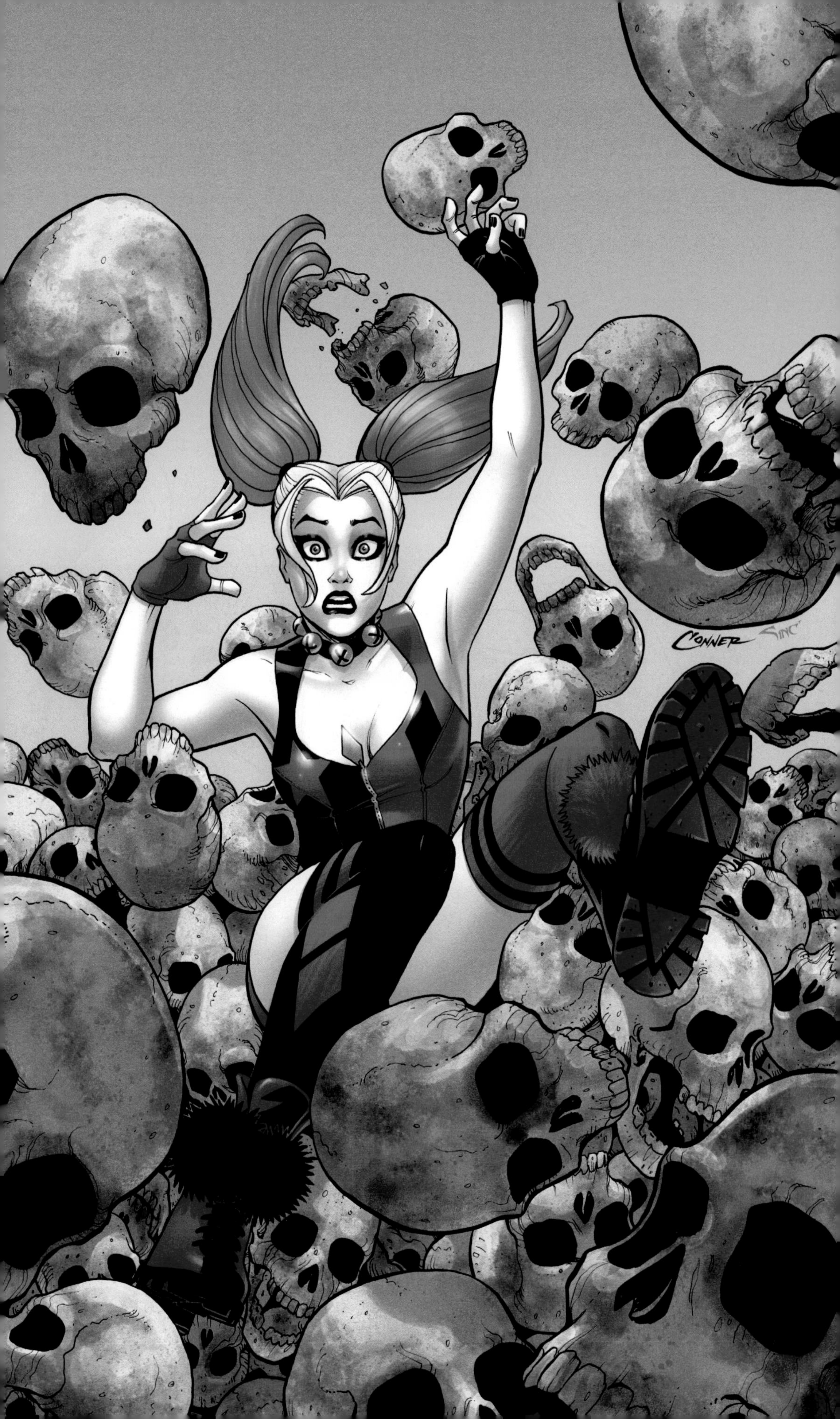
CONNER
SINC

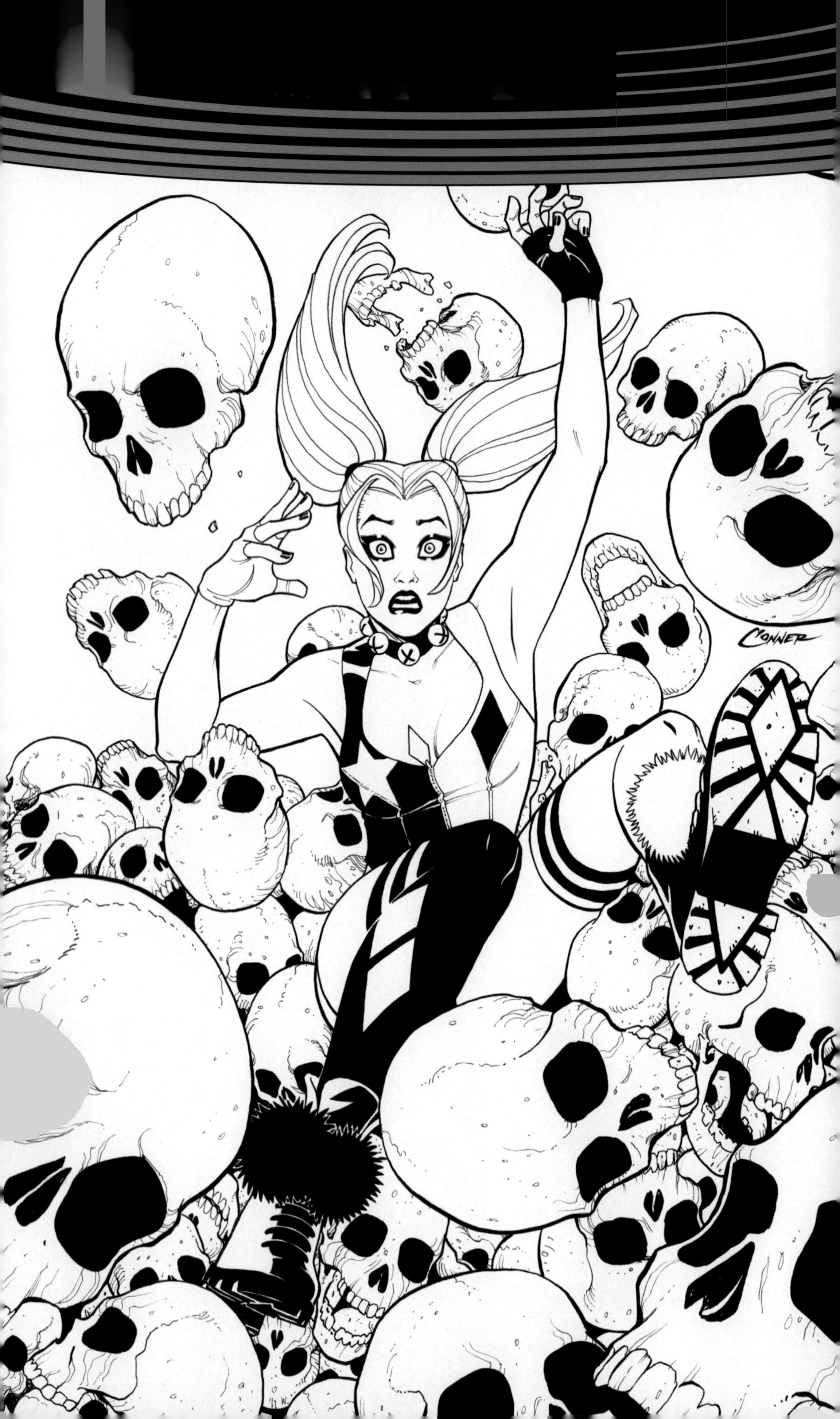
CONNER

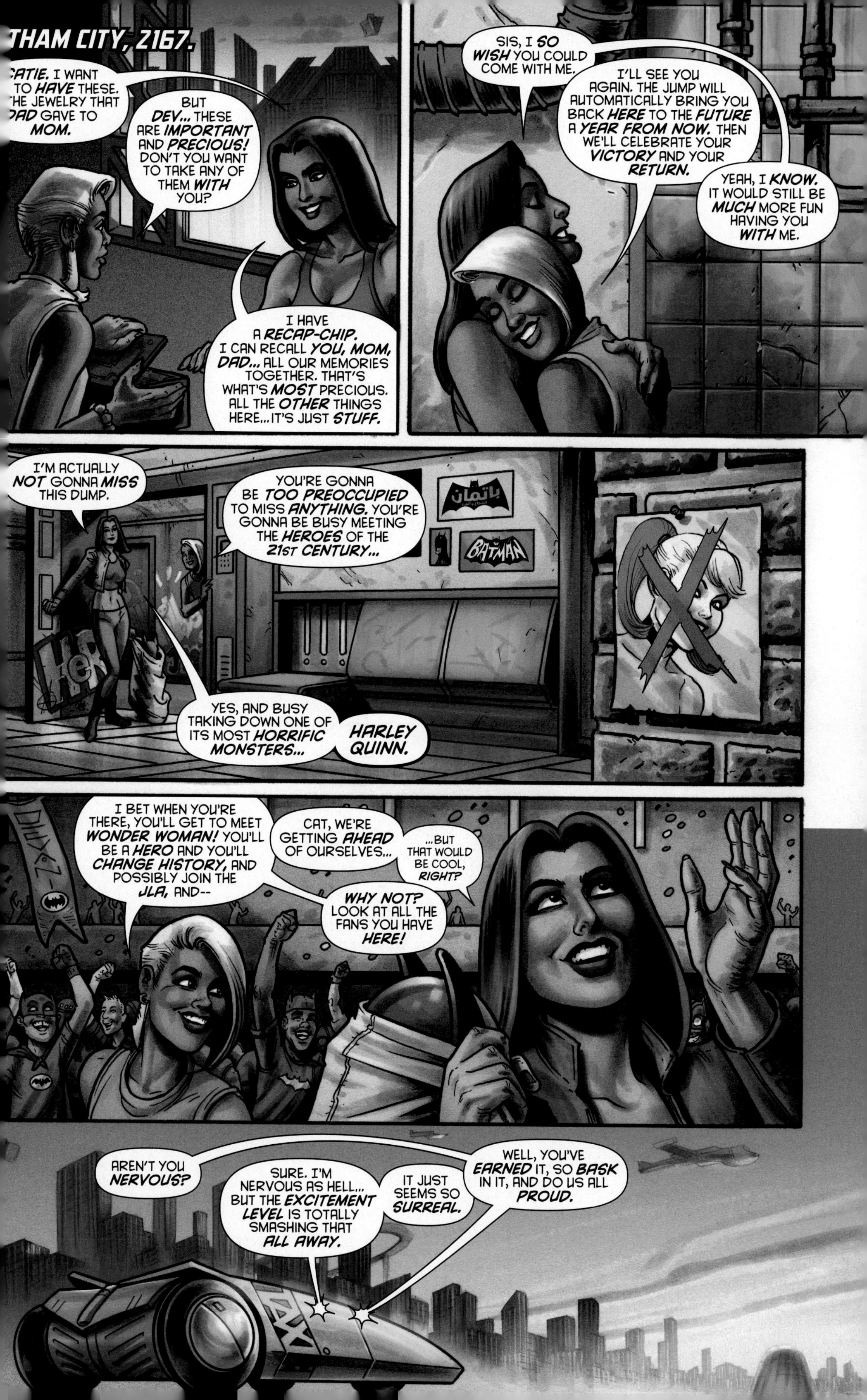
THAM CITY, 2167.
CATIE. I WANT TO HAVE THESE. THE JEWELRY THAT DAD GAVE TO MOM.
BUT DEV... THESE ARE IMPORTANT AND PRECIOUS! DON'T YOU WANT TO TAKE ANY OF THEM WITH YOU?
I HAVE A RECAP-CHIP. I CAN RECALL YOU, MOM, DAD... ALL OUR MEMORIES TOGETHER. THAT'S WHAT'S MOST PRECIOUS. ALL THE OTHER THINGS HERE... IT'S JUST STUFF.
SIS, I SO WISH YOU COULD COME WITH ME.
I'LL SEE YOU AGAIN. THE JUMP WILL AUTOMATICALLY BRING YOU BACK HERE TO THE FUTURE A YEAR FROM NOW. THEN WE'LL CELEBRATE YOUR VICTORY AND YOUR RETURN.
YEAH, I KNOW. IT WOULD STILL BE MUCH MORE FUN HAVING YOU WITH ME.
I'M ACTUALLY NOT GONNA MISS THIS DUMP.
YOU'RE GONNA BE TOO PREOCCUPIED TO MISS ANYTHING. YOU'RE GONNA BE BUSY MEETING THE HEROES OF THE 21ST CENTURY...
باتمان
BATMAN
YES, AND BUSY TAKING DOWN ONE OF ITS MOST HORRIFIC MONSTERS...
HARLEY QUINN.
I BET WHEN YOU'RE THERE, YOU'LL GET TO MEET WONDER WOMAN! YOU'LL BE A HERO AND YOU'LL CHANGE HISTORY, AND POSSIBLY JOIN THE JLA, AND--
CAT, WE'RE GETTING AHEAD OF OURSELVES...
...BUT THAT WOULD BE COOL, RIGHT?
WHY NOT? LOOK AT ALL THE FANS YOU HAVE HERE!
AREN'T YOU NERVOUS?
SURE. I'M NERVOUS AS HELL... BUT THE EXCITEMENT LEVEL IS TOTALLY SMASHING THAT ALL AWAY.
IT JUST SEEMS SO SURREAL.
WELL, YOU'VE EARNED IT, SO BASK IN IT, AND DO US ALL PROUD.

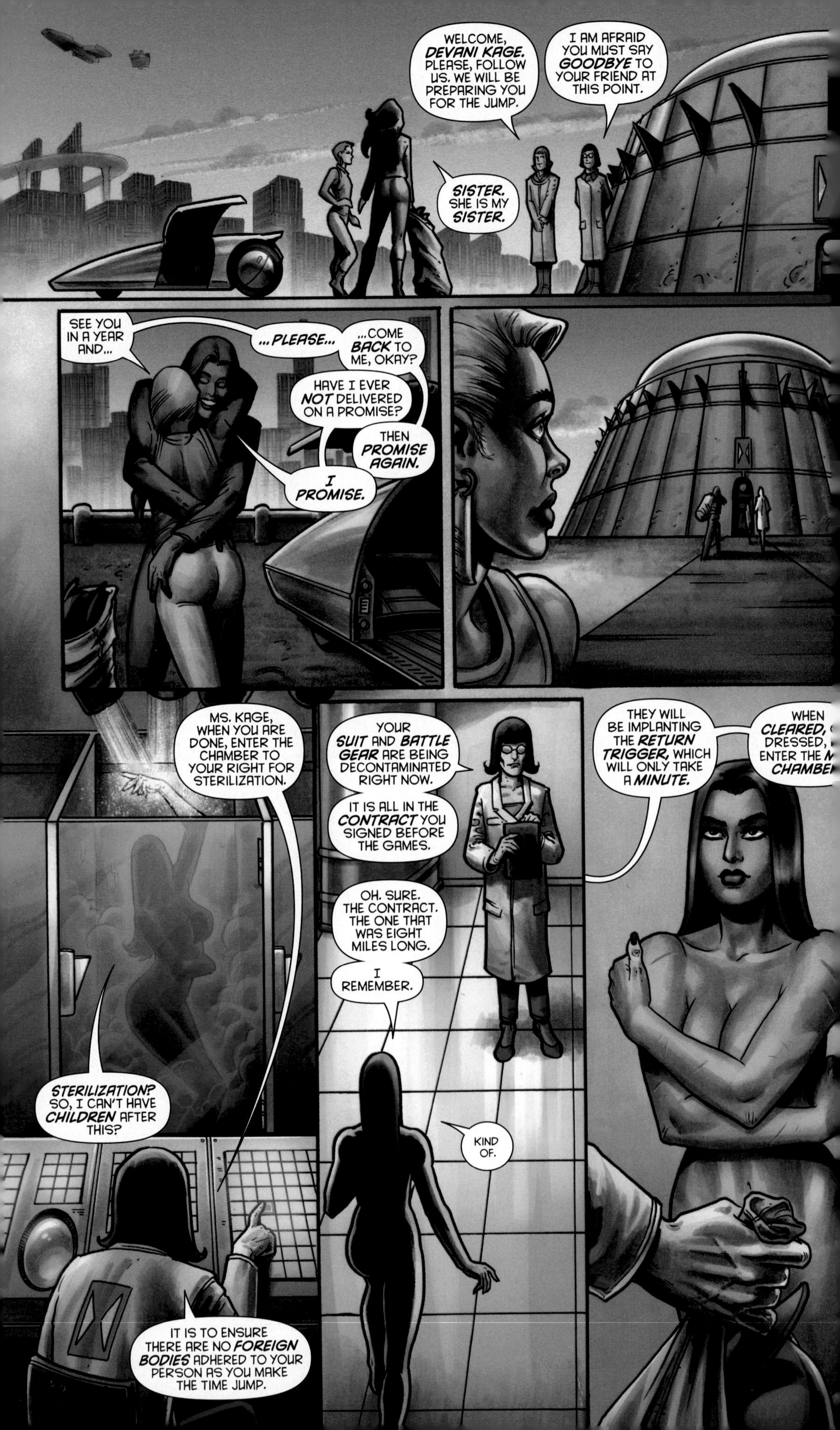
WELCOME, DEVANI KAGE. PLEASE, FOLLOW US. WE WILL BE PREPARING YOU FOR THE JUMP.
I AM AFRAID YOU MUST SAY GOODBYE TO YOUR FRIEND AT THIS POINT.
SISTER. SHE IS MY SISTER.
SEE YOU IN A YEAR AND...
...PLEASE...
...COME BACK TO ME, OKAY?
HAVE I EVER NOT DELIVERED ON A PROMISE?
THEN PROMISE AGAIN.
I PROMISE.
MS. KAGE, WHEN YOU ARE DONE, ENTER THE CHAMBER TO YOUR RIGHT FOR STERILIZATION.
STERILIZATION? SO, I CAN'T HAVE CHILDREN AFTER THIS?
IT IS TO ENSURE THERE ARE NO FOREIGN BODIES ADHERED TO YOUR PERSON AS YOU MAKE THE TIME JUMP.
YOUR SUIT AND BATTLE GEAR ARE BEING DECONTAMINATED RIGHT NOW.
IT IS ALL IN THE CONTRACT YOU SIGNED BEFORE THE GAMES.
OH. SURE. THE CONTRACT. THE ONE THAT WAS EIGHT MILES LONG.
I REMEMBER.
KIND OF.
THEY WILL BE IMPLANTING THE RETURN TRIGGER, WHICH WILL ONLY TAKE A MINUTE.

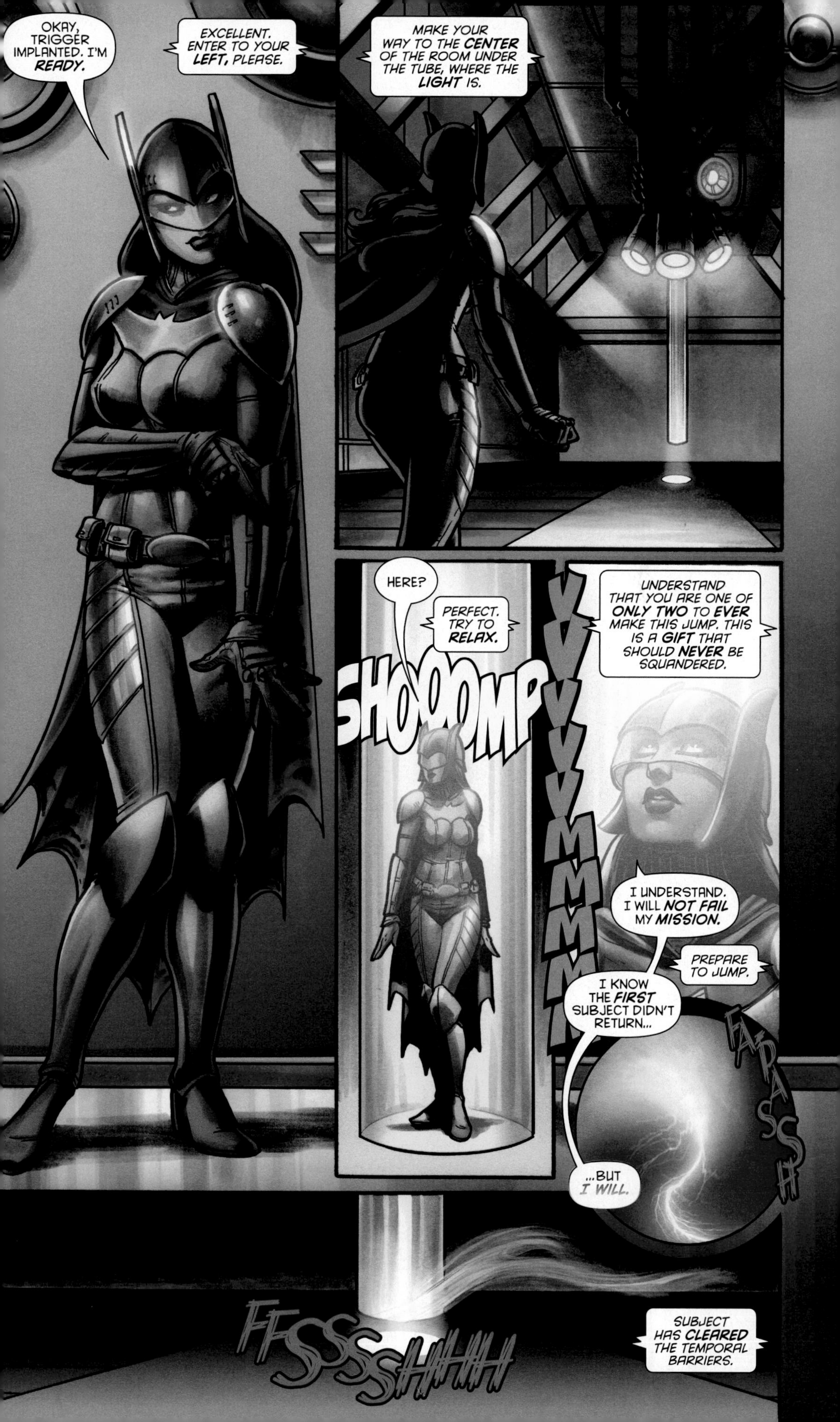

OKAY, TRIGGER IMPLANTED. I'M **READY.**
EXCELLENT. ENTER TO YOUR **LEFT,** PLEASE.
MAKE YOUR WAY TO THE **CENTER** OF THE ROOM UNDER THE TUBE, WHERE THE **LIGHT** IS.
HERE?
PERFECT. TRY TO **RELAX.**
SHOOOMP
VVVVVMMMM
UNDERSTAND THAT YOU ARE ONE OF **ONLY TWO** TO **EVER** MAKE THIS JUMP. THIS IS A **GIFT** THAT SHOULD **NEVER** BE SQUANDERED.
I UNDERSTAND. I WILL **NOT FAIL** MY **MISSION.**
PREPARE TO JUMP.
I KNOW THE **FIRST** SUBJECT DIDN'T RETURN...
...BUT *I WILL.*
FAPASSH
FFSSSSHHHH
SUBJECT HAS **CLEARED** THE TEMPORAL BARRIERS.

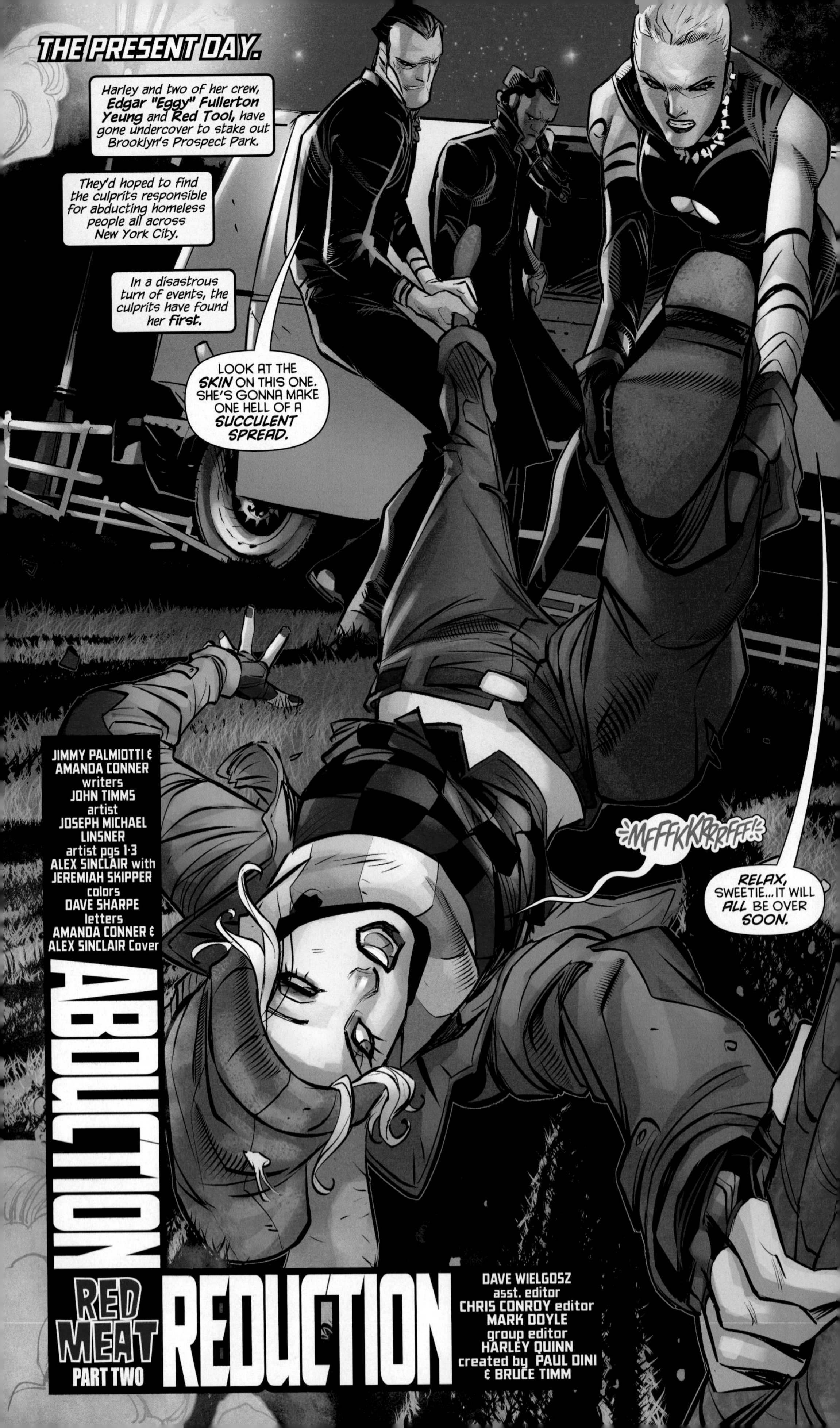
THE PRESENT DAY.
Harley and two of her crew, Edgar "Eggy" Fullerton Yeung and Red Tool, have gone undercover to stake out Brooklyn's Prospect Park.
They'd hoped to find the culprits responsible for abducting homeless people all across New York City.
In a disastrous turn of events, the culprits have found her first.
LOOK AT THE SKIN ON THIS ONE. SHE'S GONNA MAKE ONE HELL OF A SUCCULENT SPREAD.
MFFFKKRRRFFF!
RELAX, SWEETIE...IT WILL ALL BE OVER SOON.
JIMMY PALMIOTTI & AMANDA CONNER writers JOHN TIMMS artist JOSEPH MICHAEL LINSNER artist pgs 1-3 ALEX SINCLAIR with JEREMIAH SKIPPER colors DAVE SHARPE letters AMANDA CONNER & ALEX SINCLAIR Cover
ABDUCTION
RED MEAT PART TWO
REDUCTION
DAVE WIELGOSZ asst. editor CHRIS CONROY editor MARK DOYLE group editor HARLEY QUINN created by PAUL DINI & BRUCE TIMM

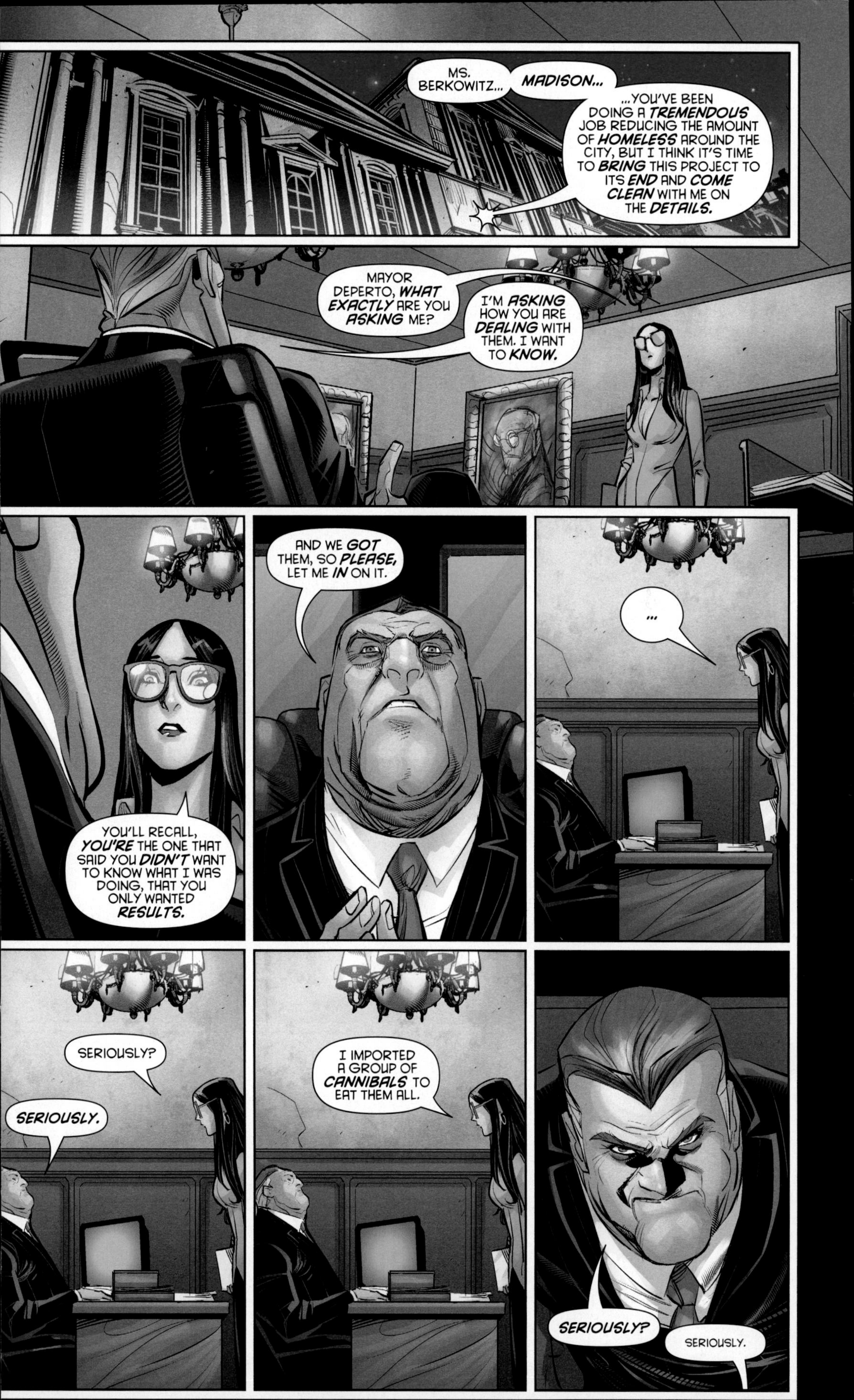
MS. BERKOWITZ...
MADISON...
...YOU'VE BEEN DOING A TREMENDOUS JOB REDUCING THE AMOUNT OF HOMELESS AROUND THE CITY, BUT I THINK IT'S TIME TO BRING THIS PROJECT TO ITS END AND COME CLEAN WITH ME ON THE DETAILS.
MAYOR DEPERTO, WHAT EXACTLY ARE YOU ASKING ME?
I'M ASKING HOW YOU ARE DEALING WITH THEM. I WANT TO KNOW.
YOU'LL RECALL, YOU'RE THE ONE THAT SAID YOU DIDN'T WANT TO KNOW WHAT I WAS DOING, THAT YOU ONLY WANTED RESULTS.
AND WE GOT THEM, SO PLEASE, LET ME IN ON IT.
...
SERIOUSLY?
SERIOUSLY.
I IMPORTED A GROUP OF CANNIBALS TO EAT THEM ALL.
SERIOUSLY?
SERIOUSLY.

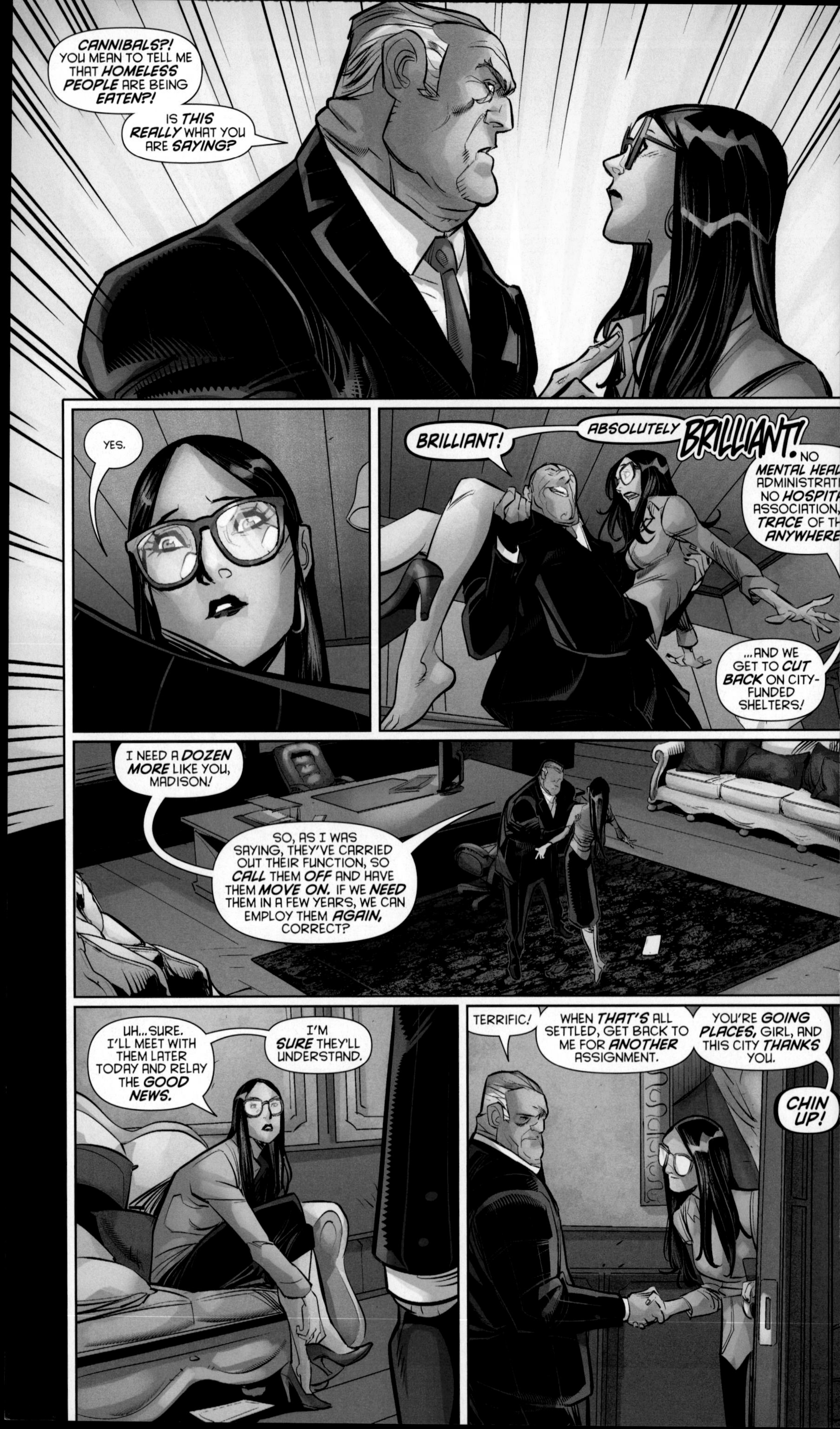

CANNIBALS?! YOU MEAN TO TELL ME THAT HOMELESS PEOPLE ARE BEING EATEN?!
IS THIS REALLY WHAT YOU ARE SAYING?
YES.
BRILLIANT!
ABSOLUTELY BRILLIANT!
NO MENTAL HEAL ADMINISTRATI NO HOSPIT ASSOCIATION, TRACE OF TH ANYWHERE
...AND WE GET TO CUT BACK ON CITY-FUNDED SHELTERS!
I NEED A DOZEN MORE LIKE YOU, MADISON!
SO, AS I WAS SAYING, THEY'VE CARRIED OUT THEIR FUNCTION, SO CALL THEM OFF AND HAVE THEM MOVE ON. IF WE NEED THEM IN A FEW YEARS, WE CAN EMPLOY THEM AGAIN, CORRECT?
UH...SURE. I'LL MEET WITH THEM LATER TODAY AND RELAY THE GOOD NEWS.
I'M SURE THEY'LL UNDERSTAND.
TERRIFIC!
WHEN THAT'S ALL SETTLED, GET BACK TO ME FOR ANOTHER ASSIGNMENT.
YOU'RE GOING PLACES, GIRL, AND THIS CITY THANKS YOU.
CHIN UP!

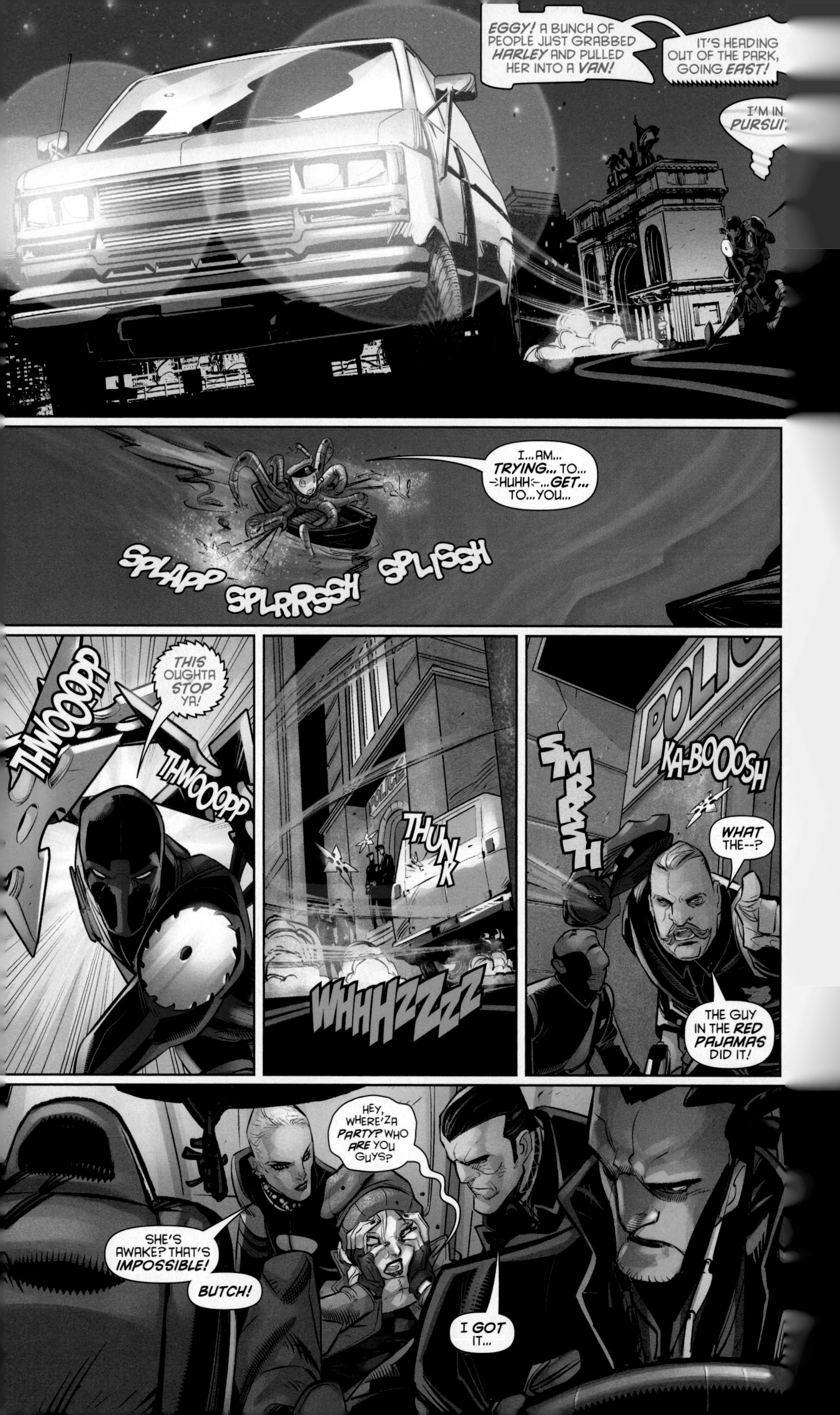
EGGY! A BUNCH OF PEOPLE JUST GRABBED HARLEY AND PULLED HER INTO A VAN!
IT'S HEADING OUT OF THE PARK, GOING EAST!
I'M IN PURSUI
I...AM... TRYING... TO... -HUHH-...GET... TO...YOU...
SPLAPP SPLRRRSSH SPLISSH
THWOOOPP
THIS OUGHTA STOP YA!
THWOOOPP
THUNK
WHHHZZZZ
SMRRSH
KA-BOOOSH
WHAT THE--?
THE GUY IN THE RED PAJAMAS DID IT!
HEY, WHERE'ZA PARTY? WHO ARE YOU GUYS?
SHE'S AWAKE? THAT'S IMPOSSIBLE!
BUTCH!
I GOT IT...

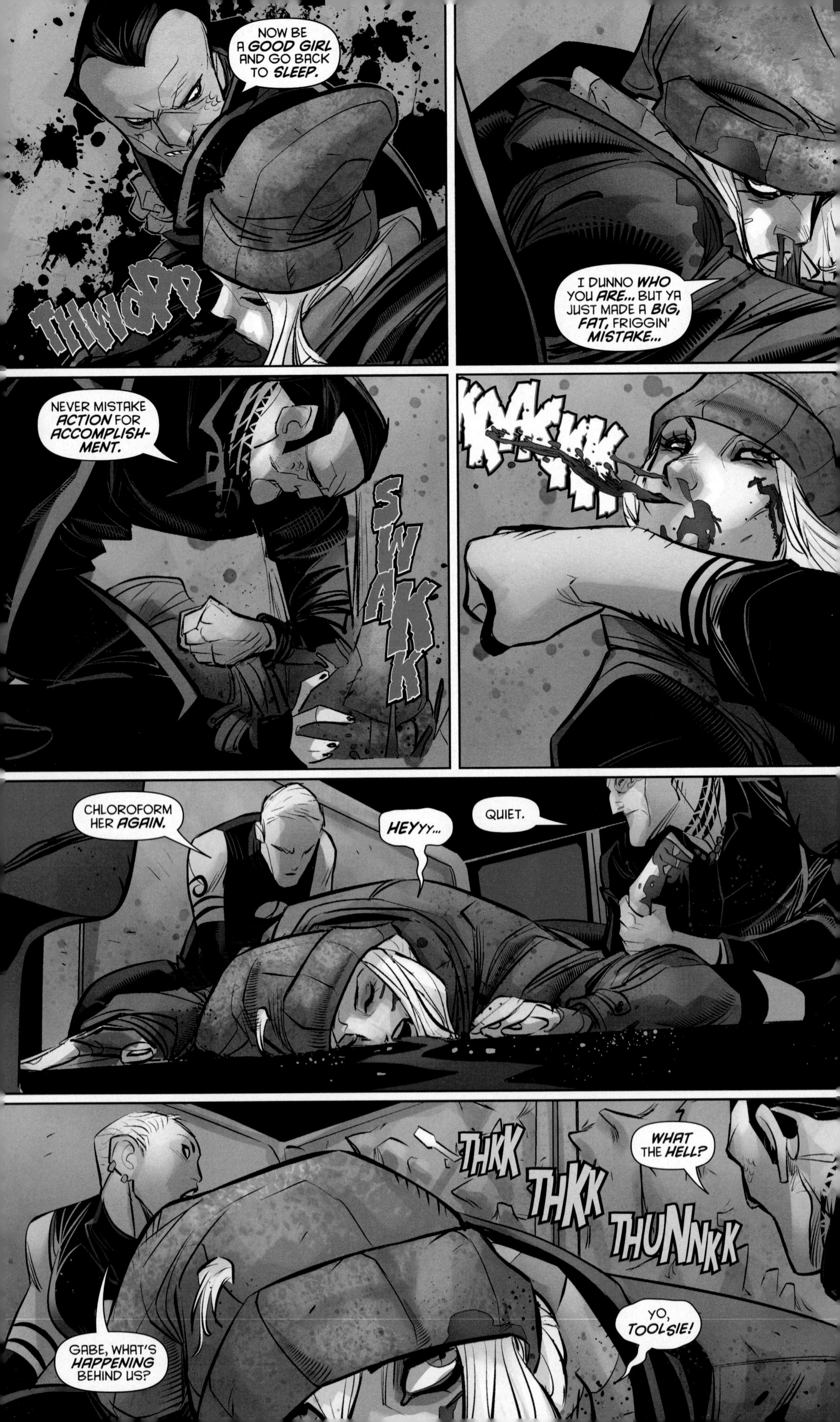
NOW BE A GOOD GIRL AND GO BACK TO SLEEP.
THWOPP
I DUNNO WHO YOU ARE... BUT YA JUST MADE A BIG, FAT, FRIGGIN' MISTAKE...
NEVER MISTAKE ACTION FOR ACCOMPLISHMENT.
SWAKK
KRAKK
CHLOROFORM HER AGAIN.
HEYYY...
QUIET.
THKK
THKK
THUNNKK
WHAT THE HELL?
GABE, WHAT'S HAPPENING BEHIND US?
YO, TOOLSIE!

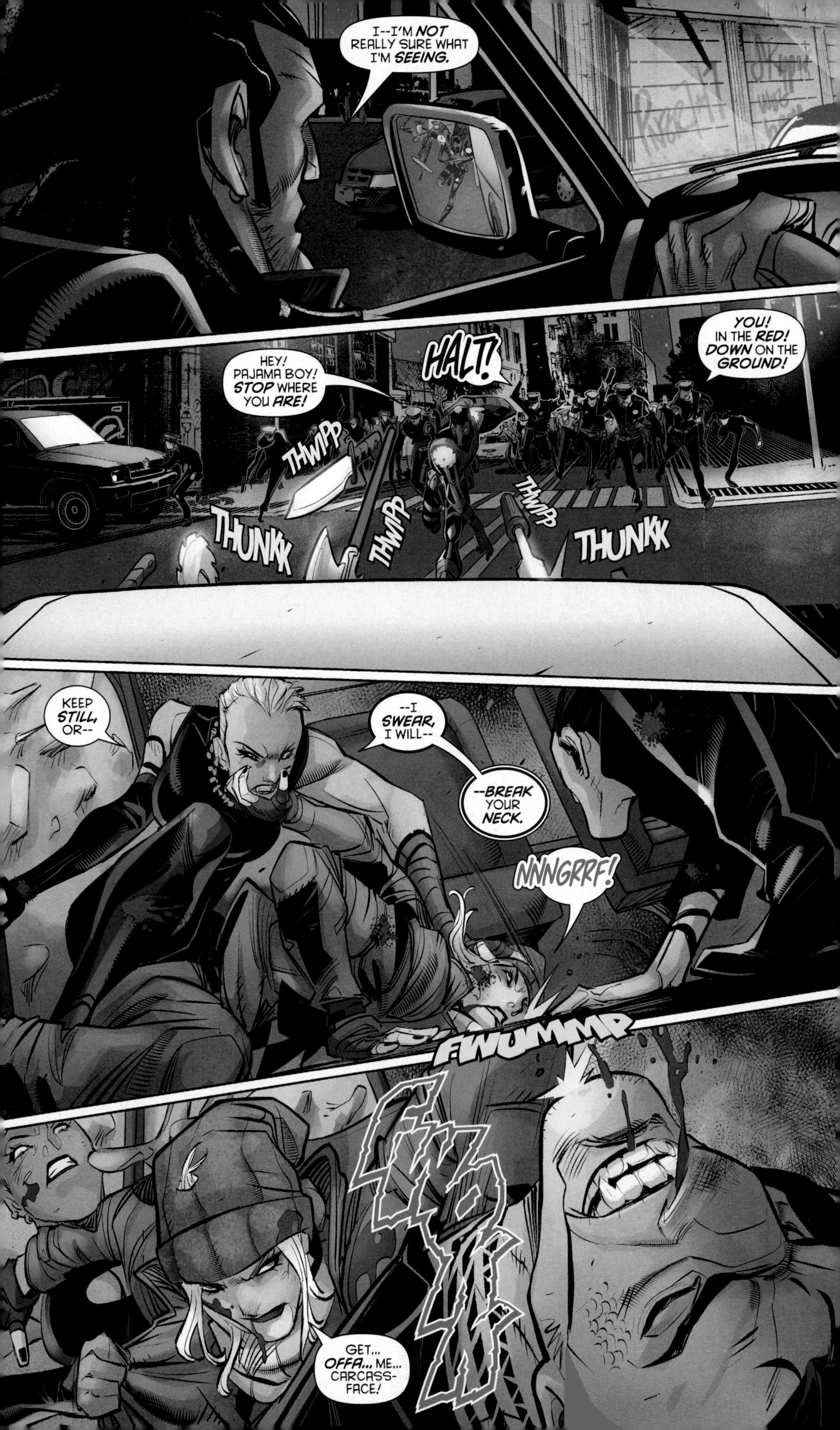
I--I'M NOT REALLY SURE WHAT I'M SEEING.
HEY! PAJAMA BOY! STOP WHERE YOU ARE!
HALT!
YOU! IN THE RED! DOWN ON THE GROUND!
THWIPP
THUNKK
THWIPP
THWIPP
THUNKK
KEEP STILL, OR--
--I SWEAR, I WILL--
--BREAK YOUR NECK.
NNNGRRF!
FWUMMP
GET... OFFA... ME... CARCASS-FACE!

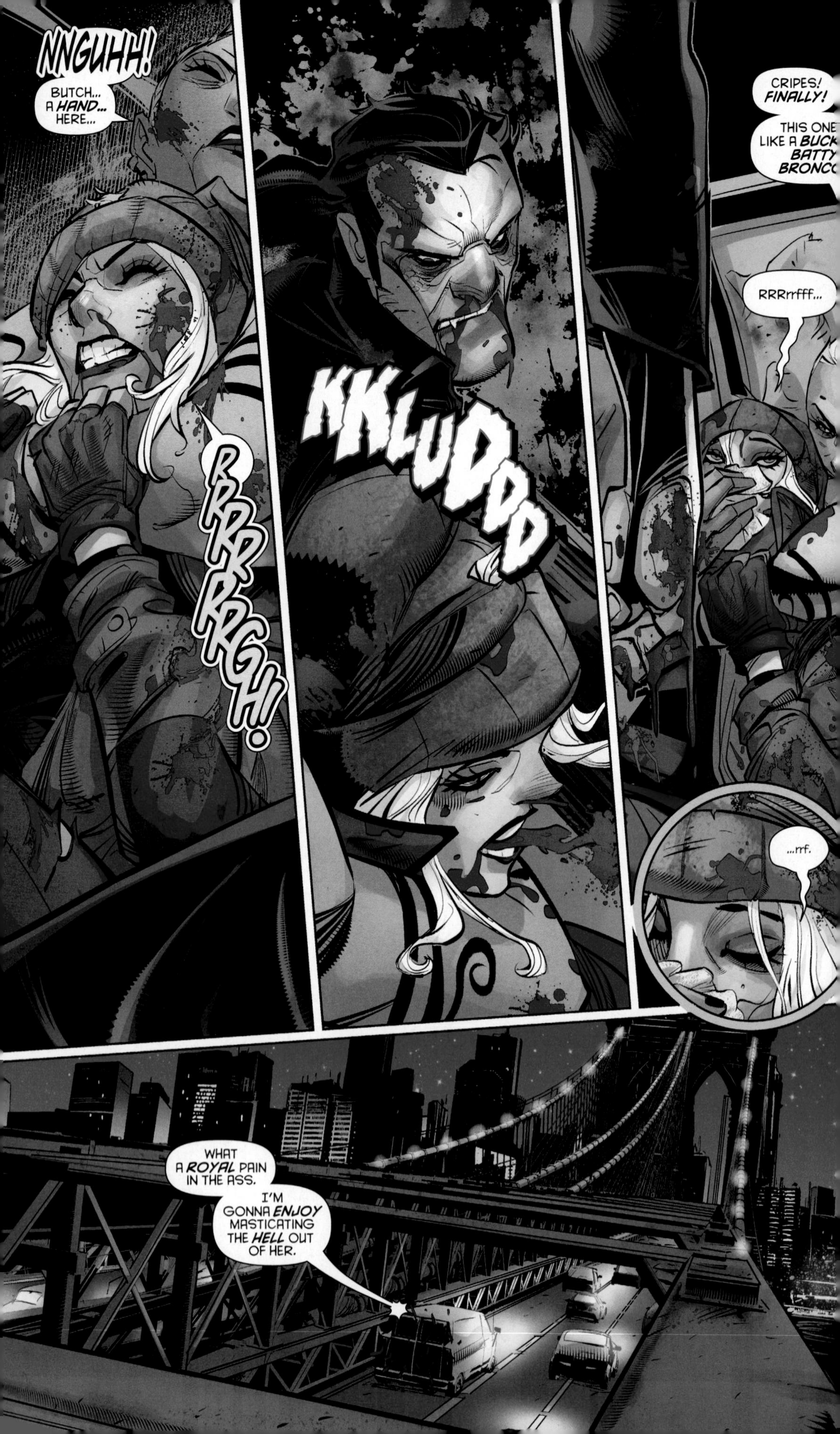
NNGUHH!
BUTCH... A HAND... HERE...
RRRRRGH!
KKLUDDD
CRIPES! FINALLY!
THIS ONE LIKE A BUCK BATTY BRONCO
RRRrrfff...
...rrf.
WHAT A ROYAL PAIN IN THE ASS.
I'M GONNA ENJOY MASTICATING THE HELL OUT OF HER.

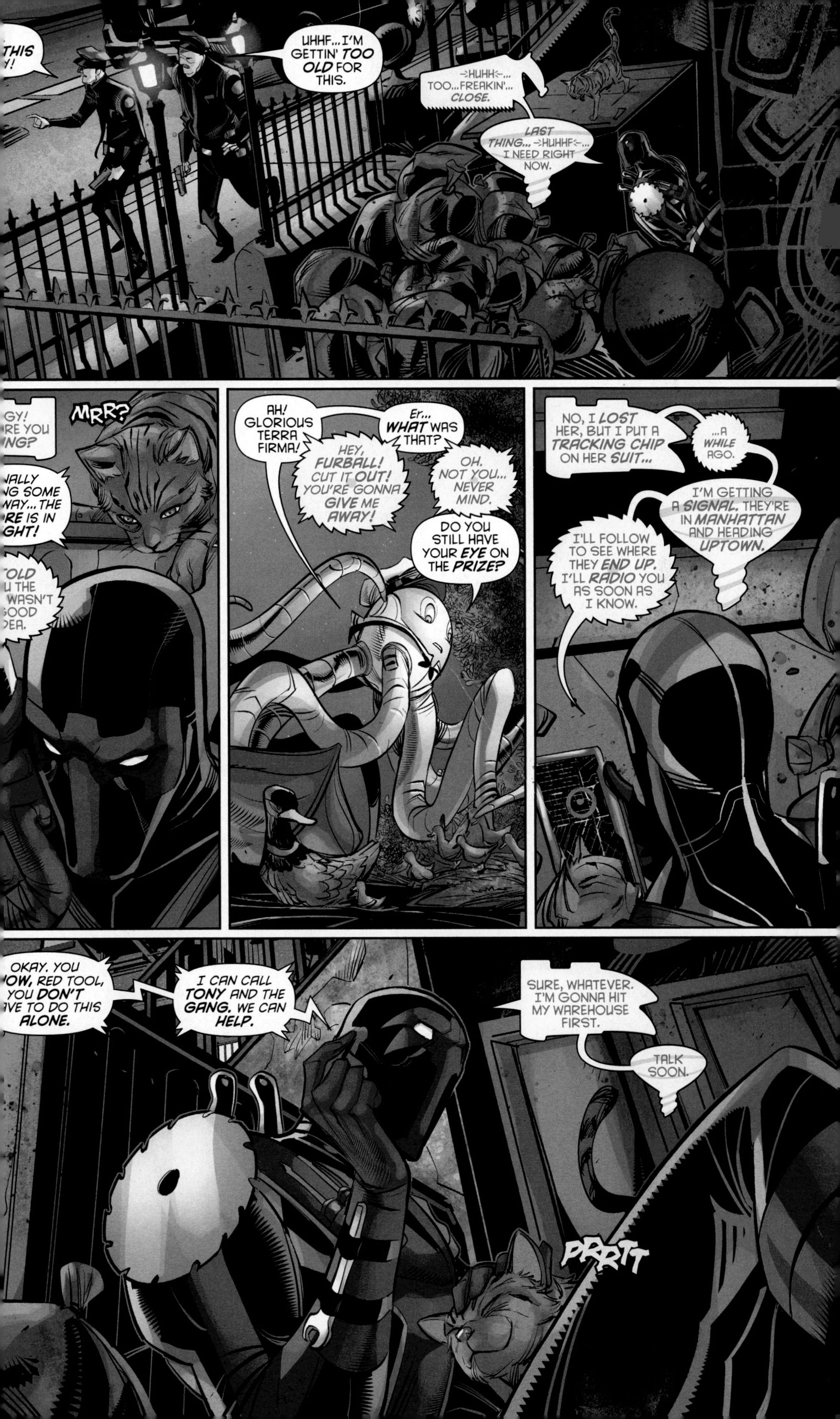
UHHF...I'M GETTIN' TOO OLD FOR THIS.
HUHH... TOO...FREAKIN'... CLOSE.
LAST THING... HUHHF... I NEED RIGHT NOW.
MRR?
AH! GLORIOUS TERRA FIRMA!
Er... WHAT WAS THAT?
HEY, FURBALL! CUT IT OUT! YOU'RE GONNA GIVE ME AWAY!
OH. NOT YOU... NEVER MIND.
DO YOU STILL HAVE YOUR EYE ON THE PRIZE?
NO, I LOST HER, BUT I PUT A TRACKING CHIP ON HER SUIT...
...A WHILE AGO.
I'M GETTING A SIGNAL. THEY'RE IN MANHATTAN AND HEADING UPTOWN.
I'LL FOLLOW TO SEE WHERE THEY END UP. I'LL RADIO YOU AS SOON AS I KNOW.
I CAN CALL TONY AND THE GANG. WE CAN HELP.
SURE, WHATEVER. I'M GONNA HIT MY WAREHOUSE FIRST.
TALK SOON.
PRRTT

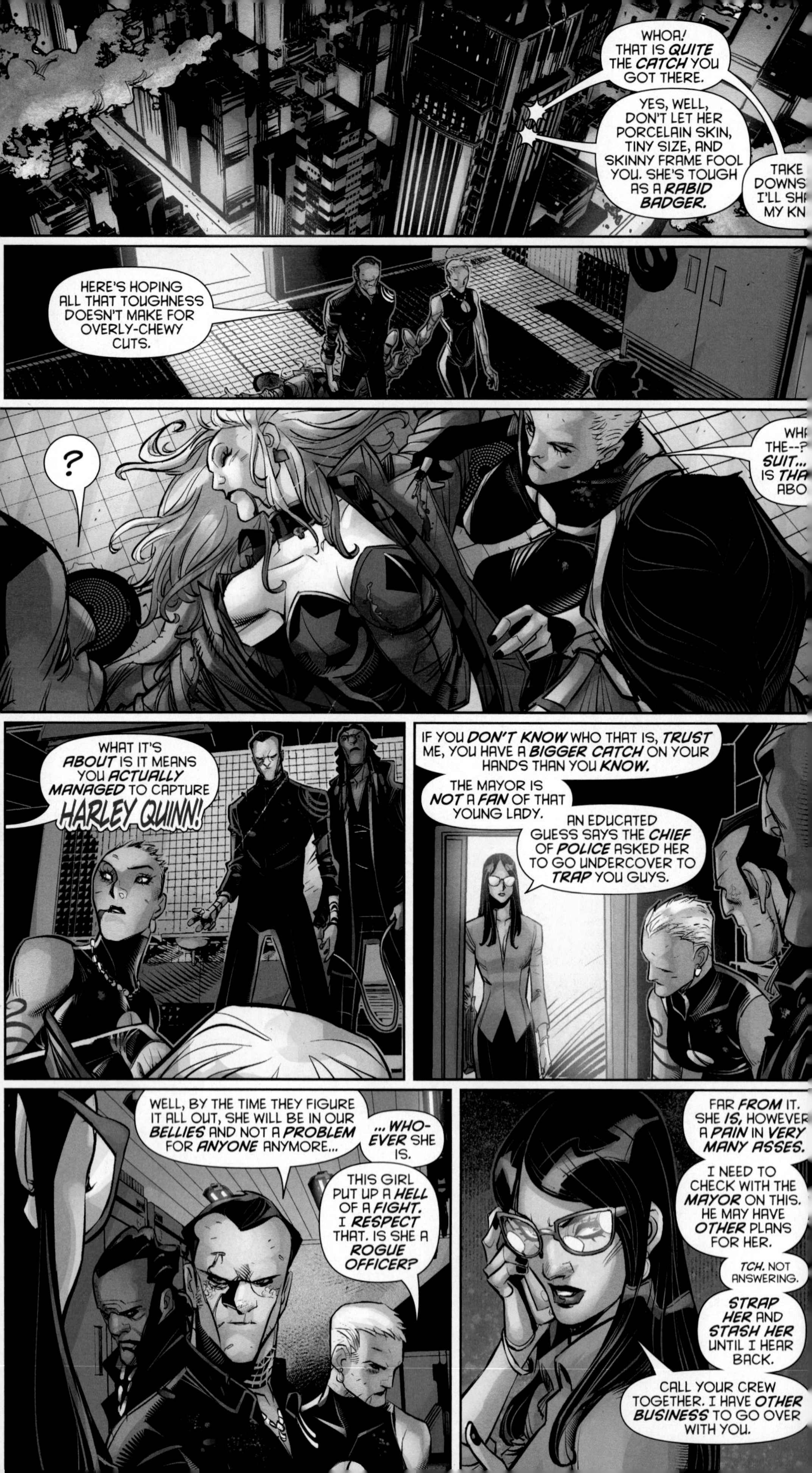

WHOA! THAT IS QUITE THE CATCH YOU GOT THERE.
YES, WELL, DON'T LET HER PORCELAIN SKIN, TINY SIZE, AND SKINNY FRAME FOOL YOU. SHE'S TOUGH AS A RABID BADGER.
TAKE DOWNS I'LL SH MY KN
HERE'S HOPING ALL THAT TOUGHNESS DOESN'T MAKE FOR OVERLY-CHEWY CUTS.
?
WH THE--? SUIT... IS THA ABO
WHAT IT'S ABOUT IS IT MEANS YOU ACTUALLY MANAGED TO CAPTURE HARLEY QUINN!
IF YOU DON'T KNOW WHO THAT IS, TRUST ME, YOU HAVE A BIGGER CATCH ON YOUR HANDS THAN YOU KNOW.
THE MAYOR IS NOT A FAN OF THAT YOUNG LADY.
AN EDUCATED GUESS SAYS THE CHIEF OF POLICE ASKED HER TO GO UNDERCOVER TO TRAP YOU GUYS.
WELL, BY THE TIME THEY FIGURE IT ALL OUT, SHE WILL BE IN OUR BELLIES AND NOT A PROBLEM FOR ANYONE ANYMORE...
...WHO-EVER SHE IS.
THIS GIRL PUT UP A HELL OF A FIGHT. I RESPECT THAT. IS SHE A ROGUE OFFICER?
FAR FROM IT. SHE IS, HOWEVER A PAIN IN VERY MANY ASSES.
I NEED TO CHECK WITH THE MAYOR ON THIS. HE MAY HAVE OTHER PLANS FOR HER.
TCH. NOT ANSWERING.
STRAP HER AND STASH HER UNTIL I HEAR BACK.
CALL YOUR CREW TOGETHER. I HAVE OTHER BUSINESS TO GO OVER WITH YOU.

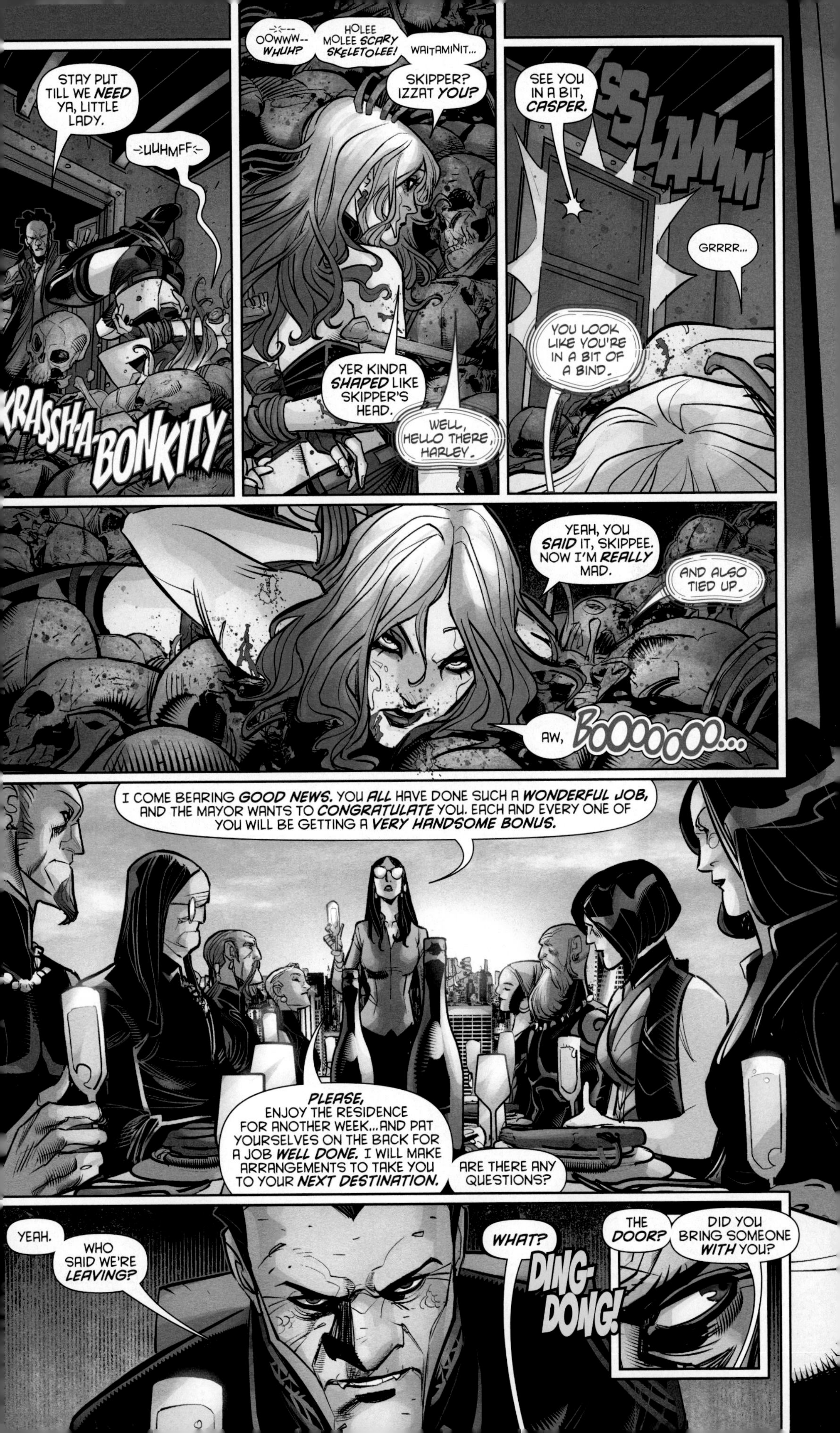
STAY PUT TILL WE NEED YA, LITTLE LADY.
UUHMFF
KRASSH-A-BONKITY
OOWWW-- WHUH?
HOLEE MOLEE SCARY SKELETOLEE!
WAITAMINIT...
SKIPPER? IZZAT YOU?
YER KINDA SHAPED LIKE SKIPPER'S HEAD.
WELL, HELLO THERE, HARLEY.
SEE YOU IN A BIT, CASPER.
SSLAMM
GRRRR...
YOU LOOK LIKE YOU'RE IN A BIT OF A BIND.
YEAH, YOU SAID IT, SKIPPEE. NOW I'M REALLY MAD.
AND ALSO TIED UP.
AW, BOOOOOOO...
I COME BEARING GOOD NEWS. YOU ALL HAVE DONE SUCH A WONDERFUL JOB, AND THE MAYOR WANTS TO CONGRATULATE YOU. EACH AND EVERY ONE OF YOU WILL BE GETTING A VERY HANDSOME BONUS.
PLEASE, ENJOY THE RESIDENCE FOR ANOTHER WEEK...AND PAT YOURSELVES ON THE BACK FOR A JOB WELL DONE. I WILL MAKE ARRANGEMENTS TO TAKE YOU TO YOUR NEXT DESTINATION.
ARE THERE ANY QUESTIONS?
YEAH.
WHO SAID WE'RE LEAVING?
WHAT?
DING-DONG!
THE DOOR?
DID YOU BRING SOMEONE WITH YOU?

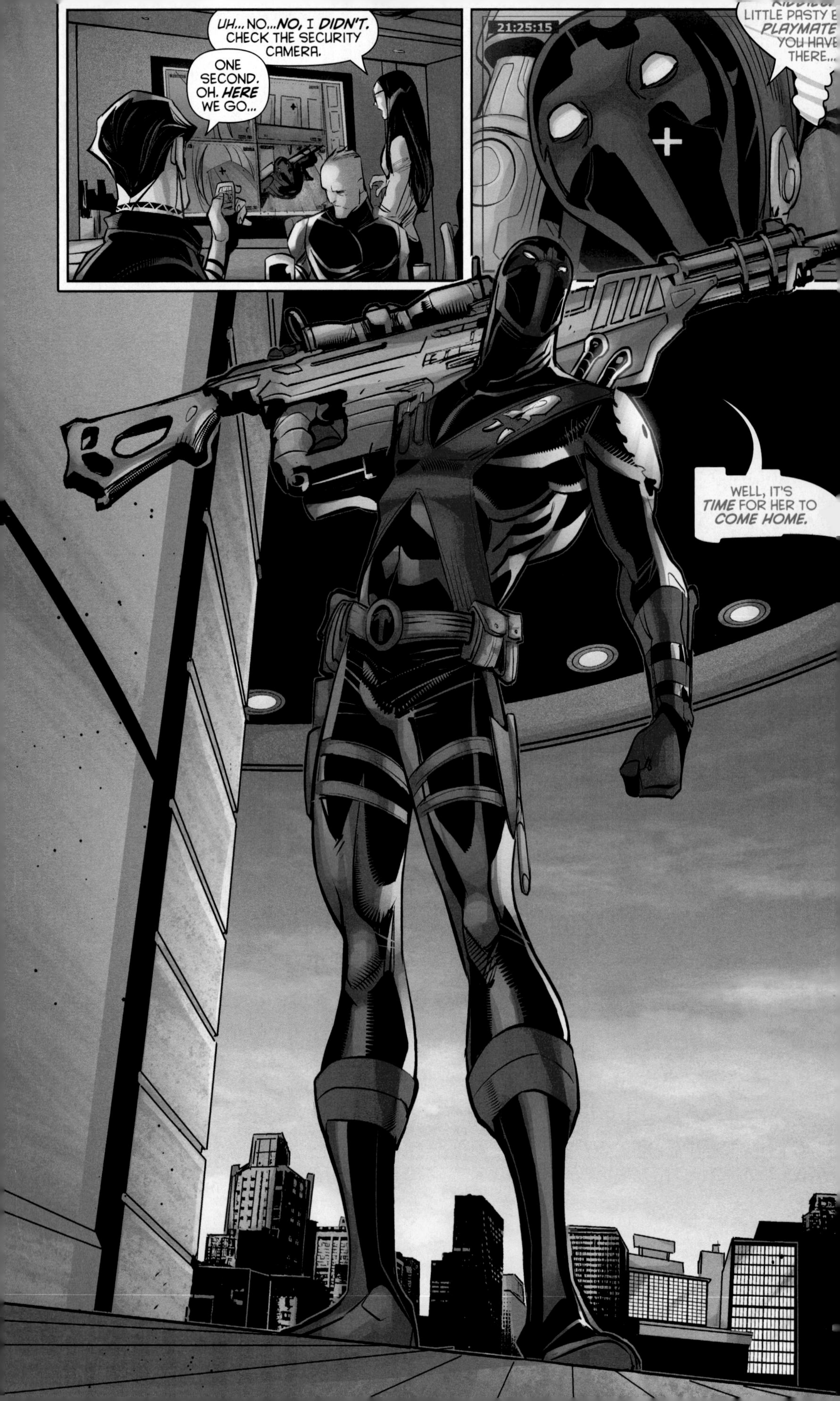
UH... NO...NO, I DIDN'T. CHECK THE SECURITY CAMERA.
ONE SECOND. OH. HERE WE GO...
21:25:15
LITTLE PASTY
PLAYMATE YOU HAVE THERE...
WELL, IT'S TIME FOR HER TO COME HOME.

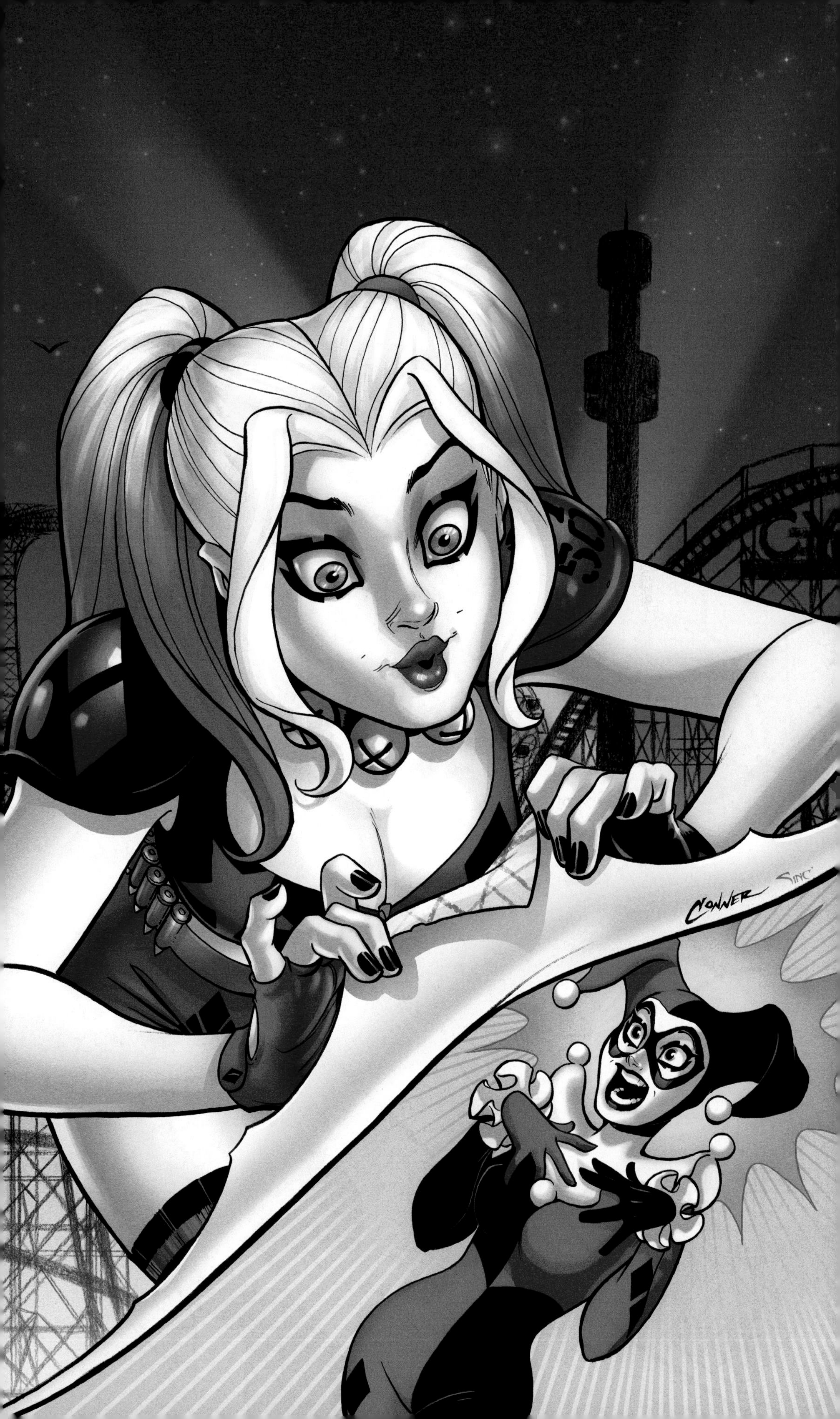

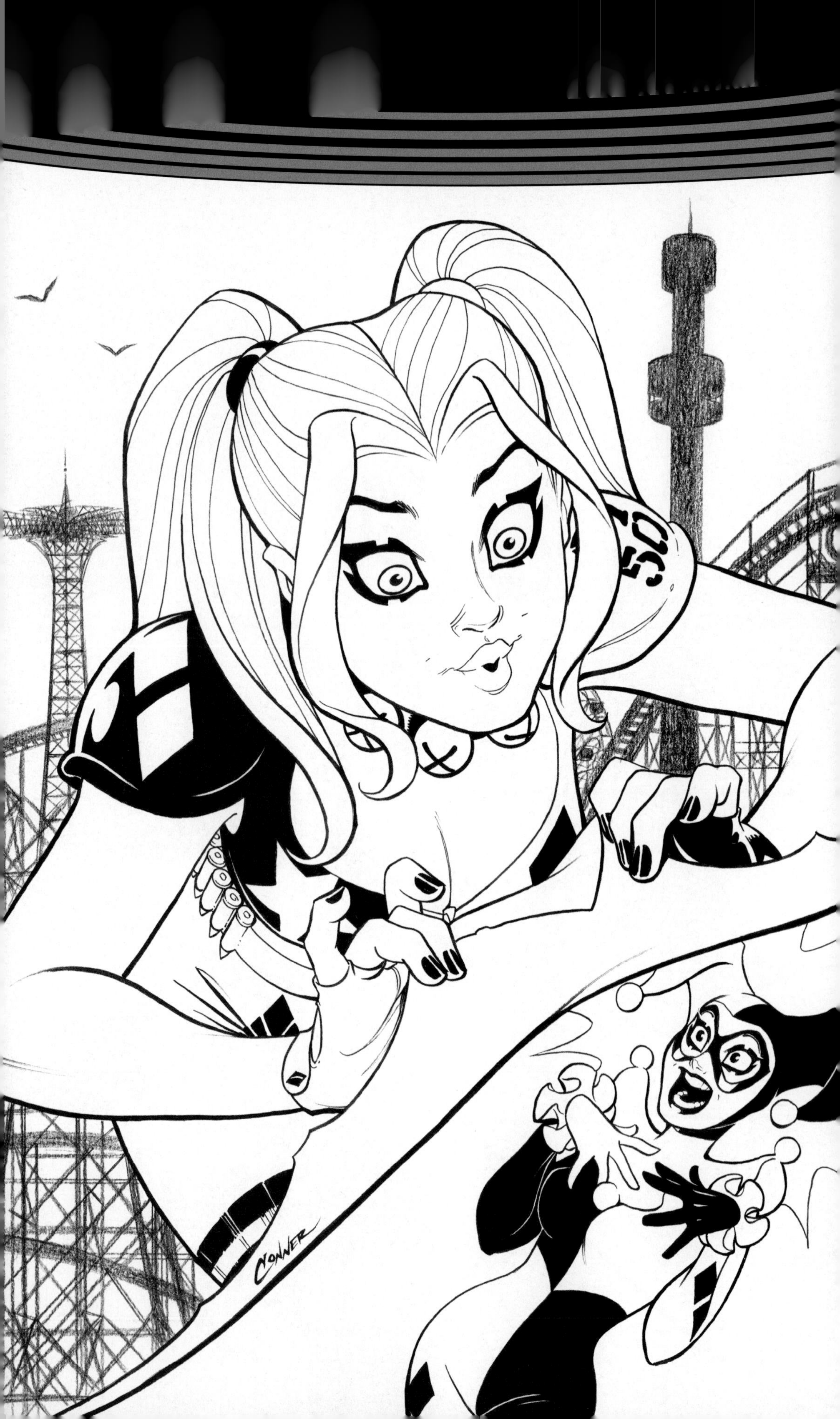
CONNER

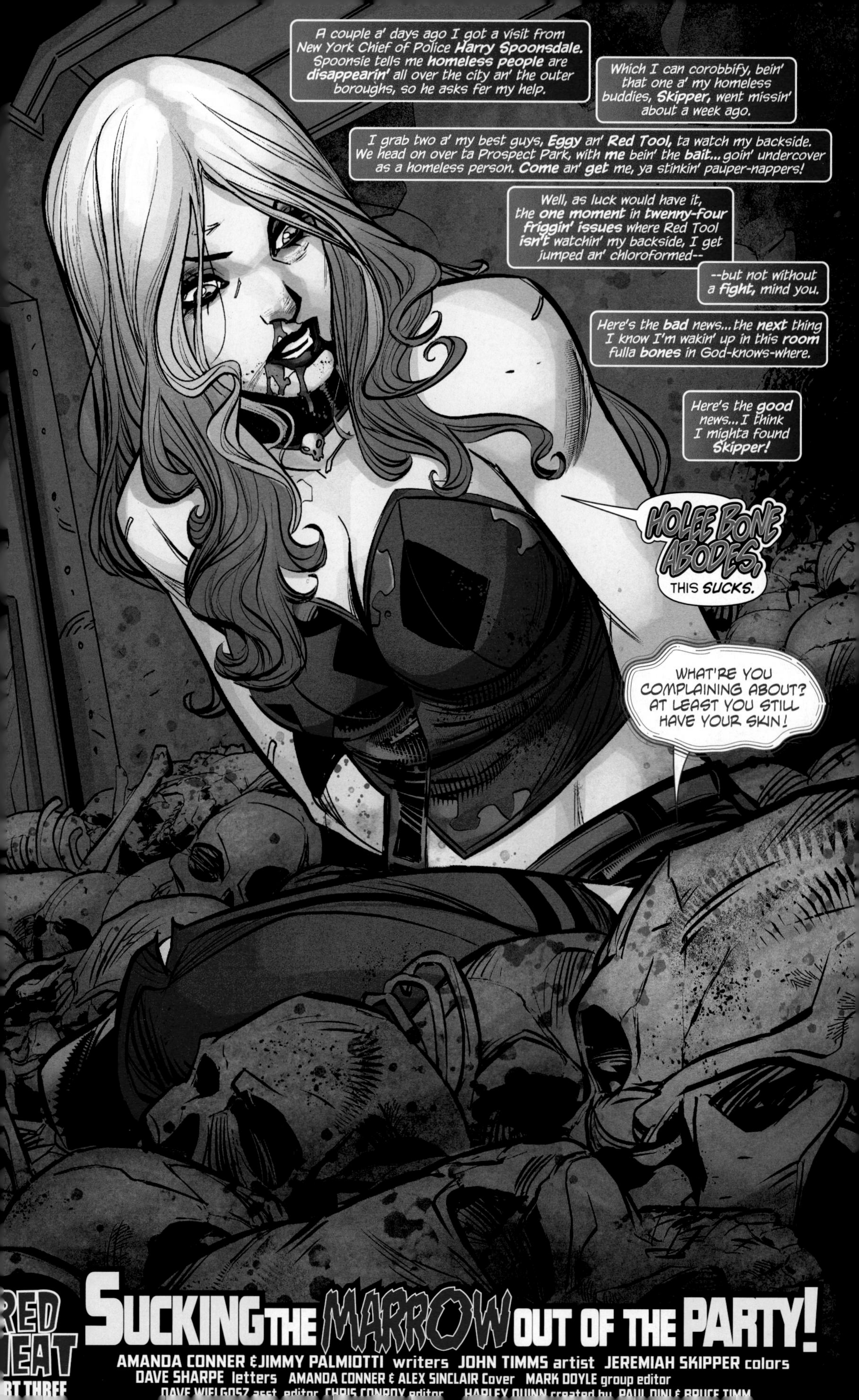
A couple a' days ago I got a visit from New York Chief of Police Harry Spoonsdale. Spoonsie tells me homeless people are disappearin' all over the city an' the outer boroughs, so he asks fer my help.
Which I can corobbify, bein' that one a' my homeless buddies, Skipper, went missin' about a week ago.
I grab two a' my best guys, Eggy an' Red Tool, ta watch my backside. We head on over ta Prospect Park, with me bein' the bait...goin' undercover as a homeless person. Come an' get me, ya stinkin' pauper-nappers!
Well, as luck would have it, the one moment in twenny-four friggin' issues where Red Tool isn't watchin' my backside, I get jumped an' chloroformed--
--but not without a fight, mind you.
Here's the bad news...the next thing I know I'm wakin' up in this room fulla bones in God-knows-where.
Here's the good news...I think I mighta found Skipper!
HOLEE BONE ABODES, THIS SUCKS.
WHAT'RE YOU COMPLAINING ABOUT? AT LEAST YOU STILL HAVE YOUR SKIN!
SUCKING THE MARROW OUT OF THE PARTY!
AMANDA CONNER & JIMMY PALMIOTTI writers JOHN TIMMS artist JEREMIAH SKIPPER colors
DAVE SHARPE letters AMANDA CONNER & ALEX SINCLAIR Cover MARK DOYLE group editor
DAVE WIELGOSZ asst. editor CHRIS CONROY editor HARLEY QUINN created by PAUL DINI & BRUCE TIMM

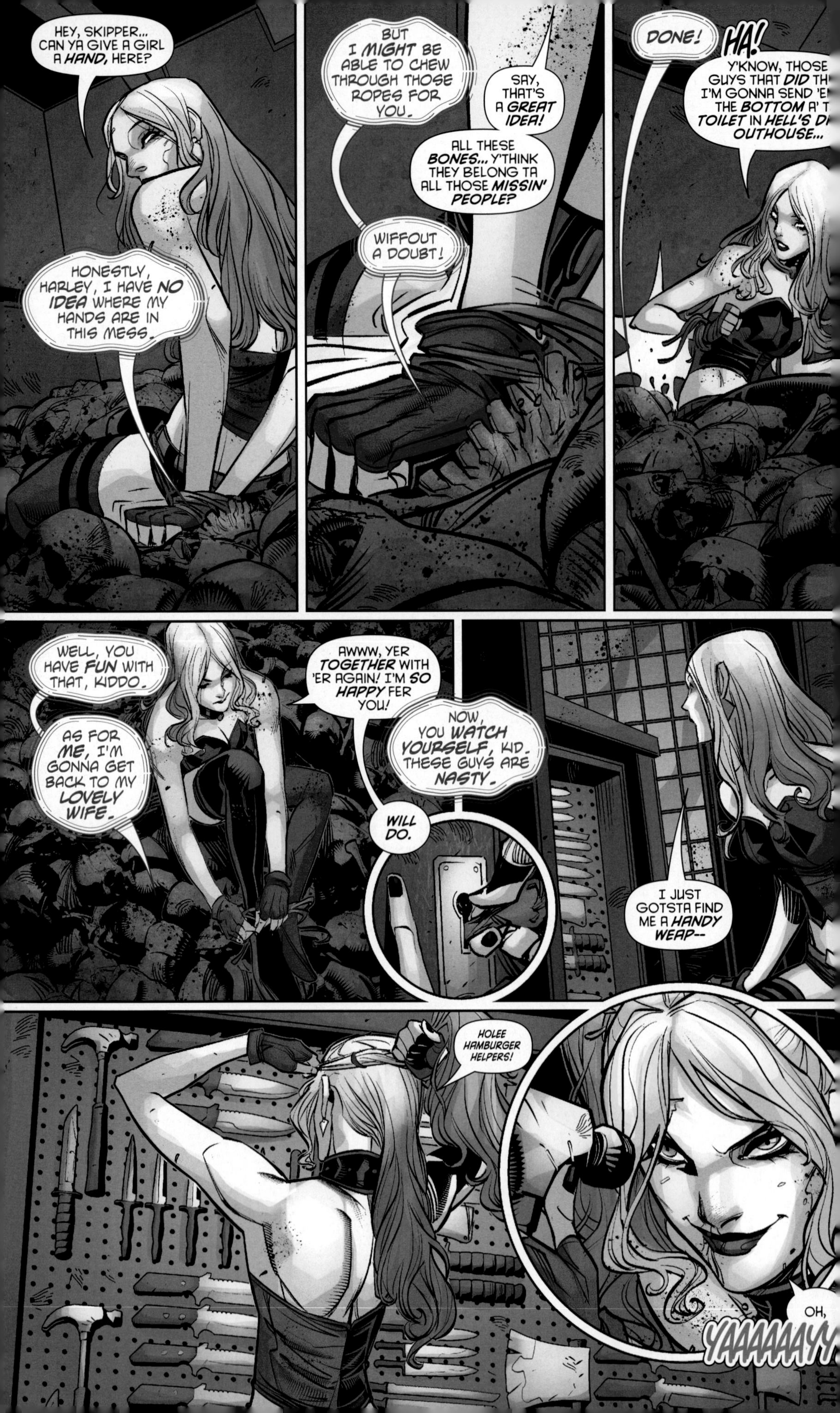
HEY, SKIPPER... CAN YA GIVE A GIRL A HAND, HERE?
HONESTLY, HARLEY, I HAVE NO IDEA WHERE MY HANDS ARE IN THIS MESS.
BUT I MIGHT BE ABLE TO CHEW THROUGH THOSE ROPES FOR YOU.
SAY, THAT'S A GREAT IDEA!
ALL THESE BONES... Y'THINK THEY BELONG TA ALL THOSE MISSIN' PEOPLE?
WIFFOUT A DOUBT!
DONE!
HA!
Y'KNOW, THOSE GUYS THAT DID TH I'M GONNA SEND 'EM THE BOTTOM A' T TOILET IN HELL'S DI OUTHOUSE...
WELL, YOU HAVE FUN WITH THAT, KIDDO.
AS FOR ME, I'M GONNA GET BACK TO MY LOVELY WIFE.
AWWW, YER TOGETHER WITH 'ER AGAIN! I'M SO HAPPY FER YOU!
NOW, YOU WATCH YOURSELF, KID. THESE GUYS ARE NASTY.
WILL DO.
I JUST GOTSTA FIND ME A HANDY WEAP--
HOLEE HAMBURGER HELPERS!
OH,
YAAAAAAYY

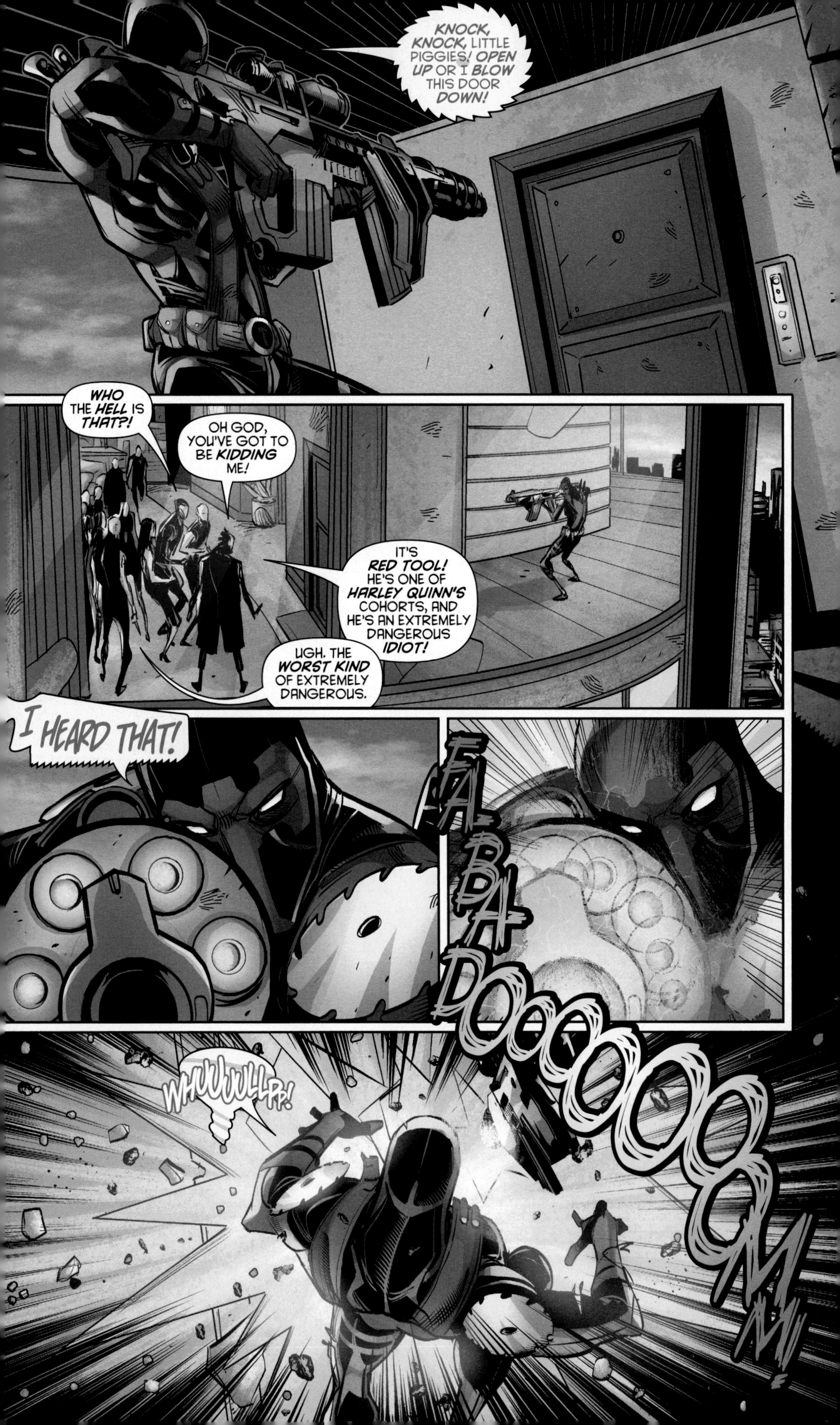
KNOCK, KNOCK, LITTLE PIGGIES! OPEN UP OR I BLOW THIS DOOR DOWN!
WHO THE HELL IS THAT?!
OH GOD, YOU'VE GOT TO BE KIDDING ME!
IT'S RED TOOL! HE'S ONE OF HARLEY QUINN'S COHORTS, AND HE'S AN EXTREMELY DANGEROUS IDIOT!
UGH. THE WORST KIND OF EXTREMELY DANGEROUS.
I HEARD THAT!
FA BA BA DOOOOOOOOM
WHUUULLPP!

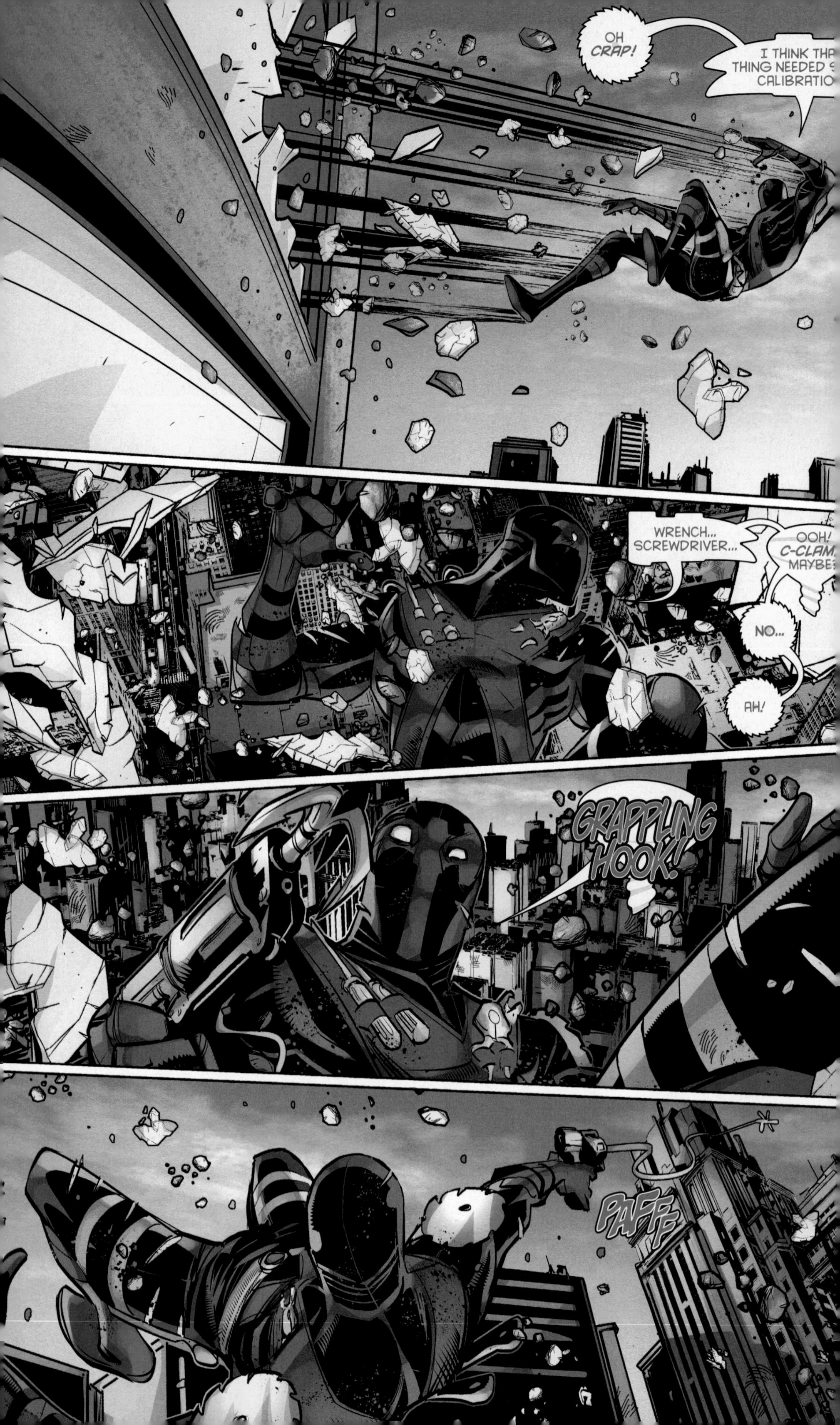
OH CRAP!
I THINK THA THING NEEDED S CALIBRATIO
WRENCH... SCREWDRIVER...
OOH! C-CLAM MAYBE
NO...
AH!
GRAPPLING HOOK!
PAFFF

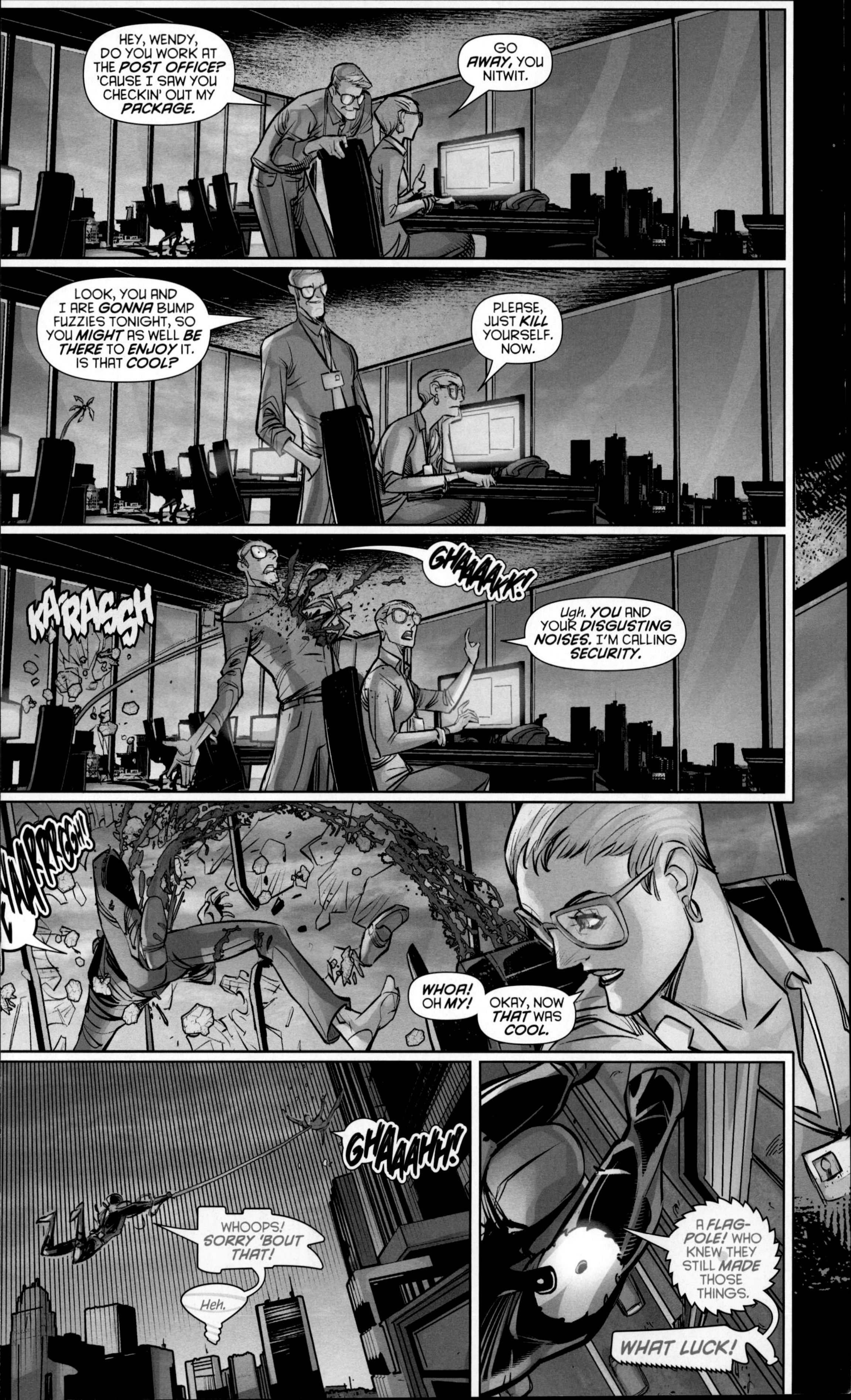

HEY, WENDY, DO YOU WORK AT THE POST OFFICE? 'CAUSE I SAW YOU CHECKIN' OUT MY PACKAGE.
GO AWAY, YOU NITWIT.
LOOK, YOU AND I ARE GONNA BUMP FUZZIES TONIGHT, SO YOU MIGHT AS WELL BE THERE TO ENJOY IT. IS THAT COOL?
PLEASE, JUST KILL YOURSELF. NOW.
KA-RASSH
GHAAAAKK!
Ugh. YOU AND YOUR DISGUSTING NOISES. I'M CALLING SECURITY.
WHOA! OH MY!
OKAY, NOW THAT WAS COOL.
GHAAAHH!
WHOOPS! SORRY 'BOUT THAT!
Heh.
A FLAG-POLE! WHO KNEW THEY STILL MADE THOSE THINGS.
WHAT LUCK!

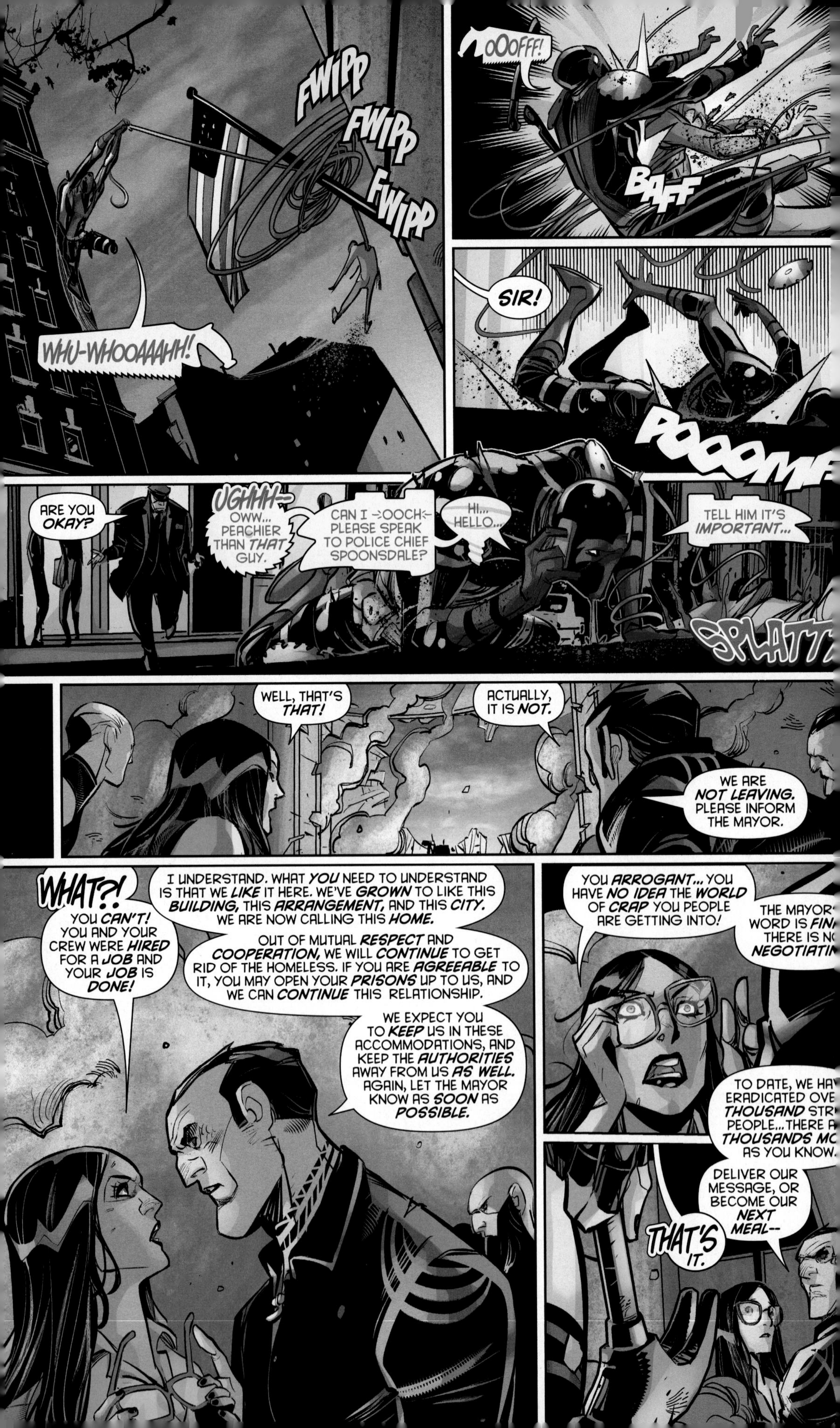

FWIPP
FWIPP
FWIPP
WHU-WHOOAAAHH!
OOOFFF!
BAFF
SIR!
POOOMF
ARE YOU OKAY?
UGHHH-- OWW... PEACHIER THAN THAT GUY.
CAN I --OOCH-- PLEASE SPEAK TO POLICE CHIEF SPOONSDALE?
HI... HELLO...
TELL HIM IT'S IMPORTANT...
SPLATT
WELL, THAT'S THAT!
ACTUALLY, IT IS NOT.
WE ARE NOT LEAVING. PLEASE INFORM THE MAYOR.
WHAT?!
YOU CAN'T! YOU AND YOUR CREW WERE HIRED FOR A JOB AND YOUR JOB IS DONE!
I UNDERSTAND. WHAT YOU NEED TO UNDERSTAND IS THAT WE LIKE IT HERE. WE'VE GROWN TO LIKE THIS BUILDING, THIS ARRANGEMENT, AND THIS CITY. WE ARE NOW CALLING THIS HOME.
OUT OF MUTUAL RESPECT AND COOPERATION, WE WILL CONTINUE TO GET RID OF THE HOMELESS. IF YOU ARE AGREEABLE TO IT, YOU MAY OPEN YOUR PRISONS UP TO US, AND WE CAN CONTINUE THIS RELATIONSHIP.
WE EXPECT YOU TO KEEP US IN THESE ACCOMMODATIONS, AND KEEP THE AUTHORITIES AWAY FROM US AS WELL. AGAIN, LET THE MAYOR KNOW AS SOON AS POSSIBLE.
YOU ARROGANT... YOU HAVE NO IDEA THE WORLD OF CRAP YOU PEOPLE ARE GETTING INTO!
THE MAYOR'S WORD IS FINA THERE IS NO NEGOTIATIN
TO DATE, WE HAV ERADICATED OVE THOUSAND STR PEOPLE... THERE A THOUSANDS MO AS YOU KNOW.
DELIVER OUR MESSAGE, OR BECOME OUR NEXT MEAL--
THAT'S IT.

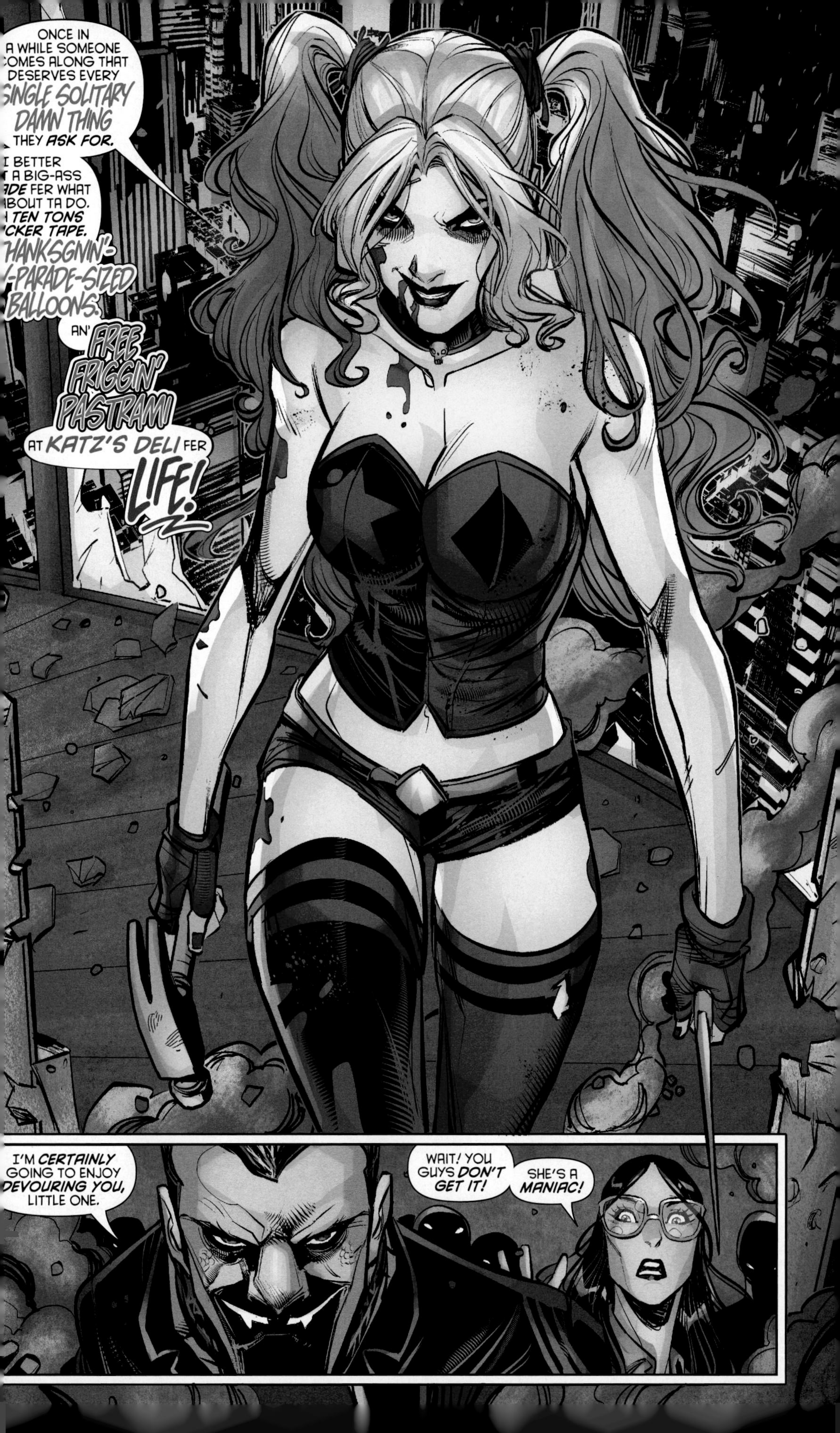
ONCE IN A WHILE SOMEONE OMES ALONG THAT DESERVES EVERY SINGLE SOLITARY DAMN THING THEY ASK FOR.
I BETTER A BIG-ASS ADE FER WHAT BOUT TA DO. TEN TONS CKER TAPE. HANKSGIVIN'- -PARADE-SIZED BALLOONS.
AN' FREE FRIGGIN' PASTRAMI AT KATZ'S DELI FER LIFE!
I'M CERTAINLY GOING TO ENJOY DEVOURING YOU, LITTLE ONE.
WAIT! YOU GUYS DON'T GET IT!
SHE'S A MANIAC!

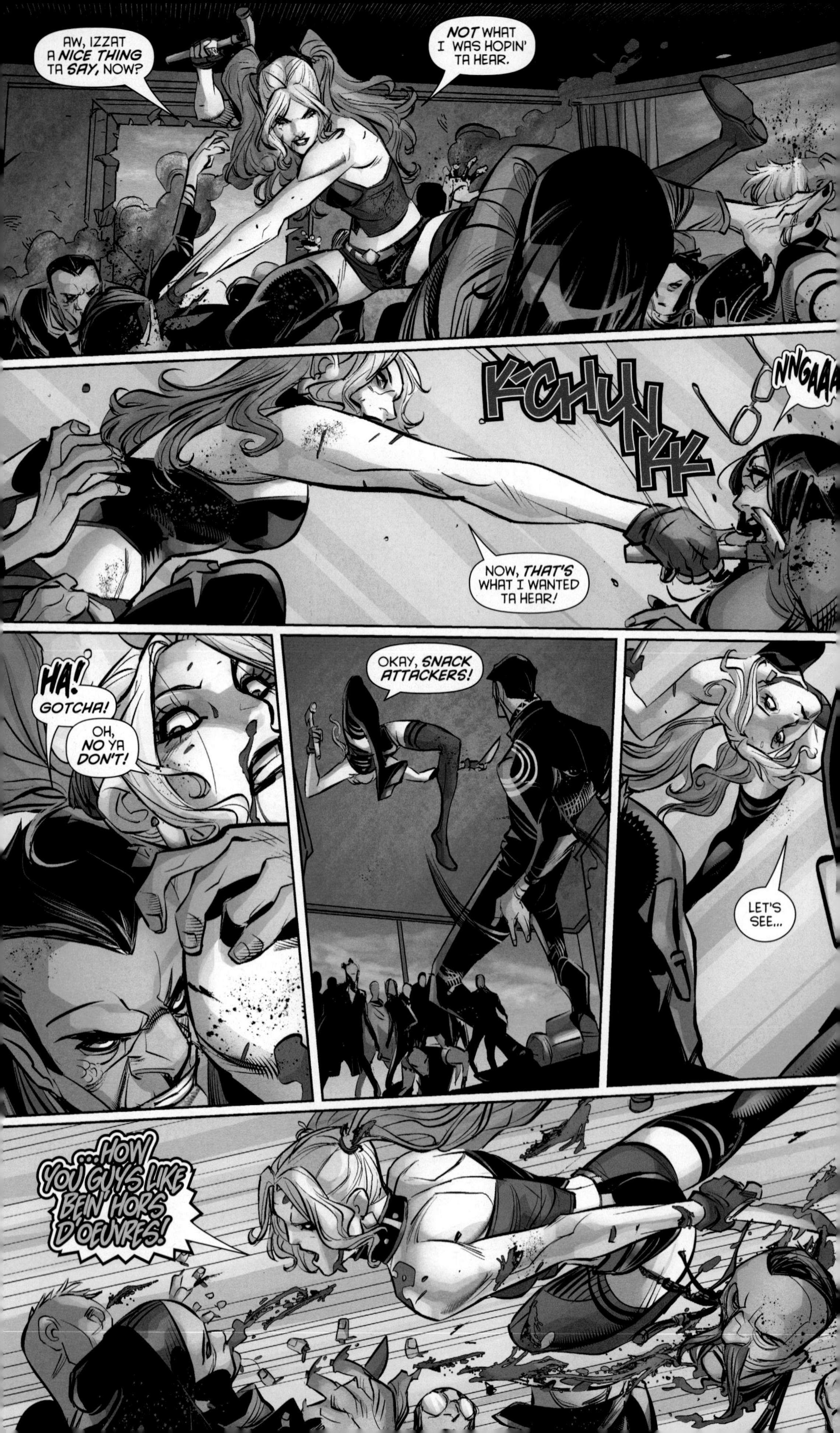
AW, IZZAT A NICE THING TA SAY, NOW?
NOT WHAT I WAS HOPIN' TA HEAR.
K'CHUNKK
NNGAAA
NOW, THAT'S WHAT I WANTED TA HEAR!
HA! GOTCHA!
OH, NO YA DON'T!
OKAY, SNACK ATTACKERS!
LET'S SEE...
...HOW YOU GUYS LIKE BEIN' HORS D'OEUVRES!

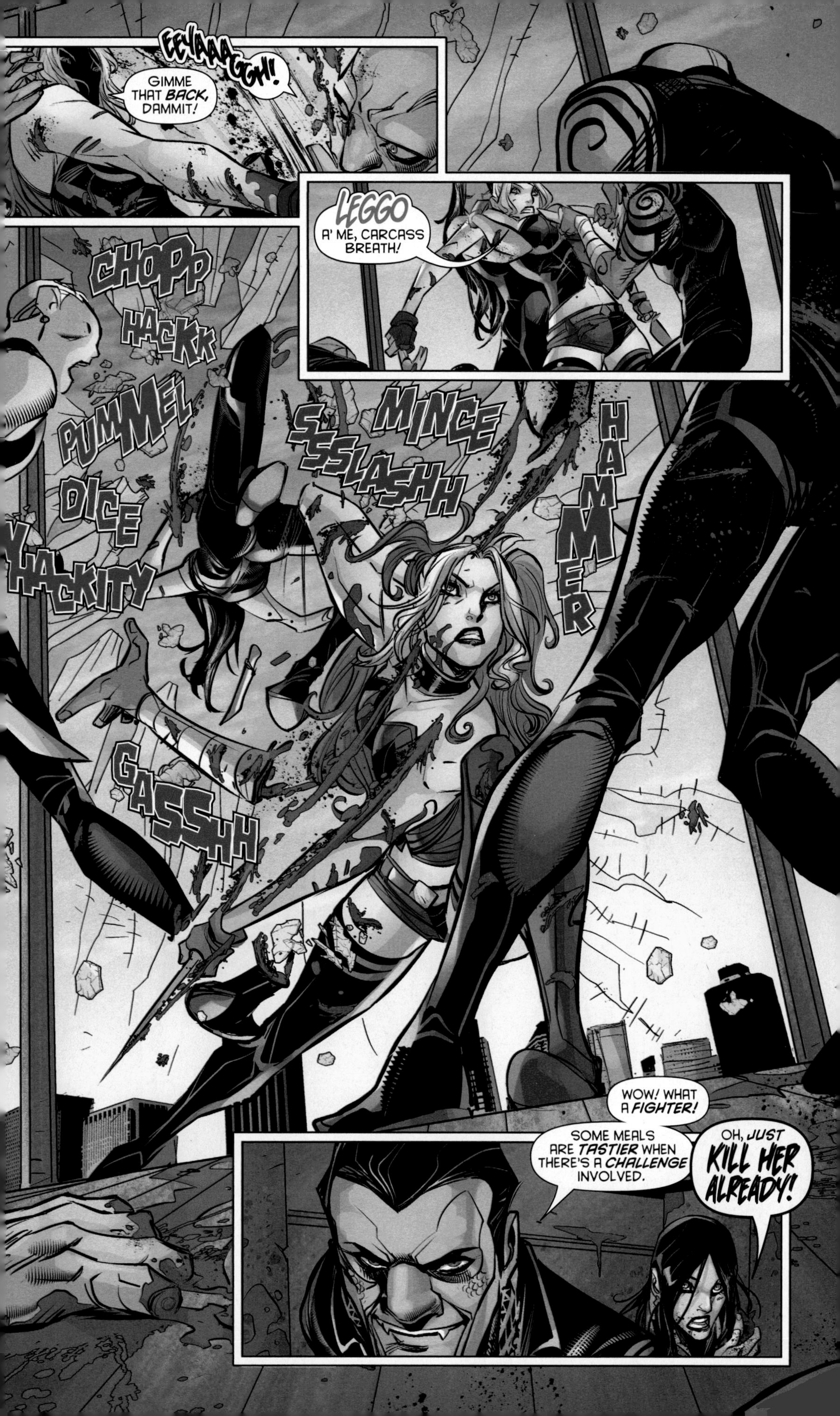
EEYAAAGGH!
GIMME THAT BACK, DAMMIT!
LEGGO A' ME, CARCASS BREATH!
CHOPP
HACKK
PUMMEL
DICE
HACKITY
MINCE
SSSLASHH
HAMMER
GASSHH
WOW! WHAT A FIGHTER!
SOME MEALS ARE TASTIER WHEN THERE'S A CHALLENGE INVOLVED.
OH, JUST KILL HER ALREADY!

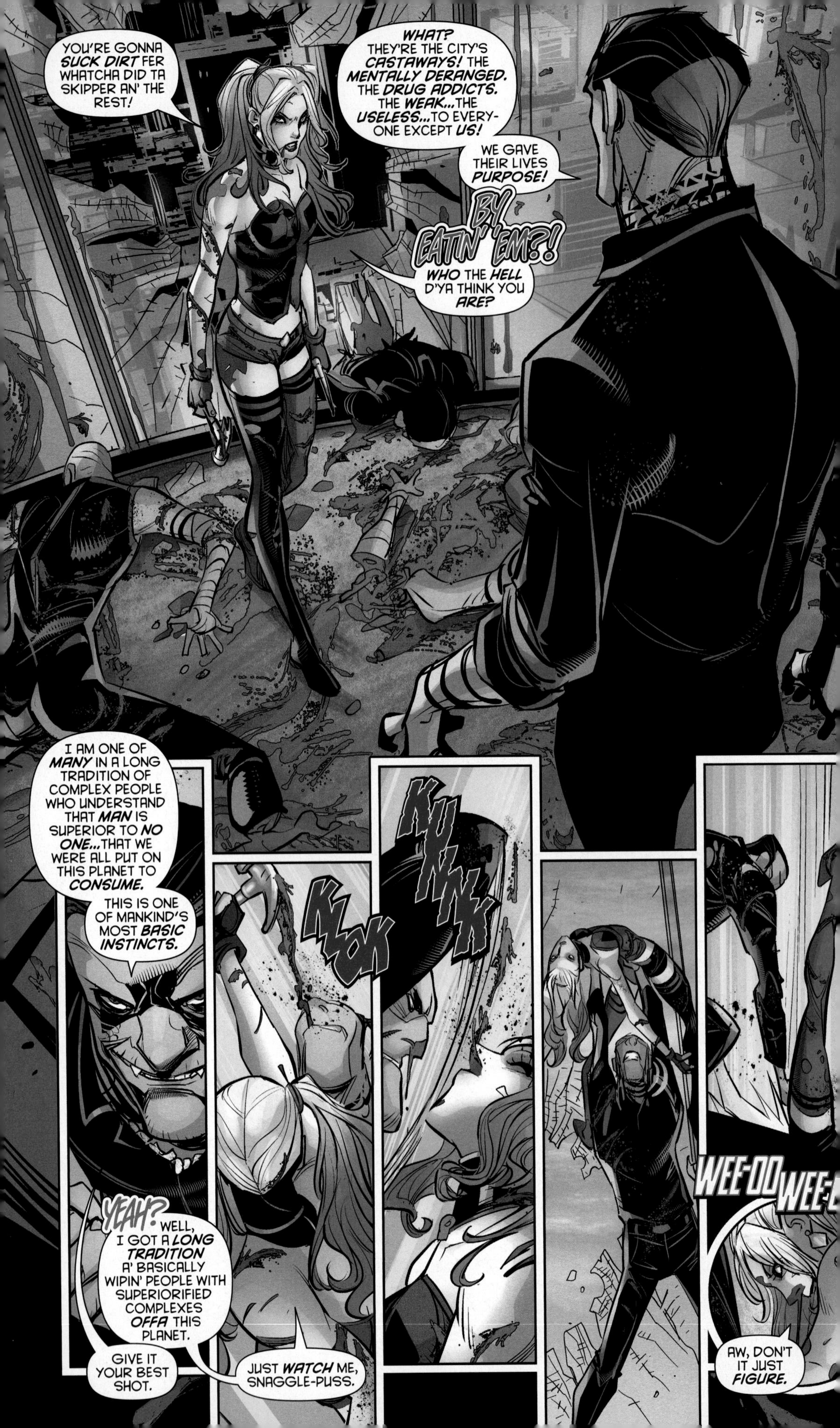

YOU'RE GONNA SUCK DIRT FER WHATCHA DID TA SKIPPER AN' THE REST!
WHAT? THEY'RE THE CITY'S CASTAWAYS! THE MENTALLY DERANGED. THE DRUG ADDICTS. THE WEAK...THE USELESS...TO EVERYONE EXCEPT US!
WE GAVE THEIR LIVES PURPOSE!
BY EATIN' 'EM?!
WHO THE HELL D'YA THINK YOU ARE?
I AM ONE OF MANY IN A LONG TRADITION OF COMPLEX PEOPLE WHO UNDERSTAND THAT MAN IS SUPERIOR TO NO ONE...THAT WE WERE ALL PUT ON THIS PLANET TO CONSUME.
THIS IS ONE OF MANKIND'S MOST BASIC INSTINCTS.
YEAH? WELL, I GOT A LONG TRADITION A' BASICALLY WIPIN' PEOPLE WITH SUPERIORIFIED COMPLEXES OFFA THIS PLANET.
GIVE IT YOUR BEST SHOT.
JUST WATCH ME, SNAGGLE-PUSS.
KLOK
KUNNK
WEE-OO WEE-
AW, DON'T IT JUST FIGURE.

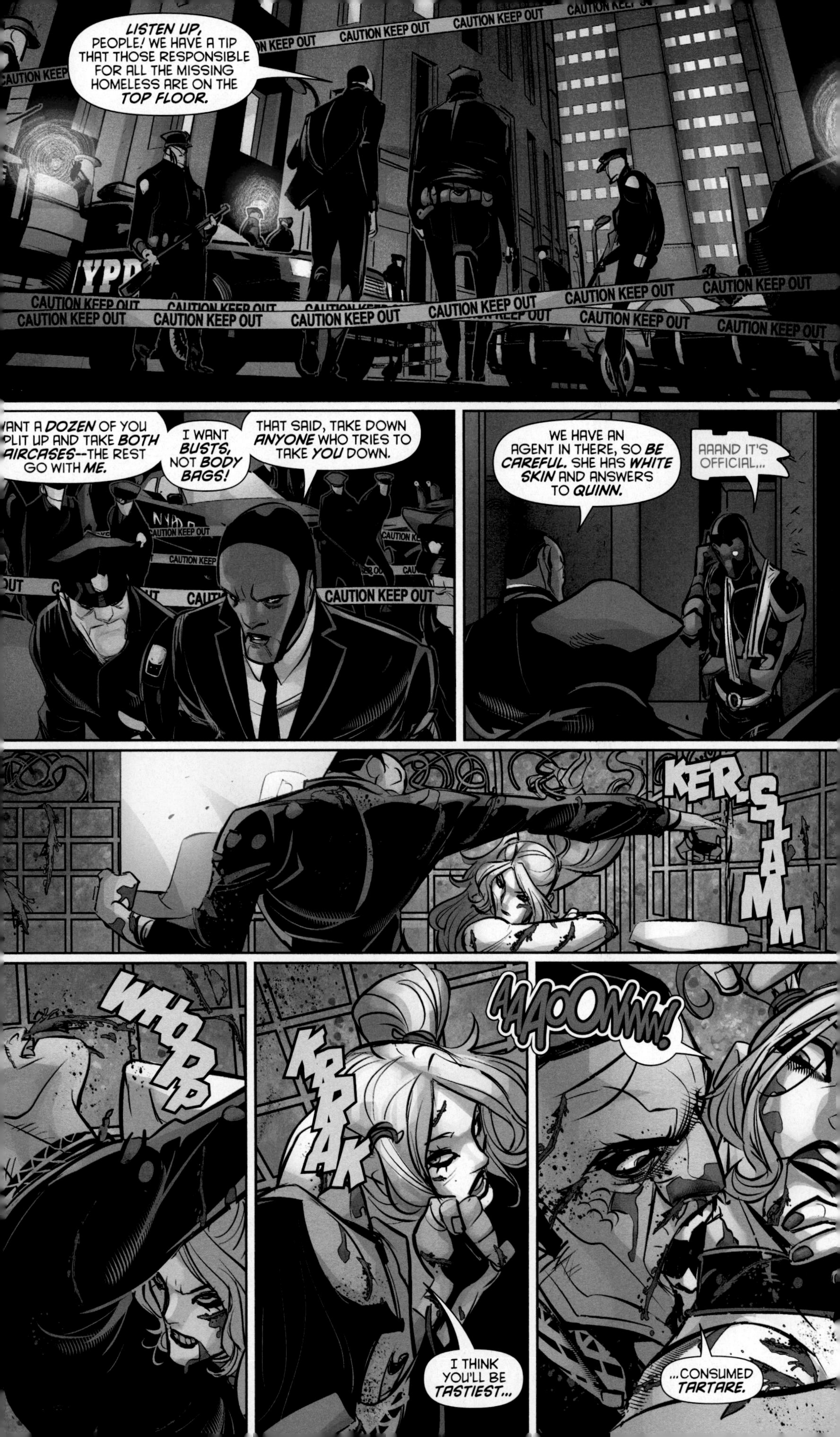
CAUTION KEEP OUT
LISTEN UP, PEOPLE! WE HAVE A TIP THAT THOSE RESPONSIBLE FOR ALL THE MISSING HOMELESS ARE ON THE TOP FLOOR.
NYPD
CAUTION KEEP OUT
WANT A DOZEN OF YOU PLIT UP AND TAKE BOTH AIRCASES--THE REST GO WITH ME.
I WANT BUSTS, NOT BODY BAGS!
THAT SAID, TAKE DOWN ANYONE WHO TRIES TO TAKE YOU DOWN.
CAUTION KEEP OUT
WE HAVE AN AGENT IN THERE, SO BE CAREFUL. SHE HAS WHITE SKIN AND ANSWERS TO QUINN.
AAAND IT'S OFFICIAL...
KER-SLAMM
WHOOD
KRAK
AAAOOWWW!
I THINK YOU'LL BE TASTIEST...
...CONSUMED TARTARE.

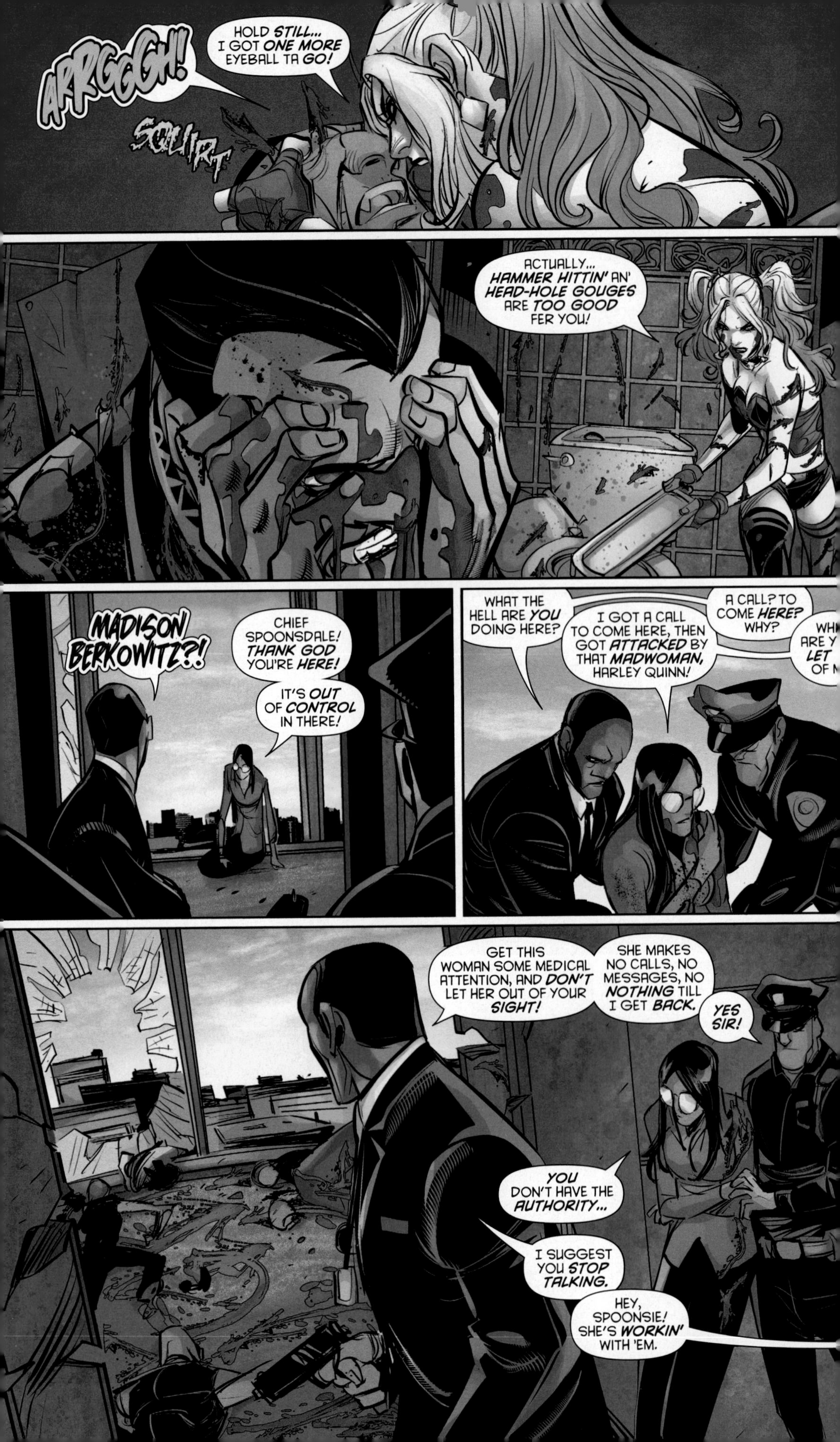
ARRGGGH!
HOLD STILL... I GOT ONE MORE EYEBALL TA GO!
SQUIRT
ACTUALLY... HAMMER HITTIN' AN' HEAD-HOLE GOUGES ARE TOO GOOD FER YOU!
MADISON BERKOWITZ?!
CHIEF SPOONSDALE! THANK GOD YOU'RE HERE!
IT'S OUT OF CONTROL IN THERE!
WHAT THE HELL ARE YOU DOING HERE?
I GOT A CALL TO COME HERE, THEN GOT ATTACKED BY THAT MADWOMAN, HARLEY QUINN!
A CALL? TO COME HERE? WHY?
GET THIS WOMAN SOME MEDICAL ATTENTION, AND DON'T LET HER OUT OF YOUR SIGHT!
SHE MAKES NO CALLS, NO MESSAGES, NO NOTHING TILL I GET BACK.
YES SIR!
YOU DON'T HAVE THE AUTHORITY...
I SUGGEST YOU STOP TALKING.
HEY, SPOONSIE! SHE'S WORKIN' WITH 'EM.

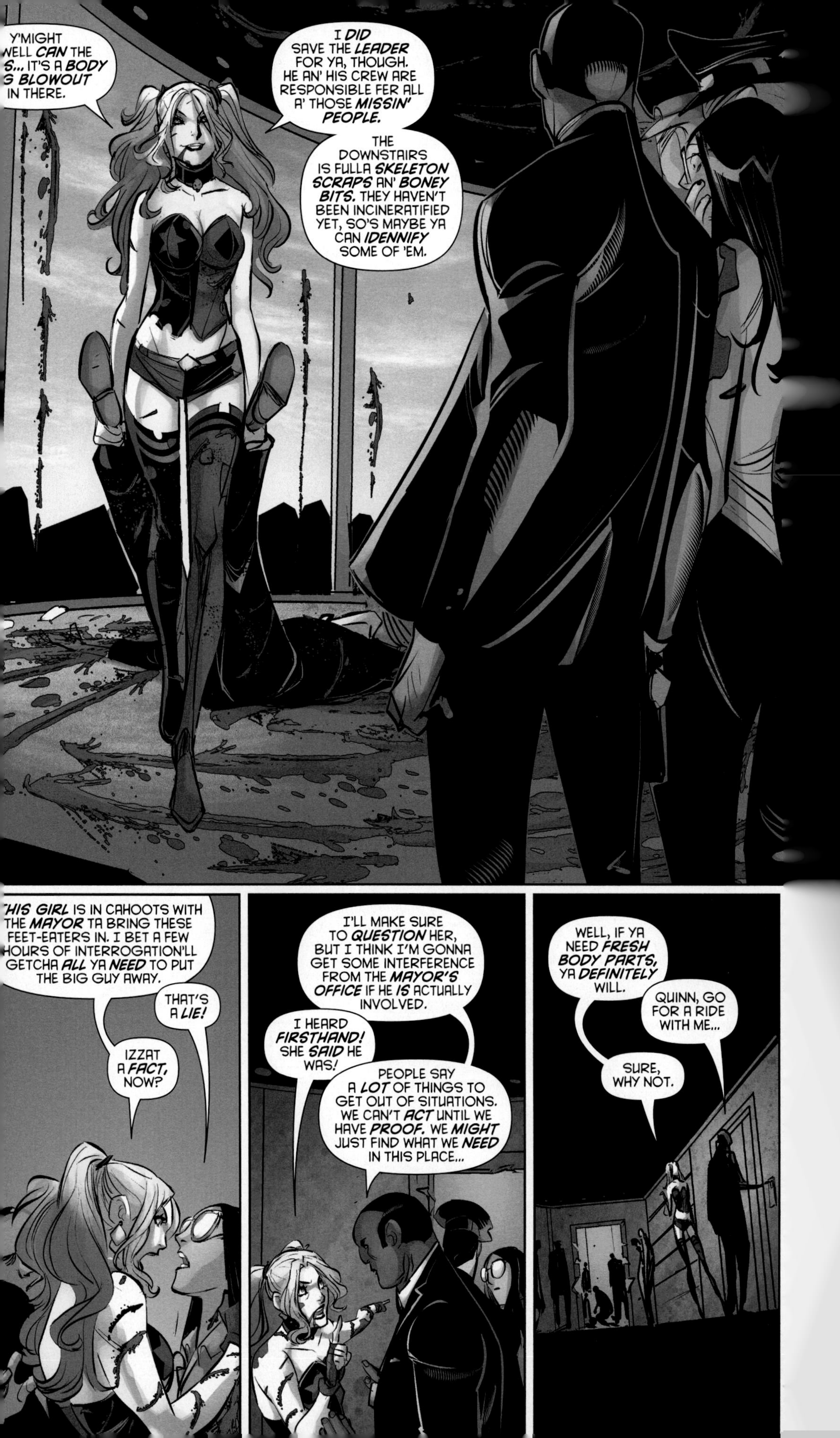
Y'MIGHT
WELL CAN THE
S... IT'S A BODY
G BLOWOUT
IN THERE.
I DID SAVE THE LEADER FOR YA, THOUGH. HE AN' HIS CREW ARE RESPONSIBLE FER ALL A' THOSE MISSIN' PEOPLE.
THE DOWNSTAIRS IS FULLA SKELETON SCRAPS AN' BONEY BITS. THEY HAVEN'T BEEN INCINERATIFIED YET, SO'S MAYBE YA CAN IDENNIFY SOME OF 'EM.
HIS GIRL IS IN CAHOOTS WITH THE MAYOR TA BRING THESE FEET-EATERS IN. I BET A FEW HOURS OF INTERROGATION'LL GETCHA ALL YA NEED TO PUT THE BIG GUY AWAY.
THAT'S A LIE!
IZZAT A FACT, NOW?
I'LL MAKE SURE TO QUESTION HER, BUT I THINK I'M GONNA GET SOME INTERFERENCE FROM THE MAYOR'S OFFICE IF HE IS ACTUALLY INVOLVED.
I HEARD FIRSTHAND! SHE SAID HE WAS!
PEOPLE SAY A LOT OF THINGS TO GET OUT OF SITUATIONS. WE CAN'T ACT UNTIL WE HAVE PROOF. WE MIGHT JUST FIND WHAT WE NEED IN THIS PLACE...
WELL, IF YA NEED FRESH BODY PARTS, YA DEFINITELY WILL.
QUINN, GO FOR A RIDE WITH ME...
SURE, WHY NOT.

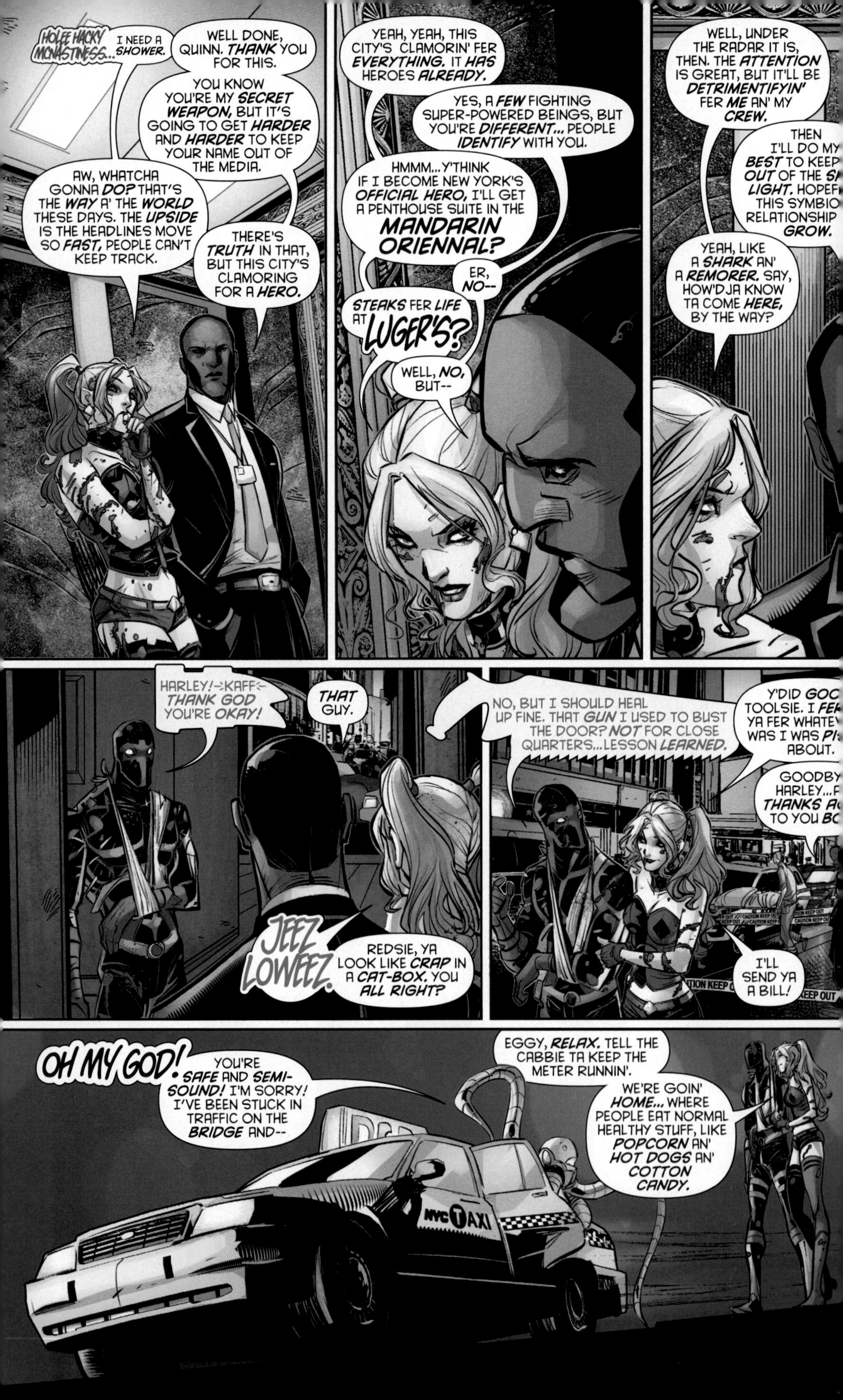

HOLEE HACKY MCNASTINESS...
I NEED A SHOWER.
WELL DONE, QUINN. THANK YOU FOR THIS.
YOU KNOW YOU'RE MY SECRET WEAPON, BUT IT'S GOING TO GET HARDER AND HARDER TO KEEP YOUR NAME OUT OF THE MEDIA.
AW, WHATCHA GONNA DO? THAT'S THE WAY A' THE WORLD THESE DAYS. THE UPSIDE IS THE HEADLINES MOVE SO FAST, PEOPLE CAN'T KEEP TRACK.
THERE'S TRUTH IN THAT, BUT THIS CITY'S CLAMORING FOR A HERO.
YEAH, YEAH, THIS CITY'S CLAMORIN' FER EVERYTHING. IT HAS HEROES ALREADY.
YES, A FEW FIGHTING SUPER-POWERED BEINGS, BUT YOU'RE DIFFERENT... PEOPLE IDENTIFY WITH YOU.
HMMM...Y'THINK IF I BECOME NEW YORK'S OFFICIAL HERO, I'LL GET A PENTHOUSE SUITE IN THE MANDARIN ORIENNAL?
ER, NO--
STEAKS FER LIFE AT LUGER'S?
WELL, NO, BUT--
WELL, UNDER THE RADAR IT IS, THEN. THE ATTENTION IS GREAT, BUT IT'LL BE DETRIMENTIFYIN' FER ME AN' MY CREW.
THEN I'LL DO MY BEST TO KEEP OUT OF THE
LIGHT. HOPEF
THIS SYMBIO
RELATIONSHIP
GROW.
YEAH, LIKE A SHARK AN' A REMORER. SAY, HOW'DJA KNOW TA COME HERE, BY THE WAY?
HARLEY! -KAFF- THANK GOD YOU'RE OKAY!
THAT GUY.
JEEZ LOWEEZ.
REDSIE, YA LOOK LIKE CRAP IN A CAT-BOX. YOU ALL RIGHT?
NO, BUT I SHOULD HEAL UP FINE. THAT GUN I USED TO BUST THE DOOR? NOT FOR CLOSE QUARTERS...LESSON LEARNED.
Y'DID
TOOLSIE. I
YA FER WHATE
WAS I WAS
ABOUT.
GOODBY
HARLEY...
THANKS
TO YOU
I'LL SEND YA A BILL!
OH MY GOD!
YOU'RE SAFE AND SEMI-SOUND! I'M SORRY! I'VE BEEN STUCK IN TRAFFIC ON THE BRIDGE AND--
EGGY, RELAX. TELL THE CABBIE TA KEEP THE METER RUNNIN'.
WE'RE GOIN' HOME... WHERE PEOPLE EAT NORMAL HEALTHY STUFF, LIKE POPCORN AN' HOT DOGS AN' COTTON CANDY.
NYC TAXI

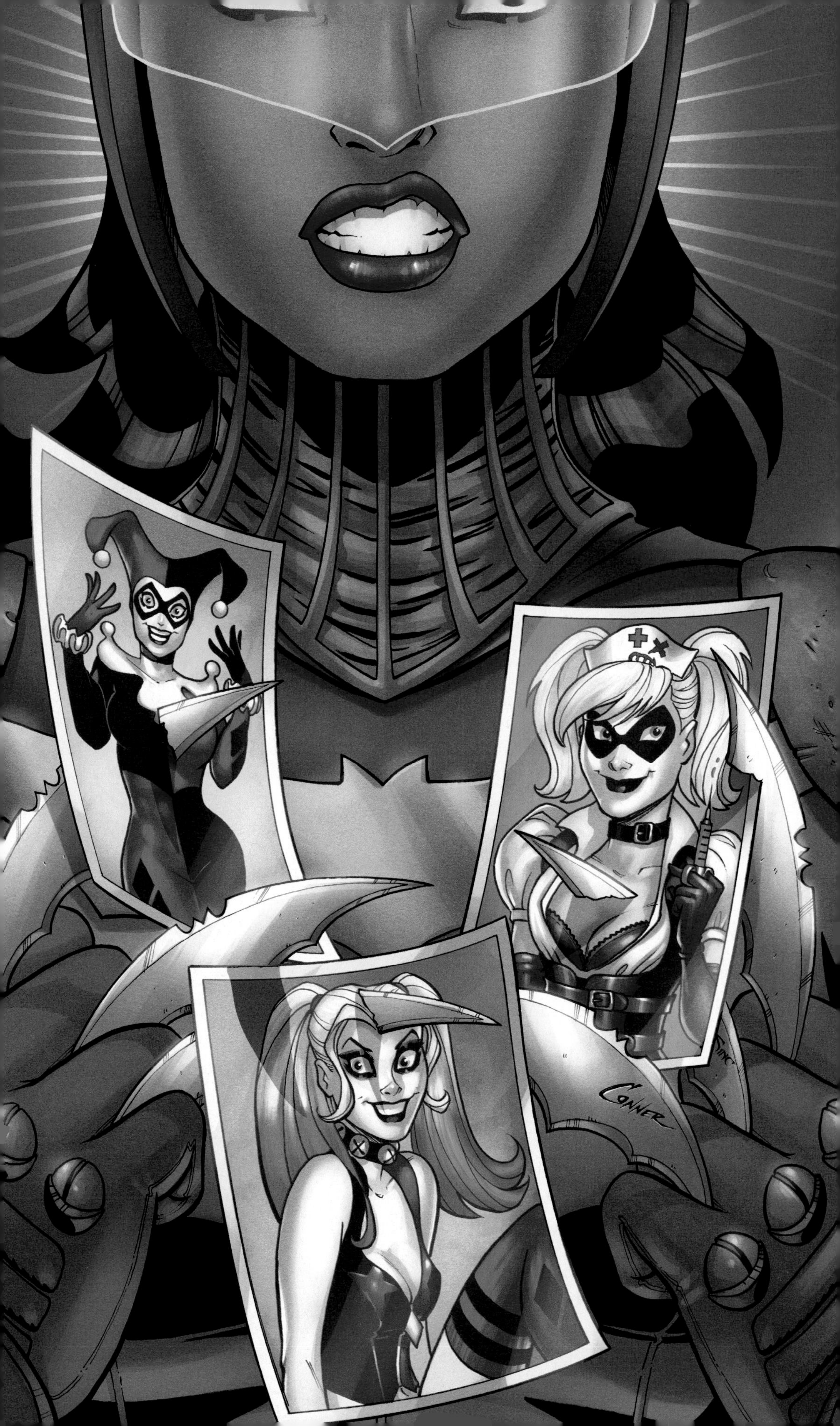
CONNER

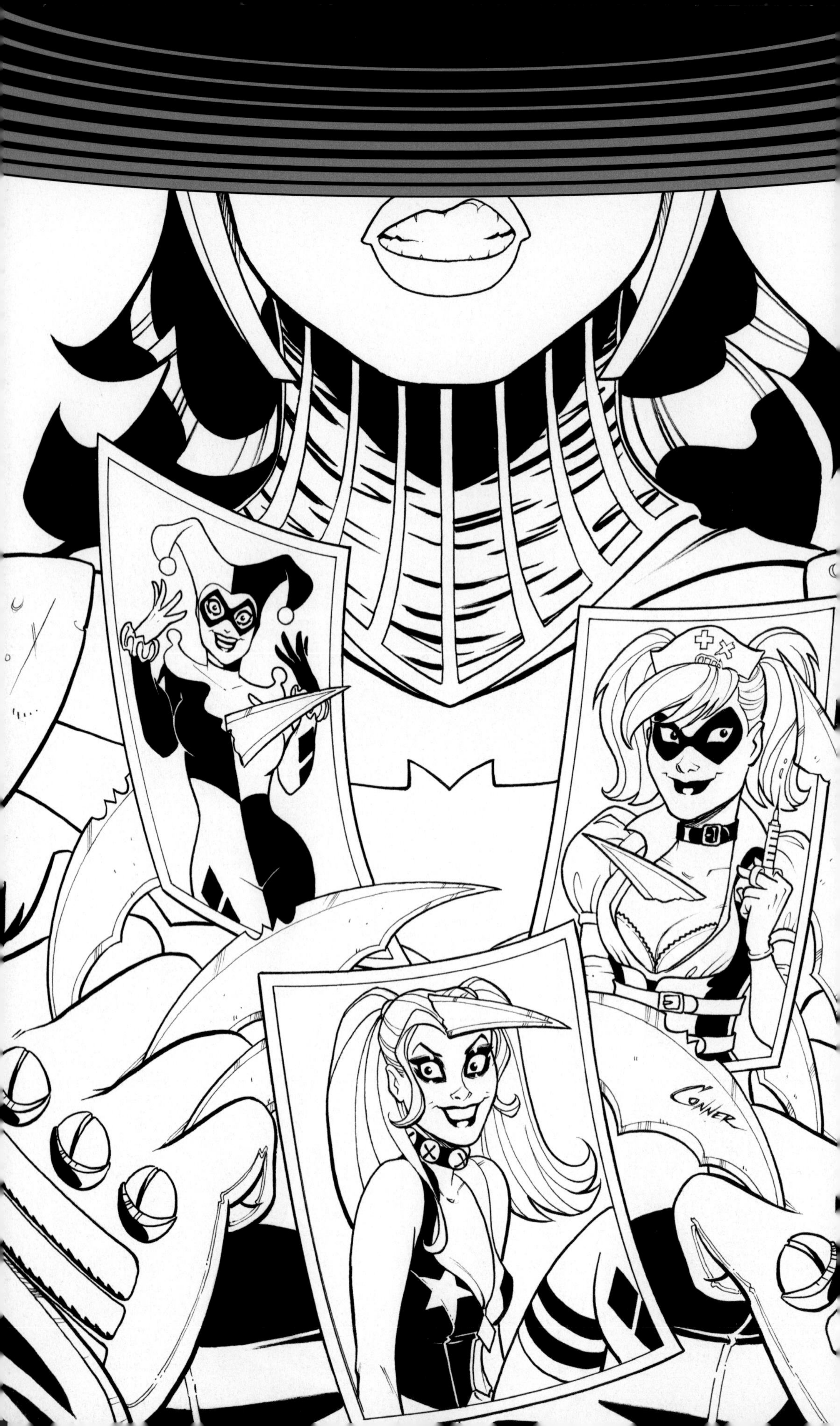
CONNER

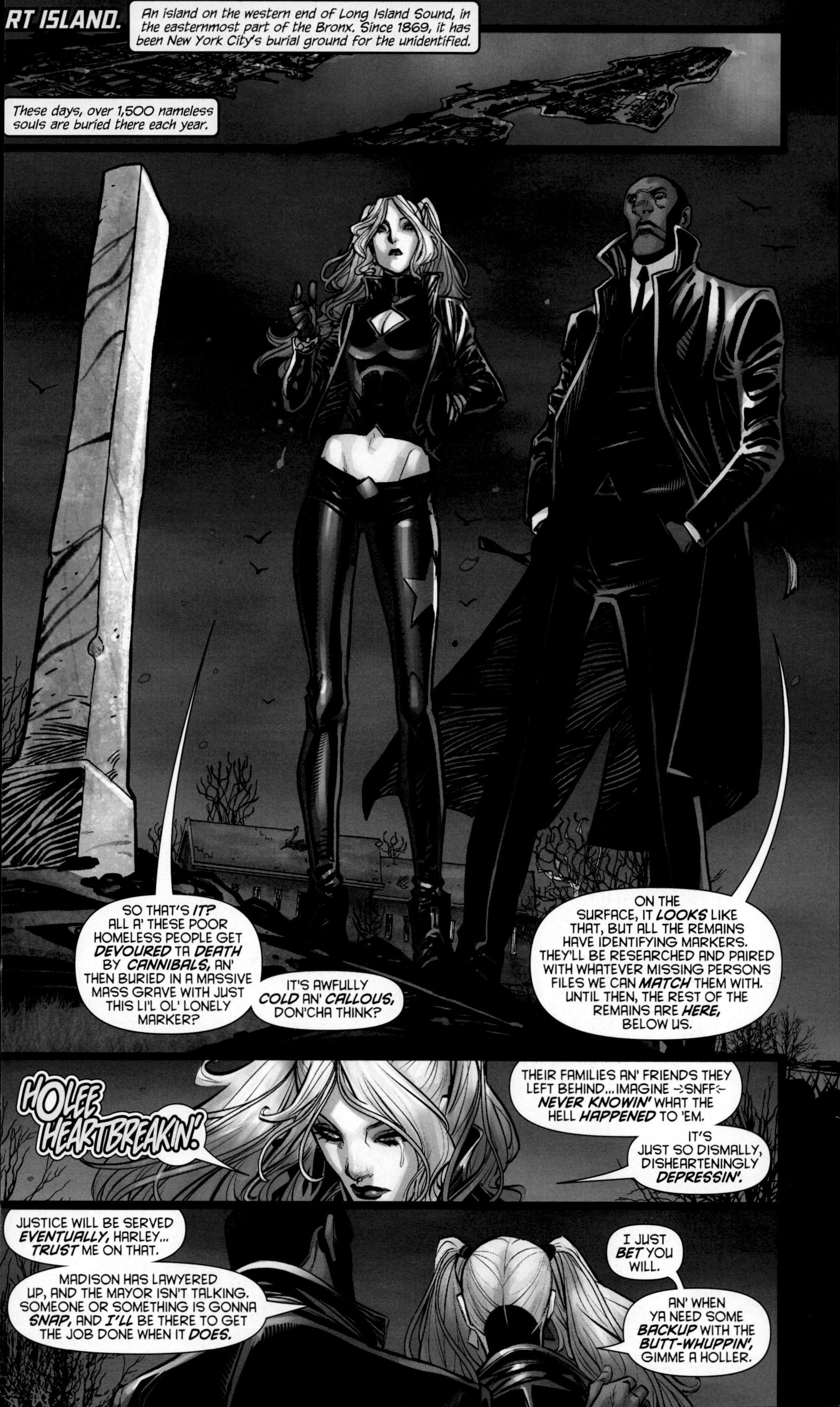

RT ISLAND.
An island on the western end of Long Island Sound, in the easternmost part of the Bronx. Since 1869, it has been New York City's burial ground for the unidentified.
These days, over 1,500 nameless souls are buried there each year.
SO THAT'S IT? ALL A' THESE POOR HOMELESS PEOPLE GET DEVOURED TA DEATH BY CANNIBALS, AN' THEN BURIED IN A MASSIVE MASS GRAVE WITH JUST THIS LI'L OL' LONELY MARKER?
IT'S AWFULLY COLD AN' CALLOUS, DON'CHA THINK?
ON THE SURFACE, IT LOOKS LIKE THAT, BUT ALL THE REMAINS HAVE IDENTIFYING MARKERS. THEY'LL BE RESEARCHED AND PAIRED WITH WHATEVER MISSING PERSONS FILES WE CAN MATCH THEM WITH. UNTIL THEN, THE REST OF THE REMAINS ARE HERE, BELOW US.
HOLEE HEARTBREAKIN'.
THEIR FAMILIES AN' FRIENDS THEY LEFT BEHIND... IMAGINE ->SNFF<- NEVER KNOWIN' WHAT THE HELL HAPPENED TO 'EM.
IT'S JUST SO DISMALLY, DISHEARTENINGLY DEPRESSIN'.
JUSTICE WILL BE SERVED EVENTUALLY, HARLEY... TRUST ME ON THAT.
MADISON HAS LAWYERED UP, AND THE MAYOR ISN'T TALKING. SOMEONE OR SOMETHING IS GONNA SNAP, AND I'LL BE THERE TO GET THE JOB DONE WHEN IT DOES.
I JUST BET YOU WILL.
AN' WHEN YA NEED SOME BACKUP WITH THE BUTT-WHUPPIN', GIMME A HOLLER.

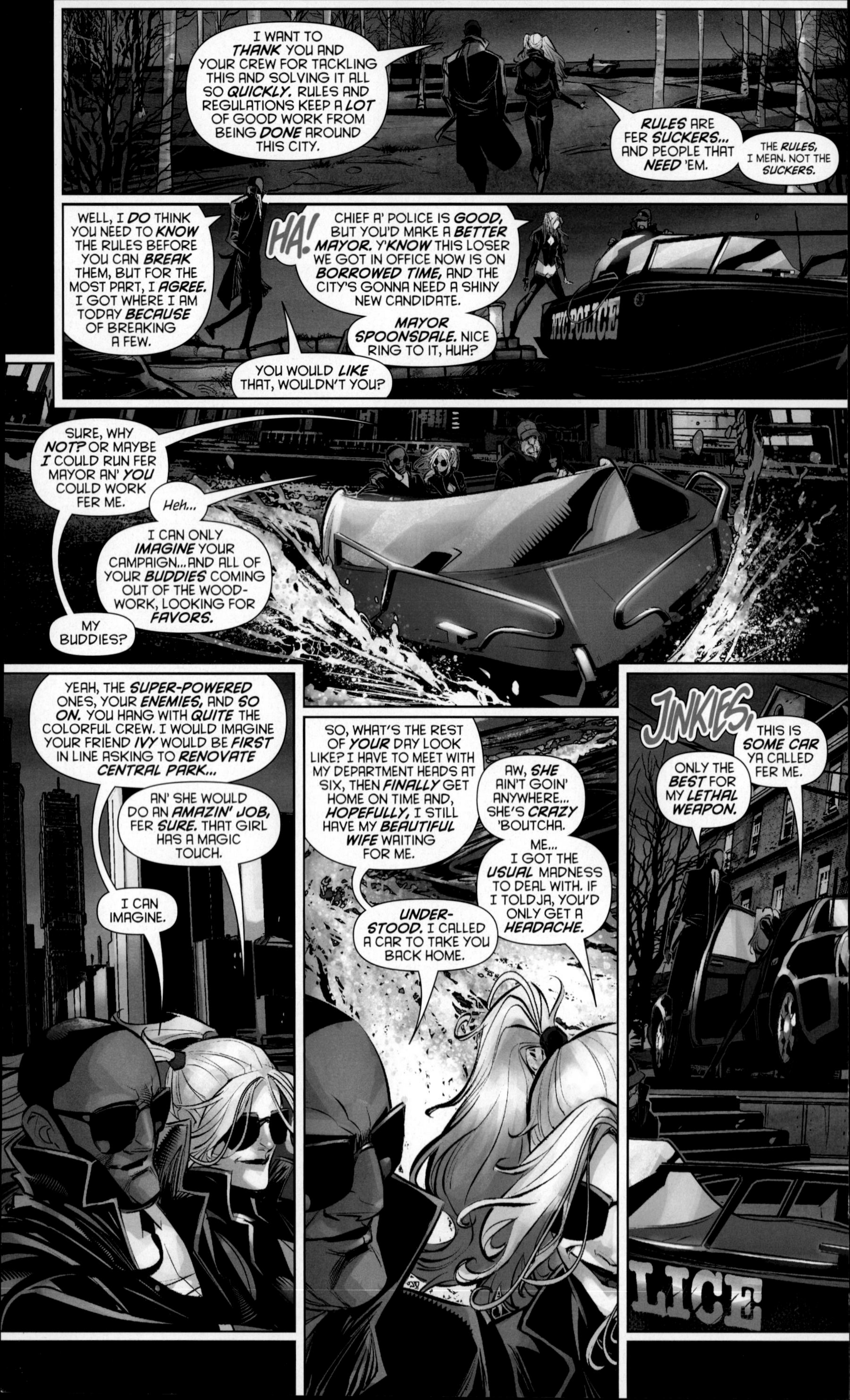
I WANT TO THANK YOU AND YOUR CREW FOR TACKLING THIS AND SOLVING IT ALL SO QUICKLY. RULES AND REGULATIONS KEEP A LOT OF GOOD WORK FROM BEING DONE AROUND THIS CITY.
RULES ARE FER SUCKERS... AND PEOPLE THAT NEED 'EM.
THE RULES, I MEAN. NOT THE SUCKERS.
WELL, I DO THINK YOU NEED TO KNOW THE RULES BEFORE YOU CAN BREAK THEM, BUT FOR THE MOST PART, I AGREE. I GOT WHERE I AM TODAY BECAUSE OF BREAKING A FEW.
HA!
CHIEF A' POLICE IS GOOD, BUT YOU'D MAKE A BETTER MAYOR. Y'KNOW THIS LOSER WE GOT IN OFFICE NOW IS ON BORROWED TIME, AND THE CITY'S GONNA NEED A SHINY NEW CANDIDATE.
MAYOR SPOONSDALE. NICE RING TO IT, HUH?
YOU WOULD LIKE THAT, WOULDN'T YOU?
NYC POLICE
SURE, WHY NOT? OR MAYBE I COULD RUN FER MAYOR AN' YOU COULD WORK FER ME.
Heh...
I CAN ONLY IMAGINE YOUR CAMPAIGN...AND ALL OF YOUR BUDDIES COMING OUT OF THE WOOD-WORK, LOOKING FOR FAVORS.
MY BUDDIES?
YEAH, THE SUPER-POWERED ONES, YOUR ENEMIES, AND SO ON. YOU HANG WITH QUITE THE COLORFUL CREW. I WOULD IMAGINE YOUR FRIEND IVY WOULD BE FIRST IN LINE ASKING TO RENOVATE CENTRAL PARK...
AN' SHE WOULD DO AN AMAZIN' JOB, FER SURE. THAT GIRL HAS A MAGIC TOUCH.
I CAN IMAGINE.
SO, WHAT'S THE REST OF YOUR DAY LOOK LIKE? I HAVE TO MEET WITH MY DEPARTMENT HEADS AT SIX, THEN FINALLY GET HOME ON TIME AND, HOPEFULLY, I STILL HAVE MY BEAUTIFUL WIFE WAITING FOR ME.
AW, SHE AIN'T GOIN' ANYWHERE... SHE'S CRAZY 'BOUTCHA.
ME... I GOT THE USUAL MADNESS TO DEAL WITH. IF I TOLDJA, YOU'D ONLY GET A HEADACHE.
UNDER-STOOD. I CALLED A CAR TO TAKE YOU BACK HOME.
JINKIES,
THIS IS SOME CAR YA CALLED FER ME.
ONLY THE BEST FOR MY LETHAL WEAPON.
LICE

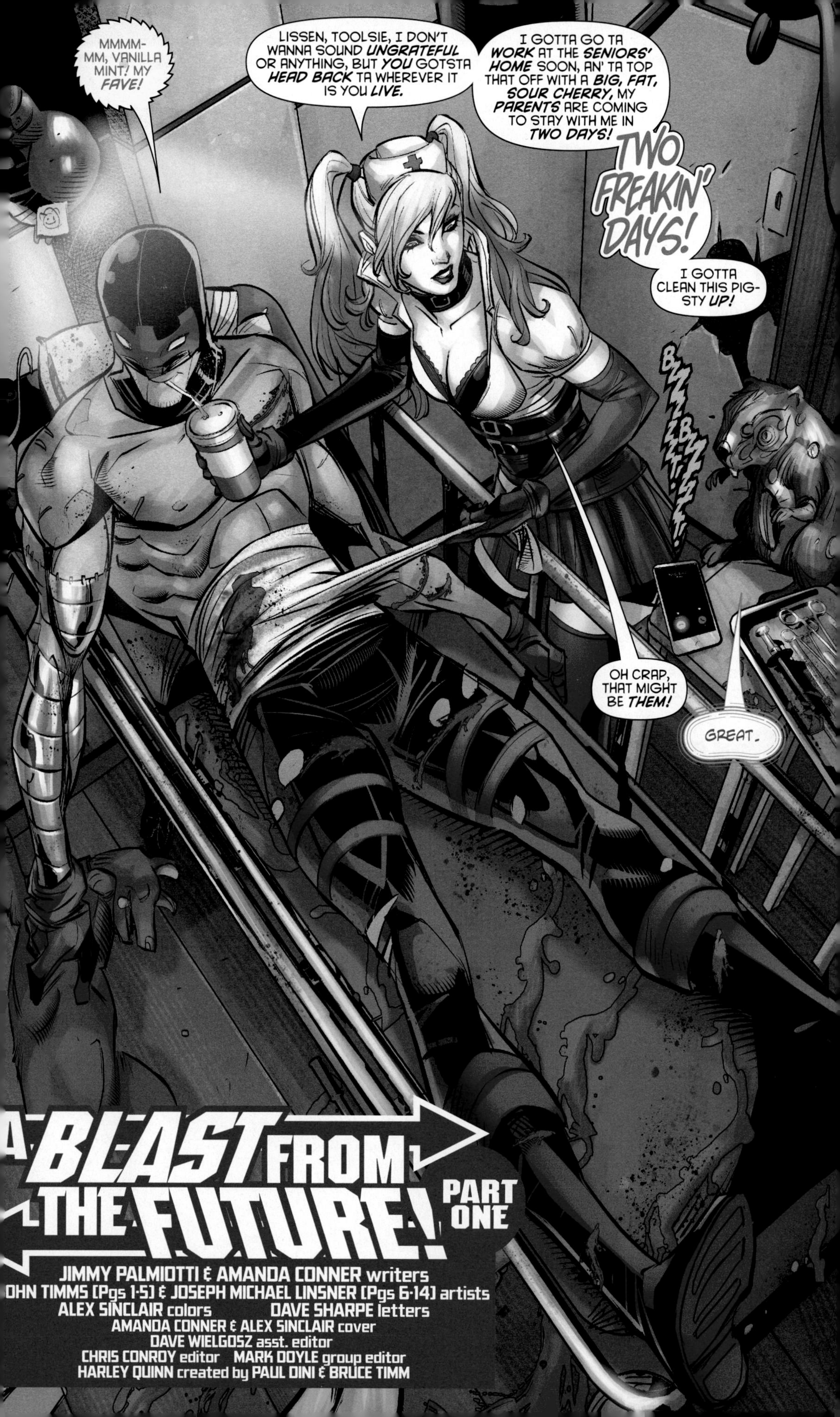
MMMM-MM, VANILLA MINT! MY FAVE!
LISSEN, TOOLSIE, I DON'T WANNA SOUND UNGRATEFUL OR ANYTHING, BUT YOU GOTSTA HEAD BACK TA WHEREVER IT IS YOU LIVE.
I GOTTA GO TA WORK AT THE SENIORS' HOME SOON, AN' TA TOP THAT OFF WITH A BIG, FAT, SOUR CHERRY, MY PARENTS ARE COMING TO STAY WITH ME IN TWO DAYS!
TWO FREAKIN' DAYS!
I GOTTA CLEAN THIS PIG-STY UP!
BZZ BZZ
OH CRAP, THAT MIGHT BE THEM!
GREAT.
A BLAST FROM THE FUTURE! PART ONE
JIMMY PALMIOTTI & AMANDA CONNER writers
OHN TIMMS [Pgs 1-5] & JOSEPH MICHAEL LINSNER [Pgs 6-14] artists
ALEX SINCLAIR colors DAVE SHARPE letters
AMANDA CONNER & ALEX SINCLAIR cover
DAVE WIELGOSZ asst. editor
CHRIS CONROY editor MARK DOYLE group editor
HARLEY QUINN created by PAUL DINI & BRUCE TIMM

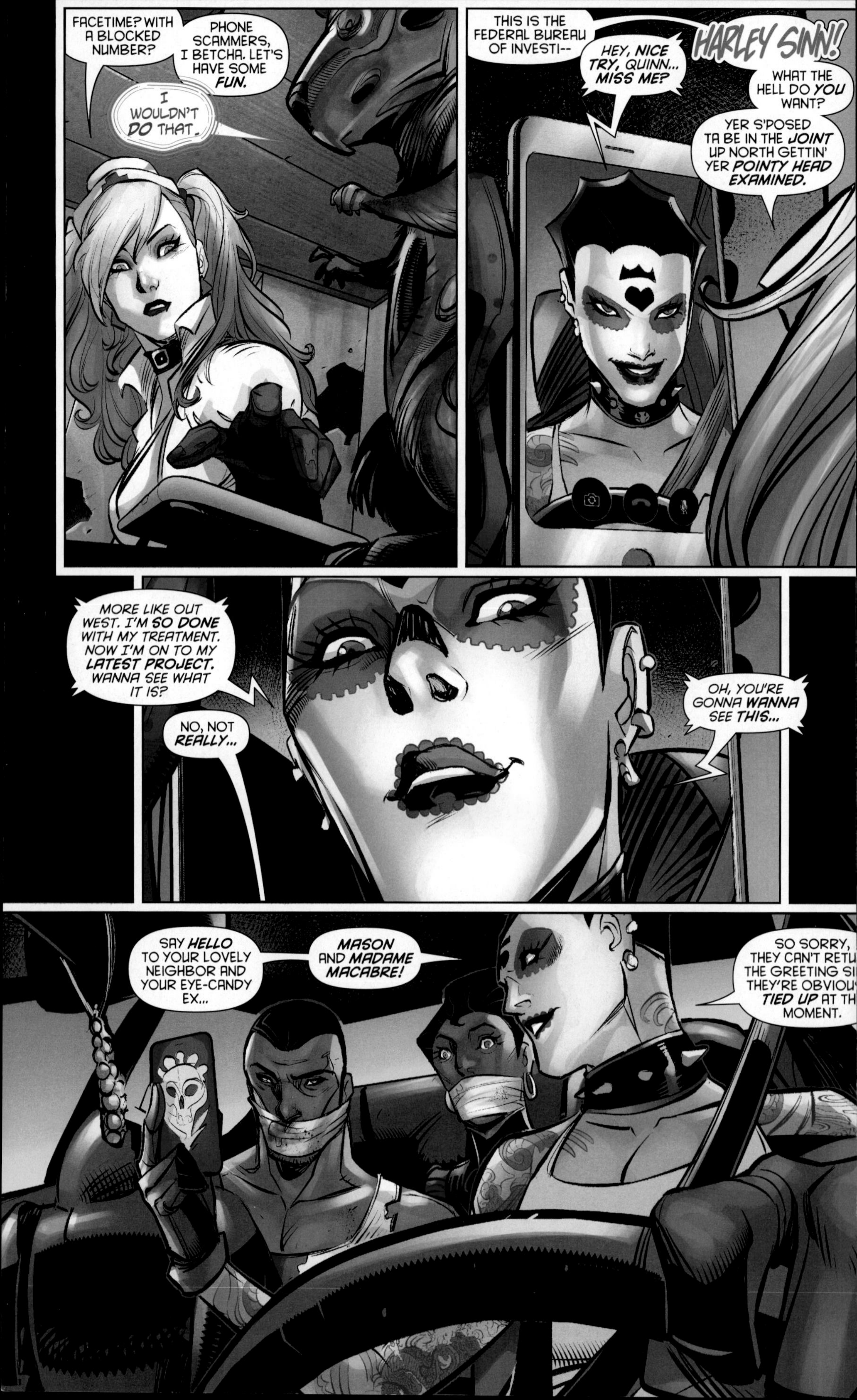
FACETIME? WITH A BLOCKED NUMBER?
PHONE SCAMMERS, I BETCHA. LET'S HAVE SOME FUN.
I WOULDN'T DO THAT.
THIS IS THE FEDERAL BUREAU OF INVESTI--
HEY, NICE TRY, QUINN... MISS ME?
HARLEY SINN!
WHAT THE HELL DO YOU WANT?
YER S'POSED TA BE IN THE JOINT UP NORTH GETTIN' YER POINTY HEAD EXAMINED.
MORE LIKE OUT WEST. I'M SO DONE WITH MY TREATMENT. NOW I'M ON TO MY LATEST PROJECT. WANNA SEE WHAT IT IS?
NO, NOT REALLY...
OH, YOU'RE GONNA WANNA SEE THIS...
SAY HELLO TO YOUR LOVELY NEIGHBOR AND YOUR EYE-CANDY EX...
MASON AND MADAME MACABRE!
SO SORRY, THEY CAN'T RETU THE GREETING SI THEY'RE OBVIOU TIED UP AT TH MOMENT.

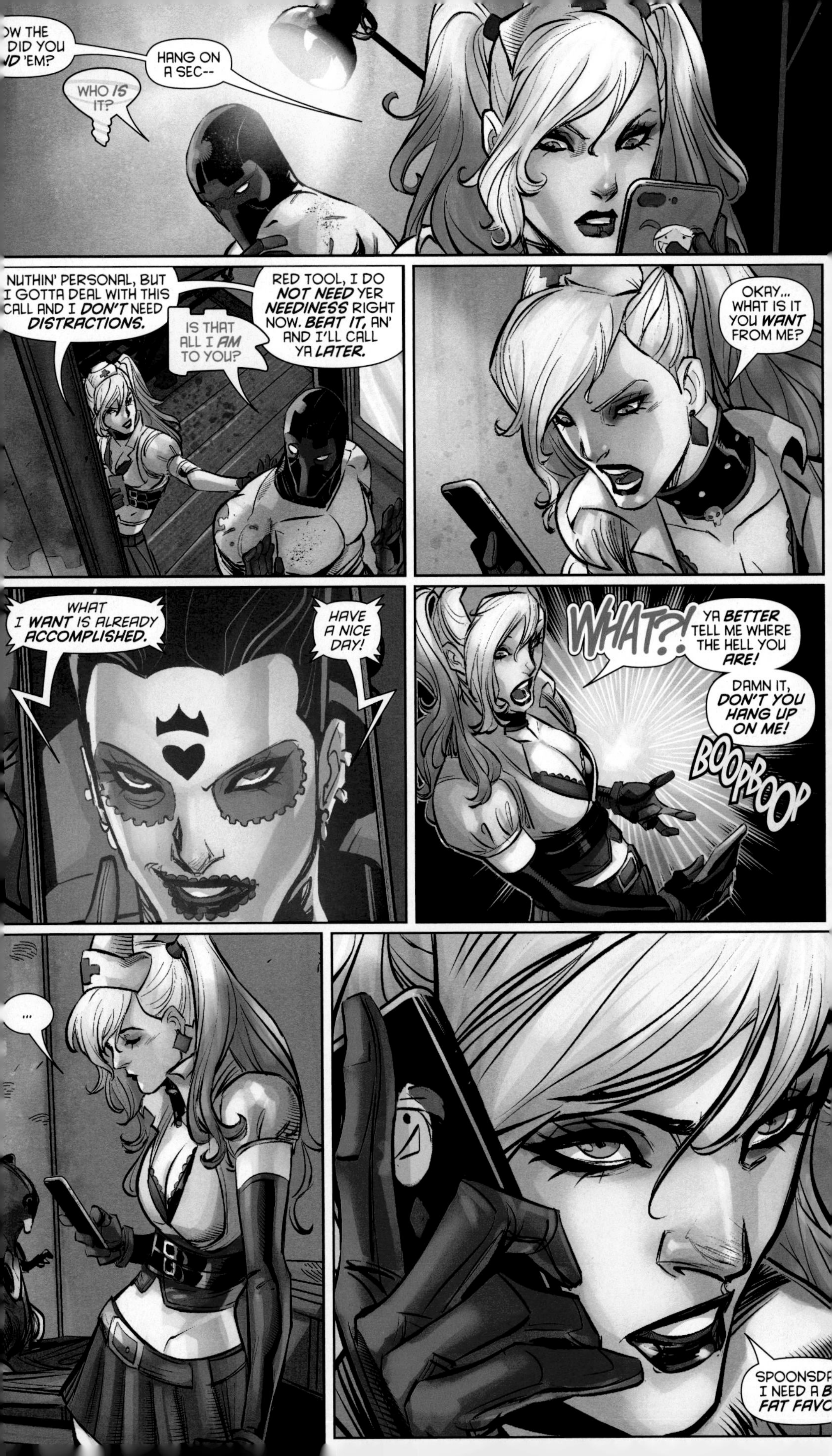
OW THE DID YOU ND 'EM?
HANG ON A SEC--
WHO *IS* IT?
NUTHIN' PERSONAL, BUT I GOTTA DEAL WITH THIS CALL AND I *DON'T* NEED *DISTRACTIONS.*
IS THAT ALL I *AM* TO YOU?
RED TOOL, I DO *NOT NEED* YER *NEEDINESS* RIGHT NOW. *BEAT IT,* AN' AND I'LL CALL YA *LATER.*
OKAY... WHAT IS IT YOU *WANT* FROM ME?
WHAT I *WANT* IS ALREADY *ACCOMPLISHED.*
HAVE A NICE DAY!
WHAT?!
YA *BETTER* TELL ME WHERE THE HELL YOU *ARE!*
DAMN IT, *DON'T YOU HANG UP ON ME!*
BOOPBOOP
...
SPOONSDR I NEED A B FAT FAVO

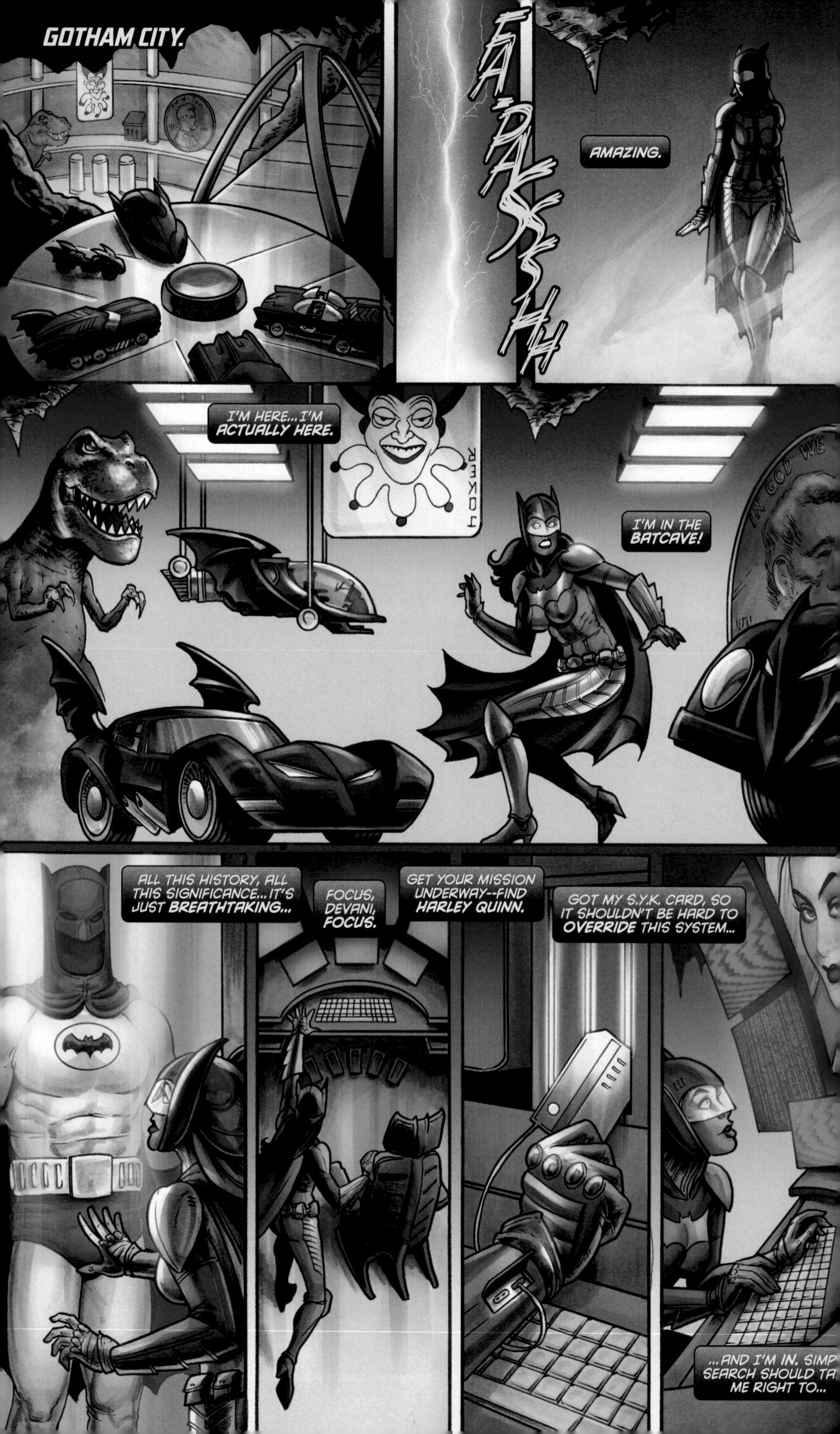
GOTHAM CITY.
FZAPASSHHH
AMAZING.
I'M HERE... I'M ACTUALLY HERE.
JOKER
I'M IN THE BATCAVE!
IN GOD WE
ALL THIS HISTORY, ALL THIS SIGNIFICANCE... IT'S JUST BREATHTAKING...
FOCUS, DEVANI, FOCUS.
GET YOUR MISSION UNDERWAY--FIND HARLEY QUINN.
GOT MY S.Y.K. CARD, SO IT SHOULDN'T BE HARD TO OVERRIDE THIS SYSTEM...
...AND I'M IN. SIMP
SEARCH SHOULD TA
ME RIGHT TO...

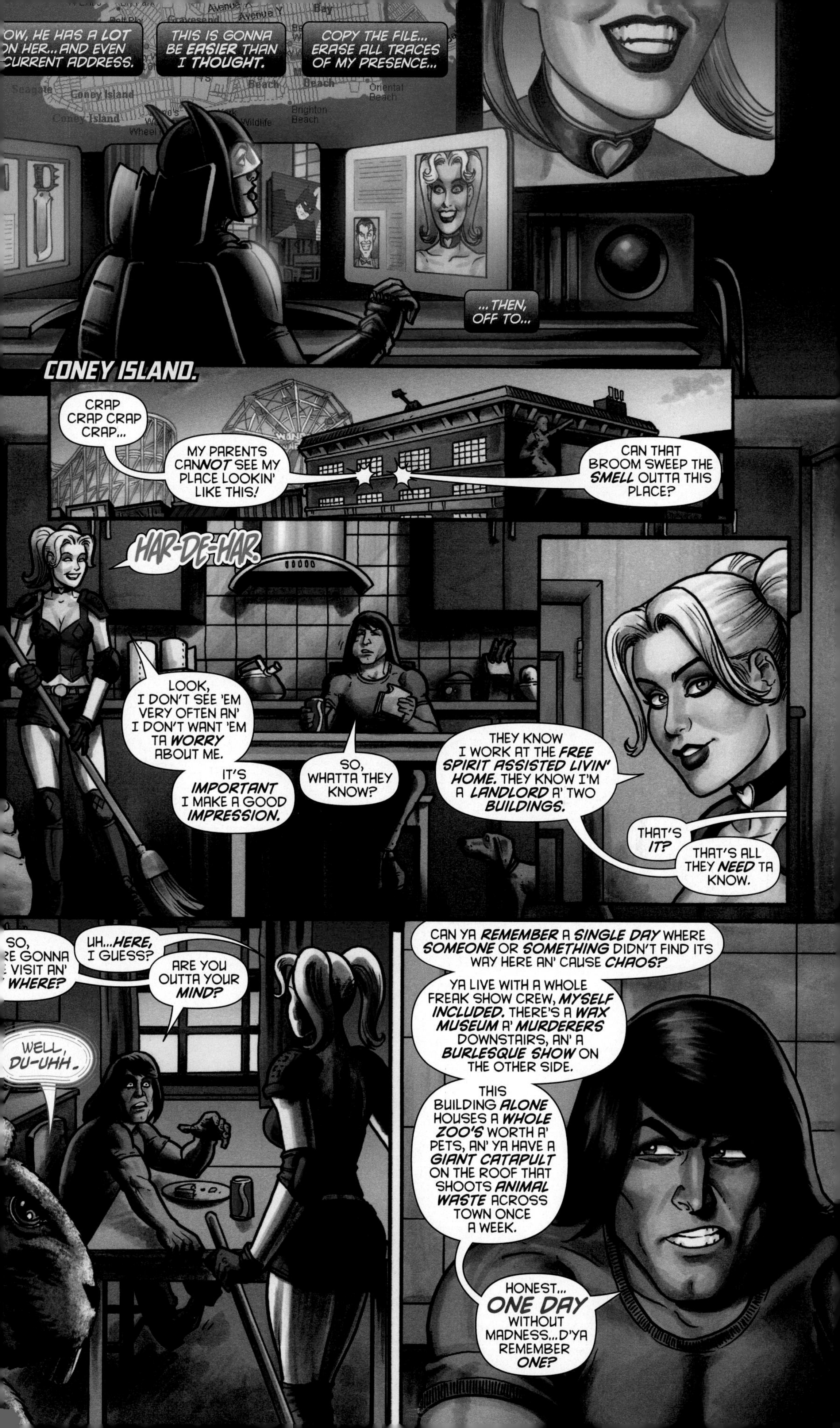

OW, HE HAS A LOT ON HER... AND EVEN CURRENT ADDRESS.
THIS IS GONNA BE EASIER THAN I THOUGHT.
COPY THE FILE... ERASE ALL TRACES OF MY PRESENCE...
...THEN, OFF TO...
CONEY ISLAND.
CRAP CRAP CRAP CRAP...
MY PARENTS CANNOT SEE MY PLACE LOOKIN' LIKE THIS!
CAN THAT BROOM SWEEP THE SMELL OUTTA THIS PLACE?
HAR-DE-HAR.
LOOK, I DON'T SEE 'EM VERY OFTEN AN' I DON'T WANT 'EM TA WORRY ABOUT ME.
IT'S IMPORTANT I MAKE A GOOD IMPRESSION.
SO, WHATTA THEY KNOW?
THEY KNOW I WORK AT THE FREE SPIRIT ASSISTED LIVIN' HOME. THEY KNOW I'M A LANDLORD A' TWO BUILDINGS.
THAT'S IT?
THAT'S ALL THEY NEED TA KNOW.
SO, RE GONNA VISIT AN' WHERE?
UH...HERE, I GUESS?
ARE YOU OUTTA YOUR MIND?
WELL, DU-UHH.
CAN YA REMEMBER A SINGLE DAY WHERE SOMEONE OR SOMETHING DIDN'T FIND ITS WAY HERE AN' CAUSE CHAOS?
YA LIVE WITH A WHOLE FREAK SHOW CREW, MYSELF INCLUDED. THERE'S A WAX MUSEUM A' MURDERERS DOWNSTAIRS, AN' A BURLESQUE SHOW ON THE OTHER SIDE.
THIS BUILDING ALONE HOUSES A WHOLE ZOO'S WORTH A' PETS, AN' YA HAVE A GIANT CATAPULT ON THE ROOF THAT SHOOTS ANIMAL WASTE ACROSS TOWN ONCE A WEEK.
HONEST... ONE DAY WITHOUT MADNESS...D'YA REMEMBER ONE?

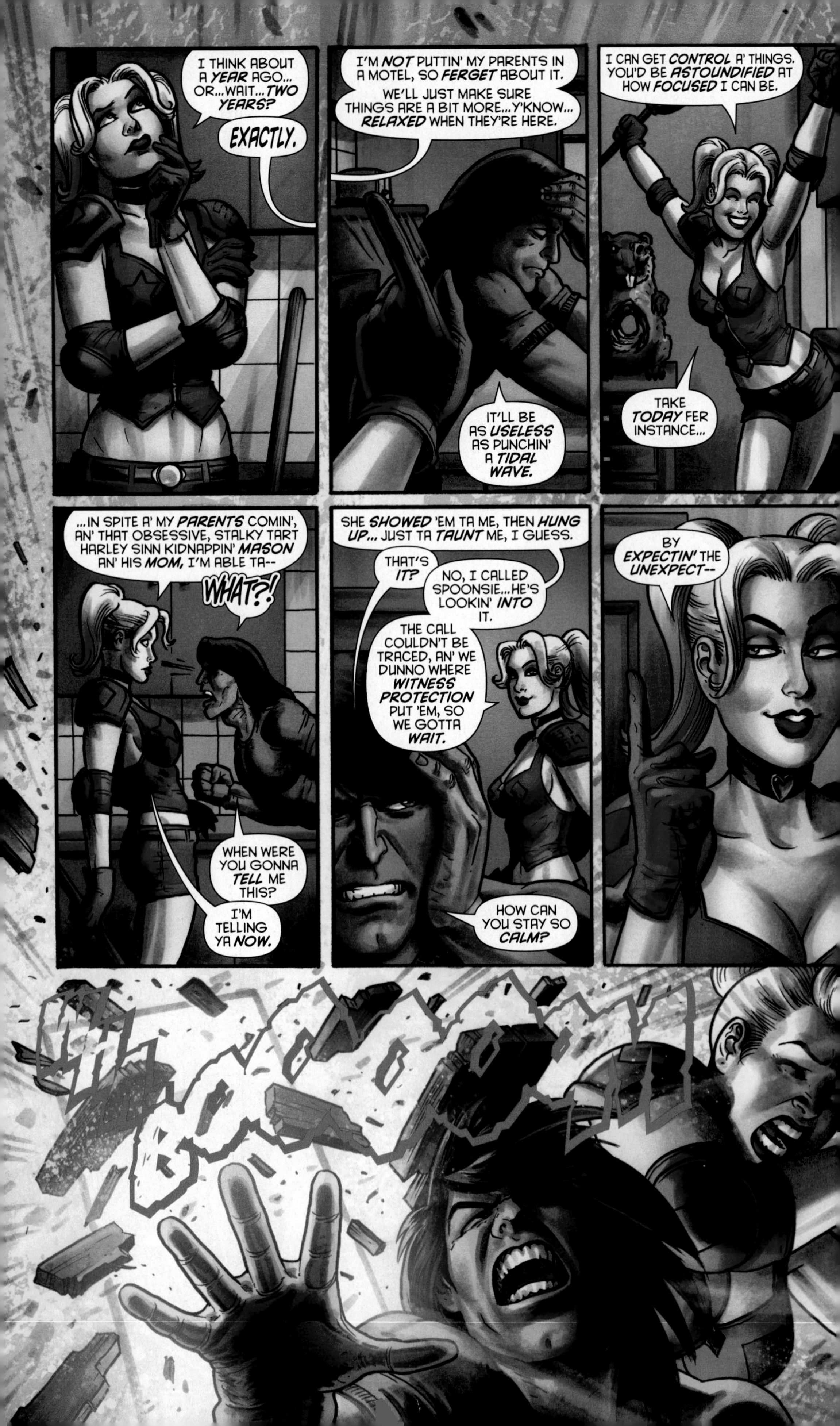

I THINK ABOUT A YEAR AGO... OR...WAIT...TWO YEARS?
EXACTLY.
I'M NOT PUTTIN' MY PARENTS IN A MOTEL, SO FERGET ABOUT IT.
WE'LL JUST MAKE SURE THINGS ARE A BIT MORE...Y'KNOW... RELAXED WHEN THEY'RE HERE.
IT'LL BE AS USELESS AS PUNCHIN' A TIDAL WAVE.
I CAN GET CONTROL A' THINGS. YOU'D BE ASTOUNDIFIED AT HOW FOCUSED I CAN BE.
TAKE TODAY FER INSTANCE...
...IN SPITE A' MY PARENTS COMIN', AN' THAT OBSESSIVE, STALKY TART HARLEY SINN KIDNAPPIN' MASON AN' HIS MOM, I'M ABLE TA--
WHAT?!
WHEN WERE YOU GONNA TELL ME THIS?
I'M TELLING YA NOW.
SHE SHOWED 'EM TA ME, THEN HUNG UP... JUST TA TAUNT ME, I GUESS.
THAT'S IT?
NO, I CALLED SPOONSIE...HE'S LOOKIN' INTO IT.
THE CALL COULDN'T BE TRACED, AN' WE DUNNO WHERE WITNESS PROTECTION PUT 'EM, SO WE GOTTA WAIT.
HOW CAN YOU STAY SO CALM?
BY EXPECTIN' THE UNEXPECT--

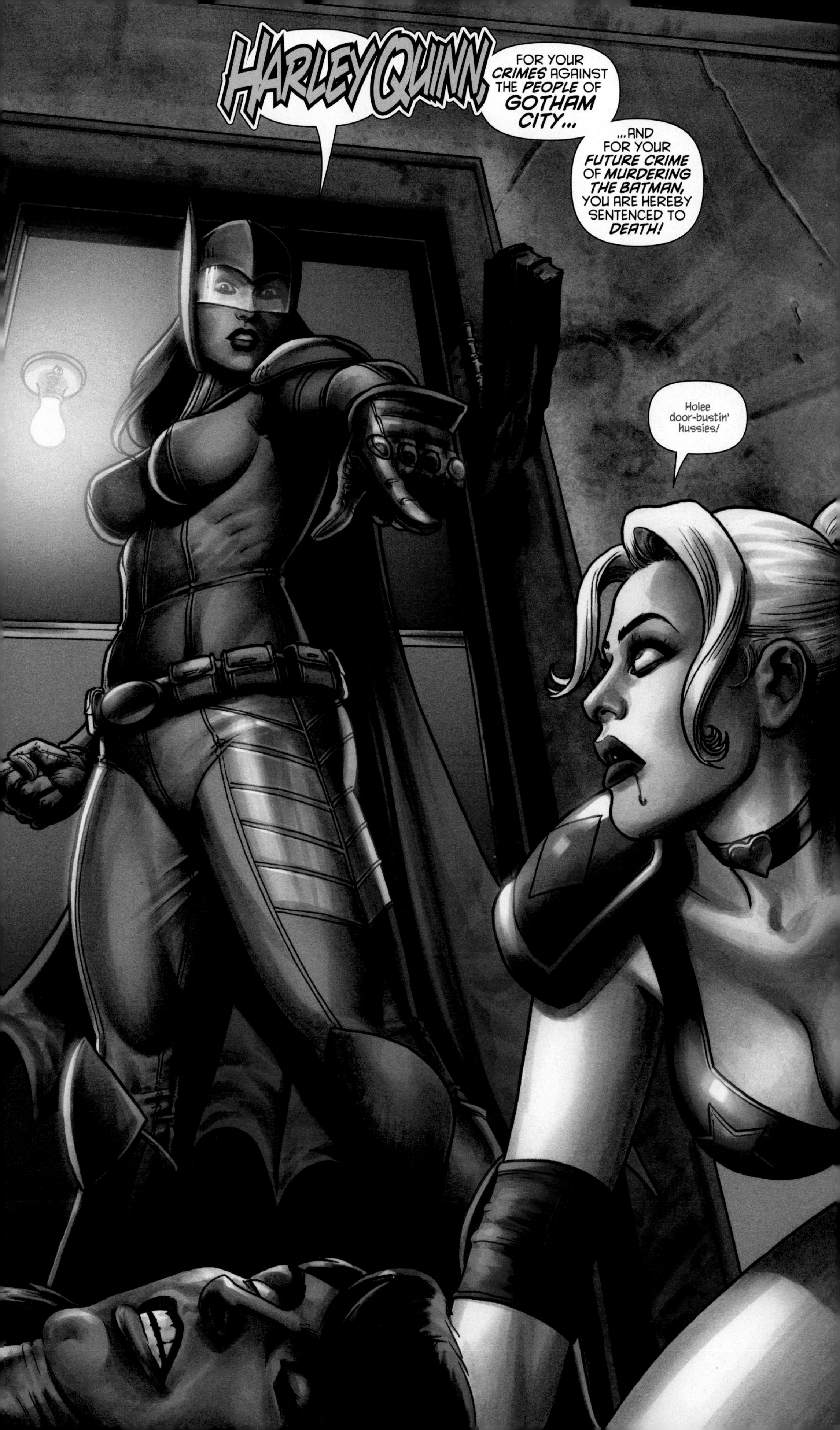
HARLEY QUINN,
FOR YOUR CRIMES AGAINST THE PEOPLE OF GOTHAM CITY...
...AND FOR YOUR FUTURE CRIME OF MURDERING THE BATMAN, YOU ARE HEREBY SENTENCED TO DEATH!
Holee door-bustin' hussies!

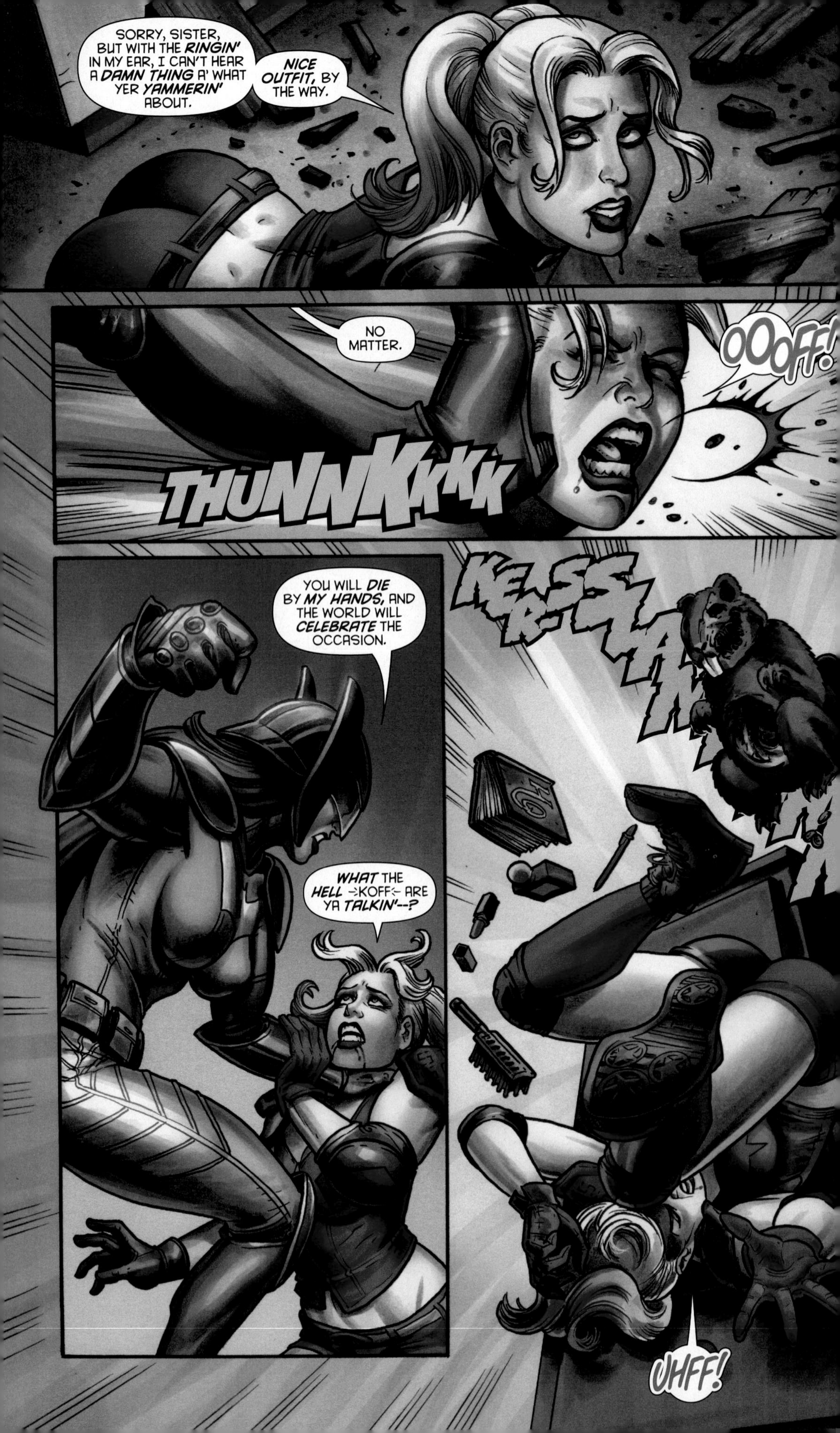
SORRY, SISTER, BUT WITH THE RINGIN' IN MY EAR, I CAN'T HEAR A DAMN THING A' WHAT YER YAMMERIN' ABOUT.
NICE OUTFIT, BY THE WAY.
NO MATTER.
OOOFF!
THUNNKKKK
YOU WILL DIE BY MY HANDS, AND THE WORLD WILL CELEBRATE THE OCCASION.
WHAT THE HELL ~KOFF~ ARE YA TALKIN'--?
KE-SS-R-LAM
UHFF!

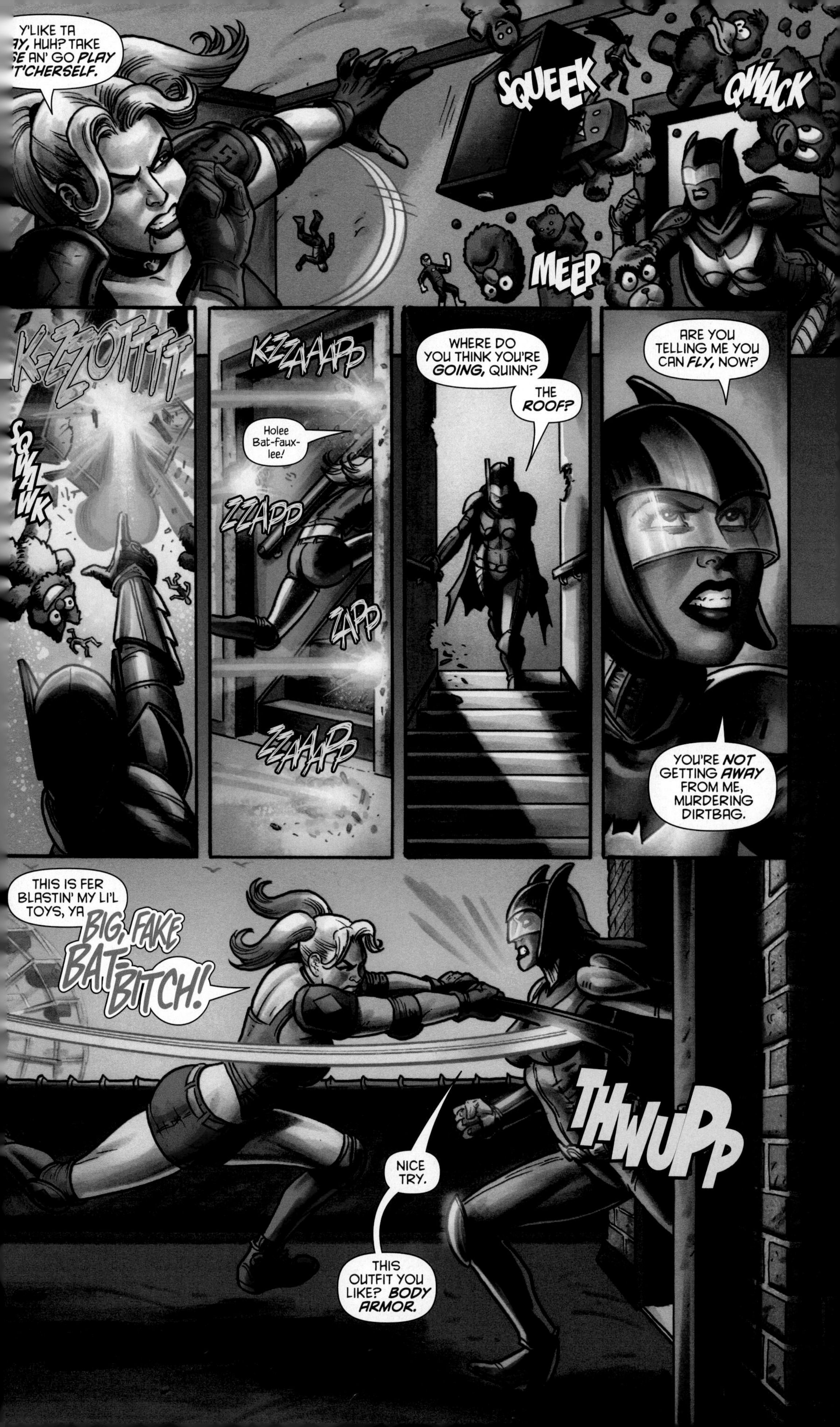
Y'LIKE TA ...AY, HUH? TAKE ...SE AN' GO PLAY ...T'CHERSELF.
SQUEEK
QWACK
MEEP
K-ZZOTTTTT
SQWAWK
KZZZAAAPP
Holee Bat-faux-lee!
ZZAPP
ZAPP
ZZZAAAPP
WHERE DO YOU THINK YOU'RE GOING, QUINN?
THE ROOF?
ARE YOU TELLING ME YOU CAN FLY, NOW?
YOU'RE NOT GETTING AWAY FROM ME, MURDERING DIRTBAG.
THIS IS FER BLASTIN' MY LI'L TOYS, YA BIG, FAKE BAT-BITCH!
THWUPP
NICE TRY.
THIS OUTFIT YOU LIKE? BODY ARMOR.

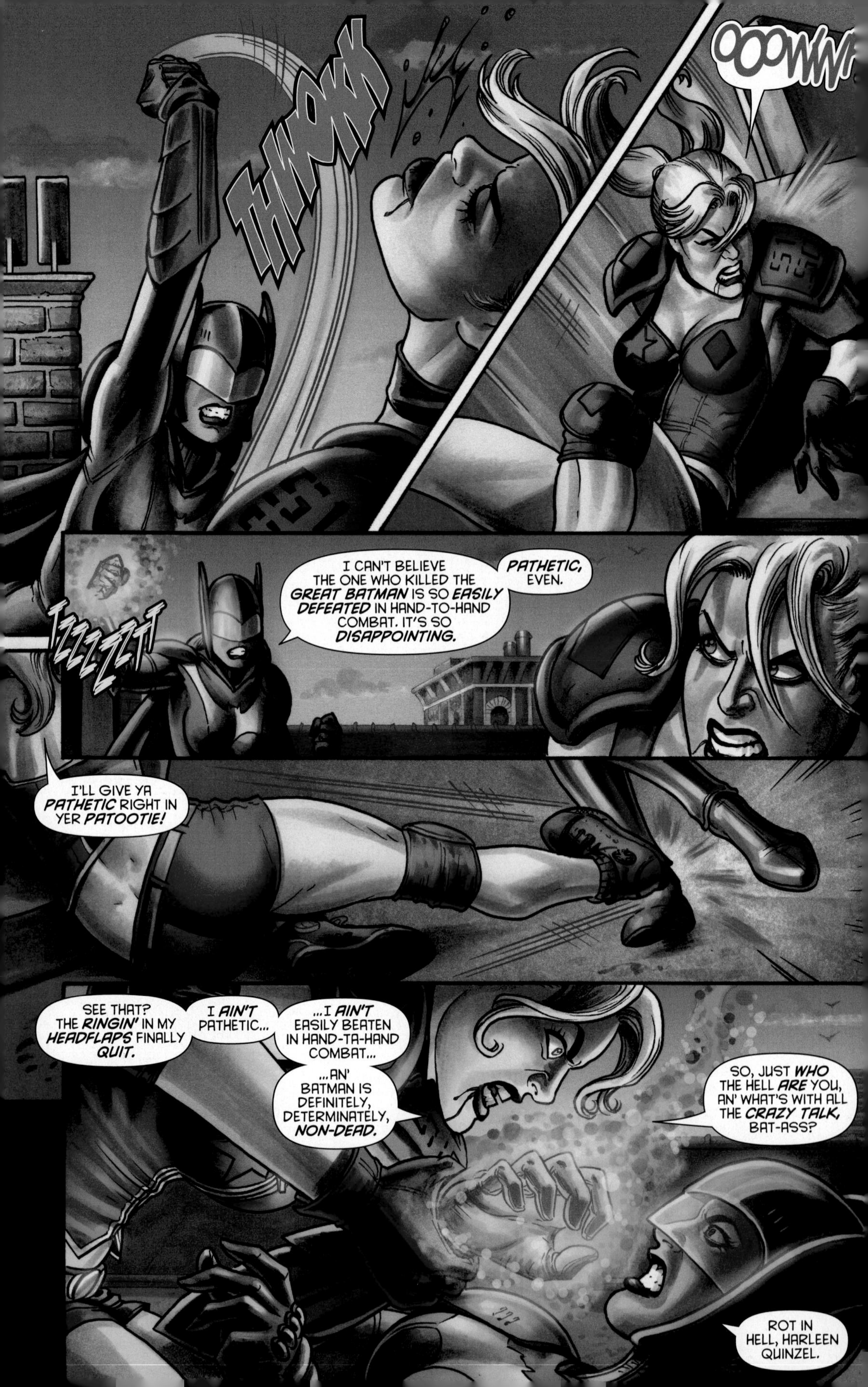
THWOKK
OOOWWW
TZZZZZZT!
I CAN'T BELIEVE THE ONE WHO KILLED THE GREAT BATMAN IS SO EASILY DEFEATED IN HAND-TO-HAND COMBAT. IT'S SO DISAPPOINTING.
PATHETIC, EVEN.
I'LL GIVE YA PATHETIC RIGHT IN YER PATOOTIE!
SEE THAT? THE RINGIN' IN MY HEADFLAPS FINALLY QUIT.
I AIN'T PATHETIC...
...I AIN'T EASILY BEATEN IN HAND-TA-HAND COMBAT...
...AN' BATMAN IS DEFINITELY, DETERMINATELY, NON-DEAD.
SO, JUST WHO THE HELL ARE YOU, AN' WHAT'S WITH ALL THE CRAZY TALK, BAT-ASS?
ROT IN HELL, HARLEEN QUINZEL.

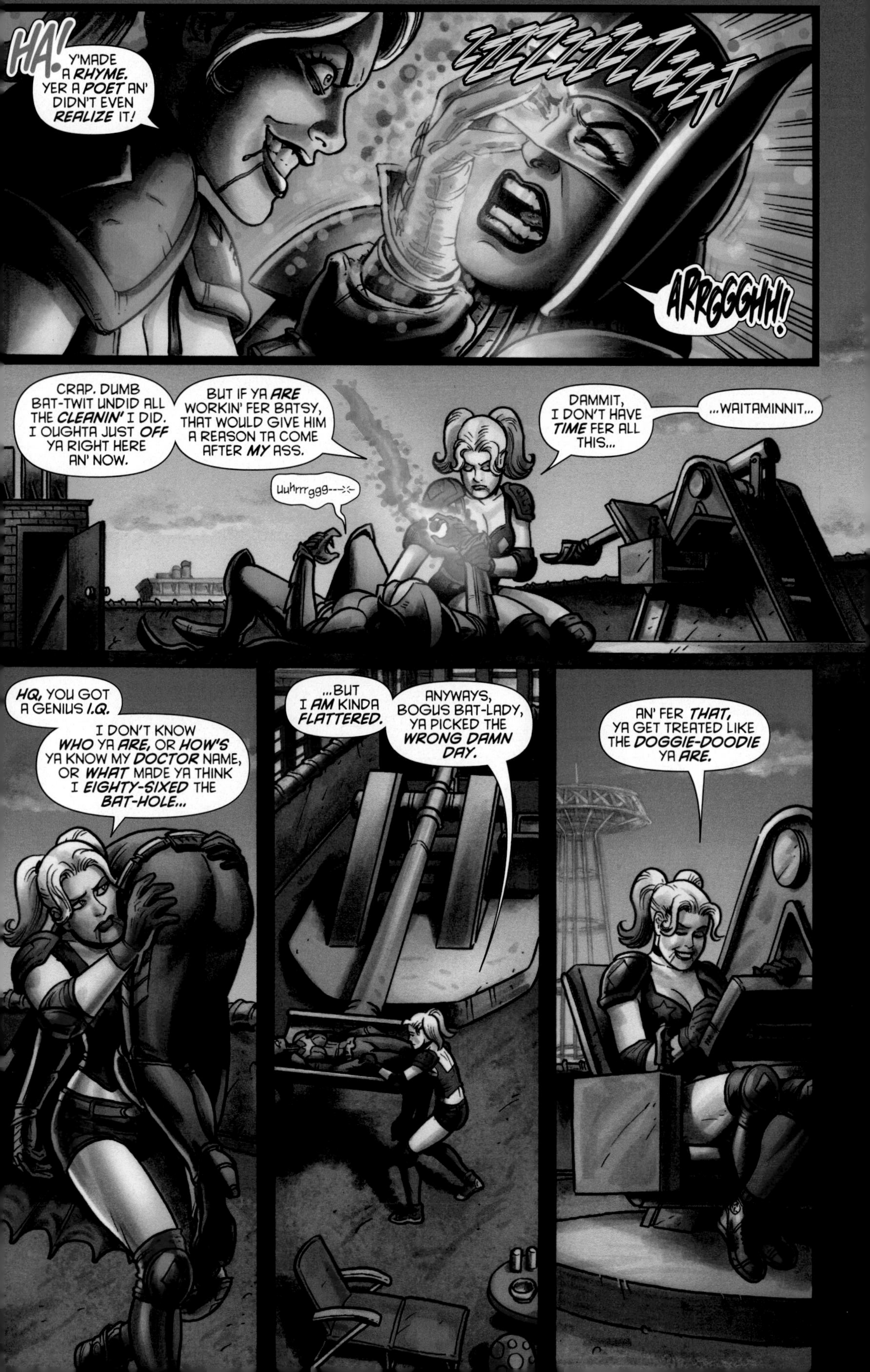
HA!
Y'MADE A RHYME. YER A POET AN' DIDN'T EVEN REALIZE IT!
ZZZZZZZZZZZZZZZT
ARRGGGHH!
CRAP. DUMB BAT-TWIT UNDID ALL THE CLEANIN' I DID. I OUGHTA JUST OFF YA RIGHT HERE AN' NOW.
BUT IF YA ARE WORKIN' FER BATSY, THAT WOULD GIVE HIM A REASON TA COME AFTER MY ASS.
Uuhrrrggg---
DAMMIT, I DON'T HAVE TIME FER ALL THIS...
...WAITAMINNIT...
HQ, YOU GOT A GENIUS I.Q.
I DON'T KNOW WHO YA ARE, OR HOW'S YA KNOW MY DOCTOR NAME, OR WHAT MADE YA THINK I EIGHTY-SIXED THE BAT-HOLE...
...BUT I AM KINDA FLATTERED.
ANYWAYS, BOGUS BAT-LADY, YA PICKED THE WRONG DAMN DAY.
AN' FER THAT, YA GET TREATED LIKE THE DOGGIE-DOODIE YA ARE.

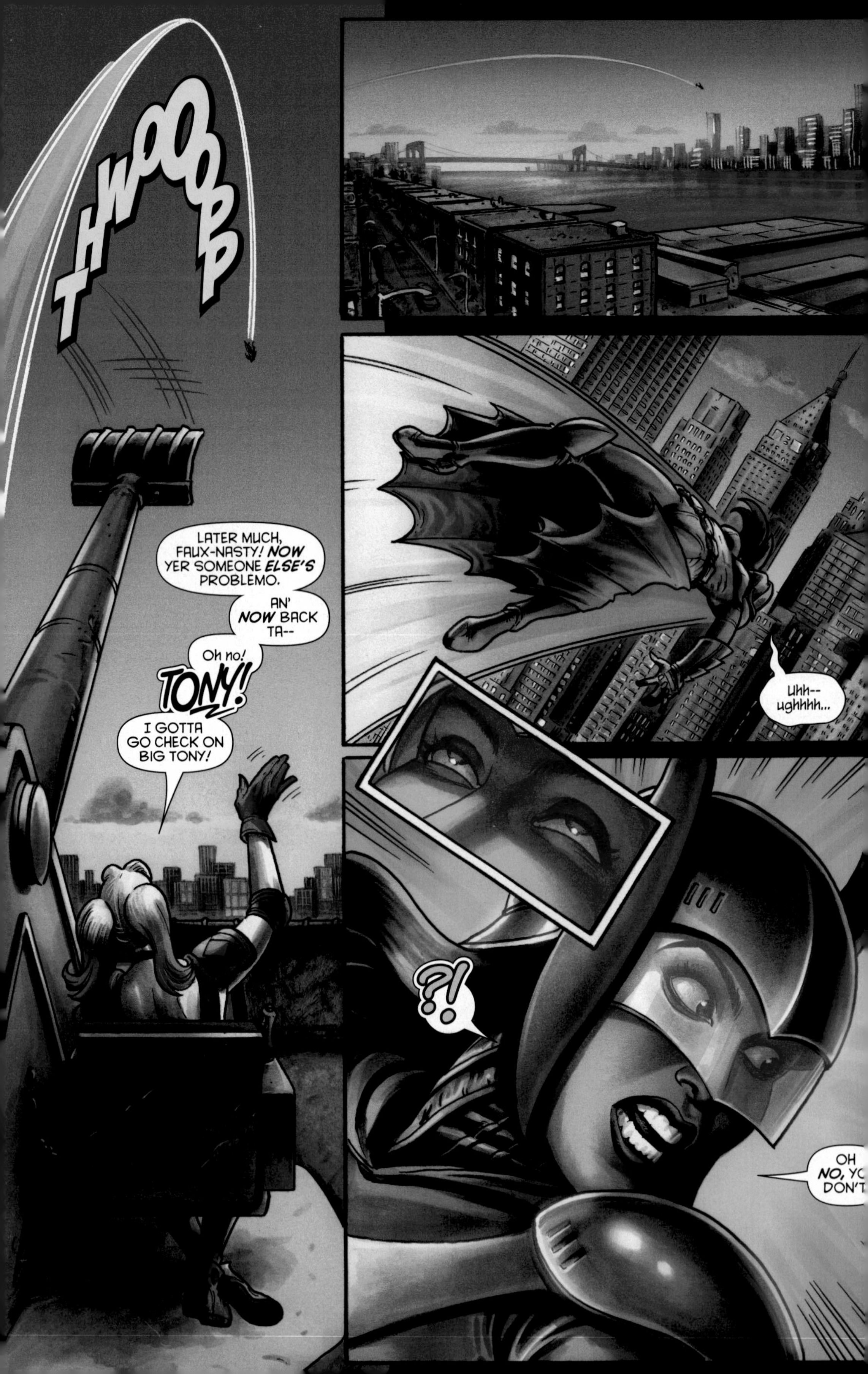
THWOOOPP
LATER MUCH, FAUX-NASTY! NOW YER SOMEONE ELSE'S PROBLEMO.
AN' NOW BACK TA--
Oh no!
TONY!
I GOTTA GO CHECK ON BIG TONY!
Uhh-- ughhhh...
?!
OH NO, YO
DON'T

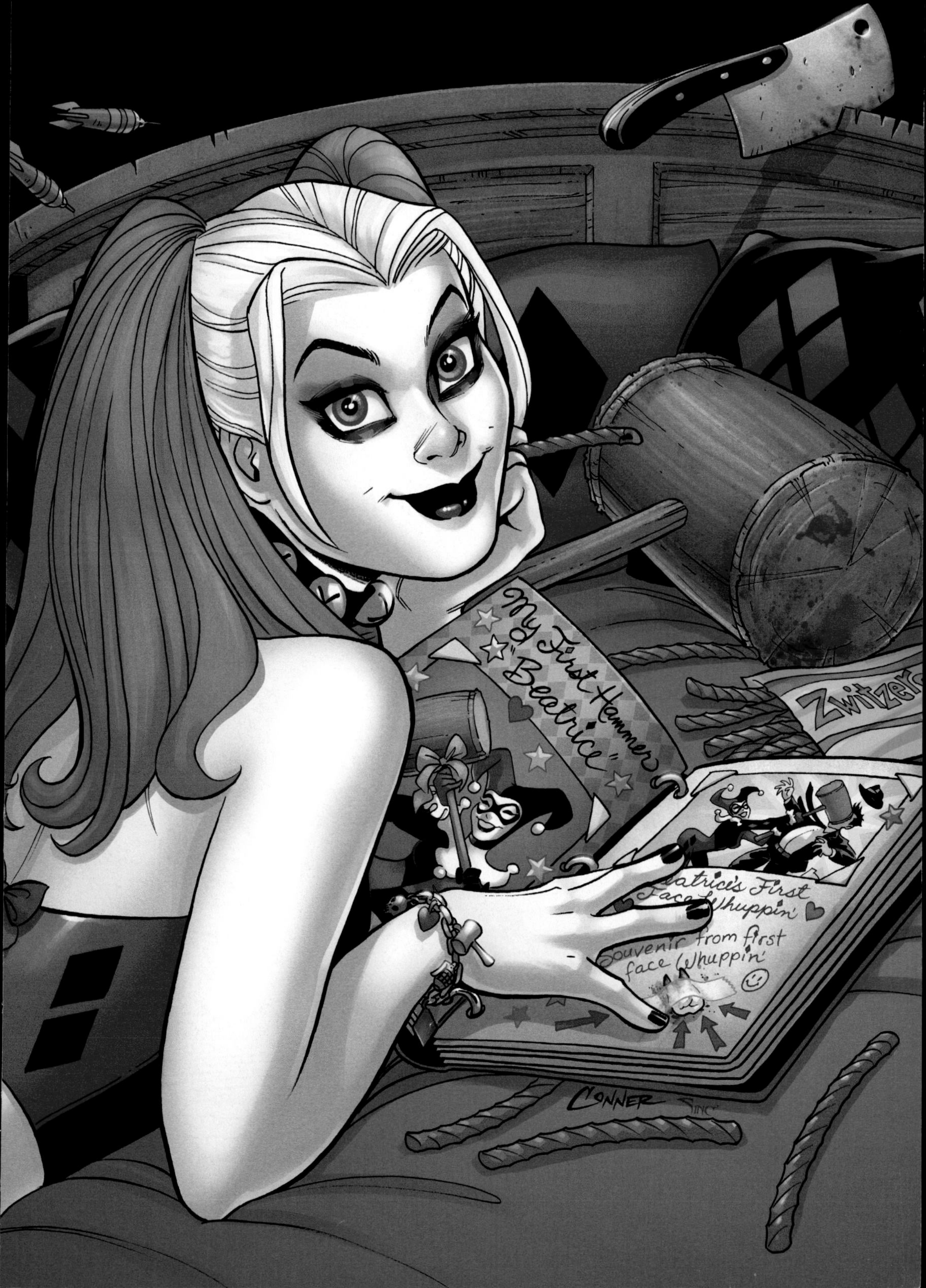
My First Hammer "Beatrice"
Zwitzer
Beatrice's First Face Whuppin'
Souvenir from first face Whuppin'
CONNER
SINC

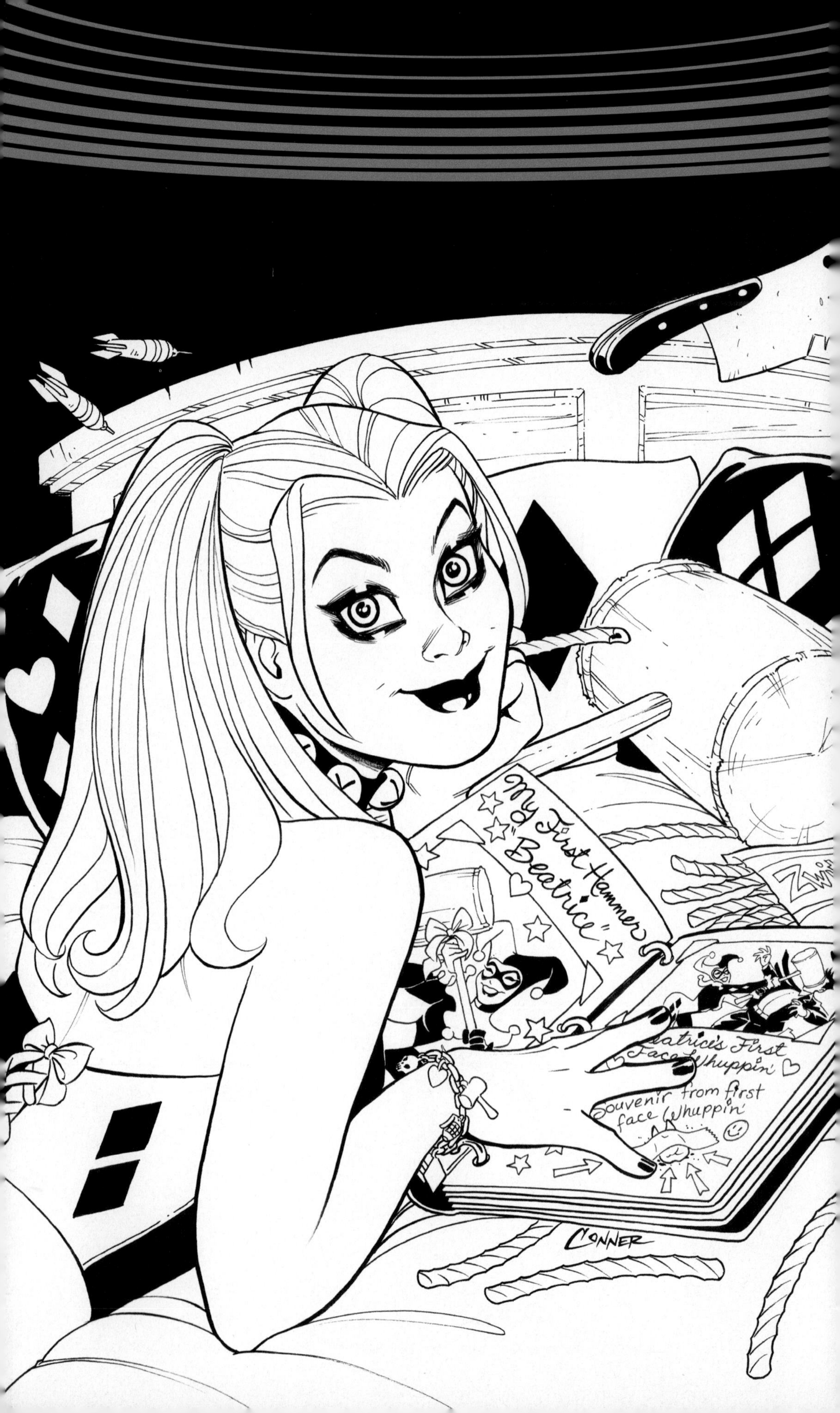

My First Hammer
"Beatrice"
Face Whuppin'
Souvenir from first face Whuppin'
CONNER

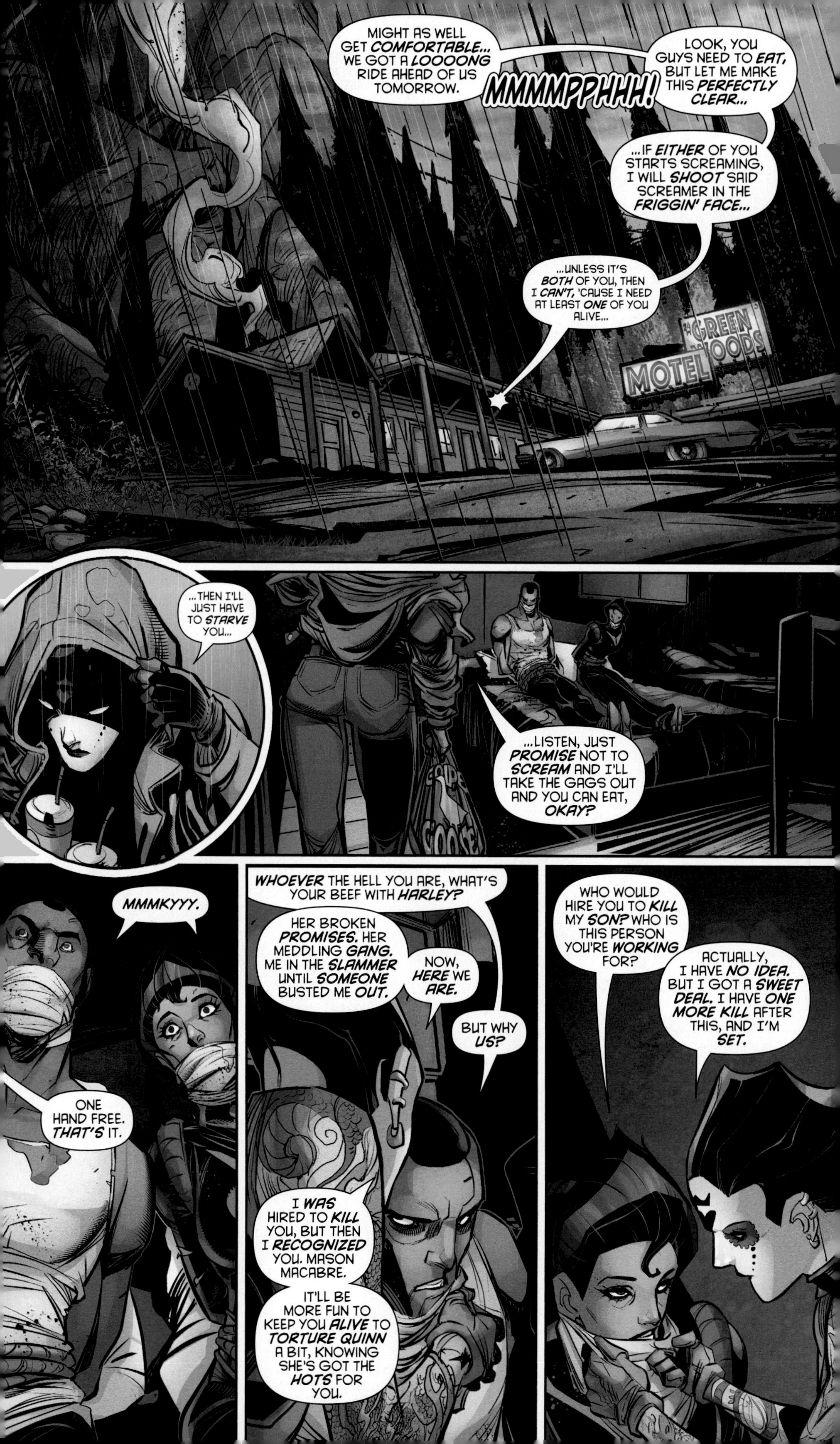

MIGHT AS WELL GET COMFORTABLE... WE GOT A LOOOONG RIDE AHEAD OF US TOMORROW.
MMMMPPHHH!
LOOK, YOU GUYS NEED TO EAT, BUT LET ME MAKE THIS PERFECTLY CLEAR...
...IF EITHER OF YOU STARTS SCREAMING, I WILL SHOOT SAID SCREAMER IN THE FRIGGIN' FACE...
...UNLESS IT'S BOTH OF YOU, THEN I CAN'T, 'CAUSE I NEED AT LEAST ONE OF YOU ALIVE...
GREEN WOODS
MOTEL
...THEN I'LL JUST HAVE TO STARVE YOU...
...LISTEN, JUST PROMISE NOT TO SCREAM AND I'LL TAKE THE GAGS OUT AND YOU CAN EAT, OKAY?
MMMKYYY.
ONE HAND FREE. THAT'S IT.
WHOEVER THE HELL YOU ARE, WHAT'S YOUR BEEF WITH HARLEY?
HER BROKEN PROMISES. HER MEDDLING GANG. ME IN THE SLAMMER UNTIL SOMEONE BUSTED ME OUT.
NOW, HERE WE ARE.
BUT WHY US?
I WAS HIRED TO KILL YOU, BUT THEN I RECOGNIZED YOU. MASON MACABRE.
IT'LL BE MORE FUN TO KEEP YOU ALIVE TO TORTURE QUINN A BIT, KNOWING SHE'S GOT THE HOTS FOR YOU.
WHO WOULD HIRE YOU TO KILL MY SON? WHO IS THIS PERSON YOU'RE WORKING FOR?
ACTUALLY, I HAVE NO IDEA. BUT I GOT A SWEET DEAL. I HAVE ONE MORE KILL AFTER THIS, AND I'M SET.

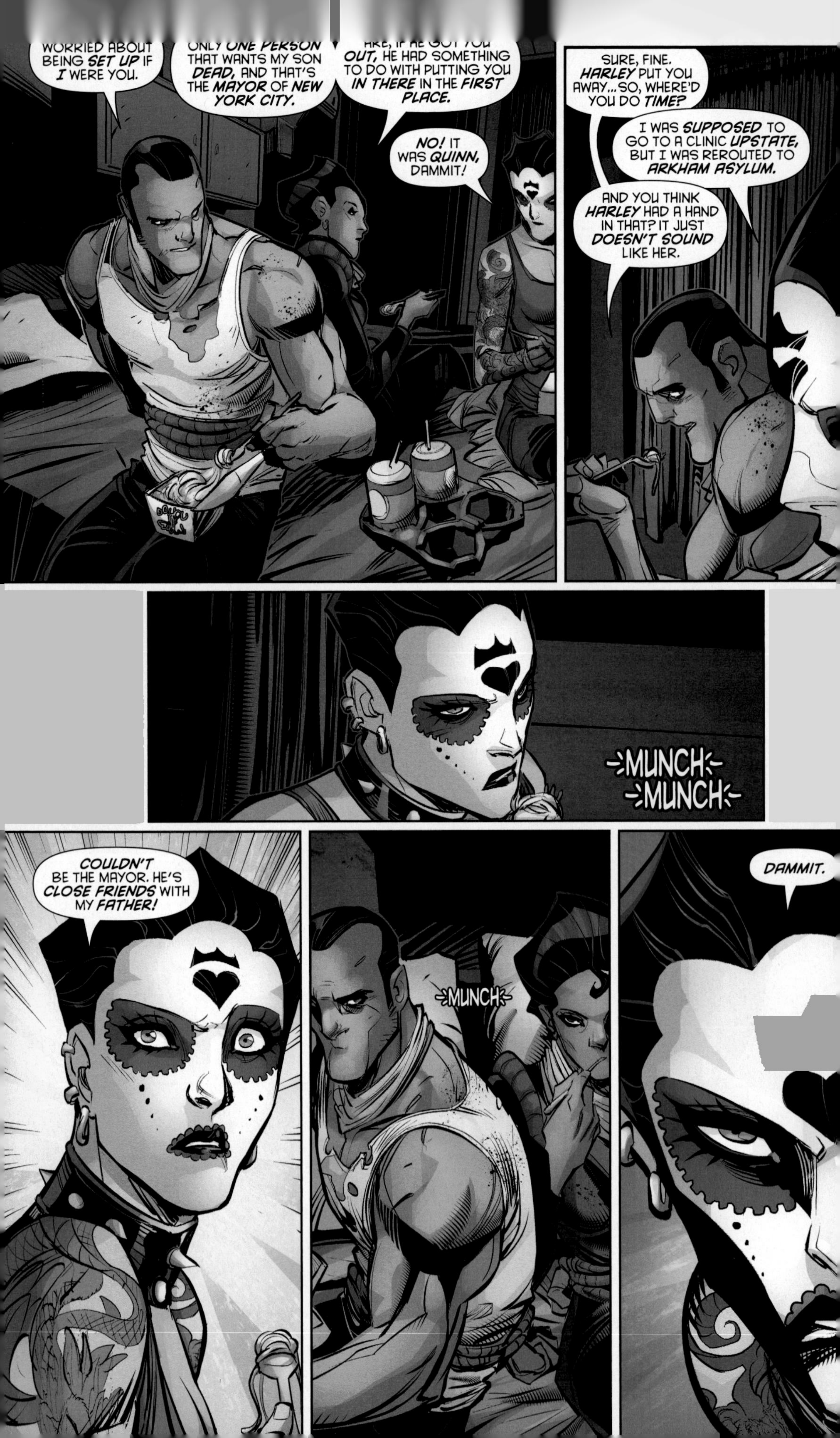
WORRIED ABOUT BEING SET UP IF I WERE YOU.
ONLY ONE PERSON THAT WANTS MY SON DEAD, AND THAT'S THE MAYOR OF NEW YORK CITY.
OUT, HE HAD SOMETHING TO DO WITH PUTTING YOU IN THERE IN THE FIRST PLACE.
NO! IT WAS QUINN, DAMMIT!
SURE, FINE. HARLEY PUT YOU AWAY... SO, WHERE'D YOU DO TIME?
I WAS SUPPOSED TO GO TO A CLINIC UPSTATE, BUT I WAS REROUTED TO ARKHAM ASYLUM.
AND YOU THINK HARLEY HAD A HAND IN THAT? IT JUST DOESN'T SOUND LIKE HER.
MUNCH
MUNCH
COULDN'T BE THE MAYOR. HE'S CLOSE FRIENDS WITH MY FATHER!
MUNCH
DAMMIT.

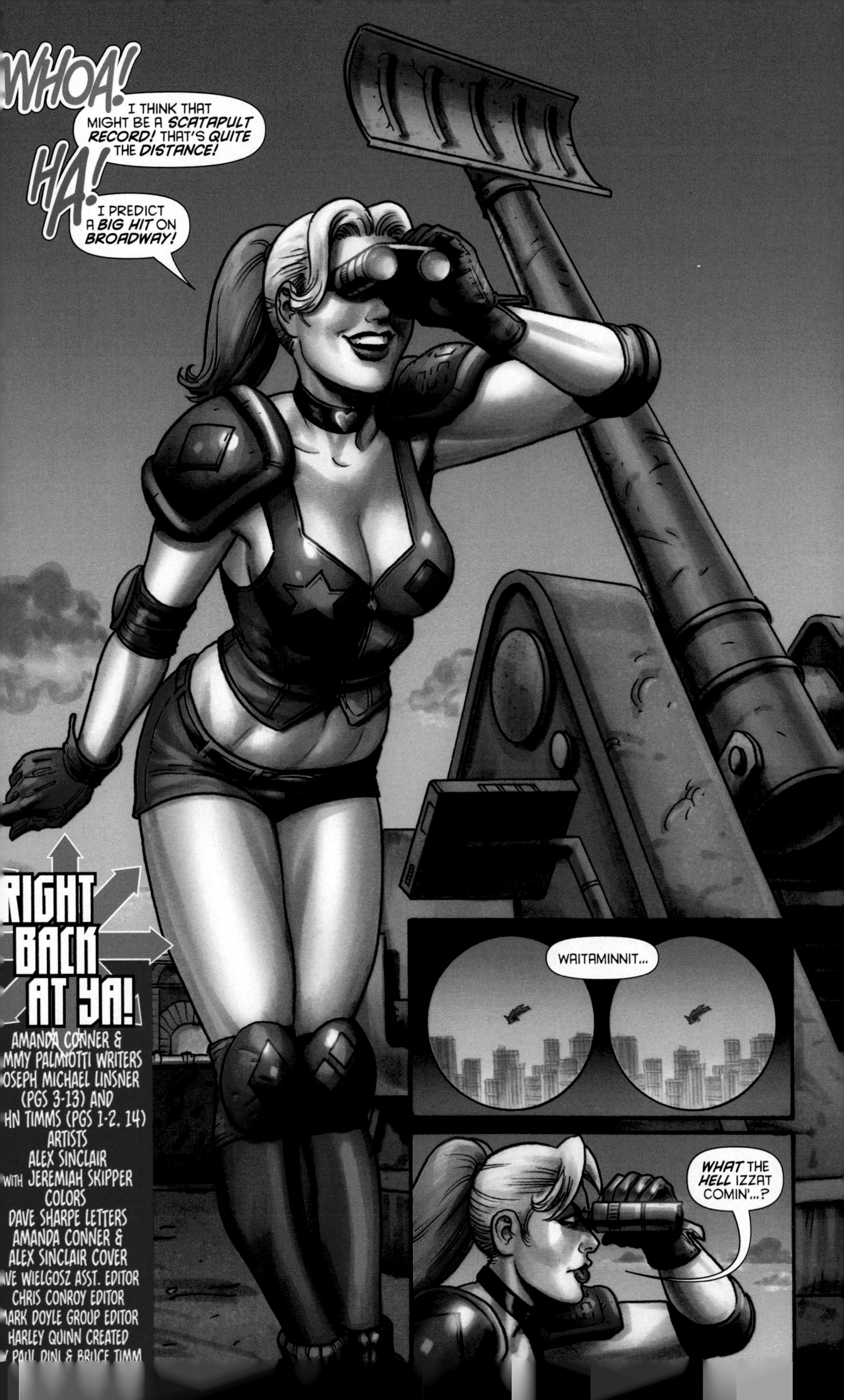
WHOA!
I THINK THAT MIGHT BE A *SCATAPULT RECORD!* THAT'S *QUITE* THE *DISTANCE!*
HA!
I PREDICT A *BIG HIT* ON *BROADWAY!*
RIGHT BACK AT YA!
AMANDA CONNER &
MMY PALMIOTTI WRITERS
OSEPH MICHAEL LINSNER
(PGS 3-13) AND
HN TIMMS (PGS 1-2, 14)
ARTISTS
ALEX SINCLAIR
WITH JEREMIAH SKIPPER
COLORS
DAVE SHARPE LETTERS
AMANDA CONNER &
ALEX SINCLAIR COVER
VE WIELGOSZ ASST. EDITOR
CHRIS CONROY EDITOR
ARK DOYLE GROUP EDITOR
HARLEY QUINN CREATED
WAITAMINNIT...
WHAT THE *HELL* IZZAT COMIN'...?

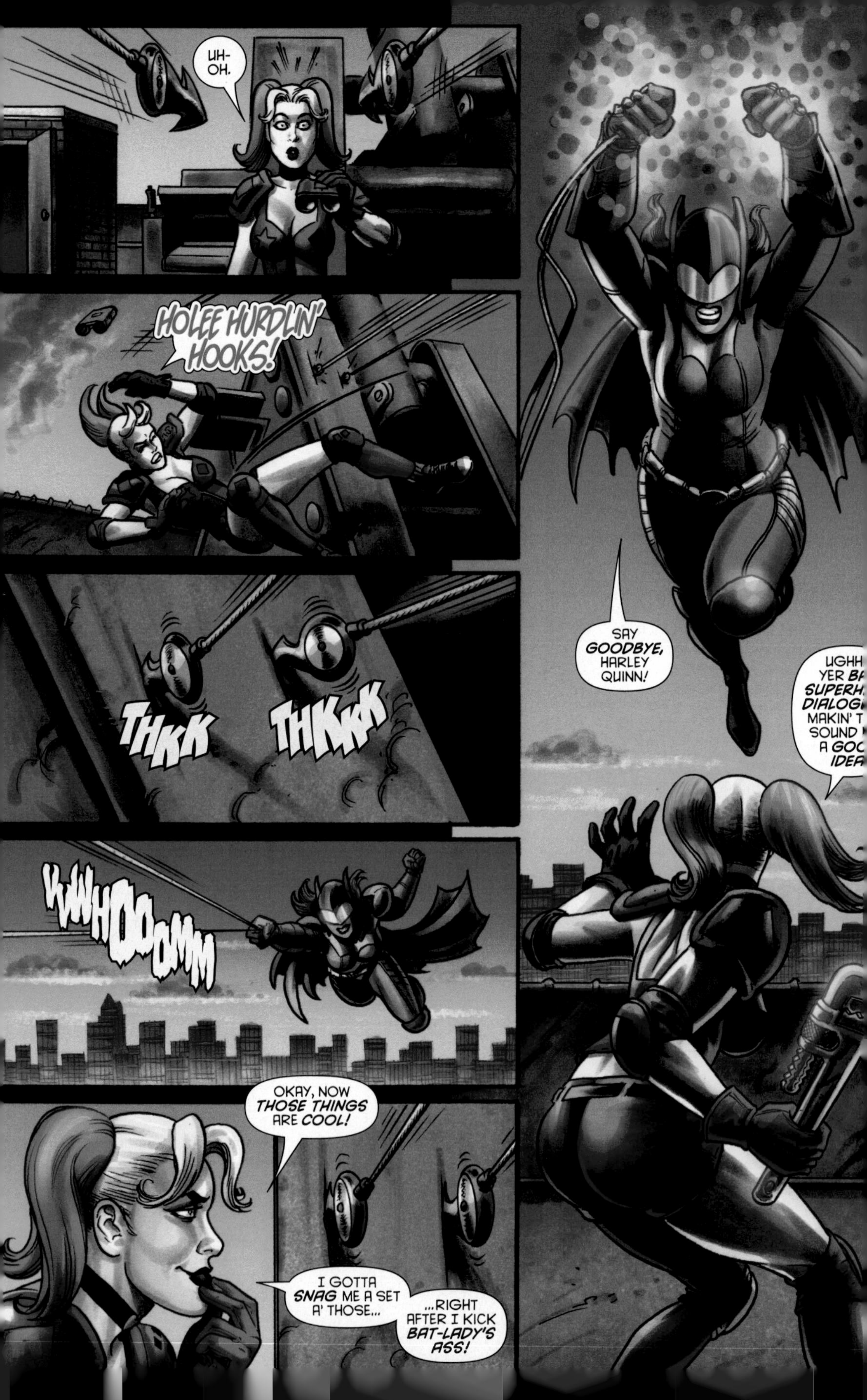
UH-OH.
HOLEE HURDLIN' HOOKS!
THKK
THKKK
VWHOOOMM
OKAY, NOW THOSE THINGS ARE COOL!
I GOTTA SNAG ME A SET A' THOSE...
...RIGHT AFTER I KICK BAT-LADY'S ASS!
SAY GOODBYE, HARLEY QUINN!
UGHH YER BA SUPERH DIALOG MAKIN' T SOUND A GOO IDEA

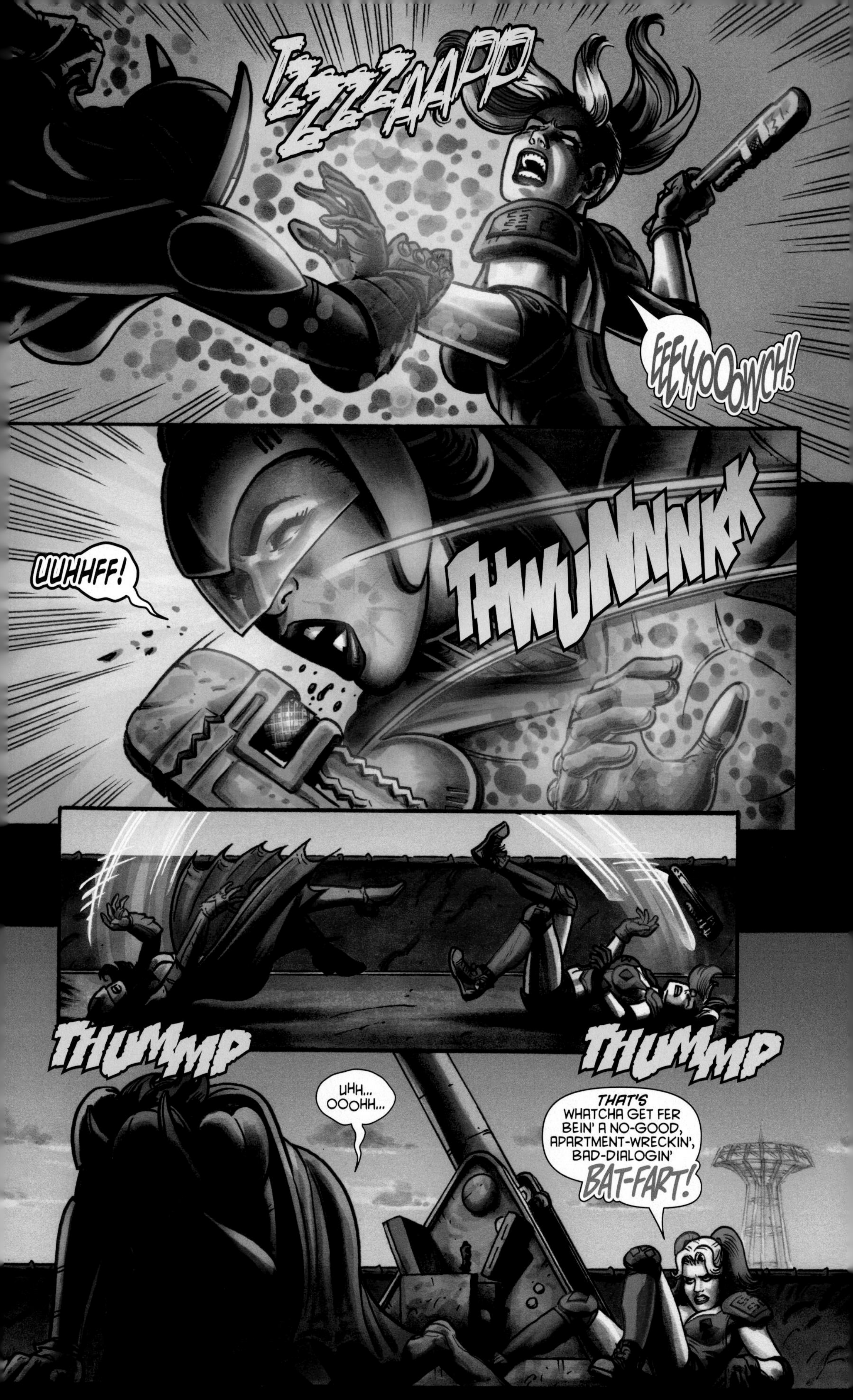
TZZZZAAPP
EEEYYOOOWCH!
THWUNNNKK
UUHHFF!
THUMMP
THUMMP
UHH... OOOHH...
THAT'S WHATCHA GET FER BEIN' A NO-GOOD, APARTMENT-WRECKIN', BAD-DIALOGIN' BAT-FART!

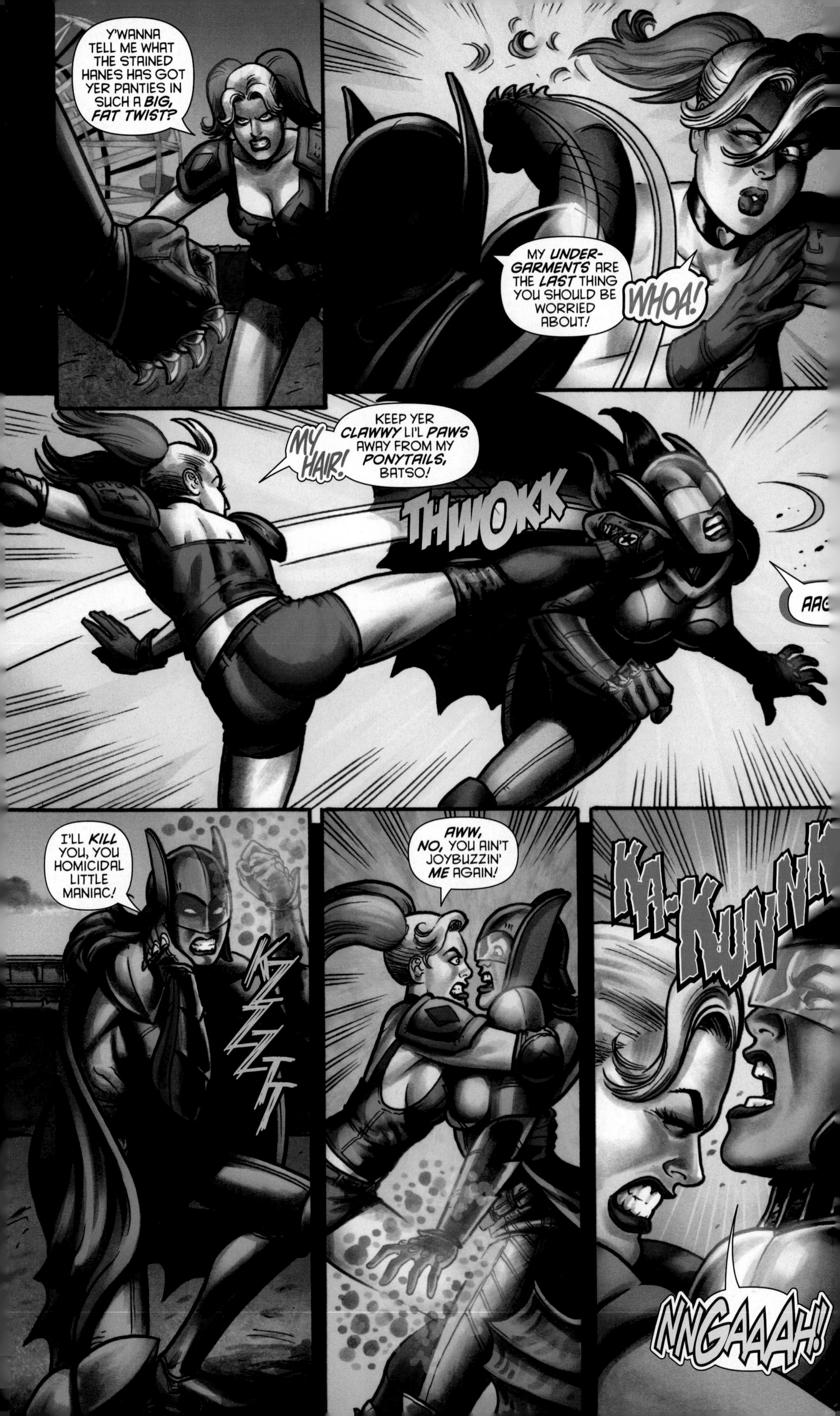
Y'WANNA TELL ME WHAT THE STAINED HANES HAS GOT YER PANTIES IN SUCH A BIG, FAT TWIST?
MY UNDER-GARMENTS ARE THE LAST THING YOU SHOULD BE WORRIED ABOUT!
WHOA!
MY HAIR!
KEEP YER CLAWWY LI'L PAWS AWAY FROM MY PONYTAILS, BATSO!
THWOKK
AAG
I'LL KILL YOU, YOU HOMICIDAL LITTLE MANIAC!
KZZZZT
AWW, NO, YOU AIN'T JOYBUZZIN' ME AGAIN!
KA-KUNNK
NNGAAAH!

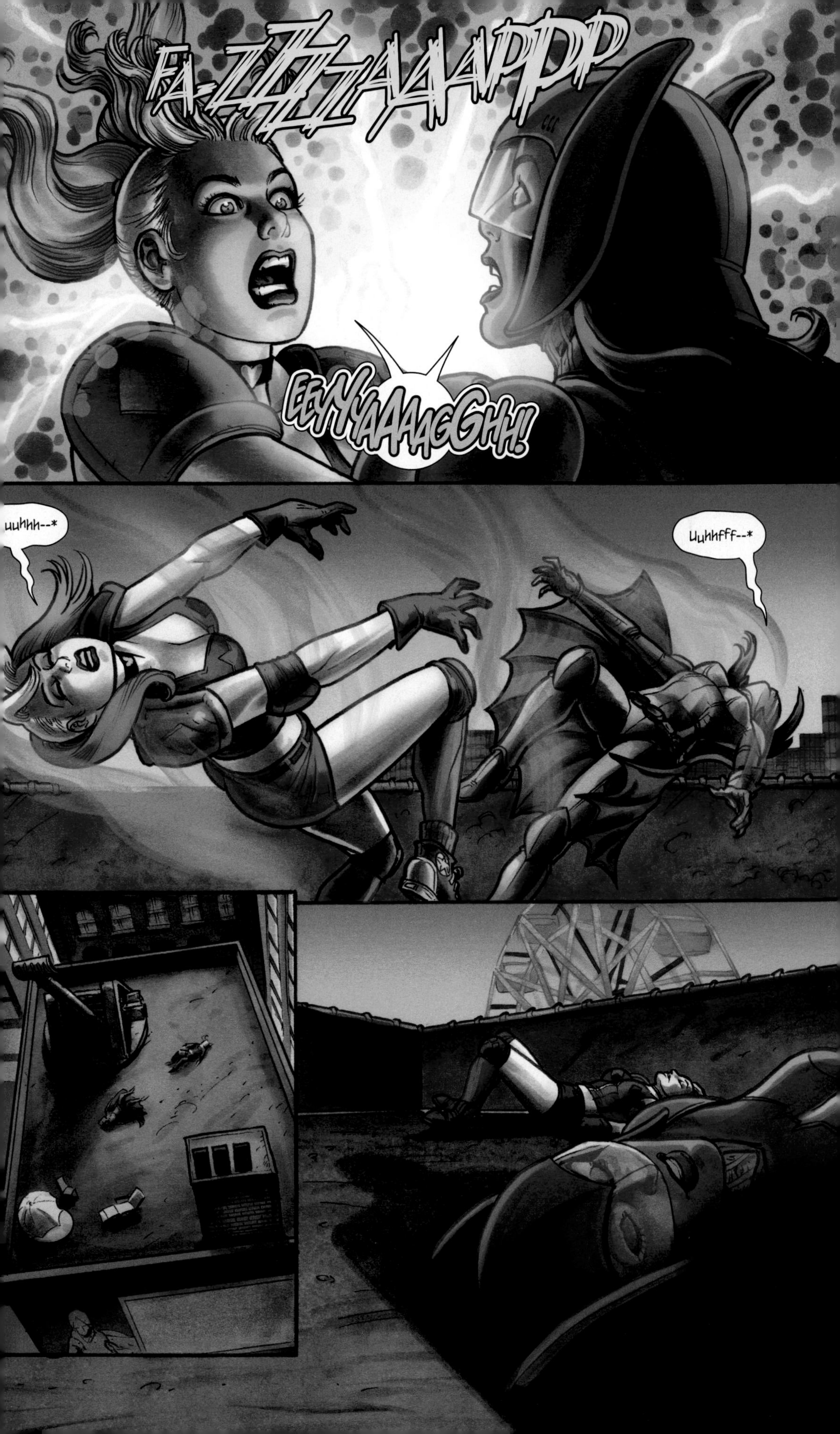
FA-ZZZZAAAAPPP
EEYYYAAAAGGHH!
uuhhh--*
Uuhhfff--*

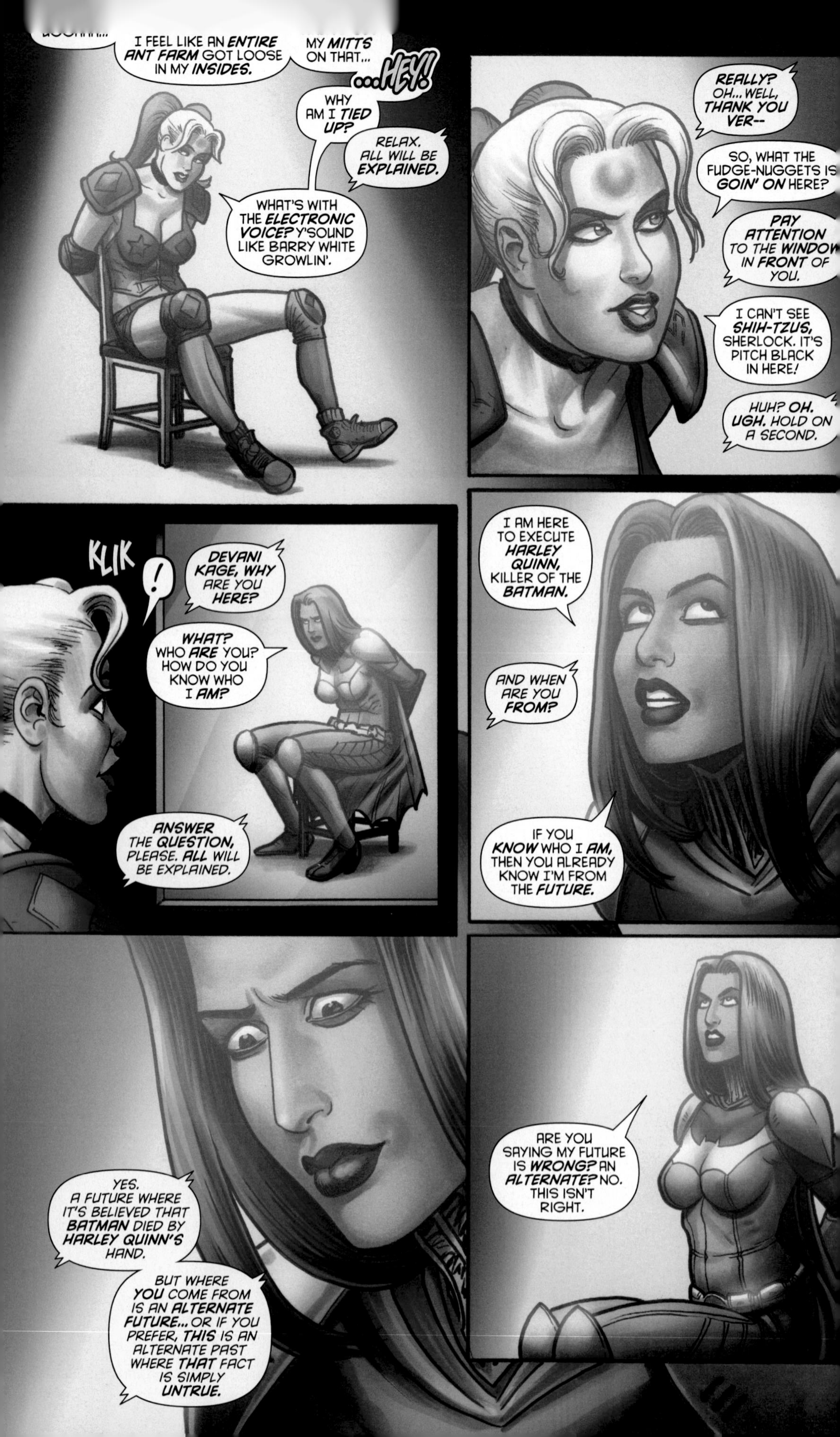
I FEEL LIKE AN ENTIRE ANT FARM GOT LOOSE IN MY INSIDES.
MY MITTS ON THAT...
...HEY!
WHY AM I TIED UP?
RELAX. ALL WILL BE EXPLAINED.
WHAT'S WITH THE ELECTRONIC VOICE? Y'SOUND LIKE BARRY WHITE GROWLIN'.
REALLY? OH... WELL, THANK YOU VER--
SO, WHAT THE FUDGE-NUGGETS IS GOIN' ON HERE?
PAY ATTENTION TO THE WINDOW IN FRONT OF YOU.
I CAN'T SEE SHIH-TZUS, SHERLOCK. IT'S PITCH BLACK IN HERE!
HUH? OH. UGH. HOLD ON A SECOND.
KLIK
!
DEVANI KAGE, WHY ARE YOU HERE?
WHAT? WHO ARE YOU? HOW DO YOU KNOW WHO I AM?
ANSWER THE QUESTION, PLEASE. ALL WILL BE EXPLAINED.
I AM HERE TO EXECUTE HARLEY QUINN, KILLER OF THE BATMAN.
AND WHEN ARE YOU FROM?
IF YOU KNOW WHO I AM, THEN YOU ALREADY KNOW I'M FROM THE FUTURE.
YES. A FUTURE WHERE IT'S BELIEVED THAT BATMAN DIED BY HARLEY QUINN'S HAND.
BUT WHERE YOU COME FROM IS AN ALTERNATE FUTURE... OR IF YOU PREFER, THIS IS AN ALTERNATE PAST WHERE THAT FACT IS SIMPLY UNTRUE.
ARE YOU SAYING MY FUTURE IS WRONG? AN ALTERNATE? NO. THIS ISN'T RIGHT.

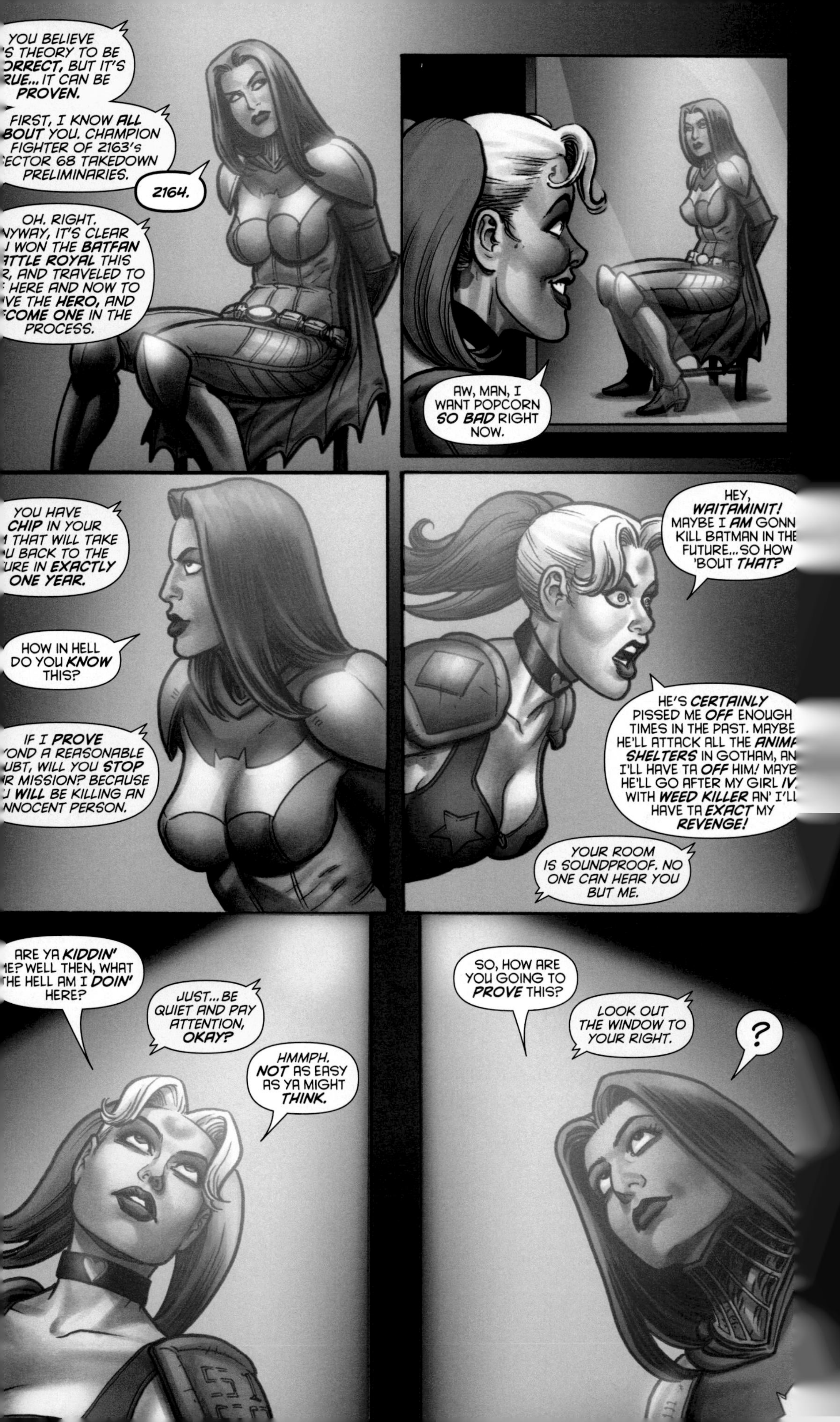
YOU BELIEVE 'S THEORY TO BE ORRECT, BUT IT'S RUE... IT CAN BE PROVEN.
FIRST, I KNOW ALL BOUT YOU. CHAMPION FIGHTER OF 2163's ECTOR 68 TAKEDOWN PRELIMINARIES.
2164.
OH. RIGHT. NYWAY, IT'S CLEAR I WON THE BATFAN ATTLE ROYAL THIS R, AND TRAVELED TO HERE AND NOW TO VE THE HERO, AND ECOME ONE IN THE PROCESS.
AW, MAN, I WANT POPCORN SO BAD RIGHT NOW.
YOU HAVE CHIP IN YOUR THAT WILL TAKE U BACK TO THE URE IN EXACTLY ONE YEAR.
HOW IN HELL DO YOU KNOW THIS?
IF I PROVE YOND A REASONABLE UBT, WILL YOU STOP R MISSION? BECAUSE U WILL BE KILLING AN NNOCENT PERSON.
HEY, WAITAMINIT! MAYBE I AM GONN KILL BATMAN IN THE FUTURE... SO HOW 'BOUT THAT?
HE'S CERTAINLY PISSED ME OFF ENOUGH TIMES IN THE PAST. MAYBE HE'LL ATTACK ALL THE ANIMA SHELTERS IN GOTHAM, AN I'LL HAVE TA OFF HIM! MAYB HE'LL GO AFTER MY GIRL IV WITH WEED KILLER AN' I'LL HAVE TA EXACT MY REVENGE!
YOUR ROOM IS SOUNDPROOF. NO ONE CAN HEAR YOU BUT ME.
ARE YA KIDDIN' ME? WELL THEN, WHAT THE HELL AM I DOIN' HERE?
JUST... BE QUIET AND PAY ATTENTION, OKAY?
HMMPH. NOT AS EASY AS YA MIGHT THINK.
SO, HOW ARE YOU GOING TO PROVE THIS?
LOOK OUT THE WINDOW TO YOUR RIGHT.
?

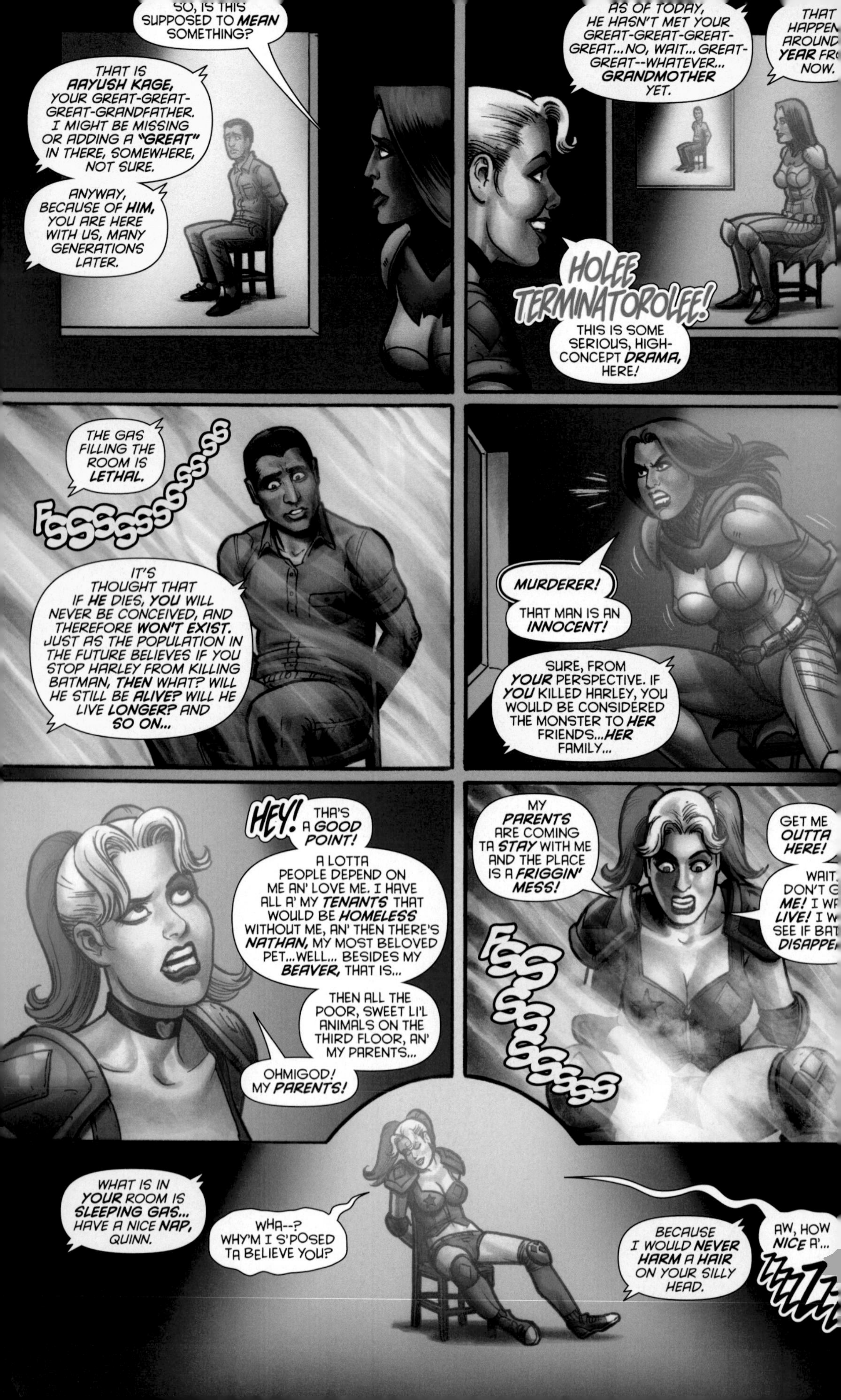

SO, IS THIS SUPPOSED TO MEAN SOMETHING?
THAT IS AAYUSH KAGE, YOUR GREAT-GREAT-GREAT-GRANDFATHER. I MIGHT BE MISSING OR ADDING A "GREAT" IN THERE, SOMEWHERE, NOT SURE.
ANYWAY, BECAUSE OF HIM, YOU ARE HERE WITH US, MANY GENERATIONS LATER.
AS OF TODAY, HE HASN'T MET YOUR GREAT-GREAT-GREAT-GREAT...NO, WAIT... GREAT-GREAT--WHATEVER... GRANDMOTHER YET.
THAT HAPPEN AROUND YEAR FR NOW.
HOLEE TERMINATOROLEE!
THIS IS SOME SERIOUS, HIGH-CONCEPT DRAMA, HERE!
THE GAS FILLING THE ROOM IS LETHAL.
FSSSSSSSSSSSSS
IT'S THOUGHT THAT IF HE DIES, YOU WILL NEVER BE CONCEIVED, AND THEREFORE WON'T EXIST. JUST AS THE POPULATION IN THE FUTURE BELIEVES IF YOU STOP HARLEY FROM KILLING BATMAN, THEN WHAT? WILL HE STILL BE ALIVE? WILL HE LIVE LONGER? AND SO ON...
MURDERER!
THAT MAN IS AN INNOCENT!
SURE, FROM YOUR PERSPECTIVE. IF YOU KILLED HARLEY, YOU WOULD BE CONSIDERED THE MONSTER TO HER FRIENDS...HER FAMILY...
HEY!
THA'S A GOOD POINT!
A LOTTA PEOPLE DEPEND ON ME AN' LOVE ME. I HAVE ALL A' MY TENANTS THAT WOULD BE HOMELESS WITHOUT ME, AN' THEN THERE'S NATHAN, MY MOST BELOVED PET...WELL... BESIDES MY BEAVER, THAT IS...
THEN ALL THE POOR, SWEET LI'L ANIMALS ON THE THIRD FLOOR, AN' MY PARENTS...
OHMIGOD! MY PARENTS!
MY PARENTS ARE COMING TA STAY WITH ME AND THE PLACE IS A FRIGGIN' MESS!
GET ME OUTTA HERE!
WAIT. DON'T G ME! I WA LIVE! I W SEE IF BAT DISAPPE
FSSSSSSSSSSS
WHAT IS IN YOUR ROOM IS SLEEPING GAS... HAVE A NICE NAP, QUINN.
WHA--? WHY'M I S'POSED TA BELIEVE YOU?
BECAUSE I WOULD NEVER HARM A HAIR ON YOUR SILLY HEAD.
AW, HOW NICE A'...
ZZZZZ

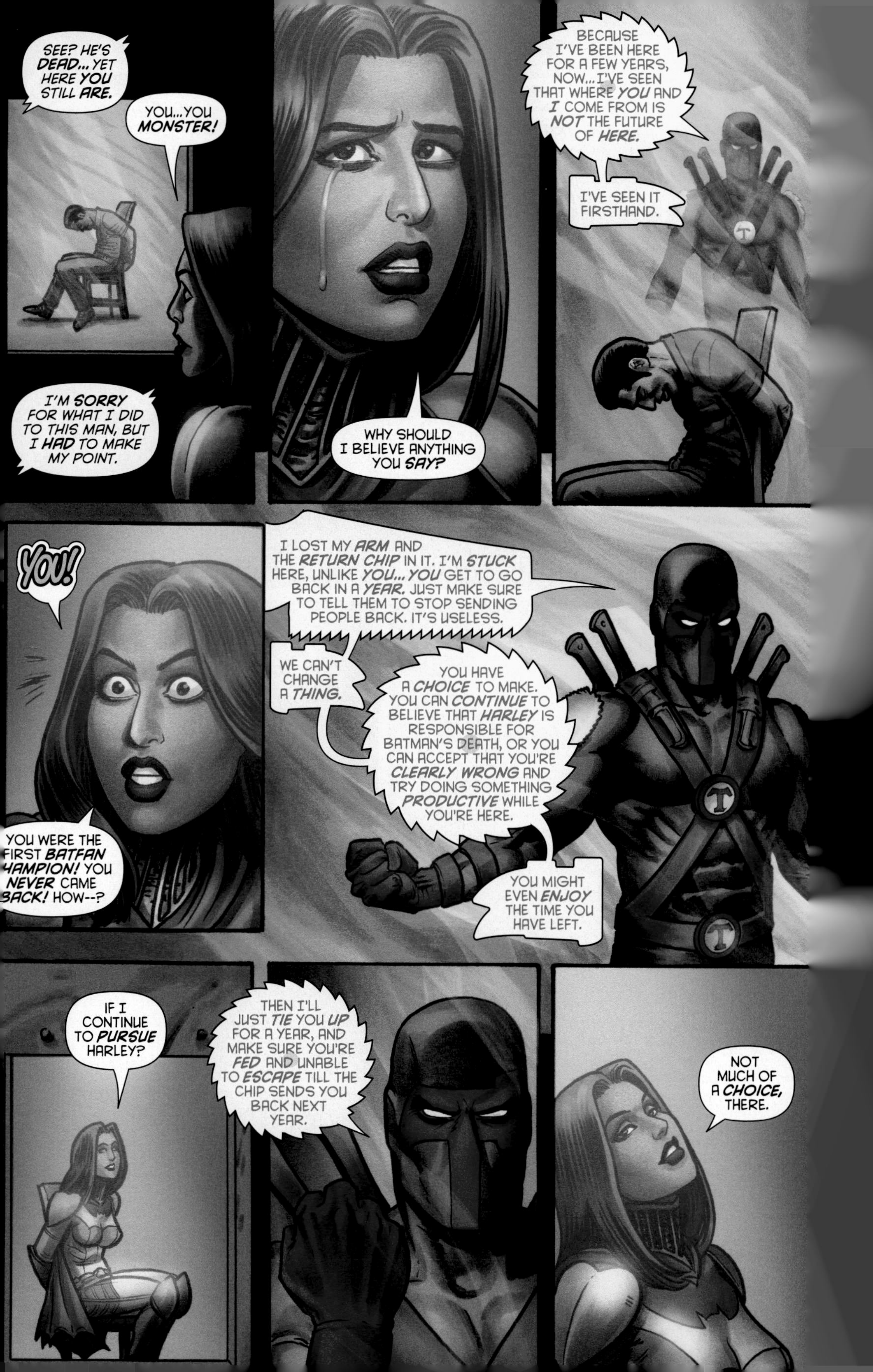
SEE? HE'S DEAD... YET HERE YOU STILL ARE.
YOU...YOU MONSTER!
I'M SORRY FOR WHAT I DID TO THIS MAN, BUT I HAD TO MAKE MY POINT.
WHY SHOULD I BELIEVE ANYTHING YOU SAY?
BECAUSE I'VE BEEN HERE FOR A FEW YEARS, NOW...I'VE SEEN THAT WHERE YOU AND I COME FROM IS NOT THE FUTURE OF HERE.
I'VE SEEN IT FIRSTHAND.
YOU!
YOU WERE THE FIRST BATFAN HAMPION! YOU NEVER CAME BACK! HOW--?
I LOST MY ARM AND THE RETURN CHIP IN IT. I'M STUCK HERE, UNLIKE YOU... YOU GET TO GO BACK IN A YEAR. JUST MAKE SURE TO TELL THEM TO STOP SENDING PEOPLE BACK. IT'S USELESS.
WE CAN'T CHANGE A THING.
YOU HAVE A CHOICE TO MAKE. YOU CAN CONTINUE TO BELIEVE THAT HARLEY IS RESPONSIBLE FOR BATMAN'S DEATH, OR YOU CAN ACCEPT THAT YOU'RE CLEARLY WRONG AND TRY DOING SOMETHING PRODUCTIVE WHILE YOU'RE HERE.
YOU MIGHT EVEN ENJOY THE TIME YOU HAVE LEFT.
IF I CONTINUE TO PURSUE HARLEY?
THEN I'LL JUST TIE YOU UP FOR A YEAR, AND MAKE SURE YOU'RE FED AND UNABLE TO ESCAPE TILL THE CHIP SENDS YOU BACK NEXT YEAR.
NOT MUCH OF A CHOICE, THERE.

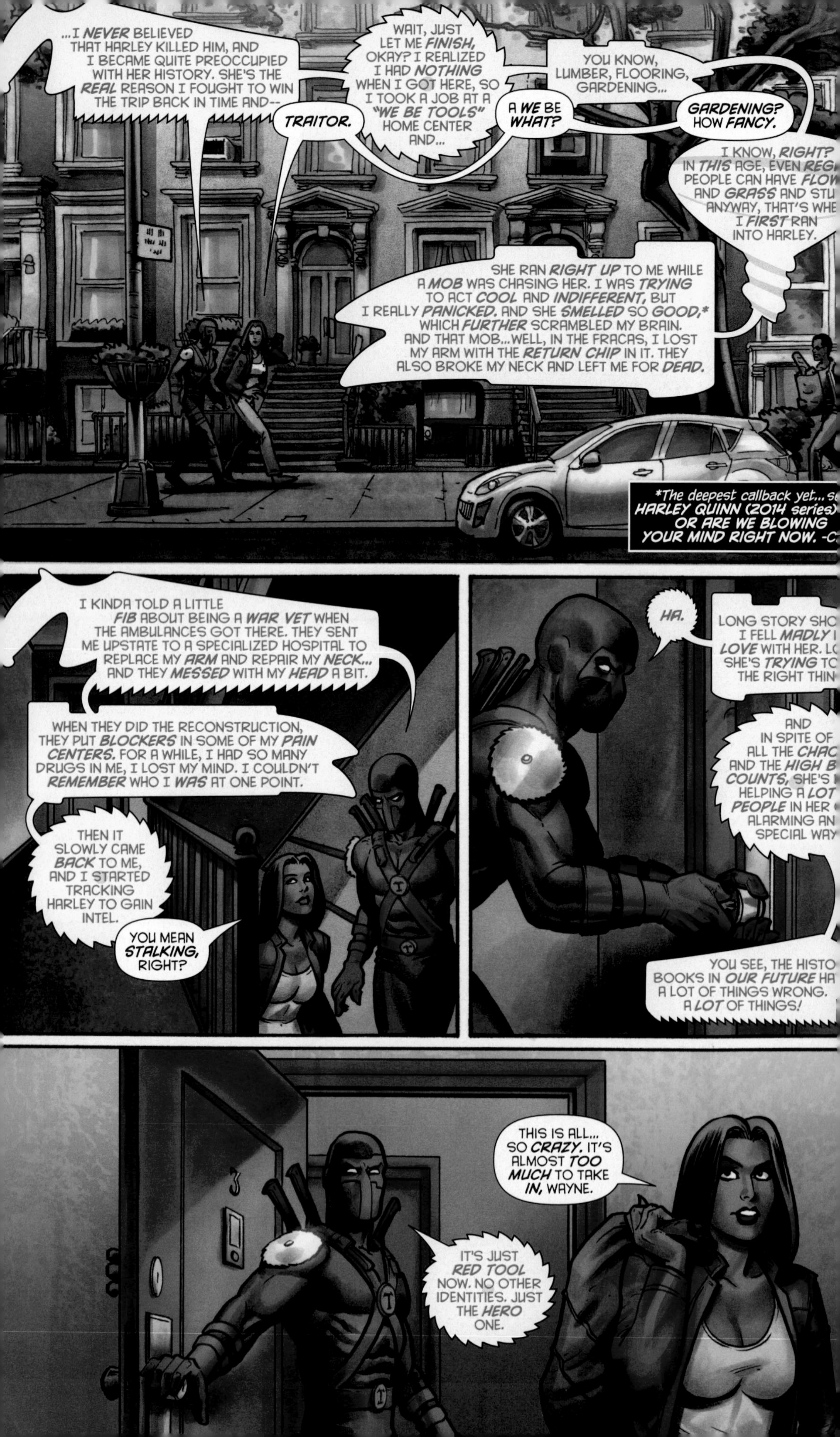
...I NEVER BELIEVED THAT HARLEY KILLED HIM, AND I BECAME QUITE PREOCCUPIED WITH HER HISTORY. SHE'S THE REAL REASON I FOUGHT TO WIN THE TRIP BACK IN TIME AND--
TRAITOR.
WAIT, JUST LET ME FINISH, OKAY? I REALIZED I HAD NOTHING WHEN I GOT HERE, SO I TOOK A JOB AT A "WE BE TOOLS" HOME CENTER AND...
A WE BE WHAT?
YOU KNOW, LUMBER, FLOORING, GARDENING...
GARDENING? HOW FANCY.
I KNOW, RIGHT? IN THIS AGE, EVEN REG PEOPLE CAN HAVE FLOW AND GRASS AND STU ANYWAY, THAT'S WHE I FIRST RAN INTO HARLEY.
SHE RAN RIGHT UP TO ME WHILE A MOB WAS CHASING HER. I WAS TRYING TO ACT COOL AND INDIFFERENT, BUT I REALLY PANICKED. AND SHE SMELLED SO GOOD,* WHICH FURTHER SCRAMBLED MY BRAIN. AND THAT MOB...WELL, IN THE FRACAS, I LOST MY ARM WITH THE RETURN CHIP IN IT. THEY ALSO BROKE MY NECK AND LEFT ME FOR DEAD.
*The deepest callback yet... se HARLEY QUINN (2014 series) OR ARE WE BLOWING YOUR MIND RIGHT NOW. -C
I KINDA TOLD A LITTLE FIB ABOUT BEING A WAR VET WHEN THE AMBULANCES GOT THERE. THEY SENT ME UPSTATE TO A SPECIALIZED HOSPITAL TO REPLACE MY ARM AND REPAIR MY NECK... AND THEY MESSED WITH MY HEAD A BIT.
WHEN THEY DID THE RECONSTRUCTION, THEY PUT BLOCKERS IN SOME OF MY PAIN CENTERS. FOR A WHILE, I HAD SO MANY DRUGS IN ME, I LOST MY MIND. I COULDN'T REMEMBER WHO I WAS AT ONE POINT.
THEN IT SLOWLY CAME BACK TO ME, AND I STARTED TRACKING HARLEY TO GAIN INTEL.
YOU MEAN STALKING, RIGHT?
HA.
LONG STORY SHO I FELL MADLY I LOVE WITH HER. L SHE'S TRYING TO THE RIGHT THIN
AND IN SPITE OF ALL THE CHAC AND THE HIGH B COUNTS, SHE'S HELPING A LOT PEOPLE IN HER ALARMING AN SPECIAL WAY
YOU SEE, THE HISTO BOOKS IN OUR FUTURE HA A LOT OF THINGS WRONG. A LOT OF THINGS!
THIS IS ALL... SO CRAZY. IT'S ALMOST TOO MUCH TO TAKE IN, WAYNE.
IT'S JUST RED TOOL NOW. NO OTHER IDENTITIES. JUST THE HERO ONE.

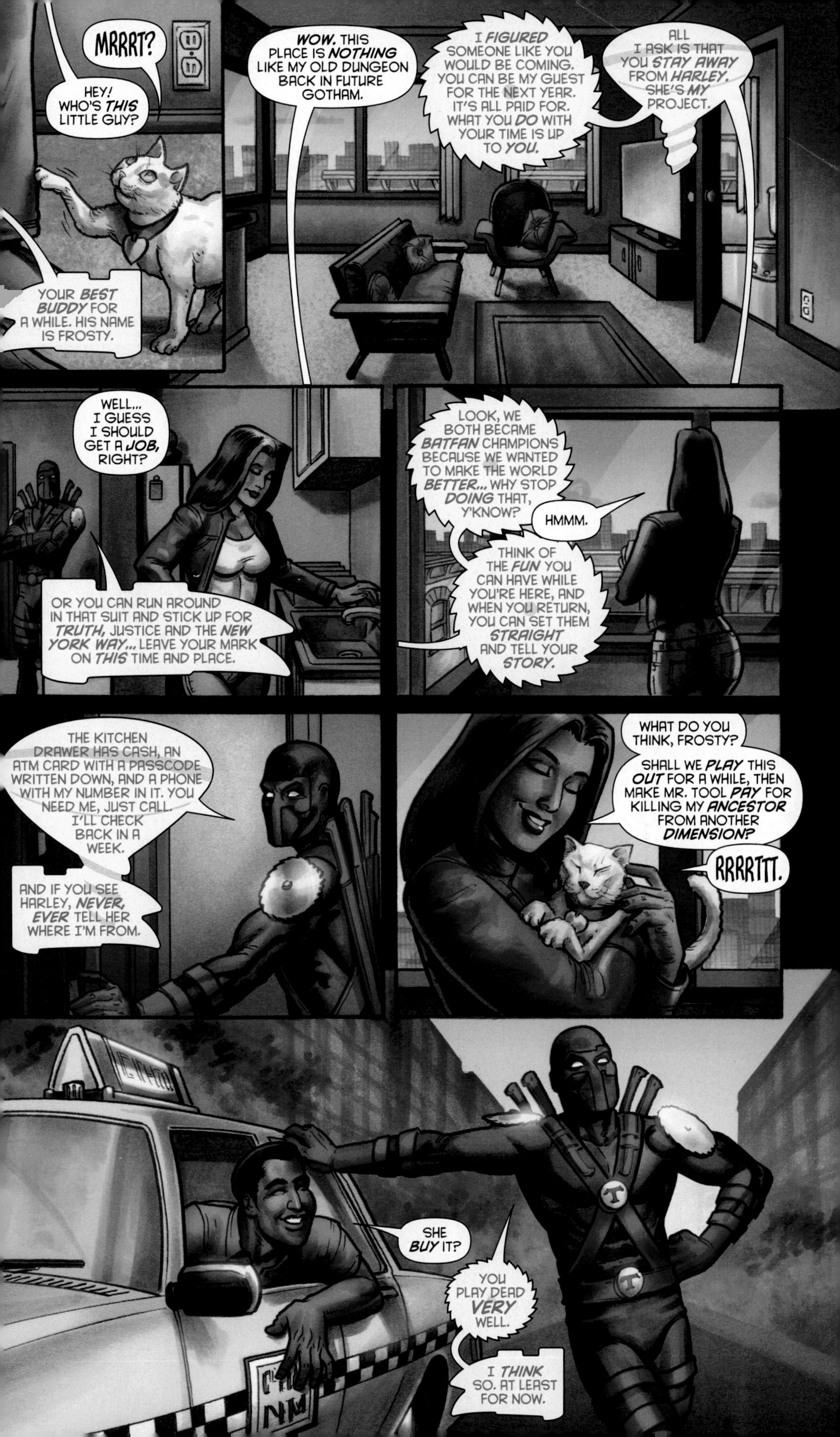
MRRRT?
HEY! WHO'S THIS LITTLE GUY?
YOUR BEST BUDDY FOR A WHILE. HIS NAME IS FROSTY.
WOW. THIS PLACE IS NOTHING LIKE MY OLD DUNGEON BACK IN FUTURE GOTHAM.
I FIGURED SOMEONE LIKE YOU WOULD BE COMING. YOU CAN BE MY GUEST FOR THE NEXT YEAR. IT'S ALL PAID FOR. WHAT YOU DO WITH YOUR TIME IS UP TO YOU.
ALL I ASK IS THAT YOU STAY AWAY FROM HARLEY. SHE'S MY PROJECT.
WELL... I GUESS I SHOULD GET A JOB, RIGHT?
OR YOU CAN RUN AROUND IN THAT SUIT AND STICK UP FOR TRUTH, JUSTICE AND THE NEW YORK WAY... LEAVE YOUR MARK ON THIS TIME AND PLACE.
LOOK, WE BOTH BECAME BATFAN CHAMPIONS BECAUSE WE WANTED TO MAKE THE WORLD BETTER... WHY STOP DOING THAT, Y'KNOW?
HMMM.
THINK OF THE FUN YOU CAN HAVE WHILE YOU'RE HERE, AND WHEN YOU RETURN, YOU CAN SET THEM STRAIGHT AND TELL YOUR STORY.
THE KITCHEN DRAWER HAS CASH, AN ATM CARD WITH A PASSCODE WRITTEN DOWN, AND A PHONE WITH MY NUMBER IN IT. YOU NEED ME, JUST CALL. I'LL CHECK BACK IN A WEEK.
AND IF YOU SEE HARLEY, NEVER, EVER TELL HER WHERE I'M FROM.
WHAT DO YOU THINK, FROSTY?
SHALL WE PLAY THIS OUT FOR A WHILE, THEN MAKE MR. TOOL PAY FOR KILLING MY ANCESTOR FROM ANOTHER DIMENSION?
RRRRTTT.
SHE BUY IT?
YOU PLAY DEAD VERY WELL.
I THINK SO. AT LEAST FOR NOW.

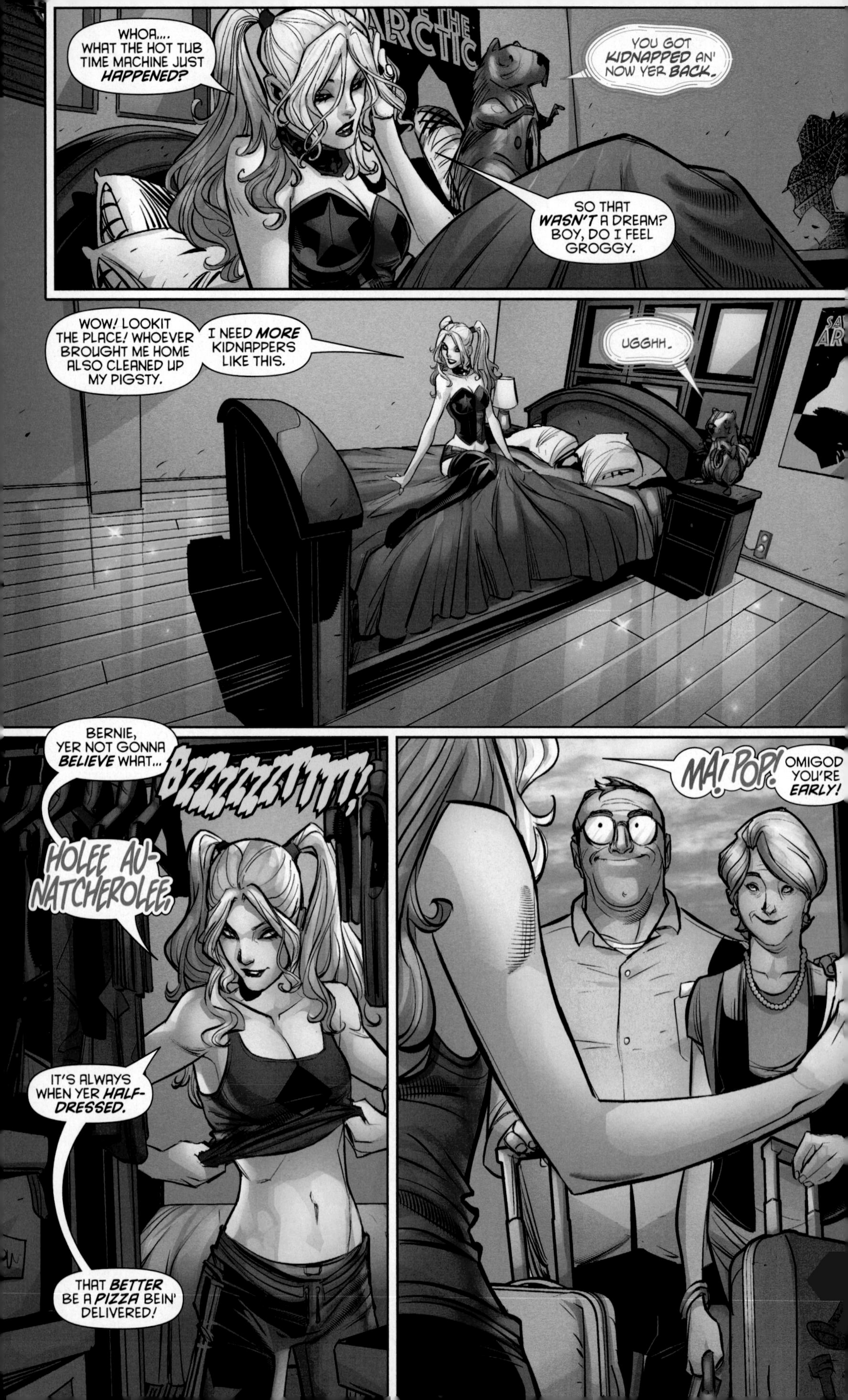
WHOA.... WHAT THE HOT TUB TIME MACHINE JUST HAPPENED?
YOU GOT KIDNAPPED AN' NOW YER BACK.
SO THAT WASN'T A DREAM? BOY, DO I FEEL GROGGY.
WOW! LOOKIT THE PLACE! WHOEVER BROUGHT ME HOME ALSO CLEANED UP MY PIGSTY.
I NEED MORE KIDNAPPERS LIKE THIS.
UGGHH.
BERNIE, YER NOT GONNA BELIEVE WHAT...
BZZZZZZZTTTT!
HOLEE AU-NATCHEROLEE.
IT'S ALWAYS WHEN YER HALF-DRESSED.
THAT BETTER BE A PIZZA BEIN' DELIVERED!
MA! POP!
OMIGOD YOU'RE EARLY!

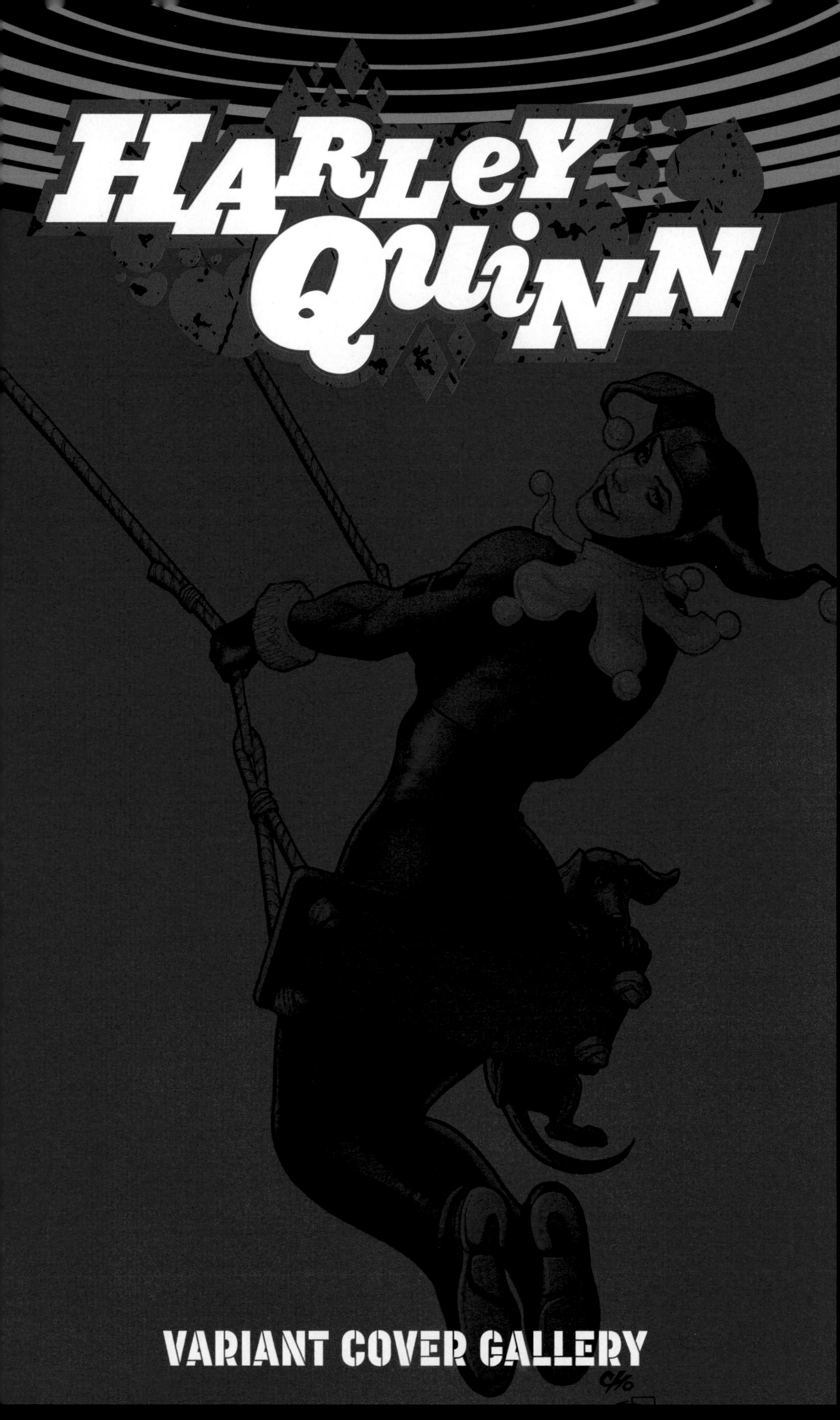
HARLEY QUINN
VARIANT COVER GALLERY

HARLEY QUINN #14 variant by FRANK CHO and LAURA MARTIN

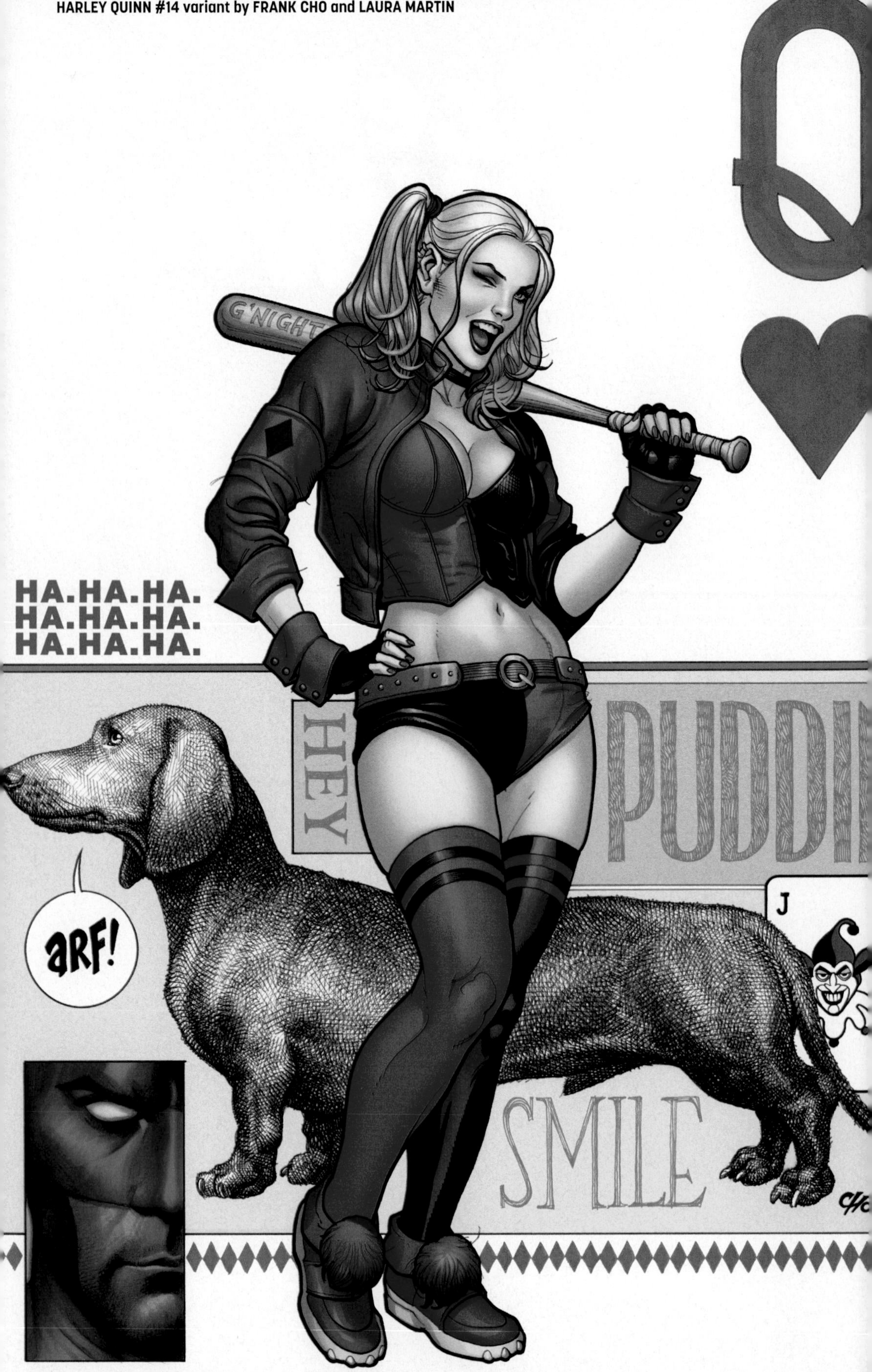

Q
G'NIGHT
HA.HA.HA.
HA.HA.HA.
HA.HA.HA.
HEY
PUDDI
J
arf!
SMILE
CHO

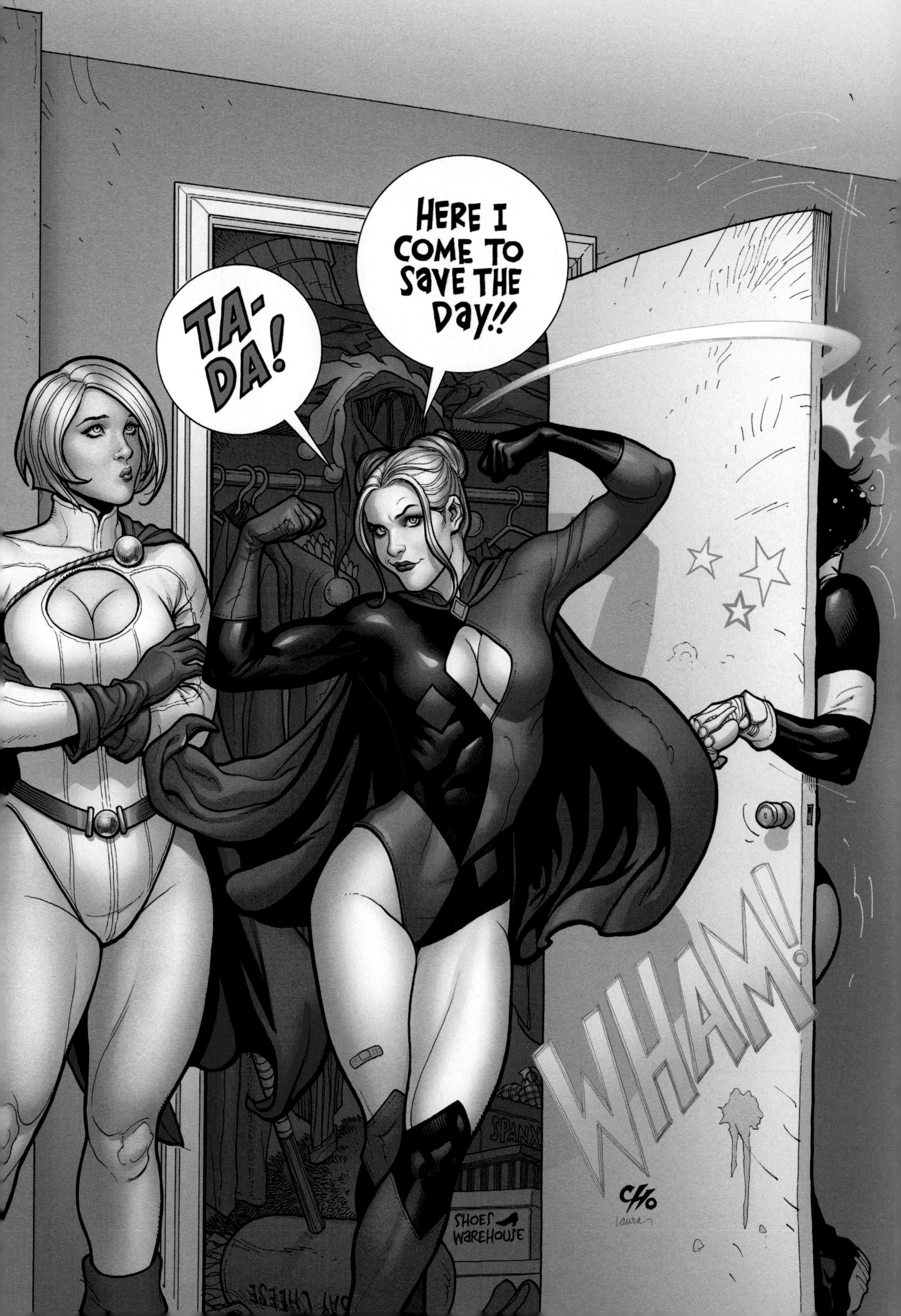
TA-DA!
HERE I COME TO SAVE THE DAY!!
WHAM!
SPANX
SHOES WAREHOUSE
CHO

HARLEY QUINN #15 variant by FRANK CHO and LAURA MARTIN

HARLEY QUINN #16 variant by FRANK CHO

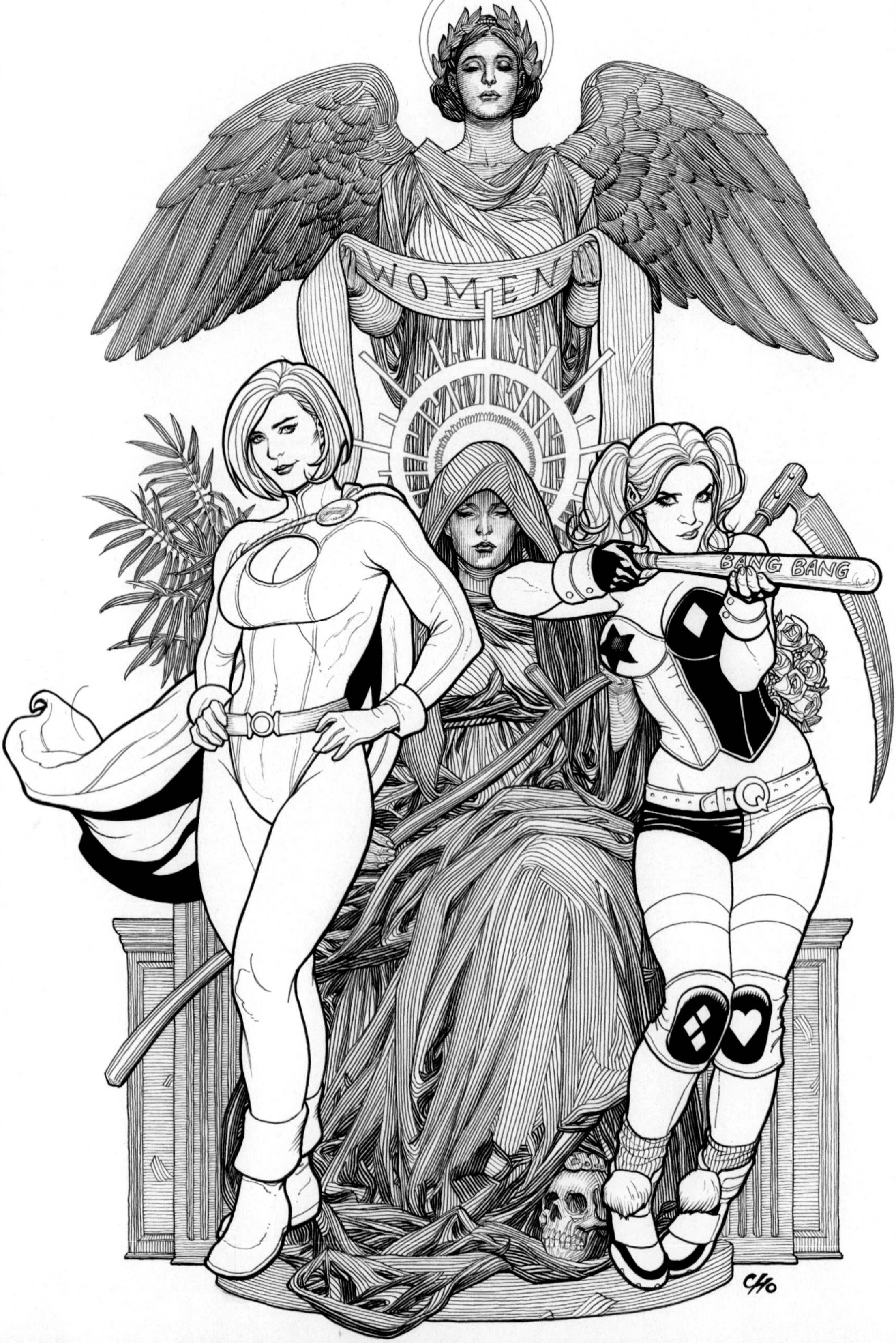
WOMEN
BANG BANG
CHO

HARLEY QUINN #17 variant by FRANK CHO and SABINE RICH

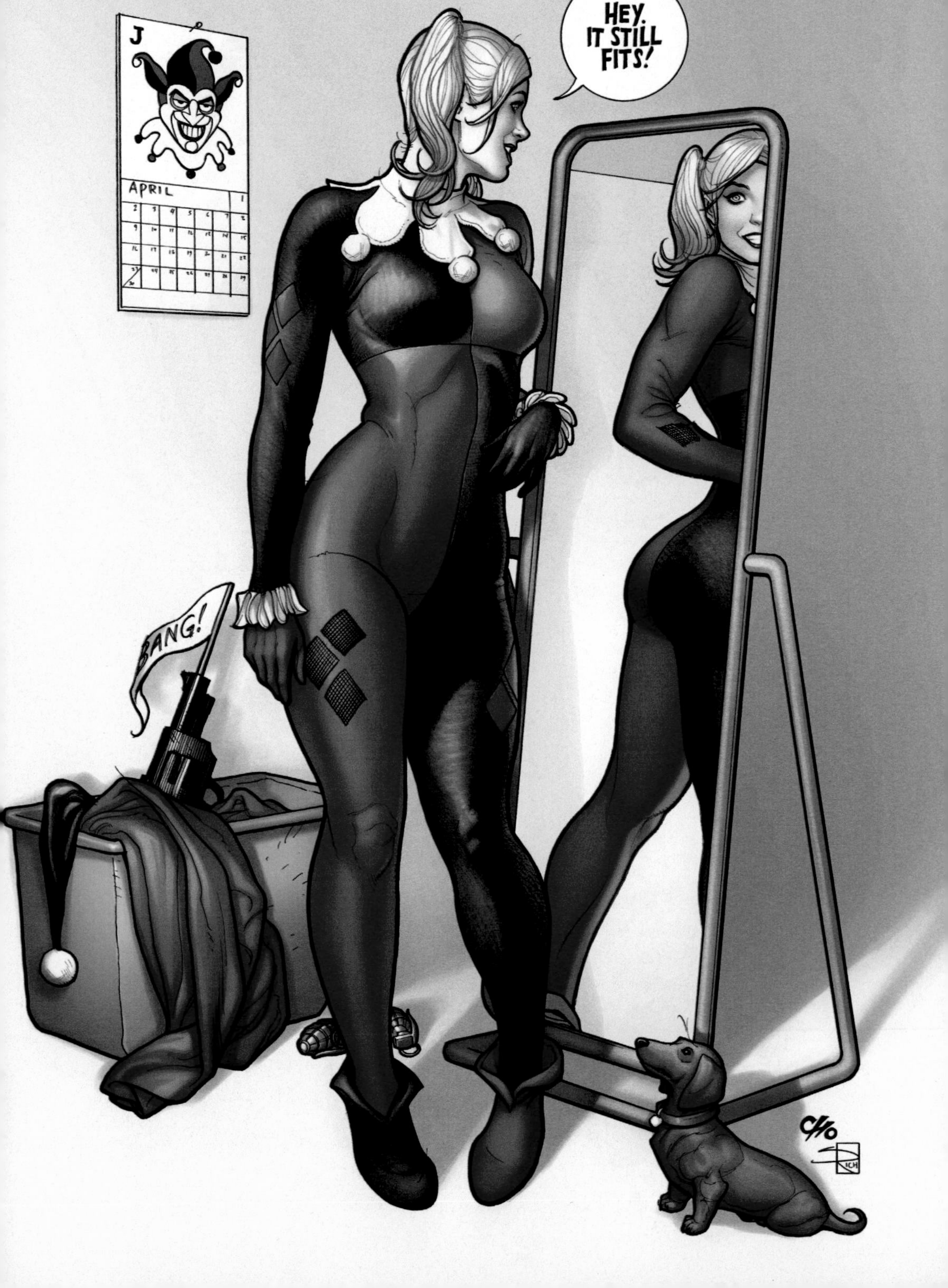
J
APRIL
HEY. IT STILL FITS!
BANG!

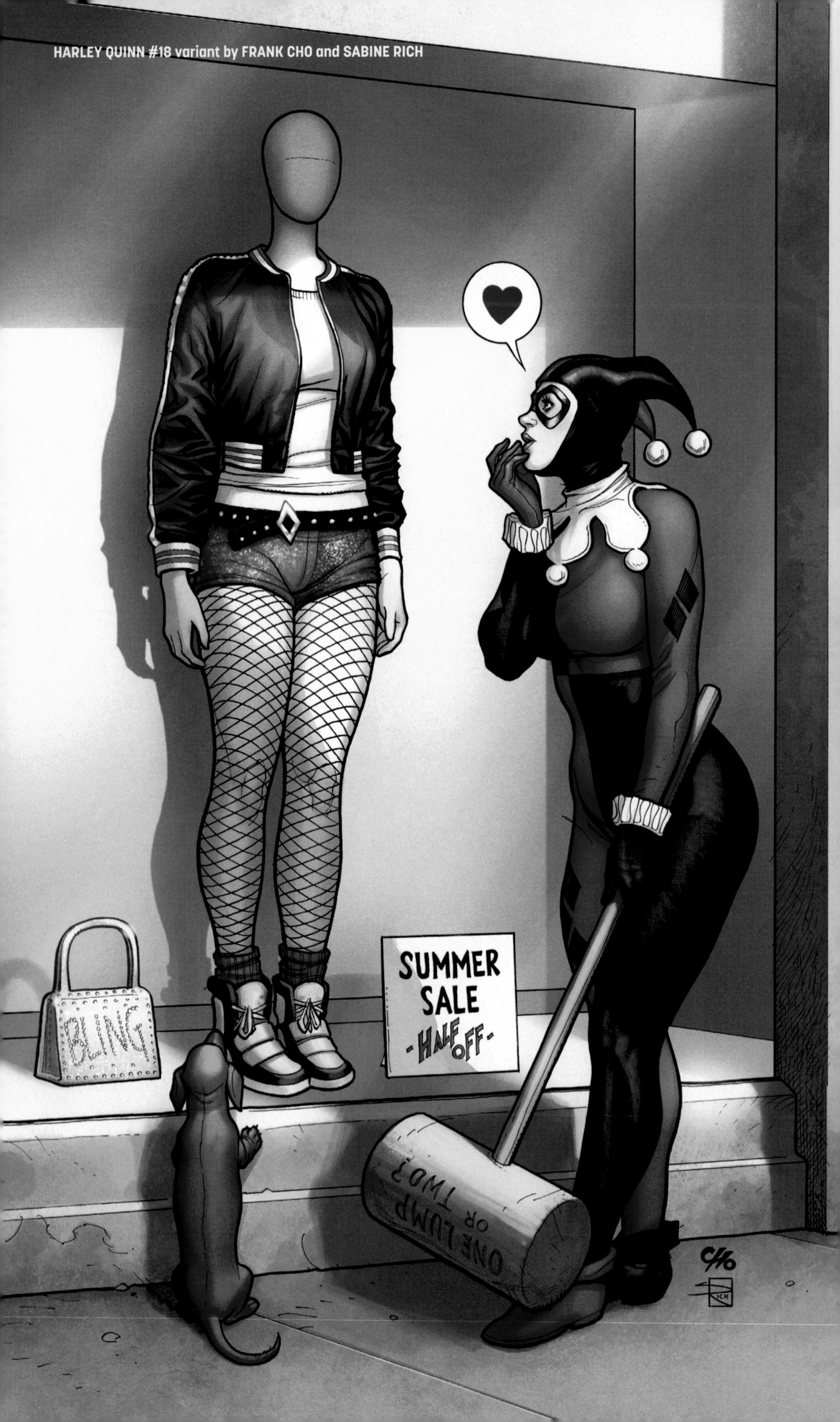
BLING
SUMMER SALE
-HALF OFF-
ONE LUMP OR TWO?
HARLEY QUINN #18 variant by FRANK CHO and SABINE RICH

HARLEY QUINN #19 variant by FRANK CHO and SABINE RICH

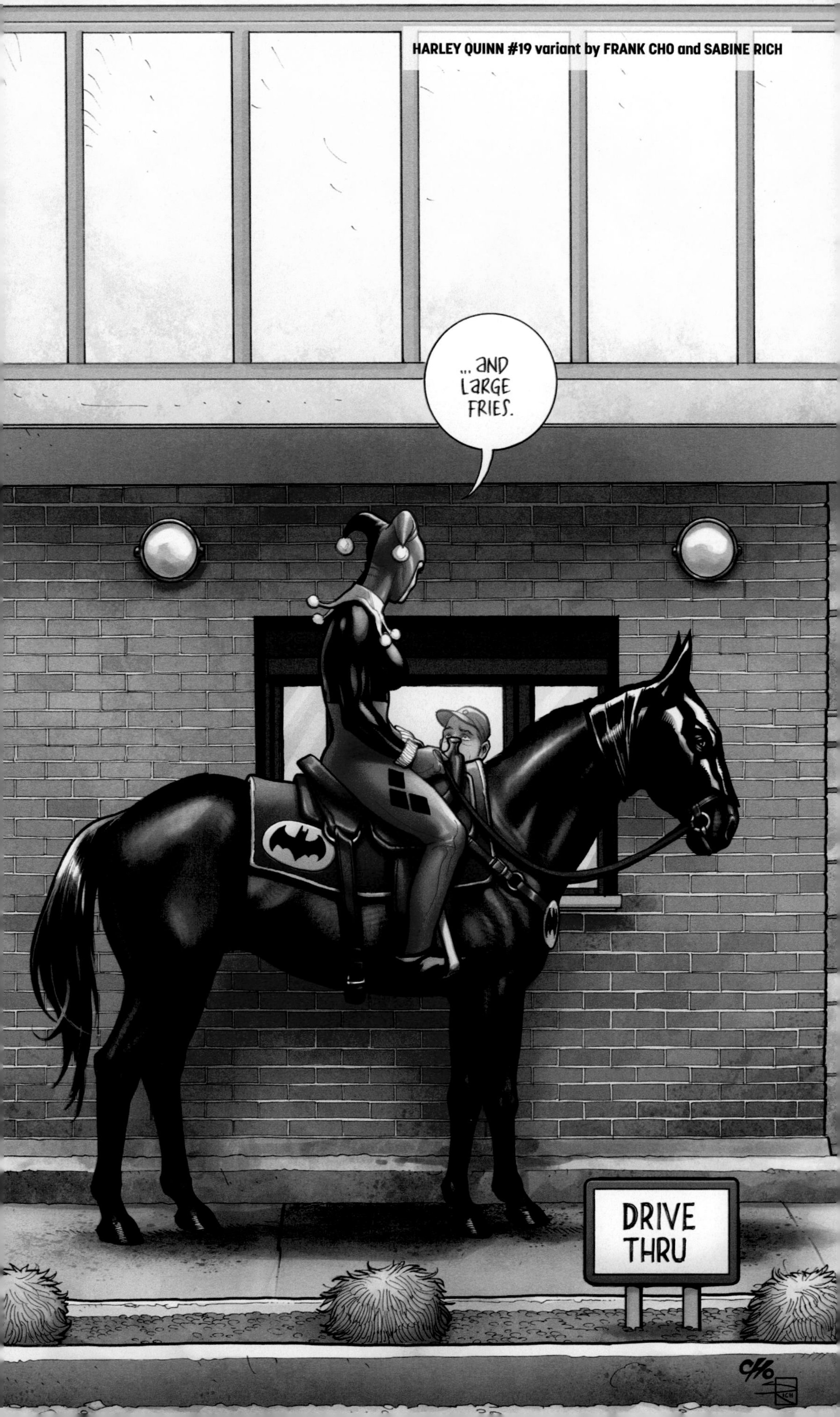
...AND LARGE FRIES.
DRIVE THRU

HARLEY QUINN #20 variant by FRANK CHO and SABINE RICH

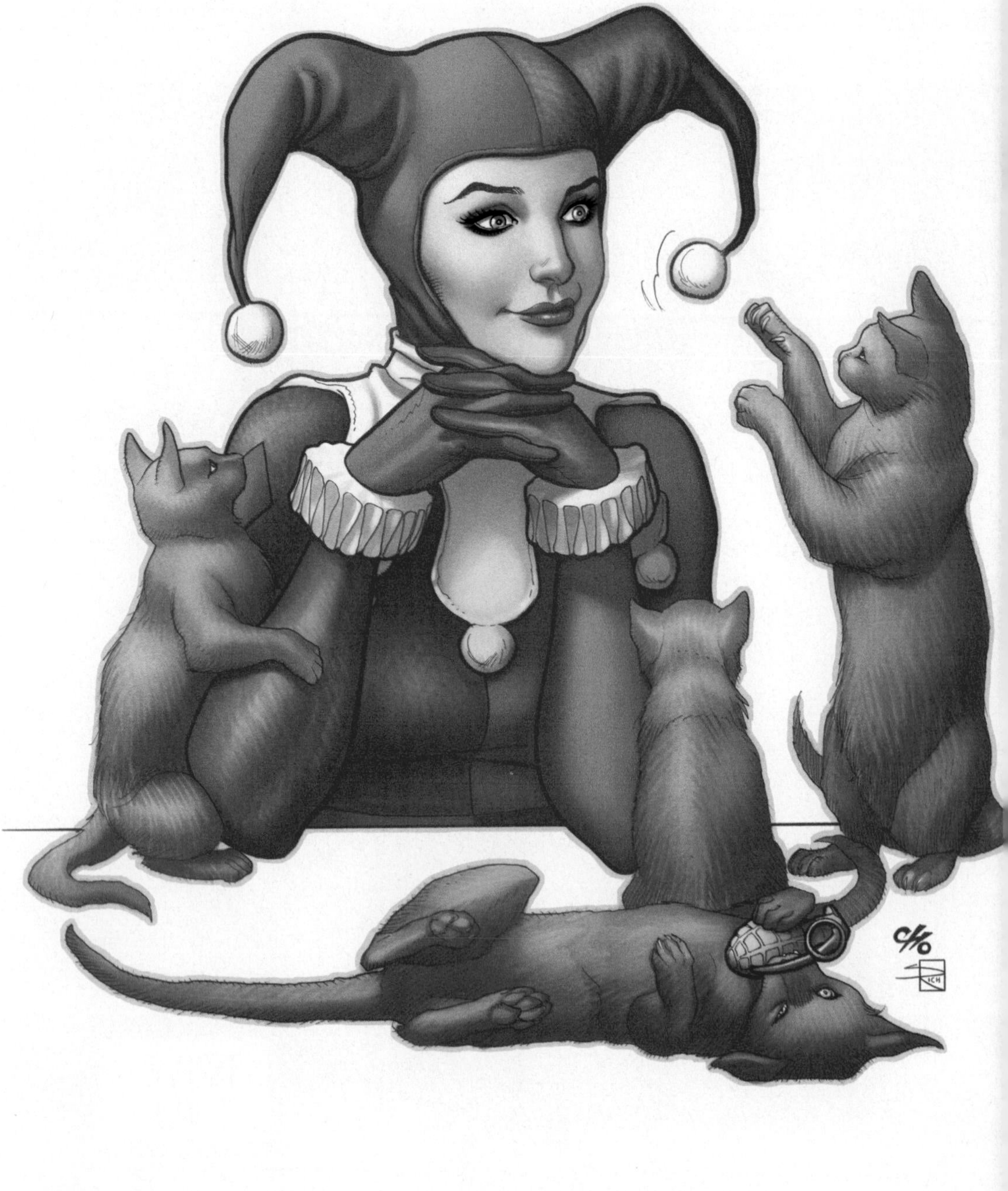

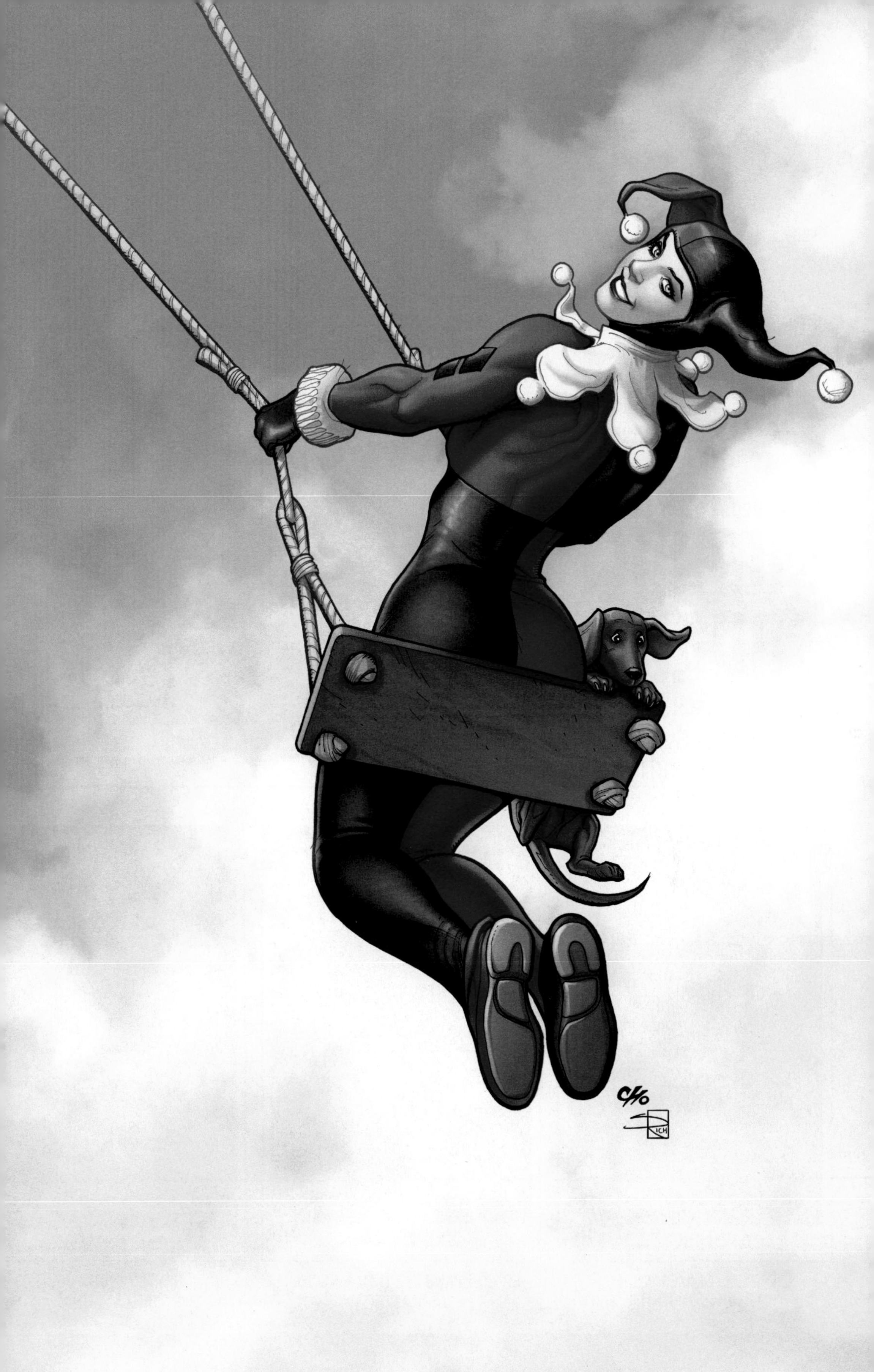
CHO
RICH

HARLEY QUINN #21 variant by FRANK CHO and SABINE RICH

"It's nice to see one of the best comics of the late '80s return so strongly."
– **Comic Book Resources**

"It's high energy from page one through to the last page." – **BATMAN NEWS**

DC UNIVERSE REBIRTH

SUICIDE SQUAD

VOL. 1: THE BLACK VAULT

ROB WILLIAMS
with JIM LEE and others

VOL.1 THE BLACK VAULT
ROB WILLIAMS • JIM LEE • PHILIP TAN • JASON FABOK • IVAN REIS • GARY FRANK

THE HELLBLAZER VOL. 1:
THE POISON TRUTH

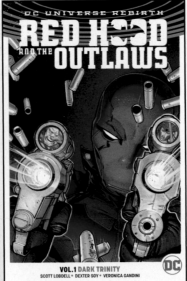

RED HOOD AND THE OUTLAWS VOL. 1:
DARK TRINITY

HARLEY QUINN VOL. 1:
DIE LAUGHING

Get more DC graphic novels wherever comics and books are sold!